NOVA SCOTIA, NEW BRUNSWICK, PRINCE EDWARD ISLAND, AND NEWFOUNDLAND AND LABRADOR

8TH EDITION

Where to Stay and Eat
for All Budgets

Must-See Sights
and Local Secrets

Ratings You Can Trust

Portions of this book appear in *Fodor's Canada*

Fodor's Travel Publications   New York, Toronto, London, Sydney, Auckland
www.fodors.com

FODOR'S NOVA SCOTIA, NEW BRUNSWICK, PRINCE EDWARD ISLAND, AND NEWFOUNDLAND AND LABRADOR
Editor: Shannon M. Kelly

Editorial Production: Tom Holton
Editorial Contributors: Tracy Barron, Shelley Cameron-McCarron, Kim Goodson, Satu Hummasti, Amy Pugsley Fraser, Susan Randles, Ana Watts
Maps: David Lindroth, *cartographer;* Bob Blake and Rebecca Baer, *map editors*
Design: Fabrizio La Rocca, *creative director;* Guido Caroti, *art director;* Melanie Marin, *senior picture editor*
Production/Manufacturing: Colleen Ziemba
Cover Photo: Greig Cranna

ISBN 1–4000–1293–7

ISSN 1079–0004

Eighth Edition

SPECIAL SALES
Fodor's Travel Publications are available at special discounts for bulk purchases for sales promotions or premiums. Special editions, including personalized covers, excerpts of existing guides, and corporate imprints, can be created in large quantities for special needs. For more information, contact your local bookseller or write to Special Markets, Fodor's Travel Publications, 1745 Broadway, New York, New York 10019. Inquiries from Canada should be directed to your local Canadian bookseller or sent to Random House of Canada, Ltd., Marketing Department, 2775 Matheson Boulevard East, Mississauga, Ontario L4W 4P7. Inquiries from the United Kingdom should be sent to Fodor's Travel Publications, 20 Vauxhall Bridge Road, London SW1V 2SA, England.

AN IMPORTANT TIP & AN INVITATION
Although all prices, opening times, and other details in this book are based on information supplied to us at press time, changes occur all the time in the travel world, and Fodor's cannot accept responsibility for facts that become outdated or for inadvertent errors or omissions. So **always confirm information when it matters,** especially if you're making a detour to visit a specific place. Your experiences—positive and negative—matter to us. If we have missed or misstated something, **please write to us.** We follow up on all suggestions. Contact the Nova Scotia editor at editors@fodors.com or c/o Fodor's at 1745 Broadway, New York, New York 10019.

PRINTED IN THE UNITED STATES OF AMERICA

10 9 8 7 6 5 4 3 2 1

DESTINATION ATLANTIC CANADA

T he rugged coastlines of the Atlantic provinces enclose ever-green forests and rolling farmland. In New Brunswick, the highest tides in the world work to carve the jagged coast. Along the shores of all four provinces, lobster boats crowd trim little harbors. Atlantic Canada can be a phenomenal adventure: kayaking, whale-watching, skiing, and dogsledding are just a few of the ways to dive in headfirst. White sandy beaches, lobsters in the pot, and cozy inns steeped in history make it easy to have a relaxing interlude, too. Prince Edward Island, for one, has uncrowded beaches and the warmest ocean water north of the Carolinas. And the easternmost province of Newfoundland and Labrador is a world unto itself, where humpback whales feed near shore and 10,000-year-old icebergs cruise by fishing villages. A wonderful assortment of cultures exists in Atlantic Canada, but it's no melting pot, as each pocket of individuality—whether Scottish, German, Mi'Kmaq, or Acadian—works fiercely to maintain its identity, traditions, and language. Cities in the Atlantic provinces thrive on a rich assortment of cultural activities and share the ability to combine metropolitan life with small-town charm. Have a fabulous trip!

Karen Cure, Editorial Director

CONTENTS

About This Book *F6*
On the Road with Fodor's *F9*
What's Where *F10*
When to Go *F13*
On the Calendar *F14*
Pleasures & Pastimes *F17*
Fodor's Choice *F20*
Smart Travel Tips *F26*

1 Nova Scotia   *1*

Halifax & Dartmouth *4*
The South Shore & the
   Annapolis Valley *18*
The Eastern Shore & Northern
   Nova Scotia *41*
Cape Breton Island *55*

2 New Brunswick   *74*

Saint John *76*
The Fundy Coast *88*
Tantramar Region *101*
The Acadian Coast &
   Peninsula *103*
St. John River Valley *109*
Fredericton *112*

3 Prince Edward Island   *121*

Charlottetown *124*
Blue Heron Drive *134*
The Kings Byway *141*
Lady Slipper Drive *145*

4 Newfoundland & Labrador   *153*

St. John's *160*
Avalon Peninsula *171*
Route 100: The Cape Shore *175*
Burin Peninsula, Gander &
   Notre Dame Bay *180*
The Great Northern
   Peninsula *185*
The Straits *194*
Coastal Labrador *195*
Labrador West *197*

Understanding Atlantic Canada   *201*

Of Sea and Land *202*
Books & Movies *204*

Index   *206*

Maps

Atlantic Canada *F8*
Nova Scotia
Nova Scotia *6–7*
Halifax *8*
Cape Breton *56*
New Brunswick
New Brunswick *80–81*
Downtown Saint John *82*
Fredericton *113*

Prince Edward Island
Prince Edward Island *126*
Charlottetown *128*
Newfoundland & Labrador
Newfoundland &
  Labrador *158–159*
St. John's *161*
Avalon Peninsula *172*

Close-Up

Acadian Culture *108*

ABOUT THIS BOOK

There's no doubt that the best source for travel advice is a like-minded friend who's just been where you're headed. But with or without that friend, you'll have a better trip with a Fodor's guide in hand. Once you've learned to find your way around its pages, you'll be in great shape to find your way around your destination.

SELECTION

Our goal is to cover the best properties, sights, and activities in their category, as well as the most interesting communities to visit. We make a point of including local food lovers' hot spots as well as neighborhood options, and we avoid all that's touristy unless it's really worth your time. You can go on the assumption that everything you read about in this book is recommended wholeheartedly by our writers and editors. Flip to On the Road with Fodor's to learn more about who they are. It goes without saying that no property mentioned in the book has paid to be included.

RATINGS

Orange stars ★ denote sights and properties that our editors and writers consider the very best in the area covered by the entire book. These, the best of the best, are listed in the Fodor's Choice section in the front of the book. Black stars ★ highlight the sights and properties we deem Highly Recommended, the don't-miss sights within any region. Fodor's Choice and Highly Recommended options in each region are usually listed on the title page of the chapter covering that region. Use the index to find complete descriptions. In cities, sights pinpointed with numbered map bullets ❶ in the margins tend to be more important than those without bullets.

SPECIAL SPOTS

Pleasures & Pastimes focuses on types of experiences that reveal the spirit of the destination. Watch for Off the Beaten Path sights. Some are out of the way, some are quirky, but all are worth your while. If the munchies hit while you're exploring, look for Need a Break? suggestions.

TIME IT RIGHT

Wondering when to go? Check On the Calendar up front and chapters' Timing sections for weather and crowd overviews and best days and times to visit.

SEE IT ALL

Use Fodor's exclusive Great Itineraries in each chapter as a model for your trip. Mix regional itineraries from several chapters to create a larger multiprovince itinerary. In cities, Good Walks guide you to important sights in each neighborhood; ▶ indicates the starting points of walks and itineraries in the text and on the map.

BUDGET WELL

Hotel and restaurant price categories from ¢ to $$$$ are defined in the opening pages of each chapter—expect to find a balanced selection for every budget. For attractions, we always give standard adult admission fees; reductions are usually available for children, students, and senior citizens. Look in Discounts & Deals in Smart Travel Tips for information on destination-wide ticket schemes. Want to pay with plastic? AE, D, DC, MC, V following restaurant and hotel listings indicate whether American Express, Discover, Diner's Club, MasterCard, or Visa are accepted.

BASIC INFO

Smart Travel Tips lists travel essentials for the entire area covered by the book; city- and region-specific basics end each chapter. To find the best way to get around, see the transportation section; see individual modes of travel ("By Car," "By Train") for details. We assume you'll check Web sites or call for particulars.

ON THE MAPS	Maps throughout the book show you what's where and help you find your way around. Black- and orange-numbered bullets ❶ ① in the text correlate to bullets on maps.
BACKGROUND	In general, we give background information within the chapters in the course of explaining sights as well as in Close-Up boxes and in Understanding Atlantic Canada at the end of the book. To get in the mood, review the suggestions in Books & Movies.
FIND IT FAST	Within the book, chapters are arranged by province in a roughly clockwise direction, starting with Nova Scotia. Chapters are divided into small regions, within which towns are covered in logical geographical order; attractive routes and interesting places between towns are flagged as En Route. Heads at the top of each page help you find what you need within a chapter.
DON'T FORGET	Restaurants are open for lunch and dinner daily unless we state otherwise; we mention dress only when there's a specific requirement and reservations only when they're essential or not accepted—it's always best to book ahead. Hotels have private baths, phones, TVs, and air-conditioning and operate on the European Plan (a.k.a. EP, meaning without meals). We always list facilities but not whether you'll be charged extra to use them, so when pricing accommodations, find out what's included.

SYMBOLS

Many Listings

★ Fodor's Choice
★ Highly recommended
⊠ Physical address
✛ Directions
🕮 Mailing address
☎ Telephone
🖷 Fax
⊕ On the Web
✉ E-mail
💳 Admission fee
🕓 Open/closed times
⚑ Start of walk/itinerary
Ⓜ Metro stations
▭ Credit cards

Outdoors

⛳ Golf
⛺ Camping

Hotels & Restaurants

🏨 Hotel
🛏 Number of rooms
👍 Facilities
🍽 Meal plans
✕ Restaurant
🪑 Reservations
👔 Dress code
🚭 Smoking
🍷 BYOB
✕🏨 Hotel with restaurant that warrants a visit

Other

🐾 Family-friendly
📱 Contact information
⇨ See also
⊠ Branch address
☞ Take note

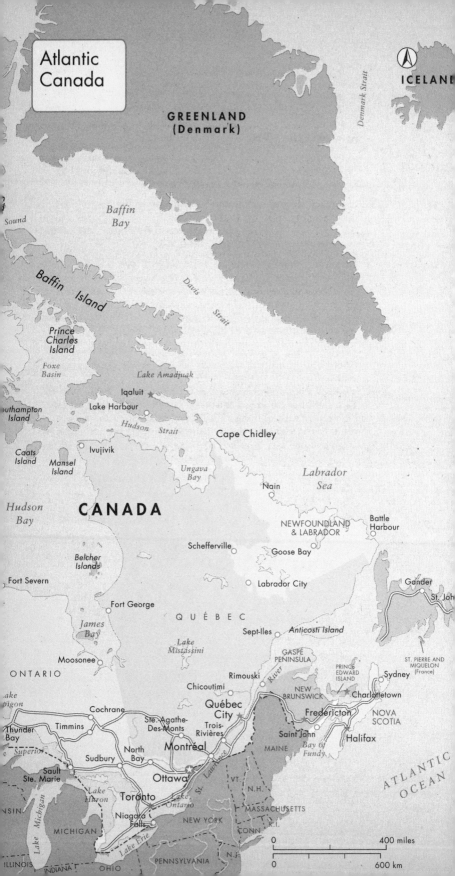

Atlantic Canada

ICELAND

GREENLAND
(Denmark)

Denmark Strait

*Baffin
Bay*

Sound

Baffin   Island

Davis

Strait

*Prince
Charles
Island*

*Foxe
Basin*

Lake Amadjuak

Iqaluit ★

Lake Harbour ○

*outhampton
Island*

Hudson   Strait

Cape Chidley

*Coats
Island*

Ivujivik ○

*Mansel
Island*

*Ungava
Bay*

Nain ○

*Labrador
Sea*

*Hudson
Bay*

CANADA

NEWFOUNDLAND
& LABRADOR

Battle
Harbour ○

*Belcher
Islands*

Schefferville ○

Goose Bay ○

Gander ○

Fort Severn ○

Labrador City ○

St. Joh

Fort George ○

Q U É B E C

*James
Bay*

Sept-Iles ○

Anticosti Island

*Lake
Mistassini*

Moosonee ○

ST. PIERRE AND
MIQUELON
(France)

GASPÉ
PENINSULA

ONTARIO

Rimouski ○

Sydney ○

River

PRINCE
EDWARD
ISLAND

Cochrane

Chicoutimi ○

Charlottetown ○

Ste.-Agathe-
Des-Monts

Québec
City ★

NEW
BRUNSWICK

Fredericton ○

NOVA
SCOTIA

*ake
pigon*

Timmins

Trois-
Rivières

Saint John ○

Halifax ○

*Thunder
Bay*

Sudbury

North
Bay

Montréal

MAINE

*Bay of
Fundy*

Superior

Sault
Ste. Marie

Ottawa ★

St. Lawrence

A T L A N T I C

O C E A N

*Lake
Huron*

Toronto

*Lake
Ontario*

VT.

N.H.

*Lake
Michigan*

Niagara
Falls

Lake Erie

MASSACHUSETTS

WISCONSIN

MICHIGAN

NEW YORK

CONN.

R.I.

0   400 miles

0   600 km

ILLINOIS

INDIANA

OHIO

PENNSYLVANIA

N.J.

ON THE ROAD WITH FODOR'S

A trip takes you out of yourself. Concerns of life at home completely disappear, driven away by more immediate thoughts—about, say, what marvels will beguile the next day, or where you'll have dinner. That's where Fodor's comes in. We make sure that you know all your options, so that you don't miss something that's around the next bend just because you didn't know it was there. Because the best memories of your trip might well have nothing to do with what you came to Atlantic Canada to see, we guide you to sights large and small all over the region. You might set out for whale-watching and lobster dinners, but back at home you find yourself unable to forget villages rich with Acadian history in Nova Scotia and New Brunswick, an evening of live jazz under the stars in PEI, or moose and caribou sightings in the wilds of Newfoundland and Labrador. With Fodor's at your side, serendipitous discoveries are never far away.

Our success in showing you every corner of Canada's Atlantic provinces is a credit to our extraordinary writers. Although there's no substitute for travel advice from a good friend who knows your style, our contributors are the next best thing—the kind of people you would poll for travel advice if you knew them.

Tracy Barron, who updated the Newfoundland and Labrador chapter, moved to St. John's in 1989 and has traveled her adopted province extensively for business and pleasure. Tracy writes for the *Telegram,* the province's daily newspaper.

Shelley Cameron-McCarron grew up on Cape Breton Island and now lives in Antigonish, Nova Scotia. She and her husband travel as much as possible in Atlantic Canada, delighting all the hidden gems in their own backyard. Shelley's articles have appeared in the *Globe and Mail,* the *Halifax Chronicle-Herald,* the *Montreal Gazette,* and a number of Canadian lifestyle magazines. Shelley updated the Eastern Shore and Northern Nova Scotia section of the Nova Scotia chapter.

Food columnist Kim Goodson, who updated Smart Travel Tips A to Z and the Halifax and Dartmouth sections of the Nova Scotia chapter, indulges her food, wine, and travel passions at every opportunity.

Amy Pugsley Fraser, a reporter at the *Halifax Herald,* spent many childhood summers in Digby and now savors the season on Nova Scotia's south shore. Fittingly, she updated the South Shore and Annapolis Valley section of the Nova Scotia chapter for this edition. Amy lives in Halifax with her husband and two young sons.

Susan Randles has written extensively on her favorite province, Prince Edward Island. In addition to coauthoring three books with her late husband, her work has been published in the *Boston Globe,* the *Toronto Star,* the *Halifax Daily News,* and in numerous magazines and on Web sites. Susan updated the Prince Edward Island chapter and the Destination: Atlantic Canada section for this edition. She lives in Dartmouth, Nova Scotia with her two children.

Writer and award-winning columnist Ana Watts, of Fredericton, is a New Brunswicker born and bred. She champions her province at every opportunity. Her travel, business, lifestyle, and parenting pieces appear in regional and national publications like *Saltscapes, Atlantic Progress,* the *Globe and Mail,* and *Today's Parent.* Her regular column in the *New Brunswick Anglican* consistently wins national press awards.

1 New Brunswick

New Brunswick is where the great Canadian forest, sliced by sweeping river valleys and modern highways, meets the Atlantic. The gentle, warm Gulf Stream washes more than 90 beaches along 2,000 km (1,240 mi) of coastline. Historic cities and quaint towns with Victorian inns and manicured gardens draw tourists year-round. Culture abounds in this province, whose population is 33% French Acadian. Whether it be salmon fishing on the Miramichi River, cycling alongside the St. John River, or experiencing the living museum at Kings Landing, New Brunswick has something for everyone.

On the Bay of Fundy, four-story sculptures are carved by the tides at Hopewell Cape. You can literally walk along the floor of the ocean during low tide. Twice daily the waters rise and fall 48 ft, producing a rich ecosystem. Plankton and mudflats provide feeding grounds for several species of whales, dolphins, seals, plovers, and sandpipers. The St. John River, nicknamed "the Rhine of North America," is the largest river on the eastern seaboard. It meanders through the length of the province from the crashing 76-foot plunge into the Grand Falls, ending in a collision with the tidal waters of the Bay of Fundy. It is here in Saint John, the largest city in the province, that the river meets the rushing waters of the bay, resulting in the Reversing Falls. The water reverses its direction when the tide comes in, causing swirling whirlpools.

New Brunswick is renowned for its covered wooden bridges. The longest one in the world, at 1,282 ft, is in Hartland. A local tradition suggests that you make a wish while crossing the St. John River on this bridge. Fredericton, the capital city, is called the City of Stately Elms. With more than 800 acres of parkland, it can be described as a city within a park. The historical grand Victorian homes line the St. John River, alive in the summer with kayakers, rowers, and canoeists. The Acadian Historical Village in Caraquet welcomes visitors to experience the life of the Acadians after they survived the expulsion of 1755. This is a province with both geographical and cultural diversity. From rugged mountains and warm sandy beaches to festivals that abound in activities reflecting the traditions of the people, New Brunswick is, indeed, a unique province.

2 Newfoundland and Labrador

The youngest member of the Canadian family, the province—which comprises Labrador on the mainland and the island of Newfoundland—joined the Confederation in 1949. This is the place where the New World begins. Norsemen settled in L'Anse aux Meadows around year 1000, followed by John Cabot in 1497. The capital city of St. John's, with its deep harbor, is the oldest settlement in the Western world. The influence of the English, Irish, and French is evident in the lively music that is played in the city's 90-plus pubs. Newfoundlanders and Labradorians are among the friendliest people in the world, always ready for a kitchen party.

Newfoundland is considered the best place in the world to view icebergs. This captivating scenery can be observed from the water in sea kayaks and tour boats as well as from the shoreline. The passage where the ice has moved for thousands of years is called Iceberg Alley. The island of Newfoundland is fondly called the Rock because of the craggy cliffs overlooking the coastline. From almost any turn in the road, spectacular vistas can be viewed, whether majestic fiords, crashing surf, or calm bays. Gros Morne National Park, on the west coast of the province's Great

Northern Peninsula, was designated a UNESCO World Heritage Site in 1987. The international science community has been drawn to the terrain which consists of rock more than a billion years old. Labrador, with a landmass of over 300,000 square km (115,000 square mi), offers unparalleled outdoor experiences. The unspoiled wilderness draws those who like to sail, hike, climb, and fish and provides a home for whales. the largest caribou herd in the world, moose, and polar bears. The Northern Lights display their colorful splendor across the sky 250 nights a year. The rugged beauty of magnificent mountains, colorfully painted wooden houses perched on cliffs, and the deep blue sea is breathtaking in Newfoundland and Labrador.

3) Nova Scotia

Almost an island, Nova Scotia is a little province on the Atlantic coast with a long history and a rich culture. Shaped by its rugged coastline and honed by the sea, over the centuries it has been a haven for blacks arriving as freemen or escaped slaves and for Scots, Germans, and Loyalists from the American Revolution, but its earliest colonial history was enriched by the Acadians and scarred by their brutal deportation. This multicultural mix, dating back 400 years, may account for Nova Scotia's rich musical climate, which includes the Gaelic ceilidh—gatherings wild with fiddles and step dancing—and the folk songs of sailors and the sea. Salty ports dot the coastline, and their extravagant Victorian mansions—many of them now hospitable bed-and-breakfasts—bespeak the wealth of shipwrights and merchants who traded with the world a century and more ago.

Cape Breton's Cabot Trail is considered one of the most scenic driving routes in the world. It winds along the coastline for almost 300 km through plateaus and highlands. Halifax, the capital city, blends the past with the present—18th- and 19th-century architecture stands alongside towering glass structures. Known as the City of Trees, Halifax is an excellent place to explore on foot. The waterfront boardwalk fringing the harbor front is embellished with outdoor cafés, pubs with traditional Irish and Scottish music, shops, and restaurants. Point Pleasant Park sits on a peninsula near the mouth of the harbor. The Halifax Citadel is a star-shaped masonry structure that dates to 1749. On a hill overlooking the commercial district, this fortress houses a museum and has commanding views of the harbor. The Annapolis Valley, sheltered on each side by the North and South mountains, is the most fertile area of the province. The meadows bordering the tranquil Annapolis River are lined with apple orchards. Wineries are newer to the region, quickly building a strong reputation, especially for ice wines. Farther south is the waterfront town of Digby, world famous for its large fresh scallops. Nova Scotia's south-shore beaches have white powdery sand and translucent turquoise water, The coastal road is lined with antiques shops, quaint art galleries, and charming seaside restaurants with outdoor patios. Today Nova Scotia maintains its unique outlook: worldly, warm, and sturdily independent.

4) Prince Edward Island

In the Gulf of St. Lawrence north of Nova Scotia and New Brunswick, Canada's smallest province, Prince Edward Island, seems too good to be true. Its manicured green fields roll down to sandy beaches, warm ocean water, and lobster boats in the harbors, and visitors are welcomed by the smiling faces of content residents. The slower paced lifestyle encourages people to gear down and relax. Almost every attraction and property is family owned and -operated. The capital city, Charlottetown, is packed with architectural heritage and culture. It is here that the Confederation of the Arts hosts the Charlottetown Festival, which features the musical *Anne of Green Gables*. In addition to its historical significance as the Cradle of Confederation, PEI is home to some of Atlantic Canada's finest inns, most ornate churches, and highly renowned lobster suppers. The Confederation Bridge has made this Garden of the Gulf easily accessible to the mainland.

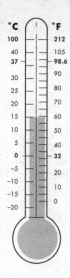

The Atlantic provinces are truly year-round destinations. Summer draws the most visitors due to the fabulous warm ocean beaches, endless activities such as sailing and kayaking, scenic hiking trails, and waterfront restaurants serving succulent lobster. Many people drive through the Maritime provinces as they are easily accessible to each other. Festivals abound in the summer season. Fall brings explosions of color to the trees with its vibrant reds, yellows, and golds; it is also the best time of the year to view many species of whales. This is a great time to travel here as the roads are less congested and the scenery is spectacular. The sea seems to transform into a deep blue that contrasts with the patchwork quilt of the forest. Generally, colors start to emerge in late September and remain until the end of October. As the temperature cools, hunting season begins. There's much to do in the winter. Downhill and cross-country skiing are popular in all four provinces. In Labrador you can ride a dogsled to view the largest caribou herd in the world. Spring brings to life colorful wild lupines and fragrant apple blossoms. Maple syrup flows from the trees, and fishing becomes a favorite pastime.

High season here is the summer and early autumn. Still, one of the pleasures of Atlantic Canada is that it remains a fairly "undiscovered" tourist destination, so you won't feel crowded even at the height of summer.

Climate

As a general rule spring arrives later in coastal regions than inland, and nights are cool by the water, even in August. Autumn can last well into November, with warm clear days and crisp nights. Most of Atlantic Canada is blanketed by snow during winter. The ocean is at its warmest in August and early September.

The following are average daily maximum and minimum temperatures for Halifax.

Forecasts **Weather Channel Connection** ☎ 900/932-8437, 95¢ (U.S.) per minute from a Touch-Tone phone.

HALIFAX, NS

Jan.	33F	1C	May	58F	14C	Sept.	67F	19C
	20	–7		41	5		53	12
Feb.	33F	1C	June	67F	19C	Oct.	58F	14C
	19	–7		50	10		44	7
Mar.	39F	4C	July	73F	23C	Nov.	48F	9C
	26	–3		57	14		36	2
Apr.	48F	9C	Aug.	73F	24C	Dec.	37F	3C
	33	1		58	13		25	4

ST. JOHN'S, NL

Jan.	32F	0C	May	50F	10C	Sept.	61F	16C
	19	–7		34	1		46	8
Feb.	32F	0C	June	61F	16C	Oct.	52F	11C
	18	–8		43	6		37	3
Mar.	34F	1C	July	68F	20C	Nov.	43F	6C
	23	–5		52	11		32	0
Apr.	41F	5C	Aug.	68F	20C	Dec.	36F 2C	
	30	–1		52	11		25	–4

ON THE CALENDAR

For festivals and events listed here that do not have contact information, get in touch with the local or provincial tourist boards (⇨ Visitor Information *in* Smart Travel Tips A to Z) for details.

SPRING	
March or April through June	The east coast of Newfoundland from St. Anthony's to St. John's is a great place to see icebergs floating by.
May	Celebrations of Loyalist Day take place on May 18 in Saint John, NB.
	Towns in the Annapolis Valley, NS, celebrate the rebirth of spring with the annual Apple Blossom Festival (☎ 902/678–8322 ⊕ www.appleblossom.com), held in late May, which includes dancing, parades, and entertainment.
	Truro, NS, pays tribute to the tulip with its three-day Tulip Festival (☎ 902/895–9258 ⊕ www.nstulips.com).

SUMMER	
May–September	The Charlottetown Festival (☎ 902/628–1864 ⊕ www.confederationcentre.com/festival.asp), in Prince Edward Island, offers musicals and concerts.
May–early June	The Scotia Festival of Music (☎ 902/429–9467 ⊕ www.scotiafestival.ns.ca) is a Halifax highlight.
June	Halifax hosts the Nova Scotia International Tattoo (☎ 902/420–1114 ⊕ www.nstattoo.ca).
	In Summerside, PE, the annual Summerside Highland Gathering (☎ 902/436–5377 or 877/224–7473 ⊕ www.collegeofpiping.com/events/highlandgathering.php3) kicks off a summer of concerts and "Come to the Ceilidh" evenings.
July	In Nova Scotia, the Antigonish Highland Games (⊕ www.antigonishhighlandgames.com), staged annually since 1861, has Scottish music, dance, and such ancient sporting events as the caber toss.
	The Atlantic Jazz Festival (☎ 902/492–2225 or 800/567–5277 ⊕ www.jazzeast.com) draws music lovers to Halifax.
	The Conception Bay Folk Festival (☎ 709/596–3324), in Carbonear, NL, highlights traditional Irish-influenced music.
	The Exploits Valley Salmon Festival (☎ 709/489–0418 ⊕ www.salmonfestival.com) is in the Grand Falls, NL, area.
	The Fish, Fun and Folk Festival (☎ 709/884–2678 ⊕ www.fishfunfolkfestival.com) is in Twillingate, NL.
	Gander's Festival of Flight, on the island of Newfoundland, celebrates the town as the aviation "Crossroads of the World" with dances, parades, and a folk festival.
	In Edmunston, NB, the francophone festival Foire Brayonne (☎ 506/739–6608 ⊕ www.foire-brayonne.nb.ca) has music, cultural events, and sports.

There's an Irish Festival (⊕ www.canadasirishfest.com) in Miramichi, NS.

Musicfest (☎ 709/643–8360), in Stephenville, NL, celebrates local music, from rock-and-roll to traditional Newfoundland.

The New Brunswick Highland Games & Scottish Festival (☎ 506/452–9244 or 888/368–4444 ⊕ www.nbhighlandgames.com) is in Fredericton.

The Summerside Lobster Carnival (☎ 902/436–4925) is a weeklong feast of lobster in PEI.

The Shediac Lobster Festival (⊕ www.lobsterfestival.nb.ca) takes place in the Nova Scotia town that calls itself the Lobster Capital of the World.

The Stan Rogers Music Festival (☎ 888/554–7826 ⊕ www.stanfest.com) presents three days of gospel, bluegrass, and folk music in an outdoor venue in Canso, NS.

August

The Acadian Festival (☎506/727–2787 ⊕www.festivalacadiencaraquet.com), at Caraquet, NB, celebrates Acadian heritage with folk singing and food.

The Burin Heritage Weekend (☎ 709/891–2297), in Newfoundland, features traditional entertainment.

The Chocolate Festival (☎ 506/466–7848 ⊕ www.town.ststephen.nb.ca), in St. Stephen, NB, includes suppers, displays, and children's events.

Festival Acadien de la Région Evangeline (☎ 902/854–3300) is an agricultural fair with Acadian music, a parade, and lobster supper, at Wellington Station, PE.

Saint John's Festival by the Sea (☎ 506/632–0086 ⊕ www.festivalbythesea.com) draws hundreds of singers, dancers, and musicians to the New Brunswick city.

The Halifax International Buskerfest has daily outdoor shows by street performers and a food festival.

Kensington, PE, stages an annual Harvest Festival (☎ 902/836–3509), the province's biggest country fair.

The Miramichi Folk Song Festival (☎ 506/623–2150 ⊕ www.miramichifolksongfestival.com), in New Brunswick, has songs steeped in Maritime lore.

At the New Brunswick Summer Music Festival (⊕ www.unb.ca/FineArts/Music/festival) in Fredericton, classical musicians perform and lecture.

The Newfoundland and Labrador Folk Festival (☎ 709/576–8508 ⊕ www.sjfac.nf.net), in St. John's, is an outstanding traditional music event.

The Nova Scotia Gaelic Mod, in St. Ann's, celebrates Scottish culture on the grounds of the only Gaelic college in North America.

Lunenburg holds the Nova Scotia Fisheries Exhibition and Fishermen's Reunion, which highlights traditional Maritime fishing skills.

PEI's Old Home Week fills Charlottetown with nostalgia.

St. John's, NL, is host to the longest-running sporting event in the world, the Royal St. John's Regatta (☎ 709/576–8921), which takes place the first Wednesday of August.

FALL

September

The Atlantic Balloon Fiesta, (☎ 506/432–9444 ⊕ www.atlanticballoonfiesta.com), in Sussex, NB, attracts about 30 brightly colored hot-air balloons; it also offers helicopter rides, parachute demonstrations, and other festival fun.

Six days of French cinema can be enjoyed at the Festival du Cinéma Francophone en Acadie (☎ 506/855–6050 ⊕ www.ficfa.com), in Moncton, NB; directors and actors from around the world attend.

World-class musicians and up-and-coming Atlantic Canadian talent flood Fredericton, NB with slick jazz, gritty blues, spicy Cajun, and world beat music for five days at the Harvest Jazz & Blues Festival (☎ 506/454–2583 or 888/622–5837 ⊕ www.harvestjazzblues.nb.ca).

October

The 10-day Celtic Colors International Festival (☎ 902/564–6668 or 888/355–7744 ⊕ www.celtic-colours.com), one of the premier Celtic events in the world, celebrates traditional music in two dozen locations across Cape Breton, NS.

November

The Prince Edward Island Crafts Council's Annual Christmas Craft Fair (☎ 902/892–5152) brings craftspeople to Charlottetown.

Prince Edward Island celebrates the winter season with Wintertide. This festival includes concerts, exhibits, winter carnivals, sleigh rides, and Christmas light displays.

PLEASURES & PASTIMES

Beaches There are so many beaches to choose from in Atlantic Canada that it's possible to be the only human strolling along a mile stretch of sand. PEI is a haven for beach lovers. Fringed with shifting dunes, the red sand reaches out to the tepid waters of the Gulf of Mexico, the warmest north of the Carolinas. The tranquil atmosphere on PEI draws clam diggers, wind surfers, beach walkers, bird-watchers, and sun worshippers alike. Many beaches have caves carved out by the tides and sandbars where you can be on an island of your own. The east coast of New Brunswick offers some of the best swimming beaches enhanced by the warm waters of the Northumberland Strait. Parlee Beach in Shediac is a paradise for those who enjoy summertime fun. Nova Scotia's south shore has lovely protected coves and long stretches of powdery white sand. The water transcends from a turquoise hue to a rich dark blue as it deepens. Coastal inns, B&Bs, and seaside cottages dot the roadside that weaves along the water's edge. In addition to the mainland beaches, Cape Breton's Ingonish Beach has crashing waves to entice body surfers. Newfoundland and Labrador's rugged coastline and cooler temperatures draw more people on the water than in it. Sea kayaking, sailing, and canoeing are popular water sports, perfect for watching birds, whales, dolphins, and porpoises.

Eating Out Although fish and seafood are the highlight of Atlantic Canadian cuisine, there are many fine-dining establishments that serve an array of international and ethnic dishes as well. If you want to go local, stick to lobster, mussels, scallops, salmon, and cod. In Newfoundland and Labrador, regional specialties include seal flipper pie and cod tongues, which are usually battered and fried. New Brunswick is known for its fiddleheads—wild ferns picked in early summer before they uncurl (hence their name). In New Brunswick you can also find dulse, which is dried, crisp seaweed that can be munched like potato chips or, in powder form, adds flavor to meat and fish.

The Great Outdoors Atlantic Canada has many provincial and national parks where campers and day-trippers engage in all kinds of outdoor activities, including water sports such as canoeing, kayaking, and sailing. Fundy National Park, one of New Brunswick's top attractions, has spectacular tides and a unique ecosystem; it is home to an abundance of wildlife such as whales, migrating seabirds, and seals. In Kouchibouguac National Park, on the northeastern shore of the province, sand dunes and grasses protect endangered piping plovers. Sand dunes are also a notable feature of Prince Edward Island National Park, where wide, sandy beaches curve around clean, warm waters that are ideal for swimming, canoeing, or windsurfing. Cape Breton Highlands National Park in Nova Scotia has spectacular drives and great opportunities for wildlife-watching as well as hiking and fishing. Newfoundland's Gros Morne National Park, a UNESCO World Heritage Site, offers rugged hiking and camping amid spectacular fjord scenery.

Biking Eastern Canada offers some of the best bicycling in the country, from the flats of Prince Edward Island to the varied terrain in New Brunswick and Nova Scotia. Write to provincial tourist boards for their road maps (which are more detailed than the maps available at gas stations) and information on local cycling associations.

Boating

With the Atlantic coastline, major rivers, and smaller lakes, boating in many forms is extremely popular throughout Atlantic Canada. Boat, canoe, and kayak rentals are widely available, and provincial tourism departments can provide lists of sources.

Fishing

Anglers can find their catch in Atlantic Canada, although restrictions, seasons, license requirements, and catch limits vary from province to province. In addition, a special fishing permit is required to fish in all national parks; it can be obtained at any national park site for a nominal fee. Nova Scotia has some of the most stringent freshwater restrictions in Canada, but the availability of Atlantic salmon, speckled trout, and striped bass makes the effort worthwhile. Salmon, trout, and black bass are abundant in the waters of New Brunswick, and although many salmon pools in the streams and rivers are leased to private freeholders, either individuals or clubs, fly fishing is still readily available for visitors. The waters surrounding Prince Edward Island have some of the best deep-sea tuna fishing. Newfoundland offers cod, mackerel, salmon, and sea trout in the Atlantic and speckled trout and rainbow trout in its fresh waters.

Golfing

Eastern Canada has become a premier golf destination hosting world-class events. Canada's golf magazine, *Score,* regards PEI as nation's best golf destination. All four Atlantic provinces have architecturally designed courses with spectacular views.

Scuba Diving

More than 3,000 shipwrecks lie off the coast of Nova Scotia, making it particularly attractive to divers. The provincial Department of Tourism can provide details on the location of wrecks and where to buy or rent equipment.

Whale-Watching

The waters around Newfoundland have excellent whale-watching in season, and giant humpbacks, right whales, finbacks, and minke whales can be seen in the Bay of Fundy. Whale-watching trips are available from Newfoundland, New Brunswick, and Nova Scotia.

Shopping

The residents of Atlantic Canada are consummate craftspeople, and the region abounds with potters, painters, glassblowers, weavers, and photographers. Good buys include hand-knitted clothing in Newfoundland; hooked rugs, quilts, pottery, and pewter objets d'art (picture frames, jewelry boxes, candlesticks, and the like) in New Brunswick and Nova Scotia; and pottery on Prince Edward Island. Many of the artisans work from home or from restored barns and farmhouses. If you're driving through the countryside, look for road signs advertising their studios. You should also look for posters listing garage and lawn sales. They're hugely popular in this part of Canada. As you sifting through the basement junk, you may find bargains, especially antiques.

Winter Activities

Life is anything but dormant in the Atlantic provinces during the winter months. Downhill and cross-country skiing are sports that continue to grow in appeal. Newfoundland has Marble Mountain, with a 1,600-foot vertical drop. Each year more than 16 feet of snow covers the area, more than anywhere else in eastern North America. Labrador has 19 runs of alpine adventure at Smokey Mountain. Nova Scotia has four ski resorts, the most popular being Wentworth and Martock, both within 1½ hours of Halifax. New Brunswick's majestic Sugarloaf is on the highest peak in the Maritimes, at Mount Carleton Provincial Park. In addition to skiing, snowmobiling is an immensely popular sport in New Brunswick. Beautifully groomed trails endlessly cut through the countryside. The Trans-Canada Trail in PEI is perfect for cross-country skiing as it goes from one end of the island to the other. Newfoundland and Labrador have 1,600 km (960 mi) of well-groomed trails for snowmobiling. Dogsledding is available to those who want a totally unique experience in outdoor adventure. In Newfoundland and Labrador snow often remains on the ground until early April, allowing for an extended winter season.

FODOR'S CHOICE

LODGING

$$$$	**Keltic Lodge,** Ingonish Beach, NS. A stunning cliffside location, the beauty of the Cape Breton Highlands, world-class golf, whale watching, and sun and sand are just a handful of the pleasures to enjoy at the Keltic Lodge.
$$$$	**Kingsbrae Arms,** St. Andrews by-the-Sea, NB. You'll be pleasantly pampered at this intimate restored 1897 estate with eclectic and amusing antiques.
$$–$$$$	**Gowrie House,** Sydney Mines, NS. Filled with art and antiques and surrounded by trees and flowerbeds, this Georgian house is a gem of a country inn; dinners are outstanding.
$$–$$$	**Fairholm National Historic Inn,** Charlottetown, PE. This inn features eight elegant suites with period antique furnishings in Olde Charlottetown.
$–$$$	**Compton House,** St. John's, NL. Charming and historic, this Victorian inn is beautifully decorated and exceptionally managed. The 12-foot high-ceilings and antiques give it an elegant quality that extends into the suites.
$–$$	**Stonehame Lodge & Chalets,** Scotsburn (near Pictou), NS. The peace and quiet of nature, and cozy, self-contained mountaintop chalets await you here.
$–$$	**West Point Lighthouse,** West Point, PE. A functioning lighthouse in a provincial park, this small inn sits next to the beach.

BUDGET LODGING

$	**Four Mile Beach Inn,** Cape North, Cape Breton, NS. Hosts are wonderful and go out of their way to help plan your Cabot Trail/Cape Breton adventure. Rooms are clean and comfortable, with great views.
$	**Islander Motor Lodge,** Charlottetown, PE. This motor lodge has many repeat visitors because it has a central location in the downtown district and it is a small, privately owned operation with friendly service and home-cooked meals.
$	**Little Shemogue Country Inn,** Little Shemogue (near Shediac), NB. This big, brick-red farmhouse is surrounded by flowers, lawns and Shemogue Bay. The food is elegant, eclectic, and authentic to the region.
¢–$	**Farmhouse Inn B&B,** Canning (near Wolfville), NS. Just a 10-minute drive from Wolfville, this cozy abode offers up whirlpool tubs and/or propane fireplaces to maximize your relaxation. Afternoon tea is complimentary.
¢–$	**Valhalla Lodge Bed & Breakfast,** St. Lunaire–Griquet (near L'Anse aux Meadows), NL. Just minutes from the community of L'Anse aux

Meadows and the National Historic Site, rooms come with ocean views and warm hospitality at this B&B. This is where Annie E. Proulx wrote her Pulitzer Prize–winning book, *The Shipping News*.

RESTAURANTS

$$$–$$$$	**La Fine Grobe-Sur-Mer,** Nigadoo (near Caraquet), NB. The food is authentic French, the service is courtly, and the view of the Bay of Chaleur is magnificent. Some diners claim to have seen the fiery phantom ship said to sail these waters.
$$–$$$$	**The Cellar,** St. John's, NL. "The Attic" would be a more appropriate name for this fine-dining establishment, given its fourth-floor location. But there's no confusion over the food, which is decidedly excellent. Rich seafood, pasta, and meat entrées are served by courteous staff and washed down with a fine selection of wines.
$$$	**Da Maurizio Dining Room,** Halifax, NS. Chef Maurizio is a local legend, but the superiority of his creative and impressive concoctions is no myth.
$$–$$$	**Acton's Grill & Café,** Wolfville, NS. Toronto restaurateurs have made this establishment a cheerful place with excellent food. The weekend buffet includes an amazing spread of seafood and greens.
$$–$$$	**Dunes Café,** Brackley Beach, PE. Enjoy a panoramic view of flowering gardens, dunes, and the ocean while savoring inspired cuisine in this dramatic cedar-and-glass structure that also houses an artist's studio and art gallery.
$–$$$	**Gabrieau's Bistro Restaurant,** Antigonish, NS. Rich pastas, gourmet thin-crust pizzas, heaping salads, international cuisine, and sinful desserts are just some of the pleasures you discover at this pleasant bistro.
$–$$$	**West Point Lighthouse,** West Point, PE. This quaint seaside restaurant has chowders, seafood, a lobster platter, and vegetarian dishes. The ocean views are panoramic both inside and outside on the patio.
$$	**The Pilot House,** Charlottetown, PE. The pub menu at this restaurant offers an extensive variety of food, from fish-and-chips and lobster BLT to curried chicken and Island Blue mussels.
$–$$	**The Norseman Restaurant,** L'Anse aux Meadows, NL. This harborfront restaurant combines dinner theater with a fine-dining menu of seafood, pasta, and caribou tenderloins. Choose from an extensive wine list to wash it all down.

BUDGET RESTAURANTS

¢–$$	**Harris' Quick 'n Tasty,** Dayton (near Yarmouth), NS. This venerable diner has sturdy dishes like turkey burgers and club sandwiches at light prices.
¢–$$	**Pump House Brewery,** Moncton, NB. This place is dedicated to fun. If there's a local festival, this is where to celebrate it. The menu is pub food with several twists.
¢–$	**Ches's,** St. John's, NL. The city's finest fast-food fish-and-chips is made with a batter from an old family recipe. It never fails.

| ¢–$ | **Julien's Pastry Shop & Bakery,** Chester, NS. If the hearty baguette sandwiches don't fill you up, there's an abundance of pastries and cookies to tempt you at this genuine French bakery. |

| ¢–$ | **Rose Arbour Café,** Windsor, NS. The floral decor in this homey eatery is as friendly as the staff. The fish-and-chips is a real delight. |

| ¢–$ | **Sugar Moon Pancake House,** Earltown, NS. Tuck into hearty buttermilk pancakes at Nova Scotia's only year-round maple farm. In season you may also see maple syrup being made over a wood-fired evaporator. |

DRIVES

Aspotogan Peninsula, between Hubbards and Chester, NS. This scenic, 45-minute coastal drive loops past picturesque working fishing villages (Northwest Cove), dramatic fjords, and sandy-white (but breezy) beaches. It's a stunning way to veer off the beaten track between two popular summer towns.

Blue Heron Drive, PE. This drive encompasses the white sweeping beaches of the North Shore through the national parks and passes Acadian villages to the red cliffs of the South Shore.

Cabot Trail, Cape Breton, NS. Regarded as one of the most scenic drives in the world, the road winds through the highlands along the coastline, providing panoramic vistas of the Atlantic Ocean.

The Discovery Trail, near Clarenville, NL. The short drive from Clarenville is rewarded with some of the most beautiful and historic communities on the island. The history is well documented in tourist attractions, which are now the area's economic backbone in the absence of the fishery. A replica of John Cabot's ship the *Matthew* can be found at Bonavista, a popular summer theater program at Trinity draws thousands, and the set of the television miniseries *Random Passage* is quickly becoming a hit with visitors.

Fundy Park to Hopewell Rocks, NB. The entire Bay of Fundy coast is carved by the highest tides in the world. The drive from Fundy National Park, through Alma, to Cape Enrage, past Mary's Point and the Shepody marshes, and on to the Hopewell Rocks includes some of its most dramatic features.

St. John River Valley, NB. The St. John River, which was once called the Rhine of North America, now it rests on its laurels. The valley is lush and much of the Trans Canada Highway (Route 2) shows it off from Edmundston to Fredericton. Take the exit to Route 102 at Long's Creek to Fredericton then on down to Gagetown, Queenstown, and Evandale to Grand Bay–Westfield. Traffic on his lower part of the river is served by free cable ferries. You can crisscross the river several times along the way.

HISTORY

Fortress of Louisbourg National Historic Site, Louisbourg, Cape Breton, NS. Costumed actors re-create the lives of 18th-century French soldiers, settlers, and tradespeople at this sprawling reconstructed fortress.

Kings Landing Historical Settlement, outside Fredericton, NB. This reconstructed village—including homes, a school, working farms, and a sawmill—illustrates life in the central St. John River valley between 1790 and 1900.

L'Anse aux Meadows National Historic Site, L'Anse aux Meadows, NL. This UNESCO World Heritage Site is the only authentic Viking settlement in North America, dating to 1000 AD.

Port-La-Joye-Fort Amherst National Historic Site, PE. Founded by the French in 1720 near the present site of Charlottetown, this was the first European settlement on the Island. Fort Amherst was built on the same location, when the British captured Port-La-Joye in 1758.

Province House National Historic Site, Charlottetown, PE. Designed in 1847, this three-story sandstone structure was the site of the Confederation Conference in 1864, the first of many meetings leading to the Canadian Confederation in 1867.

Sherbrooke Village, Sherbrooke, NS. Step back in time to the 1800s to discover a typical Nova Scotian village. Visit the blacksmith's shop and pick up a sweet at the general store.

Signal Hill National Historic Site, St. John's, NL. The site of Marconi's first wireless trans-Atlantic message includes a museum to the man and an unequaled view of the city and its famous harbor entrance, the Narrows. The water is dotted with icebergs, whales, and boats as far as the eye can see.

OUTDOOR ACTIVITIES

Boat tours, east coast of NL. An abundance of whales frolic off the Atlantic coast all summer. Tour boat operators can be found in nearly every community to take you to whales, icebergs, or large flocks of nesting seabirds. Icebergs pass along the coast from the tip of the Northern Peninsula right down the northeastern side of the island.

Cycling the Confederation Trail, PE. This well-marked trail covers 300 km (186 mi) from one end of the Island to the other. The interior has gentle rolling hills, and the coastline offers a flatter terrain. The trail passes through quaint towns with B&Bs, restaurants, and plenty of rest stops.

Exploring the ocean floor at Hopewell Rocks Hopewell Cape, NB. The Bay of Fundy tides have carved rock formations called the Giant Flowerpots that project out of the ocean floor when the tide is out.

Hiking in the Cape Mabou Highlands, Cape Breton, NS. Some of the best hiking trails in Atlantic Canada are in this region of plunging cliffs. Stunning scenery—mountains, forest, and isolated beaches—

combine with examples of the cultural heritage, reflected in the Gaelic trail markers.

Hiking the East Coast Trail, Avalon Peninsula, NL. This trail winds along 520 km (322 mi) of coastline and passes through two dozen communities, including some that have been resettled and are now abandoned. Trail sections are rated easy, moderate, difficult, or strenuous.

Kejimkujik National Park, NS. Canoers and hikers alike thrill at the opportunities inside this majestic 381-square-km (147-square-mi) national park. Spend the day swimming, hiking and spotting wildlife or spend the night in one of the tent or RV sites.

Sea Kayaking, PE. The gentle waters surrounding the Island allow for the perfect conditions to explore the bays and islets of this province on half-day or multiday excursions.

Whale-watching at Pleasant Bay, Cape Breton, NS. Several tour operators ply the waters outside this bay. Among the options is a "kitchen ceilidh" tour, complete with fiddle music. All tours offer first-class scenery and a chance to see majestic sea creatures.

NATURE

Cape Breton Highlands National Park, Cape Breton, NS. A wilderness of wooded valleys, plateau barrens, and steep cliffs, the park stretches across the Northern Peninsula of Nova Scotia's Cape Breton Island.

Cape Chignecto Provincial Park, West Advocate, NS. The community-managed Cape Chignecto Park, the province's largest park, offers days of exploring, with sea cliff rising from the Bay of Fundy and numerous hiking trails. Find views galore, rare plants, wildlife, backcountry hike-in and walk-in campsites, and access to the Bay of Fundy shoreline.

Gros Morne National Park, NL. A UNESCO World Heritage Site, this park offers great hiking and camping amid spectacular views of fjords

Prince Edward Island National Park, Cavendish, PE. Along the north shore of the Island, sky and sea meet red-sandstone cliffs, rolling dunes, and long stretches of sand.

Fundy National Park, Alma, NB. Geological diversity and the world's highest tides make this park a unique spot to visit.

VIEWS

Cape d'Or, NS. You find dory rips and the surf crashing below as you stand on the tip of the cape, a rocky, carved finger of land stretching into the turbulent Minas Channel. The vantage provides spectacular views of Cape d'Or, Cape Chignecto, and Advocate Harbour.

Highland Village Museum, Iona, Cape Breton, NS. Perched high on a hill, the view is stunning from this living-history museum that celebrates the Gaelic experience. Stand by a stone-and-sod replica of a house of old-time Highland and Island Gaels as you look down over the majestic Bras d'Or Lakes.

Morrisey Rock, near Campbellton, NB. Perched on this rocky cliff, you have a stunning view of the hills of Gaspé and of the niche the Restigouche River has carved for itself between New Brunswick and Québec.

Prince Edward Island National Park, Cavendish, PE. The Cavendish area of this park along PEI's north shore offers superb ocean views from atop the cliffs.

Signal Hill National Historic Site, St. John's, NL. Overlooking the snug punch-bowl harbor of St. John's and the sea, this hilltop was taken and retaken by opposing forces in the 17th and 18th centuries.

Swallowtail, Grand Manan Island, NB. From Lighthouse Road you can see the red-and-white light and keeper's cottage that sit on a grass-covered rocky spit of land that reaches into the Bay of Fundy. There's lots of traffic on the sea as ferries, fishing boats and whale-watching vessels scurry in and out of the harbor at North Head.

West Point Lighthouse, West Point, PE. This area and the surrounding provincial park offer a favorite vantage point to view sunsets.

SMART TRAVEL TIPS

Air Travel
Airports
Bike Travel
Boat & Ferry Travel
Business Hours
Bus Travel
Cameras & Photography
Car Rental
Car Travel
Children in Atlantic Canada
Consumer Protection
Cruise Travel
Customs & Duties
Disabilities & Accessibility
Discounts & Deals
Eating & Drinking
Ecotourism
Embassies and Consulates
Gay & Lesbian Travel
Holidays
Insurance
Language
Lodging
Mail & Shipping
Media
Money Matters
National Parks
Packing
Passports & Visas
Senior-Citizen Travel
Shopping
Sports & the Outdoors
Students in Canada
Taxes
Time
Tipping
Tours & Packages
Train Travel
Travel Agencies
Visitor Information
Web Sites

Finding out about your destination before you leave home means you won't squander time organizing everyday minutiae once you've arrived. You'll be more streetwise when you hit the ground as well, better prepared to explore the aspects of Atlantic Canada that drew you here in the first place. The organizations in this section can provide information to supplement this guide; contact them for up-to-the-minute details, and consult the A to Z sections that end each chapter for facts on the various topics as they relate to Atlantic Canada's many regions. Happy landings!

AIR TRAVEL

BOOKING

When you book, look for nonstop flights and remember that "direct" flights stop at least once. Try to avoid connecting flights, which require a change of plane. Two airlines may operate a connecting flight jointly, so ask whether your airline operates every segment of the trip; you may find that the carrier you prefer flies you only part of the way. To find more booking tips and to check prices and make online flight reservations, log on to www.fodors.com.

CARRIERS

National flag carriers have the greatest number of nonstops. Domestic carriers may have better connections to your hometown and serve a greater number of gateway cities. Foreign third-party carriers may have a price advantage.

Air Canada serves every major city in Atlantic Canada, and within Canada it has flights to most smaller cities via its regional feeder airlines. Other major airlines that serve Halifax include American Airlines (via Boston); Continental (via Newark, NJ); Delta (via Boston); and Northwest (via Detroit). Pan Am flies from Manchester, NH, and Bangor, ME, to Halifax and Saint John, and from Martha's Vineyard, MA, to Halifax. Jetsgo has direct flights to Charlottetown, Gander, Halifax, St. John's, and Stephenville from Newark. Among smaller regional carriers, Air Labrador, and CanJet serve Newfoundland and Labrador; CanJet flies to Moncton, NB and Fredericton, NB.

Air Canada dominates 90% of Canada's airline industry. Small carriers are worth investigating, especially when flying short distances between major centers. Contact regional travel agencies for charter companies. Private pilots should obtain information from the Canada Map Office, which has the *Canada Flight Supplement* (lists of airports with Canada Customs services) as well as aeronautical charts.

⚐ Major Airlines Air Canada ☎ 888/247-2262 ⊕ www.aircanada.ca. **American Airlines** ☎ 800/433-7300 ⊕ www.aa.com. **British Airways** ☎ 800/403-0882 in North America, 0870/850-9850 in the U.K. ⊕ www.ba.com. **Continental** ☎ 800/525-0280 ⊕ www.continental.com. **Delta Airlines** ☎ 800/221-1212 ⊕ www.delta.com. **Northwest** ☎ 800/225-2525 ⊕ www.nwa.com.

⚐ Smaller Airlines Air Labrador ☎ 800/563-3042. **CanJet** ☎ 800/809-7777. **Jetsgo** ☎ 866/440-0441 ⊕ www.jetsgo.ca. **Pan Am** ☎ 800/359-7262 ⊕ www.flypanam.com. **Provincial Airlines** ☎ 709/576-1666, 800/563-2800 in Atlantic Canada ⊕ www.provair.com.

⚐ Contacts for Private Pilots Canada Map Office ✉ 130 Bentley Ave., Nepean, ON K1A 0E9 ☎ 800/465-6277.

CHECK-IN & BOARDING

Always **find out your carrier's check-in policy.** Plan to arrive at the airport about two hours before your scheduled departure time for domestic flights and 2½–3 hours before international flights. You may need to arrive earlier if you're flying from one of the busier airports or during peak air-traffic times.Assuming that not everyone with a ticket will show up, airlines routinely overbook planes. When everyone does, airlines ask for volunteers to give up their seats. In return, these volunteers usually get a several-hundred-dollar flight voucher, which can be used toward the purchase of another ticket, and are rebooked on the next flight out. If there are not enough volunteers, the airline must choose who will be denied boarding. The first to get bumped are passengers who checked in late and those flying on discounted tickets, so get to the gate and check in as early as possible, especially during peak periods.

Always **bring a government-issued photo ID** to the airport; even when it's not required, a passport is best.

Departing passengers at all major airports must pay a $10 airport-improvement fee and a $24 security fee before boarding.

CUTTING COSTS

The least expensive airfares to Atlantic Canada are priced for round-trip travel and must usually be purchased at least two weeks in advance. Airlines generally allow you to change your return date for a fee; most low-fare tickets, however, are non-refundable. It's smart to call a number of airlines and check the Internet; when you are quoted a good price, book it on the spot—the same fare may not be available the next day, or even the next hour. Always check different routings and look into using alternate airports. Also, price off-peak flights, which may be significantly less expensive than others. Travel agents, especially low-fare specialists (⇨ Discounts and Deals), are helpful.

Consolidators are another good source. They buy tickets for scheduled flights at reduced rates from the airlines, then sell them at prices that beat the best fare available directly from the airlines. Sometimes you can even get your money back if you need to return the ticket. Carefully read the fine print detailing penalties for changes and cancellations, purchase the ticket with a credit card, and confirm your consolidator reservation with the airline.

⚐ Consolidators AirlineConsolidator.com ☎ 888/468-5385 ⊕ www.airlineconsolidator.com; for international tickets. **Best Fares** ☎ 800/576-8255 or 800/576-1600 ⊕ www.bestfares.com; $59.90 annual membership. **Cheap Tickets** ☎ 800/377-1000 or 888/922-8849 ⊕ www.cheaptickets.com. **Discount Travel Club** ☎ 800/409-6753. **Expedia** ☎ 800/397-3342 or 404/728-8787 ⊕ www.expedia.com. **Hotwire** ☎ 866/468-9473 or 920/330-9418 ⊕ www.hotwire.com. **Now Voyager Travel** ✉ 45 W. 21st St., 5th floor, New York, NY 10010 ☎ 212/459-1616 🖷 212/243-2711 ⊕ www.nowvoyagertravel.com. **Onetravel.com** ⊕ www.onetravel.com. **Orbitz** ☎ 888/656-4546 ⊕ www.orbitz.com. **Priceline.com** ⊕ www.priceline.com. **Travelocity** ☎ 888/709-5983, 877/282-2925 in Canada, 0870/111-7060 in the U.K. ⊕ www.travelocity.com. **Unitravel** ☎ 800/325-2222 ⊕ www.unitravel.com.

ENJOYING THE FLIGHT

State your seat preference when purchasing your ticket, and then repeat it when you confirm and when you check in. For more legroom, you can request one of the few emergency-aisle seats at check-in if you are capable of lifting at least 50 pounds—a Federal Aviation Administration requirement of passengers in these seats. Seats behind a bulkhead also offer more legroom, but they don't have under-seat storage. Don't sit in the row in front of the emergency aisle or in front of a bulkhead, where seats may not recline.

Ask the airline whether a snack or meal is served on the flight. If you have dietary concerns, request special meals when booking. These can be vegetarian, low-cholesterol, or kosher, for example. It's a good idea to pack some healthful snacks and a small (plastic) bottle of water in your carry-on bag. On long flights, try to maintain a normal routine, to help fight jet lag. At night, get some sleep. By day, eat light meals, drink water (not alcohol), and **move around the cabin** to stretch your legs. For additional jet-lag tips consult *Fodor's FYI: Travel Fit & Healthy* (available at bookstores everywhere).

All major and regional airlines and charter lines that serve Atlantic Canada prohibit smoking. All Canadian airports are also nonsmoking, with the exception of Québec, where smoking is allowed in designated areas only.

FLYING TIMES

Flying time to Halifax is 1½ hours from Montréal, 2½ hours from New York, 4½ hours from Chicago (with connection), eight hours from Los Angeles (with connection), and six hours from London.

HOW TO COMPLAIN

If your baggage goes astray or your flight goes awry, complain right away. Most carriers require that you **file a claim immediately.** The Aviation Consumer Protection Division of the Department of Transportation publishes *Fly-Rights,* which discusses airlines and consumer issues and is available online. You can also find articles and information on mytravelrights.com, the Web site of the nonprofit Consumer Travel Rights Center.

🔁 Airline Complaints **Aviation Consumer Protection Division** ✉ U.S. Department of Transportation, C-75, Room 4107, 400 7th St. SW, Washington, DC 20590 ☎ 202/366-2220 ⊕ airconsumer.ost.dot.gov. **Federal Aviation Administration Consumer Hotline** ✉ for inquiries: FAA, 800 Independence Ave. SW, Washington, DC 20591 ☎ 800/322-7873 ⊕ www.faa.gov.

RECONFIRMING

Check the status of your flight before you leave for the airport. You can do this on your carrier's Web site, by linking to a flight-status checker (many Web booking services offer these), or by calling your carrier or travel agent. Always confirm international flights at least 72 hours ahead of the scheduled departure time.

AIRPORTS

The major airport is Halifax International Airport (YHZ). For information about smaller airports, *see* the A to Z sections *in* individual chapters.

🔁 Airport Information **Halifax Internations Airport** ✉ Just off Hwy. 102, at exit 6 ☎ 902/873-4422 ⊕ www.halifax-airport.ca.

BIKE TRAVEL

Despite Canada's harsh climate and demanding landscape, bicycle travel has become very popular since the 1980s, especially on the Atlantic coast. Some terrain is steep and hilly, but it's always varied and interesting. Prince Edward Island has converted an abandoned rail line into a trail that runs from one end of the province to the other. Similar conversions are in the works in other Atlantic Provinces, but much of the terrain is gravel and unsuitable for cycling.

Nationally, the Trans-Canada Trail—linking the Atlantic to both the Pacific and Arctic oceans—allows bicycles along much of its length when the project is finished (expected date is 2006). Though cyclists aren't allowed on most multiple-lane, limited-access highways, parts of the Trans-Canada Highway are two-lane blacktop with broad, paved shoulders that are widely used by cyclists crossing the country. There are also plenty of secondary roads that see little traffic and almost no truck traffic.

For maps and information on bicycle routes, consult the provincial tourist information offices (⇨ Visitor Information).

BIKES IN FLIGHT

Most airlines accommodate bikes as luggage, provided they are dismantled and boxed; check with individual airlines about packing requirements. Some airlines sell bike boxes, which are often free at bike shops, for about $15 (bike bags can be considerably more expensive). International travelers often can substitute a bike for a piece of checked luggage at no charge; otherwise, the cost is about $100. U.S. and Canadian airlines charge $40–$80 each way.

BOAT & FERRY TRAVEL

Car ferries provide essential transportation on the east coast of Canada. Marine Atlantic runs ferries between Nova Scotia and Newfoundland. Northumberland and Bay Ferries Ltd. operates a high-speed catamaran car ferry between Bar Harbor, Maine, and Yarmouth, Nova Scotia, as well as regular car ferries between New Brunswick and Nova Scotia. Prince of Fundy Cruises sails between Portland, Maine, and Yarmouth, Nova Scotia.

For additional information about regional ferry service, *see* A to Z sections *in* individual chapters.

FARES AND SCHEDULES

All major ferry lines entering the province accept major credit cards, traveler's checks, and cash. Schedules are available through Tourism Nova Scotia outlets or online. Reservations can also be made online. Smaller independent ferries within the province that cross rivers take cash only, but the fare is usually under five dollars. **⏹ Boat & Ferry Information Marine Atlantic** ✉ 355 Purves St., North Sydney, NS B2A 3V2 ☎ 800/341-7981 ⊕ www.marine-atlantic.ca. **Northumberland and Bay Ferries Ltd.** ✉ 121 Eden St., Bar Harbor, ME 04609 ☎ 888/249-7245. **Prince of Fundy Cruises** ☎ 800/341-7540.

BUSINESS HOURS

BANKS & OFFICES

Most banks are open Monday through Thursday 10–3 and Friday 10–5 or 6. All banks are closed on national holidays. Nearly all banks have automatic teller machines (ATMs) that are accessible around the clock.

MUSEUMS & SIGHTS

Hours at museums vary, but most open at 10 or 11 and close in the evening. Many museums are closed on Monday; some stay open late one day a week, and admission is sometimes waived on that day.

SHOPS

Stores, shops, and supermarkets usually are open Monday through Saturday 9–6, although in major cities supermarkets are often open 7:30 AM–9 PM, and some food stores are open around the clock. Most large supermarkets and malls are closed on Sunday. Stores often stay open Thursday and Friday evenings, most shopping malls until 9 PM. Drugstores in major cities are often open until midnight, and convenience stores tend to be open 24 hours a day, seven days a week.

BUS TRAVEL

If you don't have a car, bus travel is essential in Atlantic Canada, especially to visit out-of-the-way towns that do not have airports or rail lines. Buses usually depart and arrive only once a day from any given departure or destination. Greyhound Lines and Voyageur offer interprovincial service. Acadian Lines operates bus service throughout Atlantic Canada. Buses are quite comfortable, have clean bathrooms, and make occasional rest stops. Smoking is not allowed on buses in Canada.

FARES & SCHEDULES

Bus terminals in major cities and even in many smaller ones are usually efficient operations with service all week and plenty of agents on hand to handle ticket sales. In villages and some smaller towns, the bus station is simply a counter in a local convenience store, gas station, or snack bar. If you ask, the bus driver will usually stop anywhere on the route to let you off, even if it is not a designated terminal.

PAYING

Visa, MasterCard, traveler's checks in U.S. or Canadian currency, and cash are all accepted when purchasing a ticket at a designated terminal.

RESERVATIONS

Bus companies do not accept reservations. Pick up your tickets at least 45 minutes before the bus's scheduled departure time. **⏹ Bus Information Acadian Lines** ☎ 506/859-5105, 800/567-5151 within Nova Scotia, New Brunswick, and Prince Edward Island ⊕ www.smtbus.com. **Voyageur** ✉ 505 E. Boulevard Maisonneuve, Montréal, QC H2L 1Y4 ☎ 514/842-2281. **Greyhound Canada** ☎ 800/661-8747 ⊕ www.greyhound.ca. **Greyhound International** ☎ 0134/231-7317 in the U.K.

CAMERAS & PHOTOGRAPHY

Atlantic Canada is one of the world's most scenic places. Particularly intriguing are the dramatic fogs of the Atlantic shore. Photographers who want to catch the country at its most strikingly beautiful should consider a winter trip. City and country take on a whole new glamour when they're buried deep in snow.

The *Kodak Guide to Shooting Great Travel Pictures* (available at bookstores everywhere) is loaded with tips.
Photo Help Kodak Information Center ☎ 800/242-2424.

EQUIPMENT PRECAUTIONS

Don't pack film or equipment in checked luggage, where it is much more susceptible to damage. X-ray machines used to view checked luggage are extremely powerful and therefore are likely to ruin your film. Try to ask for hand inspection of film, which becomes clouded after repeated exposure to airport X-ray machines, and keep videotapes and computer disks away from metal detectors. Always keep film, tape, and computer disks out of the sun. Carry an extra supply of batteries, and be prepared to turn on your camera, camcorder, or laptop to prove to airport security personnel that the device is real.

CAR RENTAL

Some companies, such as Avis, don't rent manual-transmission cars in Canada.
Major Agencies Alamo ☎ 800/327-9633 ⊕ www.alamo.com. **Avis** ☎ 800/331-1084, 800/879-2847 in Canada, 02/9353-9000 in Australia, 09/525-1982 in New Zealand, 0870/606-0100 in the U.K. ⊕ www.avis.com. **Budget** ☎ 800/527-0700, 0870/156-5656 in the U.K. ⊕ www.budget.com. **Dollar** ☎ 800/800-4000, 0124/622-0111 in the U.K., where it's affiliated with Sixt, 02/9223-1444 in Australia ⊕ www.dollar.com. **Hertz** ☎ 800/654-3001, 800/263-0600 in Canada, 02/9669-2444 in Australia, 09/256-8690 in New Zealand, 020/8897-2072 in the U.K. ⊕ www.hertz.com. **National Car Rental** ☎ 800/227-7368, 020/8680-4800 in the U.K. ⊕ www.nationalcar.com.

CUTTING COSTS

For a good deal, book through a travel agent who will shop around. Price local car-rental companies—whose prices may be lower, although their service and maintenance may not be as good as those of major rental agencies—and research rates on the Internet. Remember to ask about required deposits and cancellation penalties. If you're traveling during a holiday period, also make sure that a confirmed reservation guarantees you a car.

INSURANCE

When driving a rented car, you are generally responsible for any damage to or loss of the vehicle. You also may be liable for any property damage or personal injury that you may cause while driving. Before you rent, see what coverage you already have under the terms of your personal auto-insurance policy and credit cards. A "no fault" policy is offered by all major car-rental companies for about $30 a day and will cover virtually any mishap.

REQUIREMENTS & RESTRICTIONS

You must be 21 years old to rent an economy or midsize car and 25 years old to rent an SUV or other specialty vehicle. Rental-car companies have not set an upper age limit.

SURCHARGES

Before you pick up a car in one city and leave it in another, ask about drop-off charges or one-way service fees, which can be substantial. Note, too, that some rental agencies charge extra if you return the car before the time specified in your contract. To avoid a hefty refueling fee, fill the tank just before you turn in the car, but be aware that gas stations near the rental outlet may overcharge. It's almost never a deal to buy the tank of gas that's in the car when you rent it; the understanding is that you'll return it empty, but some fuel usually remains.

CAR TRAVEL

In Atlantic Canada your own driver's license is acceptable for up to three months. Atlantic Canada's highway system is excellent. It includes the Trans-Canada Highway, the longest highway in the world—running about 8,000 km (5,000 mi) from Victoria, British Columbia, to St. John's, Newfoundland, using ferries to bridge coastal waters at each end.

FROM THE U.S.

Drivers must carry owner registration and proof of insurance coverage, which is compulsory in Canada. The Canadian Non-Resident Inter-Provincial Motor Vehicle Liability Insurance Card, available from any U.S. insurance company, is accepted as evidence of financial responsibility in Canada. The minimum liability coverage in Atlantic Canada is C$200,000. If you are driving a car that is not registered in your name, carry a letter from the owner that authorizes your use of the vehicle.

The U.S. Interstate Highway System leads directly into Canada along I–95 from Maine to New Brunswick. There are many smaller highway crossings between the two countries as well.

🔹 Insurance Information **Insurance Bureau of Canada** ☎ 416/362–2031 in Canada ⊕ www.ibc.ca.

EMERGENCY SERVICES

In case of an accident or emergency call 911. If you are a member of the American Automobile Association, you are automatically covered by the Canadian Automobile Association while traveling in Canada.

🔹 **Canadian Automobile Association** ☎ 800/222–4357.

GASOLINE

At this writing, the per-liter price of gas is 85¢ ($3.23 per gallon), but gas prices in Canada are expected to decrease. Gasoline tends to be most expensive in places such as Newfoundland, where transport costs and high provincial taxes boost the price.

Distances are always shown in kilometers, and gasoline is always sold in liters. (A gallon has 3.8 liters.)

RULES OF THE ROAD

By law, you are required to wear seat belts (and to use infant seats). Some provinces have a statutory requirement to drive with vehicle headlights on for extended periods after dawn and before sunset. Radar-detection devices are illegal. Speed limits, given in kilometers, vary from province to province, but they are usually within the 90–110 kph (50–68 mph) range outside cities. Speed limits are strictly enforced, and tickets start at $75. Drinking and driving (anything over a .08 blood alcohol level) is considered a serious crime with serious penalties, including loss of driving privileges, impoundment of your vehicle, and jail. Roadblock checks are not unusual, especially on holiday weekends. Parking tickets start at $12 and are common, especially in larger urban centers.

Always strap children under 40 pounds into approved child-safety seats. Children must wear seat belts regardless of where they're seated. You may turn right at a red light after stopping if there is no oncoming traffic. When in doubt, wait for the green.

CHILDREN IN ATLANTIC CANADA

If you are crossing the border with children, carry identification for them similar to that required by adults (i.e., passport or birth certificate). Children traveling with one parent or other adult should bring a letter of permission from the other parent, parents, or legal guardian. Divorced parents with shared custody rights should carry legal documents establishing their status.

If you are renting a car, don't forget to arrange for a car seat when you reserve. For general advice about traveling with children, consult *Fodor's FYI: Travel with Your Baby* (available in bookstores everywhere).

FLYING

If your children are two or older, ask about children's airfares. As a general rule, infants under two not occupying a seat fly at greatly reduced fares or even for free. But if you want to guarantee a seat for an infant, you have to pay full fare. Consider flying during off-peak days and times; most airlines will grant an infant a seat without a ticket if there are available seats. When booking, confirm carry-on allowances if you're traveling with infants. In general, for babies charged 10%–50% of the adult fare, you are allowed one carry-on bag and a collapsible stroller; if the flight is full, the stroller may have to be checked, or you may be limited to less.

Experts agree that it's a good idea to use safety seats aloft for children weighing less than 40 pounds. Airlines set their own policies: if you use a safety seat, U.S. carriers usually require that the child be ticketed, even if he or she is young enough to ride free, because the seats must be strapped into regular seats. And even if you pay the full adult fare for the seat, it may be worth it, especially on longer trips. Do **check your airline's policy about using safety seats during takeoff and landing.** Safety seats are not allowed everywhere in the plane, so get your seat assignments as early as possible.

When reserving, request children's meals or a freestanding bassinet (not available at all airlines) if you need them. But note that bulkhead seats, where you must sit to use the bassinet, may lack an overhead bin or storage space on the floor.

LODGING

Most hotels in Canada allow children under a certain age to stay in their parents' room at no extra charge, but others charge for them as extra adults; be sure to find out the cutoff age for children's discounts.

SIGHTS & ATTRACTIONS

Places that are especially appealing to children are indicated by a rubber-duckie icon (🦆) in the margin.

CONSUMER PROTECTION

Whether you're shopping for gifts or purchasing travel services, **pay with a major credit card** whenever possible, so you can cancel payment or get reimbursed if there's a problem (and you can provide documentation). If you're doing business with a particular company for the first time, contact your local Better Business Bureau and the attorney general's offices in your state and (for U.S. businesses) the company's home state as well. Have any complaints been filed? Finally, if you're buying a package or tour, always consider travel insurance that includes default coverage (⇨ Insurance).

🚩 BBBs **Council of Better Business Bureaus** ✉ 4200 Wilson Blvd., Suite 800, Arlington, VA 22203 ☎ 703/276-0100 🖷 703/525-8277 ⊕ www. bbb.org.

CRUISE TRAVEL

Most major cruise lines call at Halifax from New York, Boston, and Montréal. Halifax Harbour's proximity to downtown makes the city ideal for short stopovers. All cruise ships entering the harbor are scheduled by the Halifax Port Authority.

To learn how to plan, choose, and book a cruise-ship voyage, consult *Fodor's FYI: Plan & Enjoy Your Cruise* (available in bookstores everywhere).

🚩 Cruise Lines and Contacts **Carnival Cruise Lines** ☎ 800/438-6744 ⊕ www.carnival.com. **Halifax Port Authority** ✉ 1215 Marginal Rd., ☎ 902/426-8222 ⊕ www.portofhalifax.ca. **Holland America** ✉ 300 Elliott Ave. W. Seattle ☎ 800/426-0327.

CUSTOMS & DUTIES

When shopping abroad, keep receipts for all purchases. Upon reentering the country,

be ready to show Customs officials what you've bought. Pack purchases together in an easily accessible place. If you think a duty is incorrect, appeal the assessment. If you object to the way your clearance was handled, note the inspector's badge number. In either case, first ask to see a supervisor. If the problem isn't resolved, write to the appropriate authorities, beginning with the port director at your point of entry.

IN AUSTRALIA

Australian residents who are 18 or older may bring home A$400 worth of souvenirs and gifts (including jewelry), 250 cigarettes or 250 grams of cigars or other tobacco products, and 1,125 ml of alcohol (including wine, beer, and spirits). Residents under 18 may bring back A$200 worth of goods. Members of the same family traveling together may pool their allowances. Prohibited items include meat products. Seeds, plants, and fruits need to be declared upon arrival.

🚩 **Australian Customs Service** ⬙ Regional Director, Box 8, Sydney, NSW 2001 ☎ 02/9213-2000 or 1300/363263, 02/9364-7222 or 1800/803-006 quarantine-inquiry line 🖷 02/9213-4043 ⊕ www. customs.gov.au.

IN CANADA

U.S. Customs and Immigration (⇨ In the U.S.) has preclearance services at international airports in Calgary, Edmonton, Montréal, Ottawa, Vancouver, and Winnipeg. This allows U.S.-bound air passengers to depart their airplane directly on arrival at their U.S. destination without further inspection and delays.

American and British visitors may bring the following items into Canada duty-free: 200 cigarettes, 50 cigars, and 7 ounces of tobacco; 1 bottle (1.1 liters or 40 imperial ounces) of liquor or wine, or 24 355-ml (12-ounce) bottles or cans of beer for personal consumption. Any alcohol and tobacco products in excess of these amounts is subject to duty, provincial fees, and taxes. You can also bring in gifts up to a total value of C$750.

A deposit is sometimes required for trailers (refunded upon return). Cats and dogs must have a certificate issued by a licensed veterinarian that clearly identifies the animal and certifies that it has been vaccinated against rabies during the preceding 36 months. Seeing-eye dogs are allowed into Canada without restriction. Plant material must be declared and inspected. There may be restrictions on some live plants, bulbs, and seeds. With certain restrictions or prohibitions on some fruits and vegetables, visitors may bring food with them for their own use, providing the quantity is consistent with the duration of the visit.

Canada's firearms laws are significantly stricter than those in the United States. Only sporting rifles and shotguns may be imported provided they are to be used for sporting, hunting, or competition while in Canada. All firearms must be declared to Canadian Customs at the first point of entry. Failure to declare firearms will result in their seizure, and criminal charges may be made. Regulations require visitors to have a confirmed "Firearms Declaration" to bring any guns into Canada; a fee of $50 applies, good for one year. For more information contact the Canadian Firearms Centre. **Revenue Canada** ✉ 2265 St. Laurent Blvd. S, Ottawa, ON K1G 4K3 ☎ 613/993-0534, 800/461-9999 in Canada. **Canadian Firearms Centre** ☎ 800/731-4000.

IN NEW ZEALAND

All homeward-bound residents may bring back NZ$700 worth of souvenirs and gifts; passengers may not pool their allowances, and children can claim only the concession on goods intended for their own use. For those 17 or older, the duty-free allowance also includes 4.5 liters of wine or beer; one 1,125-ml bottle of spirits; and either 200 cigarettes, 250 grams of tobacco, 50 cigars, *or* a combination of the three up to 250 grams. Meat products, seeds, plants, and fruits must be declared upon arrival to the Agricultural Services Department. **New Zealand Customs** ✉ Head office: The Customhouse, 17-21 Whitmore St., Box 2218, Wellington ☎ 09/300-5399 or 0800/428-786 ⊕ www.customs.govt.nz.

IN THE U.K.

From countries outside the European Union, including Canada, you may bring home, duty-free, 200 cigarettes or 50 cigars; 1 liter of spirits or 2 liters of fortified or sparkling wine or liqueurs; 2 liters of still table wine; 60 ml of perfume; 250 ml of toilet water; plus £145 worth of other goods, including gifts and souvenirs. Prohibited items include meat products, seeds, plants, and fruits.

HM Customs and Excise ✉ Portcullis House, 21 Cowbridge Rd. E, Cardiff CF11 9SS ☎ 0845/010-9000 or 0208/929-0152, 0208/929-6731 or 0208/910-3602 complaints ⊕ www.hmce.gov.uk.

IN THE U.S.

U.S. residents who have been out of the country for at least 48 hours may bring home, for personal use, $800 worth of foreign goods duty-free, as long as they haven't used the $800 allowance or any part of it in the past 30 days. This exemption may include 1 liter of alcohol (for travelers 21 and older), 200 cigarettes, and 100 non-Cuban cigars. Family members from the same household who are traveling together may pool their $800 personal exemptions. For fewer than 48 hours, the duty-free allowance drops to $200, which may include 50 cigarettes, 10 non-Cuban cigars, and 150 ml of alcohol (or 150 ml of perfume containing alcohol). The $200 allowance cannot be combined with other individuals' exemptions, and if you exceed it, the full value of all the goods will be taxed. Antiques, which the U.S. Bureau of Customs and Border Protection defines as objects more than 100 years old, enter duty-free, as do original works of art done entirely by hand, including paintings, drawings, and sculptures. This doesn't apply to folk art or handicrafts, which are in general dutiable.

You may also send packages home duty-free, with a limit of one parcel per addressee per day (except alcohol or tobacco products or perfume worth more than $5). You can mail up to $200 worth of goods for personal use; label the package PERSONAL USE and attach a list of its contents and their retail value. If the package contains your used personal belongings, mark it AMERICAN GOODS RETURNED to avoid paying duties. You may send up to $100 worth of goods as a gift; mark the package UNSOLICITED GIFT. Mailed items do not affect your duty-free allowance on your return.

To avoid paying duty on foreign-made high-ticket items you already own and will take on your trip, register them with Customs before you leave the country. Consider filing a Certificate of Registration for laptops, cameras, watches, and other digital devices identified with serial numbers or other permanent markings; you can keep the certificate for other trips. Otherwise, bring a sales receipt or insurance form to show that you owned the item before you left the United States.

🔒 U.S. Bureau of Customs and Border Protection ✉ for inquiries and equipment registration, 1300 Pennsylvania Ave. NW, Washington, DC 20229 🌐 www.customs.gov ☎ 877/287-8667, 202/354-1000 ✉ for complaints, Customer Satisfaction Unit, 1300 Pennsylvania Ave. NW, Room 5.5D, Washington, DC 20229.

DISABILITIES & ACCESSIBILITY

Travelers with disabilities do not have the same blanket legal protection in Canada that they have in the United States, but things are constantly improving. The Canadian Paraplegic Association National Office has information about touring in Canada. To file a complaint about transportation obstacles at Canadian airports (including flights), railroads, or ferries, contact the director's office at the Accessible Transportation Directorate, part of the Canadian Transportation Agency.

🔒 Local Resources Canadian Paraplegic Association National Office ✉ 1101 Prince of Wales Dr., Prom. Suite 230, Ottawa, ON K2C 3W7 ☎ 613/723-1033 🌐 www.canparaplegic.org. **Canadian Transportation Agency** ☎ 800/387-4999 in Canada 🌐 www.cta-otc.gc.ca

LODGING

The definition of accessibility seems to differ from hotel to hotel. Some properties may be accessible for people with mobility problems but not for people with hearing or vision impairments, for example.

If you have mobility problems, ask for the lowest floor on which accessible services are offered. If you have a hearing impairment, check whether the hotel has devices to alert you visually to the ring of the telephone, a knock at the door, and the sound of a fire/emergency alarm. Some hotels provide these devices without charge. Discuss your needs with hotel personnel if this equipment isn't available, so that a staff member can personally alert you in the event of an emergency.

If you're bringing a guide dog, get authorization ahead of time and write down the name of the person with whom you spoke.

RESERVATIONS

When discussing accessibility with an operator or reservations agent, ask hard questions. Are there any stairs, inside *or* out? Are there grab bars next to the toilet *and* in the shower/tub? How wide is the doorway to the room? To the bathroom? For the most extensive facilities meeting the latest legal specifications, opt for newer accommodations. If you reserve through a toll-free number, consider also calling the hotel's local number to confirm the information from the central reservations office. Get confirmation in writing when you can.

SIGHTS & ATTRACTIONS

Thanks to increased awareness and government-incentive programs, most major attractions—museums, churches, theaters—are equipped with ramps and lifts for wheelchairs. National and provincial institutions like parks, public monuments, and government buildings are almost always accessible although not always with the same level of convenience as found in the United States.

TRANSPORTATION

In larger communities some buses and some taxis are wheelchair-accessible. With a minimum of 48 hours' notice, the National Car Rental hand-control reservations center can arrange for a car to be picked up at an airport or other metropolitan location. Vans with seats removed to accommodate wheelchairs are also available. Windshield cards from other countries are recognized in Atlantic Canada, and specifically allocated parking spots are readily available.

🔒 Complaints Aviation Consumer Protection Division (⇨ Air Travel) for airline-related problems. In Canada: **Accessible Transportation Directorate** ✉ 15 Eddy St., Hull, QC K1A 0N9 ☎ 819/997-6828 or 800/883-1813. **Abilities Foundation of Nova Scotia** ✉ 3670 Kempt Rd., Halifax, NS B3K 4X8 ☎ 902/453-6000 🖷 902/464-6121 🌐 www.abilitiesfoundations.ca. In the U.S.: **Departmental Office of Civil Rights** ✉ for general inquiries, U.S. Department of Transportation, S-30, 400 7th St. SW, Room 10215, Washington, DC 20590 ☎ 202/366-4648 🖷 202/366-9371 🌐 www.dot.gov/ost/docr/index.htm. **Disability Rights Section** ✉ NYAV, U.S. Department of Justice, Civil Rights Division, 950 Pennsylvania Ave. NW, Washington, DC 20530 ☎ ADA information line 202/514-0301, 800/514-0301, 202/514-0383 TTY, 800/514-0383 TTY 🌐 www.ada.gov. **U.S. Department of Transportation Hotline** ☎ for disability-related air-travel problems, 800/778-4838 or 800/455-9880 TTY.

🔒 Car Rental ☎ 800/651-1223, Ext. 5149

TRAVEL AGENCIES

In the United States, the Americans with Disabilities Act requires that travel firms serve the needs of all travelers. Some agencies specialize in working with people with disabilities.

⚡ Travelers with Mobility Problems **Access Adventures/B. Roberts Travel** ⊠ 206 Chestnut Ridge Rd., Scottsville, NY 14624 ☎ 585/889-9096 ⊕ www.brobertstravel.com ⬧ dltravel@prodigy. net, run by a former physical-rehabilitation counselor. **CareVacations** ⊠ No. 5, 5110-50 Ave., Leduc, Alberta, Canada T9E 6V4 ☎ 780/986-6404 or 877/ 478-7827 ⬟ 780/986-8332 ⊕ www.carevacations. com, for group tours and cruise vacations. **Flying Wheels Travel** ⊠ 143 W. Bridge St., Box 382, Owatonna, MN 55060 ☎ 507/451-5005 ⬟ 507/451-1685 ⊕ www.flyingwheelstravel.com.

DISCOUNTS & DEALS

Be a smart shopper and compare all your options before making decisions. A plane ticket bought with a promotional coupon from travel clubs, coupon books, and direct-mail offers or purchased on the Internet may not be cheaper than the least expensive fare from a discount ticket agency. And always keep in mind that what you get is just as important as what you save.

DISCOUNT RESERVATIONS

To save money, look into discount reservations services with Web sites and toll-free numbers, which use their buying power to get a better price on hotels, airline tickets (⇨ Air Travel), even car rentals. When booking a room, always **call the hotel's local toll-free number** (if one is available) rather than the central reservations number—you'll often get a better price. Always ask about special packages or corporate rates.

When shopping for the best deal on hotels and car rentals, look for guaranteed exchange rates, which protect you against a falling dollar. With your rate locked in, you won't pay more, even if the price goes up in the local currency.

⚡ Airline Tickets **Air 4 Less** ☎ 800/AIR4LESS; low-fare specialist.

⚡ Hotel Rooms **Accommodations Express** ☎ 800/444-7666, 800/277-1064 ⊕ www. accommodationsexpress.com. **Hotels.com** ☎ 800/ 246-8357 ⊕ www.hotels.com. **RMC Travel** ☎ 800/ 245-5738 ⊕ www.rmcwebtravel.com. **Steigenberger Reservation Service** ☎ 800/223-5652

⊕ www.srs-worldhotels.com. **Turbotrip.com** ☎ 800/473-7829 ⊕ www.turbotrip.com.

PACKAGE DEALS

Don't confuse packages and guided tours. When you buy a package, you travel on your own, just as though you had planned the trip yourself. Fly/drive packages, which combine airfare and car rental, are often a good deal. In cities, ask the local visitor bureau about hotel packages that include tickets to major museum exhibits or other special events.

EATING & DRINKING

The Atlantic Provinces are a preferred destination for seafood lovers. Excellent fish is available in all types of dining establishments. Menu prices do not include applicable taxes or gratuities. The restaurants we list are the cream of the crop in each price category. Properties indicated by a ✕⊡ are lodging establishments whose restaurant warrants a special trip.

WHAT IT COSTS (in Canadian Dollars)					
	$$$$	$$$	$$	$	¢
AT DINNER	over $30	$20–$30	$12–$20	$8–$12	under $8

Prices are for a main course at dinner.

MEALTIMES

Unless otherwise noted, the restaurants listed in this guide are open daily for lunch and dinner.

RESERVATIONS & DRESS

Reservations are always a good idea; we mention them only when they're essential or not accepted. Book as far ahead as you can, and reconfirm as soon as you arrive. (Large parties should always call ahead to check the reservations policy.) We mention dress only when men are required to wear a jacket or a jacket and tie.

WINE, BEER & SPIRITS

Locally produced wines, ranging from young table wines to excellent vintages, are offered in most licensed restaurants and are worth a try. Some pubs are producing their own microbrews with excellent results, but these beers are not available in liquor stores. Propeller, a local brewery, produces fine beers available in the liquor stores and at most pubs and taverns. The brewery also makes a nonalcoholic ginger beer and a naturally flavored orange soda. Stutz hard apple cider is produced in the Annapolis Valley in limited quantities. If you are lucky enough to find some, don't pass it by. Liquor outlets, the only place to purchase alcoholic beverages, are closed on Sunday and holidays.

ECOTOURISM

Wilderness areas often have very delicate ecosystems. Sand dunes in eastern Canada and important nesting grounds for seabirds are often protected. Areas where sensitivity is required are well posted with signs that designate rules.

EMBASSIES & CONSULATES

All embassies are in Ottawa. There is a United States consulate in Halifax.
🛂 Australia **Australian High Commission** ⊠ 50 O'Connor St., Suite 710, Ottawa 🖀 613/236-0841.
🛂 New Zealand **New Zealand High Commission** ⊠ 99 Bank St., Suite 727, Ottawa 🖀 613/238-5991.
🛂 United Kingdom **British High Commission** ⊠ 80 Elgin St., Ottawa 🖀 613/237-1530.
🛂 United States **U.S. Consulate** ⊠ 1969 Upper Water St., Halifax NS 🖀 902/429-2480 **U.S. Embassy** ⊠ 490 Sussex Dr., Ottawa 🖀 613/238-5335.

GAY & LESBIAN TRAVEL

Atlantic Canada is generally a fairly tolerant place, and same-sex couples should face few problems. The larger cities actively and avidly compete for gay visitors. Rural areas are dotted with gay-friendly B&Bs and camping facilities.
🛂 Gay- & Lesbian-Friendly Travel Agencies **Different Roads Travel** ⊠ 8383 Wilshire Blvd., Suite 520, Beverly Hills, CA 90211 🖀 323/651-5557 or 800/429-8747 (Ext. 14 for both) 🖷 323/651-3678 ✍ lgernert@tzell.com. **Kennedy Travel** ⊠ 130 W. 42nd St., Suite 401, New York, NY 10036 🖀 212/840-8659, 800/237-7433 🖷 212/730-2269 🌐 www.kennedytravel.com. **Now, Voyager** ⊠ 4406 18th St., San Francisco, CA 94114 🖀 415/626-1169 or 800/255-6951 🖷 415/626-8626 🌐 www.nowvoyager.com. **Skylink Travel and Tour** ⊠ 1455 N. Dutton Ave., Suite A, Santa Rosa, CA 95401 🖀 707/546-9888 or 800/225-5759 🖷 707/636-0951; serving lesbian travelers.

HOLIDAYS

Canadian national holidays are as follows: New Year's Day (January 1), Good Friday (late March or early April), Easter Monday (the Monday following Good Friday), Victoria Day (late May), Canada Day (July 1), Labour Day (first Monday in September), Thanksgiving (mid-October), Remembrance Day (November 11), Christmas, and Boxing Day (December 26).

The following are provincial holidays: New Brunswick Day (August 4); St. Patrick's Day (March 20), St. George's Day (April 24), Discovery Day (June 26), Memorial Day (July 1), and Orangemen's Day (July 10) in Newfoundland; and Civic Holiday (August 4) in Nova Scotia.

INSURANCE

The most useful travel-insurance plan is a comprehensive policy that includes coverage for trip cancellation and interruption, default, trip delay, and medical expenses (with a waiver for preexisting conditions).

Without insurance you'll lose all or most of your money if you cancel your trip, regardless of the reason. Default insurance covers you if your tour operator, airline, or cruise line goes out of business. Trip-delay covers expenses that arise because of bad weather or mechanical delays. Study the fine print when comparing policies.

U.K. residents can buy a travel-insurance policy valid for most vacations taken during the year in which it's purchased (but check preexisting-condition coverage). British and Australian citizens need extra medical coverage when traveling overseas.

Always **buy travel policies directly from the insurance company**; if you buy them from a cruise line, airline, or tour operator that goes out of business, you probably won't be covered for the agency's or operator's default, a major risk. Before making any purchase, review your existing health and home owner's policies to find what they cover away from home.
🛂 Travel Insurers In the U.S.: **Access America** ⊠ 6600 W. Broad St., Richmond, VA 23230 🖀 800/284-8300 🖷 804/673-1491 or 800/346-9265 🌐 www.accessamerica.com. **Travel Guard International** ⊠ 1145 Clark St., Stevens Point, WI 54481 🖀 715/345-0505 or 800/826-1300 🖷 800/955-8785 🌐 www.travelguard.com.
🛂 In the U.K.: **Association of British Insurers** ⊠ 51 Gresham St., London EC2V 7HQ 🖀 020/7600-3333 🖷 020/7696-8999 🌐 www.abi.org.uk. In Canada: **RBC Insurance** ⊠ 6880 Financial Dr., Mississauga, ON L5N 7Y5 🖀 800/565-3129 🖷 905/813-4704 🌐 www.rbcinsurance.com. In Australia: **Insurance Council of Australia** ⊠ Insurance Enquiries and Complaints, Level 3, 56 Pitt

St., Sydney, NSW 2000 ☎ 1300/363683 or 02/ 9251-4456 ⎙ 02/9251-4453 ⊕ www.iecltd.com.au. In New Zealand: **Insurance Council of New Zealand** ✉ Level 7, 111-115 Customhouse Quay, Box 474, Wellington ☎ 04/472-5230 ⎙ 04/473-3011 ⊕ www.icnz.org.nz.

LANGUAGE

Canada's two official languages are English and French. New Brunswick is Canada's only officially bilingual province. English is widely spoken in the French-Canadian communities in Atlantic Canada, making it unnecessary to speak any French.

LODGING

In the cities you have a choice of luxury hotels, moderately priced modern properties, and smaller older hotels with perhaps fewer conveniences but more charm. Options in smaller towns and in the country include large full-service resorts, small privately owned inns, roadside motels, and bed-and-breakfasts.

Expect accommodations to cost more in summer than in the off-season (except for places where winter is high season, such as ski resorts). Book well in advance for high-season accommodations. When making reservations, ask about special deals and packages. Big-city hotels that cater to business travelers often offer weekend packages. Discounts are common when you book for a week or longer, and many city hotels offer rooms at up to 50% off in winter. Also be aware of any special events or festivals that may coincide with your visit and fill every room for miles around.

The lodgings we list are the cream of the crop in each price category. We always list the facilities that are available, but we don't specify whether they cost extra; when pricing accommodations, always ask what's included and what costs extra. Properties are assigned price categories based on the range between their least and most expensive standard double rooms at high season (excluding holidays). Properties marked ✕⊡ are lodging establishments whose restaurants warrant a special trip.

Assume that hotels operate on the European Plan (EP, with no meals) unless we specify that they use the Continental Plan

(CP, with a Continental breakfast), Modified American Plan (MAP, with breakfast and dinner), or the Full American Plan (FAP, with all meals).

WHAT IT COSTS (in Canadian Dollars)					
	$$$$	$$$	$$	$	¢
FOR 2 PEOPLE	over $250	$175-$250	$125-$175	$75-$125	under $75

Prices are for two people in a standard double room in high season, excluding 15% harmonized sales tax (HST) in NB, NL, and NS.

APARTMENT & VILLA RENTALS

If you want a home base that's roomy enough for a family and comes with cooking facilities, consider a furnished rental. These can save you money, especially if you're traveling with a group. Home-exchange directories sometimes list rentals as well as exchanges.

🏠 International Agents **Hideaways International** ✉ 767 Islington St., Portsmouth, NH 03801 ☎ 603/430-4433 or 800/843-4433 ⎙ 603/430-4444 ⊕ www.hideaways.com, membership $145.
🏠 Rental Listings **Halifax Chronicle-Herald** ☎ 902/426-2811.

BED & BREAKFASTS

For assistance in booking B&B rooms, contact the appropriate provincial tourist board (⇨ Visitor Information), which either will have a listing of B&Bs or will be able to refer you to an association that can help you secure reservations.

CAMPING

Campgrounds in Atlantic Canada range from rustic woodland settings far from the nearest paved road to facility-packed open fields full of sleek motor homes next to major highways. Some of the best sites are in national and provincial parks. These sites are well cared for, well equipped, and close to plenty of nature and activity programs for both children and adults. The campgrounds in the coastal regions of the Maritime Provinces are particularly beautiful. Wilderness camping for hikers and canoeists is available in national and provincial parks.

HOME EXCHANGES

If you would like to exchange your home for someone else's, join a home-exchange organization, which will send you its updated listings of available exchanges for a year and will include your own listing in at least one of them. It's up to you to make specific arrangements.

F Exchange Clubs **HomeLink International** Box 47747, Tampa, FL 33647 ☎ 813/975-9825 or 800/638-3841 ⊟ 813/910-8144 ⊕ www.homelink. org; $110 yearly for a listing, online access, and catalog; $70 without catalog. **Intervac U.S.** ⊠ 30 Corte San Fernando, Tiburon, CA 94920 ☎ 800/756-4663 ⊟ 415/435-7440 ⊕ www.intervacus.com; $105 yearly for a listing, online access, and a catalog; $50 without catalog.

HOSTELS

No matter what your age, you can save on lodging costs by staying at hostels. In some 4,500 locations in more than 70 countries around the world, Hostelling International (HI), the umbrella group for a number of national youth-hostel associations, offers single-sex dorm-style beds and, at many hostels, rooms for couples and family accommodations. Membership in any HI national hostel association, open to travelers of all ages, allows you to stay in HI-affiliated hostels at member rates; one-year membership is about $28 for adults (C$35 for a two-year minimum membership in Canada, £13.50 in the U.K., A$52 in Australia, and NZ$40 in New Zealand); hostels charge about $10–$30 per night. Members have priority if the hostel is full; they're also eligible for discounts around the world, even on rail and bus travel in some countries.

F Organizations **Hostelling International–USA** ⊠ 8401 Colesville Rd., Suite 600, Silver Spring, MD 20910 ☎ 301/495-1240 ⊟ 301/495-6697 ⊕ www. hiayh.org. **Hostelling International–Canada** ⊠ 205 Catherine St., Suite 400, Ottawa, ON K2P 1C3 ☎ 613/237-7884 or 800/663-5777 ⊟ 613/237-7868 ⊕ www.hihostels.ca. **YHA England and Wales** ⊠ Trevelyan House, Dimple Rd., Matlock, Derbyshire DE4 3YH ☎ 0870/870-8808, 0870/ 770-8868, 0162/959-2700 ⊟ 0870/770-6127 ⊕ www.yha.org.uk. **YHA Australia** ⊠ 422 Kent St., Sydney, NSW 2001 ☎ 02/9261-1111 ⊟ 02/9261-1969 ⊕ www.yha.com.au. **YHA New Zealand** ⊠ Level 4, Torrens House, 195 Hereford St., Box 436, Christchurch ☎ 03/379-9970 or 0800/278-299 ⊟ 03/365-4476 ⊕ www.yha.org.nz.

HOTELS

Canada doesn't have a national government rating system for hotels, but many provinces do rate their accommodations. Most hotel rooms have air-conditioning, private baths with tubs and showers, and two double beds. All hotels we list have air-conditioning and private bath unless otherwise noted.

F Toll-Free Numbers **Best Western** ☎ 800/528-1234 ⊕ www.bestwestern.com. **Clarion** ☎ 800/ 424-6423 ⊕ www.choicehotels.com. **Comfort Inn** ☎ 800/424-6423 ⊕ www.choicehotels.com. **Days Inn** ☎ 800/325-2525 ⊕ www.daysinn.com. **Hilton** ☎ 800/445-8667 ⊕ www.hilton.com. **Holiday Inn** ☎ 800/465-4329 ⊕ www.sixcontinentshotels. com. **Howard Johnson** ☎ 800/446-4656 ⊕ www. hojo.com. **Quality Inn** ☎ 800/424-6423 ⊕ www. choicehotels.com. **Radisson** ☎ 800/333-3333 ⊕ www.radisson.com. **Ramada** ☎ 800/228-2828, 800/854-7854 international reservations ⊕ www. ramada.com. **Sheraton** ☎ 800/325-3535 ⊕ www. starwood.com/sheraton. **Sleep Inn** ☎ 800/424-6423 ⊕ www.choicehotels.com. **Westin Hotels & Resorts** ☎ 800/228-3000 ⊕ www.starwood.com/ westin.

MAIL & SHIPPING

In Canada you can buy stamps at the post office or from convenience stores, hotel lobbies, railway stations, airports, bus terminals, many retail outlets, and some newsstands. Note that the suite number often appears before the street number in an address, followed by a hyphen.

Following are postal abbreviations for provinces and territories: Alberta, AB; British Columbia, BC; Manitoba, MB; New Brunswick, NB; Newfoundland and Labrador, NL Northwest Territories and Nunavut, NT; Nova Scotia, NS; Ontario, ON; Prince Edward Island, PE; Québec, PQ; Saskatchewan, SK; Yukon, YT.

POSTAL RATES

Within Canada, postcards and letters cost 48¢ for up to 30 grams, 77¢ for between 31 and 50 grams, and 96¢ for between 51 and 100 grams. Letters and postcards to the United States cost 65¢ for up to 30 grams, 90¢ for between 31 and 50 grams, and $1.40 for up to 100 grams.

International mail and postcards are $1.25 for up to 20 grams, $1.75 for between 21 and 50 grams, and $3 for between 51 and 100 grams.

RECEIVING MAIL

You may have mail sent to you c/o General Delivery in the town you are visiting, for pickup in person within 15 days, after which it will be returned to the sender.

MEDIA

NEWSPAPERS & MAGAZINES

Maclean's and *Saturday Night* are Canada's two main general-interest magazines. Both cover arts and culture as well as politics. Canada has two national newspapers, the *National Post* and the *Globe and Mail*—both are published in Toronto, and both are available at newsstands in major foreign cities, especially the big weekend editions, which are published on Saturday. The arts-and-entertainment sections of both papers have advance news of major events and exhibitions across the country. Both also have Web sites with limited information on cultural events. For more detailed information, rely on the metropolitan papers. Provincial daily newspapers in Atlantic Canada include the *Halifax Herald* and the *Daily News* in Nova Scotia, the *Telegraph-Journal* in New Brunswick, the *Guardian* in Prince Edward Island, and the *Telegram* in Newfoundland and Labrador.

RADIO & TELEVISION

U.S. television dominates Canada's airwaves. In border areas—where most Canadians live—Fox, PBS, NBC, CBS, and ABC are readily available. Canada's two major networks, the state-owned Canadian Broadcasting Corporation (CBC) and the private CTV, and the smaller Global Network broadcast a steady diet of U.S. sitcoms and dramas, with only a scattering of Canadian-produced shows. The selection of Canadian-produced current-affairs programs, however, is much wider. The CBC also has a parallel French-language network, Radio-Canada. Canadian cable subscribers have a vast menu of specialty channels to choose from, including the all-news outlets operated by the CTV and CBC.

The CBC operates the country's only truly national radio network. In fact, it operates four of them, two in English and two in French. Its Radio 1 network, usually broadcast on the FM band, has a daily schedule rich in news, current-affairs, and discussion programs. One of the most popular shows, *As It Happens*, takes a quirky and highly entertaining look at national, world, and weird events every evening at 6. Radio 2, usually broadcast on FM, emphasizes music and often features live classical concerts by some of Canada's best orchestras, opera companies, and choral groups. The two French-language networks follow formats similar to their English-language counterparts.

MONEY MATTERS

At this writing, the exchange rate is favorable for Americans traveling in Canada. Taxes are high, but most of these expenses can be reclaimed if you save your receipts.

Throughout this book, unless otherwise stated, all prices are given in Canadian dollars. Prices throughout this guide are given for adults. Substantially reduced fees are almost always available for children, students, and senior citizens. For information on taxes, *see* Taxes.

ATMS

Most banks, gas stations, malls, and convenience stores have automatic teller machines (ATMs) that are accessible around the clock.

CREDIT CARDS

Throughout this guide, the following abbreviations are used: **AE**, American Express; **D**, Discover; **DC**, Diners Club; **MC**, MasterCard; and **V**, Visa.

⬚ Reporting Lost Cards American Express ☎ 800/441-0519. **Diners Club** ☎ 800/234-6377. **Discover** ☎ 800/347-2683. **MasterCard** ☎ 800/622-7747. **Visa** ☎ 800/847-2911.

CURRENCY

U.S. dollars are accepted in much of Canada (especially in communities near the border). However, to get the most favorable exchange rate, exchange at least some of your money into Canadian funds. Traveler's checks (some are available in Canadian dollars) and major U.S. credit cards are accepted in most areas.

The units of currency in Canada are the Canadian dollar (C$) and the cent, in almost the same denominations as U.S. currency ($5, $10, $20, 1¢, 5¢, 10¢, 25¢, etc.). The $1 and $2 bill are no longer used; they have been replaced by $1 and $2 coins (known as a "loonie," because of the loon that appears on the coin, and a "toonie," respectively). At this writing, US$1 is equivalent to C$1.33, £1 to C$2.23, €1 to C$1.53, A$1 to C$.93, and NZ$1 to C$.82.

CURRENCY EXCHANGE

For the most favorable rates, **change money through banks.** Although ATM transaction fees may be higher abroad than at home, ATM rates are excellent because they're based on wholesale rates offered only by major banks. You won't do as well at exchange booths in airports or rail and bus stations, in hotels, in restaurants, or in stores. To avoid lines at airport exchange booths, get a bit of local currency before you leave home.

⚑ Exchange Services International Currency Express ⊠ 427 N. Camden Dr., Suite F, Beverly Hills, CA 90210 ☎ 888/278-6628 orders ☎ 310/278-6410 ⊕ www.foreignmoney.com. **Thomas Cook International Money Services** ☎ 800/287-7362 orders and retail locations ⊕ www.us.thomascook.com.

NATIONAL PARKS

If you plan to visit several parks in a region, you may be able to save money on park fees by buying a multipark pass. Parks Canada passes include the PEI Combo Pass, the Atlantic Regional National Park Pass, and the Eastern Newfoundland National Historic Sites Pass. Parks Canada is decentralized, so it's best to contact the park you plan to visit for information. You can buy passes at the parks covered by the pass.

⚑ Park Passes Parks Canada national office ⊠ 25 Eddy St., Hull, PQ K1A 0M5 ☎ 800/213-7275 ⊕ www.parkscanada.pch.gc.ca.

PACKING

If you plan on camping or hiking in the deep woods in summer, particularly in northern Canada, always carry insect repellent, especially in June, which is blackfly season. Consider investing in specially designed hats, jackets, and pants constructed of very fine mesh material.

Atlantic Canada experiences a wide range of weather and temperatures throughout the year. Even an August evening can be quite cold, especially if you are close to the water. A waterproof wind-breaking jacket is essential.

In your carry-on luggage, pack an extra pair of eyeglasses or contact lenses and enough of any medication you take to last a few days longer than the entire trip. You may also ask your doctor to write a spare prescription using the drug's generic name, as brand names may vary from country to country. In luggage to be checked, **never pack prescription drugs, valuables, or undeveloped film.** And don't forget to carry with you the addresses of offices that han-

dle refunds of lost traveler's checks. Check *Fodor's How to Pack* (available at online retailers and bookstores everywhere) for more tips.

To avoid Customs and security delays, carry medications in their original packaging. Don't pack any sharp objects in your carry-on luggage, including knives of any size or material, scissors, and corkscrews, or anything else that might arouse suspicion.

To avoid having your checked luggage chosen for hand inspection, don't cram bags full. The U.S. Transportation Security Administration suggests packing shoes on top and placing personal items you don't want touched in clear plastic bags.

CHECKING LUGGAGE

You're allowed to carry aboard one bag and one personal article, such as a purse or a laptop computer. Make sure what you carry on fits under your seat or in the overhead bin. Get to the gate early, so you can board as soon as possible, before the overhead bins fill up.

Baggage allowances vary by carrier, destination, and ticket class. On international flights, you're usually allowed to check two bags weighing up to 70 pounds (32 kilograms) each, although a few airlines allow checked bags of up to 88 pounds (40 kilograms) in first class. Some international carriers don't allow more than 66 pounds (30 kilograms) per bag in business class and 44 pounds (20 kilograms) in economy. On domestic flights the limit is usually 50–70 pounds (23–32 kilograms) per bag. In general, carry-on bags shouldn't exceed 40 pounds (18 kilograms). Most airlines won't accept bags that weigh more than 100 pounds (45 kilograms) on domestic or international flights. Check baggage restrictions with your carrier before you pack.

Airline liability for baggage is limited to $2,500 per person on flights within the United States. On international flights it amounts to $9.07 per pound or $20 per kilogram for checked baggage (roughly $640 per 70-pound bag), with a maximum of $634.90 per piece and $400 per passenger for unchecked baggage. You can buy additional coverage at check-in for about $10 per $1,000 of coverage, but it often excludes a rather extensive list of items, shown on your airline ticket.

Before departure, itemize your bags' contents and their worth, and label the bags with your name, address, and phone number. (If you use your home address, cover it so potential thieves can't see it readily.) Include a label inside each bag and **pack a copy of your itinerary.** At check-in make sure each bag is correctly tagged with the destination airport's three-letter code. Because some checked bags will be opened for hand inspection, the U.S. Transportation Security Administration recommends that you leave luggage unlocked or use the plastic locks offered at check-in. TSA screeners place an inspection notice inside searched bags, which are resealed with a special lock.

If your bag has been searched and contents are missing or damaged, file a claim with the TSA Consumer Response Center as soon as possible. If your bags arrive damaged or fail to arrive at all, file a written report with the airline before leaving the airport.

🛂 Complaints **U.S. Transportation Security Administration Consumer Response Center** ☎ 866/289-9673 ⊕ www.tsa.gov.

PASSPORTS & VISAS

When traveling internationally, carry your passport even if you don't need one (it's always the best form of ID) and **make two photocopies of the data page** (one for someone at home and another for you, carried separately from your passport). If you lose your passport, promptly call the nearest embassy or consulate and the local police.

U.S. passport applications for children under age 14 require consent from both parents or legal guardians; both parents must appear together to sign the application. If only one parent appears, he or she must submit a written statement from the other parent authorizing passport issuance for the child. A parent with sole authority must present evidence of it when applying; acceptable documentation includes the child's certified birth certificate listing only the applying parent, a court order specifically permitting this parent's travel with the child, or a death certificate for the nonapplying parent. Application forms and instructions are available on the Web site of the U.S. State Department's Bureau of Consular Affairs (⊕ www.travel.state.gov).

ENTERING CANADA

Citizens and legal residents of the United States do not need a passport or a visa to enter Canada, but proof of citizenship (a birth certificate or valid passport) and some form of photo identification will be requested. Naturalized U.S. residents should carry their naturalization certificate. Permanent residents who are not citizens should carry their "green card." U.S. residents entering Canada from a third country must have a valid passport, naturalization certificate, or "green card."

Citizens of the United Kingdom, Australia, and New Zealand need only a valid passport to enter Canada for stays of up to six months.

PASSPORT OFFICES

The best time to apply for a passport or to renew is in fall and winter. Before any trip, check your passport's expiration date, and, if necessary, renew it as soon as possible.

🛂 Australian Citizens **Passports Australia** ☎ 131-232 ⊕ www.passports.gov.au.
🛂 New Zealand Citizens **New Zealand Passports Office** ☎ 0800/22-5050 or 04/474-8100 ⊕ www.passports.govt.nz.
🛂 U.K. Citizens **U.K. Passport Service** ☎ 0870/521-0410 ⊕ www.passport.gov.uk.

SENIOR-CITIZEN TRAVEL

To qualify for age-related discounts, mention your senior-citizen status up front when booking hotel reservations (not when checking out) and before you're seated in restaurants (not when paying the bill). Be sure to have identification on hand. When renting a car, ask about promotional car-rental discounts, which can be cheaper than senior-citizen rates.

🛂 Educational Programs **Elderhostel** ✉ 11 Ave. de Lafayette, Boston, MA 02111-1746 ☎ 877/426-8056, 978/323-4141 international callers, 877/426-2167 TTY 🖷 877/426-2166 ⊕ www.elderhostel.org. **Interhostel** ✉ University of New Hampshire, 6 Garrison Ave., Durham, NH 03824 ☎ 603/862-1147 or 800/733-9753 🖷 603/862-1113 ⊕ www.learn.unh.edu.

SHOPPING

Some smaller regions and towns in Atlantic Canada have become known for particular products. Craftswomen in the tiny Newfoundland outport of St. Anthony, for example, make parkas, caps, and mittens out of heavy fabric called Grenfell cloth.

SMART SOUVENIRS

The hooked rugs produced by Acadian artisans (usually women) are either kitschy or naively charming, depending on your point of view. The best are available in the Cape Breton village of Chéti-camp for prices that range from $15 into the hundreds.

WATCH OUT

Americans should note that it is illegal both to buy Cuban cigars and to take them home.

SPORTS & THE OUTDOORS

BICYCLING

Canadian Cycling Association ✉ 702-2197 Riverside Dr., Ottawa, ON K1H 7X3 ☎ 613/248-1353 🖷 613/248-9311 ⊕ www.canadian-cycling.com.

CANOEING AND KAYAKING

Provincial tourist offices (⇨ Visitor Information) can be of assistance, especially in locating an outfitter to suit your needs. You may also contact the Canadian Recreational Canoeing Association. **Canadian Recreational Canoeing Association** ✉ 446 Main St. W., Merrickville, ON K0G 1N0 ☎ 613/269-2910 or 888/252-6292 🖷 613/269-2908 ⊕ www.crca.ca.

CLIMBING/MOUNTAINEERING

Alpine Club of Canada ✉ Indian Flats Rd., Canmore, AB T1W 2T8 ☎ 403/678-3200 🖷 403/678-3224 ⊕ www.alpineclubofcanada.ca.

FISHING

You can get a nonresident fishing license from a Department of Natural Resources office or at a sporting-goods store. Before casting a line in national park waters, you must obtain a National Parks Fishing License at park offices. **Licenses New Brunswick Department of Natural Resources** ☎ 506/453-3826. **Newfoundland and Labrador Department of Natural Resources** ☎ 709/729-6704. **Nova Scotia Department of Agriculture and Fisheries** ☎ 902/424-4467. **Prince Edward Island Department of Agriculture, Fisheries, Aquaculture and Forestry** ☎ 902/368-4880.

GOLF

Royal Canadian Golf Association ✉ 1333 Dorval Dr., Oakville, ON L6J 4Z3 ☎ 905/849-9700 🖷 905/845-7040 ⊕ www.rcga.org.

SCUBA DIVING

Canadian Amateur Diving Association ✉ 703-2197 Riverside Dr., Ottawa, ON K1H 7X3 ☎ 613/736-5238 🖷 613/736-0409 ⊕ www.diving.ca.

TENNIS

Tennis Canada ✉ 3111 Steeles Ave. W, Downsview, ON M3J 3H2 ☎ 800/263-9039, 416/665-9777 🖷 416/665-6480 ⊕ www.tenniscanada.com.

STUDENTS IN CANADA

Persons under 18 years of age who are not accompanied by their parents should bring a letter from a parent or guardian giving them permission to travel to Canada. **IDs & Services STA Travel** ✉ 10 Downing St., New York, NY 10014 ☎ 212/627-3111, 800/777-0112 24-hr service center 🖷 212/627-3387 ⊕ www.sta.com. **Travel Cuts** ✉ 187 College St., Toronto, ON M5T 1P7 ☎ 800/592-2887 in the U.S., 416/979-2406 or 866/246-9762 in Canada 🖷 416/979-8167 ⊕ www.travelcuts.com.

TAXES

A goods and services tax (GST) of 7% applies on virtually every transaction in Canada except for the purchase of basic groceries. Newfoundland and Labrador, Nova Scotia, and New Brunswick have a 15% single harmonized sales tax (HST), which combines the GST and the provincial sales tax.

You must pay a $10 airport-improvement tax and a $24 security tax at airports when you leave Canada.

GST REFUNDS

You can get a GST refund on purchases taken out of the country and on short-term accommodations of less than one month, but not on food, drink, tobacco, car or motor-home rentals, or transportation. Rebate forms, which must be submitted within 60 days of leaving Canada, may be obtained from certain retailers, tourist information outlets, duty-free shops, and Customs officials, or from the Canada Customs and Revenue Agency. Instant cash rebates up to a maximum of $500 are provided by some duty-free shops when you leave Canada, and most provinces do not tax goods that are shipped directly by the vendor to the purchaser's home. Always **save your original receipts** from stores and hotels (not just credit-card receipts), and be sure the name and address of the establishment is shown on the receipt. Original receipts are not returned. To be eligible for a refund, receipts must total at least $200, and each individual receipt must show a minimum purchase of $50.

🔂 **Canada Customs and Revenue Agency** ✉ Visitor Rebate Program, Summerside Tax Centre, 275 Pope Rd., Suite 104, Summerside, PE C1N 6C6 ☎ 902/432–5608, 800/668–4748 in Canada ⊕ www.ccra-adrc.gc.ca.

PROVINCIAL TAX REFUNDS

Call the provincial toll-free visitor information lines for details (⇨ Visitor Information) on provincial tax refunds. Most provinces do not tax goods shipped directly by the vendor to the visitor's home address.

TIME

New Brunswick, Nova Scotia, and Prince Edward Island are on Atlantic Time, which is (during daylight savings) three hours earlier than Greenwich meant time (GMT) and one hour later than eastern daylight time (EDT). Newfoundland and Labrador are on Newfoundland time, which is −2:30 GMT and +1:30 EDT.

TIPPING

Tips and service charges are not usually added to a bill in Canada. In general, tip 15% of the total bill. This goes for waiters and waitresses, barbers and hairdressers, and taxi drivers. Porters and doormen should get about $2 a bag. For maid service, leave at least $2 per person a day ($3 in luxury hotels).

TOURS & PACKAGES

Because everything is prearranged on a prepackaged tour or independent vacation, you spend less time planning—and often get it all at a good price.

BOOKING WITH AN AGENT

Travel agents are excellent resources. But it's a good idea to collect brochures from several agencies, as some agents' suggestions may be influenced by relationships with tour and package firms that reward them for volume sales. If you have a special interest, find an agent with expertise in that area; the American Society of Travel Agents (ASTA; ⇨ Travel Agencies) has a database of specialists worldwide. You can log on to the group's Web site to find an ASTA travel agent in your neighborhood.

Make sure your travel agent knows the accommodations and other services of the place being recommended. Ask about the hotel's location, room size, beds, and whether it has a pool, room service, or programs for children, if you care about these? Has your agent been there in person or sent others whom you can contact?

Do some homework on your own, too: local tourism boards can provide information about lesser-known and small-niche operators, some of which may sell only direct.

THEME TRIPS

The companies listed below offer multiday tours in Canada. Additional local or regionally based companies that have different-length trips with these themes are listed in each chapter, either with information about the town or in the A to Z section that concludes the chapter.

🔂 Adventure **Gorp Travel** ✉ Box 1486, Boulder, CO 80306 ☎ 303/444–2622 or 800/444–0099 🖷 303/635–0658 ⊕ www.gorptravel.com.

🔂 Bicycling **Backroads** ✉ 801 Cedar St., Berkeley, CA 94710-1800 ☎ 510/527–1555 or 800/462–2848 🖷 510/527–1444 ⊕ www.backroads.com. **Bike Rider Tours** ✉ Box 130254, Boston, MA 02113 ☎ 617/723–2354 or 800/473–7040 🖷 617/723–2355 ⊕ www. bikeriderstours.com. **Butterfield & Robinson** ✉ 70 Bond St., Toronto, ON M5B 1X3 ☎ 416/864–1354 or 800/678–1147 🖷 416/864–0541 ⊕ www.butterfield. com. **Easy Rider Tours** ✉ Box 228, Newburyport, MA 01950 ☎ 978/463–6955 or 800/488–8332 🖷 978/463–6988 ⊕ www.easyridertours.com. **Vermont Bicycle Touring** ✉ Box 711, Bristol, VT 05443-0711 ☎ 800/245–3868 or 802/453–4811 🖷 802/453–4806 ⊕ www.vbt.com.

🔂 Fishing **Fishing International** ✉ Box 2132, Santa Rosa, CA 95405 ☎ 707/542–4242 or 800/950–4242 🖷 707/526–3474 ⊕ www.travelsource.com/fishing.

🔂 Walking/Hiking **Backroads** ✉ 801 Cedar St., Berkeley, CA 94710-1800 ☎ 510/527–1555 or 800/462–2848 🖷 510/527–1444 ⊕ www.backroads.com. **Butterfield & Robinson** ✉ 70 Bond St., Toronto, ON M5B 1X3 ☎ 416/864–1354 or 800/678–1147 🖷 416/864–0541 ⊕ www.butterfield.com. **Country Walkers** ✉ Box 180, Waterbury, VT 05676-0180 ☎ 802/244–1387 or 800/464–9255 🖷 802/244–5661 ⊕ www. countrywalkers.com. **New England Hiking Holidays** ✉ Box 1648, North Conway, NH 03860 ☎ 603/356–9696 or 800/869–0949 ⊕ www.nehikingholidays. com. **Walking the World** ✉ Box 1186, Fort Collins, CO 80522 ☎ 970/498–0500 or 800/340–9255 🖷 970/

498-9100 ⊕ www.gorp.com/walkingtheworld; specializes in tours for ages 50 and older.

TRAIN TRAVEL

VIA Rail, Canada's Amtrak counterpart, provides transcontinental rail service to Atlantic Canada.

CUTTING COSTS

If you're planning to travel a lot by train, **look into the Canrail pass.** It allows 12 days of coach-class travel within a 30-day period; sleeping cars are available, but they sell out very early and must be reserved at least a month in advance during the high season (June–mid-October), when the pass is $780 (discounts for youths and seniors). The low-season rate (October 16–May) is $490. The pass is not valid during the Christmas period (December 15 through January 5). For more information and reservations, contact a travel agent in the United States. In the United Kingdom, Long-Haul Leisurail represents VIA Rail.

Train travelers can **check out the 30-day North American RailPass** offered by VIA Rail. It allows unlimited coach–economy travel in the United States and Canada. You must indicate the itinerary when purchasing the pass. The cost is $1,029 from June to October 15, $725 at other times.
🚆 Train Information **Long-Haul Leisurail** ⊠ Box 113, Peterborough, PE3 8HY U.K. ☎ 01733/335599. **VIA Rail Canada** ☎ 800/561-3949, 888/842-7245.

TRAVEL AGENCIES

A good travel agent puts your needs first. Look for an agency that has been in business at least five years, emphasizes customer service, and has someone on staff who specializes in your destination. In addition, **make sure the agency belongs to a professional trade organization.** The American Society of Travel Agents (ASTA)—the largest and most influential in the field with more than 20,000 members in some 140 countries—maintains and enforces a strict code of ethics and will step in to help mediate any agent-client disputes involving ASTA members if necessary. ASTA (whose motto is "Without a travel agent, you're on your own") also maintains a Web site that includes a directory of agents. (If a travel agency is also acting as your tour operator, *see* Buyer Beware *in* Tours and Packages.)

🚆 Local Agent Referrals **American Society of Travel Agents (ASTA)** ⊠ 1101 King St., Suite 200, Alexandria, VA 22314 ☎ 703/739-2782 or 800/965-2782 24-hr hot line ⅏ 703/739-3268 ⊕ www. astanet.com. **Association of British Travel Agents** ⊠ 68-71 Newman St., London W1T 3AH ☎ 020/7637-2444 ⅏ 020/7637-0713 ⊕ www.abta.com. **Association of Canadian Travel Agencies** ⊠ 130 Albert St., Suite 1705, Ottawa, ON K1P 5G4 ☎ 613/237-3657 ⅏ 613/237-7052 ⊕ www.acta.ca. **Australian Federation of Travel Agents** ⊠ Level 3, 309 Pitt St., Sydney, NSW 2000 ☎ 02/9264-3299 ⅏ 02/9264-1085 ⊕ www.afta.com.au. **Travel Agents' Association of New Zealand** ⊠ Level 5, Tourism and Travel House, 79 Boulcott St., Box 1888, Wellington 6001 ☎ 04/499-0104 ⅏ 04/499-0786 ⊕ www.taanz.org.nz.

VISITOR INFORMATION

Learn more about foreign destinations by checking government-issued travel advisories and country information. For a broader picture, consider information from more than one country.
🚆 Tourist Information **Canadian Tourism Commission** ☎ 613/946-1000 ⊕ www.canadatourism.com. **Nova Scotia Tourism** ⊠ Box 519, Halifax, B3J 2R7 ☎ 800/565-0000 ⊕ www.gov.ns.ca/tourism. **Tourism New Brunswick** ⊠ Box 12345, Campbellton, E3N 3T6 ☎ 800/561-0123 ⊕ www.tourismnewbrunswick.ca. **Newfoundland and Labrador Tourism** ⊠ Box 8730, St. John's, A1B 4K2 ☎ 800/563-6353 ⊕ www.gov.nl.ca/tourism. **Tourism PEI** ⊠ Box 940, Charlottetown, C1A 7M5 ☎ 888/734-7529 ⊕ www.peiplay.com.
🚆 In the U.K. **Visit Canada Center** ⊠ 62-65 Trafalgar Sq., London, WC2 5DY ☎ 0891/715-000, 50p per minute peak rate and 45p per minute cheap rate.

WEB SITES

Do check out the World Wide Web when planning your trip. You'll find everything from weather forecasts to virtual tours of famous cities. Be sure to visit Fodors.com (⊕ www.fodors.com), a complete travel-planning site. You can research prices and book plane tickets, hotel rooms, rental cars, vacation packages, and more. In addition, you can post your pressing questions in the Travel Talk section. Other planning tools include a currency converter and weather reports, and there are loads of links to travel resources. For festivals, check out ⊕ www.festivalseeker.com.

NOVA SCOTIA

1

FODOR'S CHOICE

Acton's Grill & Café, *Wolfville*
Aspotogan Peninsula drive
Cabot Trail drive
Cape Breton Highlands National Park, *Cape Breton*
Cape Chignecto Park, *West Advocate*
Cape d'Or
Da Maurizio Dining Room, *Halifax*
Farmhouse Inn B&B, *near Wolfville*
Fortress of Louisbourg, *Louisbourg, Cape Breton*
Four Mile Beach Inn, *Cape North, Cape Breton*
Gabrieau's Bistro Restaurant, *Antigonish*
Gowrie House, *Sydney Mines*
Harris' Quick 'n Tasty, *Dayton*
Highland Village Museum, *Iona*
Hiking trails, *Mabou Mines, Cape Breton*
Julien's Pastry Shop & Bakery, *Chester*
Kejimkujik National Park
Keltic Lodge, *Ingonish Beach*
Rose Arbour Café, *Windsor*
Sherbrooke Village
Stonehame Lodge & Chalets, *Scotsburn*
Sugar Moon Farm Pancake House, *Earltown*
Whale-watching at Pleasant Bay, *Cape Breton*

HIGHLY RECOMMENDED

SIGHTS Alexander Graham Bell National Historic Site, *Baddeck*
Atlantic Theatre Festival, *Wolfville*
Bluenose II, *Lunenburg*
Fortress of Louisbourg National Historic Site, *Louisbourg*
Glace Bay Miners' Museum, *Quarry Point*
Halifax Citadel National Historic Site, *Halifax*
Peggy's Cove
Ross Farm Living Museum of Agriculture, *New Ross*
Rossignol Cultural Centre, *Liverpool*
Salty's on the Waterfront, *Halifax*

Many other great hotels and restaurants enliven Nova Scotia.
For other favorites, look for the black stars as you read this chapter.

Updated by
Kim Goodson,
Amy Pugsley
Fraser, and
Shelley
Cameron-
McCarron

"INFINITE RICHES IN A LITTLE ROOM," wrote Elizabethan playwright Christopher Marlowe. He might have been referring to Nova Scotia, Canada's second-smallest province, which packs an impossible variety of cultures and landscapes into an area half the size of Ohio.

Water, water everywhere, but that's not all. Within the convoluted coastline of Nova Scotia, you find highlands that rival Scotland's; rugged fjords; rolling farmland; and networks of rivers, ponds, and lakes calling out to kayakers and canoers. Fifty-six kilometers (35 miles) is the farthest you can get from the sea anywhere in the province. Pounding waves in summer and the grinding ice of winter storms have sculpted the coastal rocks and reduced sandstone cliffs to stretches of sandy beach. Inland, the fertile fields of the Annapolis Valley yield peaches, corn, apples, and plums, sold at farm stands in summer and fall. A succession of wildflowers covers the roadside with blankets of color: purple and blue lupines; yellow coltsfoot; pink fireweed. Each of the wild habitats—bogs, dry barrens, tidal wetlands, open fields, dense spruce woods, and climax hardwood forests—has its own distinctive plant life. Thousands of years ago, scouring glaciers left scars on the land; the Halifax Citadel stands atop a drumlin, a round-top hill left by the retreating ice. Wildlife abounds: ospreys and bald eagles, moose and deer, whales in the waters off Cape Breton and Brier Island.

The original people of Nova Scotia, the Mi'Kmaqs, have been here for 10,000 years. In the early days of European exploration, the French and English navigators found them settled on the shores and harvesting the sea. In later years waves of immigrants filled the province: Germans in Lunenburg County; Highland Scots displaced by their landlords' preference for sheep; New England Loyalists escaping the American Revolution; blacks arriving as freemen or escaped slaves; Jews in Halifax, Sydney, and industrial Cape Breton; Ukranians, Poles, West Indians, Italians, and Lebanese drawn to the Sydney steel mill. As a result, there are Gaelic signs in Mabou and Iona, German sausage and sauerkraut in Lunenburg, and Greek music festivals in Halifax. The Acadians fly their tricolor flag with pride. Scots step-dance to antique fiddle airs. The fragrance of burning sweetgrass mingles with the prayers of the Mi'Kmaqs' Catholic mass, blending the old ways with the new.

This is a little, buried nation, with a capital city the same size as Marlowe's London. Before Canada was formed in 1867, Nova Scotians were prosperous shipwrights and merchants, trading with the world. Who created Cunard Lines? A Haligonian, Samuel Cunard. Those days brought democracy to the British colonies, left Victorian mansions in the salty little ports, and created a uniquely Nova Scotian outlook: worldly, approachable, and sturdily independent.

Exploring Nova Scotia

When arriving in Nova Scotia from New Brunswick via the Trans-Canada Highway (Highway 104), you have three ways to proceed into the province. Amherst is the first community after the border. From Amherst, Highway 104 takes you toward Halifax, a two-hour drive. Touring alternatives lie to the north and south. Highway 6, to the north, follows the shore of the Northumberland Strait; farther east is Cape Breton. Highway 2, to the south, is a less-traveled road and a favorite because of nearby fossil-studded shores. Branch roads lead to the Annapolis Valley and other points south. Drivers should be aware that the sharply curving rural roads warrant careful attention.

Numbers in the text correspond to numbers in the margin and on the Nova Scotia, Halifax, and Cape Breton Island maps.

If you have
3 days

Start in **Halifax** ①–⑭, a port city that combines old and new. Explore the South Shore and the Annapolis Valley, taking in the Lighthouse Route and Evangeline Trail, which loop back to Halifax. Head for **Peggy's Cove** ⑯, a fishing village perched on sea-washed granite and surrounded by coastal barrens. Explore the crafts shops of **Mahone Bay** ⑰ and travel on to **Lunenburg** ⑱ and the Fisheries Museum. Continue on Highway 3 or 103 to **Shelburne** ⑳ on Day 2. Visit **Yarmouth** ㉑ and travel on to **Digby** ㉓ to try its famous scallops. **Annapolis Royal** ㉔ is a lovely spot to spend an afternoon, or drive down Digby Neck to visit **Long Island and Brier Island** ㉕ and catch a whale-watching cruise in season. Travel on to the elm-lined streets of **Wolfville** ㉖, home of Acadia University, and explore nearby Grand Pré National Historic Site. On Day 3 check tide times and drive to Minas Basin, where the tides are the highest in the world. A leisurely drive puts you back in Halifax by late afternoon.

If you have
5 days

Spend a day or two in **Halifax** ①–⑭ before exploring the Eastern Shore along Highway 7, which winds along a dramatic coastline. **Musquodoboit Harbour** ㉘ is a haven for fishing enthusiasts. Nearby is Martinique Beach, one of Nova Scotia's best. Spend some time in **Sherbrooke Village** ㉙. Continue on Highway 7 toward **Antigonish** ㉛, on the Sunrise Trail. Visit Hector Heritage Quay in **Pictou** ㉝, where the Scots landed in 1773. From Pictou Highway 6 runs beside a string of beaches. Turn right to **Malagash** ㉟ and the Jost Vineyards. A half-hour drive takes you to **Amherst** ㊲. Continue on to **Joggins** ㊳ and search for souvenirs in its sandstone cliffs. For more fossils, head to **Parrsboro** ㊴.

If you have
7 days

Cape Breton Island is the perfect place for a leisurely seven-day tour. The coastal route takes you on a west-to-east loop from the Canso Strait Causeway. Overnight in **Mabou** ㊸, the heart of the island's rich musical tradition. From a base in **Margaree Harbour** ㊹, take a day or more to explore the Cabot Trail and Cape Breton Highlands National Park. Peruse crafts stores along St. Ann's Bay, but allow time to visit the Alexander Graham Bell National Historic Site in **Baddeck** ㊼. Spend the night in **Iona** ㊽. A day or two in **Sydney** ㊾ positions you for an afternoon excursion to the Glace Bay Miners' Museum in **Glace Bay** ㊿ and a daylong visit to Fortress of Louisbourg National Historic Park and the town of **Louisbourg** (51). Take Highway 4 back to Canso Causeway through **Big Pond** (52), and spend a day wandering one or more of the colorful Acadian villages of Isle Madame, such as **Arichat** (53).

About the Restaurants

Helping travelers discover for themselves the best tastes of the province, the Nova Scotian culinary industry has formed an organization called the Taste of Nova Scotia. It pulls together the producers and the preparers, setting quality standards to ensure that patrons at member restaurants receive authentic Nova Scotian food. Look for their symbol: a golden oval porthole framing food and a ship.

About the Hotels

Nova Scotia's strength lies in a sprinkling of first-class resorts that have retained a traditional feel, top country inns with a dedication to fine dining and high-level accommodations, and a few superior corporate hotels. Bed-and-breakfasts, particularly those in smaller towns, are often exceptional. Most resorts and many B&Bs are seasonal, closing during the winter. Expect to pay considerably more in Halifax and Dartmouth than elsewhere. Nova Scotia's computerized system **Check In** (☎ 902/425–5781 or 800/565–0000 ⊕ www.checkinnovascotia.com) provides information about and makes reservations with more than 700 hotels, motels, inns, campgrounds, and car rental agencies.

WHAT IT COSTS In Canadian Dollars				
	$$$$	$$$	$$	$	¢
RESTAURANTS	over $30	$20–$30	$12–$20	$8–$12	under $8
HOTELS	over $250	$175–$250	$125–$175	$75–$125	under $75

Restaurant prices are per person for a main course at dinner. Hotel prices are for two people in a standard double room in high season, excluding 15% harmonized sales tax (HST).

Timing

The best time of year to visit is mid-June through mid-September; in fact, many resorts, hotels, and attractions are open only during July and August. Nova Scotia, particularly the Cape Breton area, is very popular in fall because of the foliage and the 10-day Celtic Colours International Festival in October. And October—with blazing autumn colors, warm and sunny days, and cool nights—can be spectacular. Lobster is plentiful in May and June. Whale-watching and wildlife cruises and sea-kayaking outfitters generally operate from July to mid-September. Most golf courses stay open from June until late September, and some into October. Skiing season (both downhill and cross-country) is from mid-December to early April.

HALIFAX & DARTMOUTH

Updated by
Kim Goodson

Halifax and Dartmouth, combined with the surrounding County of Halifax and known as the Halifax Regional Municipality (HRM), gaze upon each other across Halifax Harbour, the second-largest natural harbor in the world. Once the point of entry to Canada for refugees and immigrants, the port remains a busy shipping center, with a flow of container ships and tugboats. Pleasure boats and yachts tie up alongside historic schooners at the Historic Properties Wharf. Pubs, shops, museums, and parks welcome visitors and locals. In summer jazz concerts and buskers, music festivals and sports events enliven the outdoor atmosphere. Art on exhibit, crafts sales, live theater, and fine food bring people here in all seasons. The film *Titanic* brought fresh attention to part of Halifax's history. Some 150 victims of the disaster are buried in three cemeteries here, and the Maritime Museum of the Atlantic has a *Titanic* display.

Halifax

1,137 km (705 mi) northeast of Boston; 275 km (171 mi) southeast of Moncton, New Brunswick.

Halifax is an intimate city that retains the ease of a small town. From harbor-front life to Victorian public gardens, it is large enough to have

1

Bird-Watching

A healthy population of bald eagles nests in Cape Breton, where they reel above Bras d'Or Lake or perch in trees along riverbanks. The Bird Islands boat tour from Big Bras d'Or circles islands where Atlantic puffins, kittiwakes, and guillemots nest in rocky cliffs. In May and August, the Bay of Fundy teems with migrating shorebirds, and the tidal marshes near the end of the Bird Islands are home to great blue-heron rookeries. The useful *Where to Find the Birds in Nova Scotia*, published by the Nova Scotia Bird Society, is available locally in shops.

Fresh- & Saltwater Fishing

Nova Scotia has more than 9,000 lakes and 100 brooks; practically all lakes and streams are open to anglers. The catch includes Atlantic salmon (June–September), brook and sea trout, bass, rainbow trout, and shad. The most prosperous fishing region in the province stretches from Barrington to Digby. Limited quantities of smelt and *gaspereaux* (river herring or alewives), abundant in May and June, can be taken without a license. Licenses are not required for saltwater fishing. *See* Sports & the Outdoors *in* Nova Scotia A to Z and *in* Smart Travel Tips A to Z for information about licenses.

Tastes of Nova Scotia

Succulent blueberries, crisp apples, wild mushrooms, home-raised poultry, quality beef, fresh-from-the-sea lobster, cultivated mussels, Digby scallops, and fine Atlantic salmon are just some of the highlights of Nova Scotia cuisine. The quality of ingredients comes from the closeness of the harvest. Agriculture and fisheries (wild harvest and aquaculture) are never far away.

Fossil Hunting

Coal seams and shale cliffs along Cape Breton's shores yield fossilized ferns, leaves, and petrified wood. Kempt Head on Boularderie Island, Sutherland's Corner on Sydney Mines' Shore Road, and the beach at Point Aconi are good places to search. The province's richest source of fossils is the Minas Basin, near Joggins and Parrsboro, where dinosaur fossils, agate, and amethyst are found. You are welcome to gather what rocks you find along the beaches, but a permit from the Nova Scotia Museum of Natural History is required to dig along the cliffs.

Celtic Music

Scottish immigrants brought fiddles and folk airs to eastern Nova Scotia and Cape Breton, where Highland music mingled with that of the Acadians and, later, with that of the Irish. Today the region enjoys world renown as a center of distinctive Celtic music. Watch for concerts by Jimmy Rankin or the Barra MacNeils, Gaelic-punk singer Mary Jane Lamond, and outstanding fiddlers such as Natalie MacMaster, Ashley MacIsaac, Buddy MacMaster, and Wendy MacIsaac. You can often catch these acts at a square dance in Inverness County or a milling frolic on Bras d'Or Lake. In October the Celtic Colours International Festival brings musicians from around the world to Cape Breton.

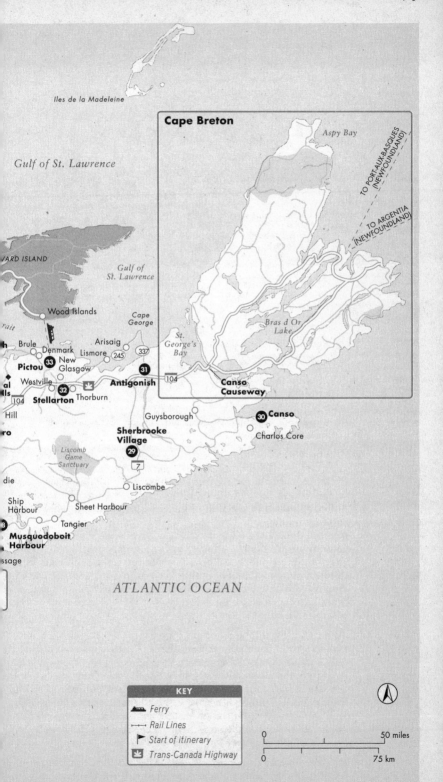

Iles de la Madeleine

Gulf of St. Lawrence

Cape Breton

Aspy Bay

TO PORT-AUX-BASQUES
(NEWFOUNDLAND)

TO ARGENTIA
(NEWFOUNDLAND)

VARD ISLAND

Gulf of
St. Lawrence

Wood Islands

Cape
George

Bras d Or
Lake

rait

Brule

Arisaig

Denmark   Lismore   245   337

St.
George's
Bay

Pictou 33 New
Glasgow

Westville 31 104

Antigonish

Canso
Causeway

al   32
lls

104 Stellarton Thorburn

Hill

Guysborough

30 **Canso**

ro

Sherbrooke
Village

Charlos Core

Liscomb
Game
Sanctuary

29

7

die

Liscombe

Ship
Harbour

Sheet Harbour

8

Tangier

**Musquodoboit
Harbour**

ssage

ATLANTIC OCEAN

KEY

Ferry

Rail Lines

Start of itinerary

Trans-Canada Highway

0   50 miles

0   75 km

Anna
Leonowens
Gallery **12**

Art Gallery of
Nova
Scotia **11**

Brewery
Market. **4**

Government
House **5**

Halifax Citadel
National
Historic Site. . . **8**

Halifax Public
Gardens. **6**

Historic
Properties **2**

Maritime
Museum of
the Atlantic . . . **3**

Mary E. Black
Gallery **13**

Nova Scotia
Museum of
Natural
History. **7**

Pier 21 . . . . . . **14**

Province
House **10**

Purdy's
Wharf **1**

St. Paul's
Church. **9**

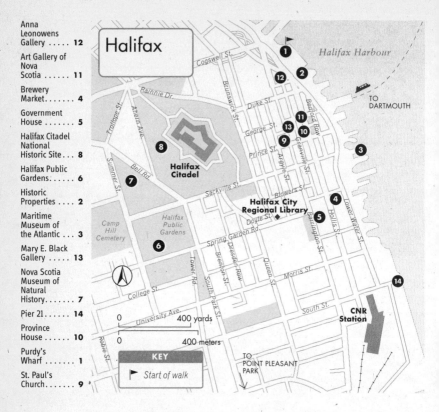

the trappings of a capital city yet small enough that many of its sights can be seen on a pleasant walk downtown.

A Good Walk

Begin on Upper Water Street at **Purdy's Wharf ❶ ▶** for unobstructed views of Halifax Harbour and the pier and office towers of this wharf. Continue south on Lower Water Street to the restored warehouses of the **Historic Properties ❷**, a cluster of boutiques and restaurants linked by cobblestone footpaths. Stroll south several blocks along the piers to the **Maritime Museum of the Atlantic ❸**: the wharves outside frequently welcome visiting transatlantic yachts and sail-training ships. Walk to the end of the block and cross Lower Water Street to **Brewery Market ❹**, a restored waterfront property. Take the elevator at the office end of Brewery Market and emerge on Hollis Street. Turn left, past several elegant Victorian town houses—notably Keith Hall—once the executive offices of the brewery.

Turn right onto Bishop Street and right again onto Barrington Street, Halifax's main downtown thoroughfare. The stone mansion on your right is **Government House ❺**, the official residence of Nova Scotia's lieutenant governor. Take a detour from Barrington Street onto Spring Garden Road and the attractive shops in the Park Lane and Spring Garden Place shopping centers; then walk west to the **Halifax Public Gardens ❻**, where you can rest your legs on shaded benches amid flower beds and rare trees. A block to the north, on Summer Street, is the **Nova Scotia Museum of Natural History ❼**.

On your way back to Barrington Street, on Bell Road and Sackville Street, you'll notice the **Halifax Citadel National Historic Site ❽**, dominated by the fortress that once commanded the city. On a lot defined by Barrington,

Argyle, and Prince streets lies **St. Paul's Church** ❾; one wall within its historic confines contains a fragment of the great Halifax Explosion of 1917. A block north and facing City Hall is the Grand Parade, where musicians perform at noon on summer days. From here, the waterfront side of Citadel Hill, look uphill: the tall, stylish brick building is the World Trade and Convention Centre and is attached to the 10,000-seat Halifax Metro Centre—the site of hockey games, rock concerts, and political conventions. Head down the hill on Prince Street, making a left on Hollis Street to **Province House** ❿, Canada's oldest legislative building. North of Province House, at Cheapside, is the **Art Gallery of Nova Scotia** ⓫, which showcases a large collection of folk art. Walk a block west to Granville Street and two blocks north to the **Anna Leonowens Gallery** ⓬, where you can peruse the work of local artists. Return south two blocks on Barrington to stop by the crafts displays at the **Mary E. Black Gallery** ⓭. A final stop lies to the south: **Pier 21** ⓮, a former immigration center, houses a museum of immigration.

TIMING   The city of Halifax is fairly compact: depending on your tendency to stop and study, the above tour can take from a half to a full day. Pier 21 could take several hours in itself, so you may want to visit it separately from the walk. You can drive from sight to sight, but parking is a problem, and you will miss out on much of the flavor of the city.

Sights to See

⓬ **Anna Leonowens Gallery.** The gallery is named for the Victorian woman who served the king of Siam as governess and whose memoirs served as inspiration for Rodgers and Hammerstein's *The King and I*. Founding the Nova Scotia College of Art and Design was just another of her life's chapters. Three exhibition spaces serve as a showcase for the college faculty and students. The displays focus on contemporary studio and media art. ⊠ *1891 Granville St.* ☎ *902/494–8223* ⊠ *Free* ☉ *Tues.–Fri. 11–5, Sat. noon–4.*

⓫ **Art Gallery of Nova Scotia.** Sheltered within this historic building is an extensive permanent collection of more than 4,000 works, including an internationally recognized collection of Maritime and folk art by artists such as wood-carver Sydney Howard and painter Joe Norris. Also here is the actual home of the late folk painter Maude Lewis, whose bright, cheery paintings cover the tiny structure inside and out. The collection of contemporary art has major works by Christopher Pratt, Alex Colville, John Nesbitt, and Dawn McNutt. ⊠ *1741 Hollis St., at Cheapside* ☎ *902/424–7542* ⊕ *www.agns.gov.ns.ca* ⊠ *$5* ☉ *June–Aug., Mon.–Wed. and Fri. 10–6, Thurs. 10–9, weekends noon–5; Sept.–May, Tues.–Fri. 10–5, weekends noon–5.*

❹ **Brewery Market.** A popular Saturday market takes place at this sprawling stone complex where Alexander Keith once brewed the beer that still bears his name. You can browse stalls laden with hand-dyed silk scarves, leather work, paintings, and stone carvings. Culinary temptations include Chinese and Indian snacks, farm cheese, and home-smoked sausage. Golden mountains of freshly baked bread; colorful displays of fresh local fruits and vegetables; and stalls with lamb, rabbit, and big brown eggs make this a true farmer's market. Many of the city's finest chefs are regularly seen shopping here. ⊠ *Between Hollis and Lower Water Sts.* ☎ *902/423–2279* ☉ *Sat. 7 AM–1 PM.*

off the
beaten
path

FAIRVIEW CEMETERY – This cemetery is the final resting place of 121 victims of the *Titanic*. The graves can easily be located in a graceful arc of granite tombstones. One grave—marked J. DAWSON— attracts particular attention from visitors. It's not the fictional

Minnesota artist featured in the 1998 film, but James Dawson, a coal trimmer from Ireland. Nineteen other victims are buried in Mount Olivet Catholic Cemetery, 10 in the Baron de Hirsch Jewish Cemetery. The Maritime Museum of the Atlantic has an exhibit about the disaster. ⊠ *3720 Windsor St., 3 km (2 mi) north of downtown.*

❺ Government House. Built between 1799 and 1805 for Sir John Wentworth, the Loyalist governor of New Hampshire, and his racy wife, Fannie (Thomas Raddall's novel *The Governor's Lady* tells their story), this house has since been the official residence of the province's lieutenant governor (currently Myra Freeman, the first woman to hold the post in almost 400 years). It is North America's oldest consecutively occupied government residence, as the older President's House (the White House) was evacuated and burned during the War of 1812. Its construction, of Nova Scotian stone, was engineered by a Virginian Loyalist, Isaac Hildrith. The house, which has been restored to its original elegance, isn't open to the public. ⊠ *1451 Barrington St.*

★ ❽ Halifax Citadel National Historic Site. The Citadel, erected between 1826 and 1856, was the heart of the city's fortifications and was linked to smaller forts and gun emplacements on the harbor islands and on the bluffs above the harbor entrance. Several other forts stood on the site before the present one. Kilted soldiers drill in front of the **Army Museum,** once the barracks, and a cannon is fired every day at noon. Before leaving, take in the view from the Citadel: the spiky downtown crowded between the hilltop and the harbor; the wooded islands at the harbor's mouth; and the naval dockyard under the Angus L. Macdonald Bridge, the nearer of the two bridges connecting Halifax with Dartmouth. The handsome, four-sided **Town Clock** on Citadel Hill was given to Halifax by Prince Edward, duke of Kent, military commander from 1794 to 1800. ⊠ *Citadel Hill* ☎ *902/426–5080* ⊕ *www.pc.gc. ca* ⌨ *June–Sept. 15 $9, May 7–31 and Sept. 16–Oct. $5.75* ☉ *May 7–June 30 and Sept.–Oct., daily 9–5; July–Aug., daily 9–6.*

❻ Halifax Public Gardens. One of the oldest formal Victorian gardens in North America, this city oasis had its start in 1753 as a private garden. Its layout was completed in 1875 by Richard Power, former gardener to the duke of Devonshire in Ireland. Gravel paths wind among ponds, trees, and flower beds, revealing an astonishing variety of plants from all over the world. The centerpiece is a gazebo erected in 1887 for Queen Victoria's Golden Jubilee. The gardens are closed during the winter, but you can take a pleasant walk around the perimeter along the cast-iron fence. ⊠ *Bounded by Sackville, Summer, and S. Park Sts. and Spring Garden Rd.*

❷ Historic Properties. These waterfront warehouses date from the early 19th century, when trade and war made Halifax prosperous. They were built by such raffish characters as Enos Collins, a privateer, smuggler, and shipper whose vessels defied Napoléon's blockade to bring American supplies to the duke of Wellington. The buildings have since been taken over by quality shops, chic offices, and restaurants, including those in Privateer's Warehouse. ⊠ *Lower Water and Hollis Sts.*

Khyber Center for the Arts. Primarily a gallery for young and emerging artists, the Khyber hosts works in numerous genres, including performance art. Its various galleries are in a historic, turreted building. Also in the building is the Khyber Club bar, where young artists spend time discussing their work and drinking Khybeer. ⊠ *1588 Barrington St.* ☎ *902/422–9668* ⌨ *By donation* ☉ *Wed.–Sat. noon–5.*

③ Maritime Museum of the Atlantic. The exhibits in this restored chandlery and warehouse on the waterfront include small boats once used around the coast, as well as displays describing Nova Scotia's proud sailing heritage, from the days when the province, on its own, was one of the world's foremost shipbuilding and trading nations. Other exhibits explore the Halifax Explosion of 1917, shipwrecks, and lifesaving. Permanently moored outside, after a long life of charting the coasts of Labrador and the Arctic, is the hydrographic steamer *Acadia*. At the next wharf (summer only) is Canada's naval memorial, **HMCS *Sackville*,** the sole survivor of a fleet that escorted convoys of ships from Halifax to England during World War II.

The museum has a permanent exhibit about the *Titanic* disaster. With many victims buried in Halifax, the city was, in a sense, the ship's final destination. The display includes 20 artifacts and dozens of photographs. The centerpiece is the only surviving deck chair. Also on display are a section of wall paneling, a balustrade molding and part of a newel from the dual curving staircase, a cribbage board carved from *Titanic* oak by the carpenter of one of the rescue ships, and the log kept by a wireless operator at Cape Race, Newfoundland, on the fateful night. An extensive research library is open to the public by appointment only. ✉ *1675 Lower Water St.* ☎ *902/424–7490 or 902/424–7491* ⊕ *museum.gov. ns.ca/mma* ☞ *$8* ⊘ *May–Oct., Mon. and Wed.–Sat. 9:30–5:30, Tues. 9:30–8; May and Oct., Sun. 1–5:30; June–Sept., Sun. 9:30–5:30; Nov.–Apr., Wed.–Sat. 9:30–5, Tues. 9:30–8, Sun. 1–5.*

⑬ Mary E. Black Gallery. The exhibit space for the Nova Scotia Centre for Craft and Design presents rotating shows of quality crafts. ✉ *1683 Barrington St.* ☎ *902/424–4062* ☞ *Free* ⊘ *Weekdays 9–4:30, Sat. 10–4.*

☾ ⑦ Nova Scotia Museum of Natural History. You can learn about whales, fossils, dinosaurs, birds, and mushrooms here. The Nature Centre is home to live snakes, frogs, insects, and other creatures; the Butterfly Pavilion is filled with species from around the world. Nature talks, walks, and workshops are designed to appeal to all interests and ages. The museum is most easily recognized by the huge fiberglass model of the tiny northern spring peeper (a frog) that "clings" to the side of the building May through October. ✉ *1747 Summer St.* ☎ *902/424–7353* ⊕ *nature. museum.gov.ns.ca* ☞ *$4* ⊘ *Mid-May–Oct., Mon., Tues., and Thurs.–Sun. 1–5:30, Wed. 9:30–8; Nov.–mid-May, Tues. and Thurs.–Sun. 9:30–5, Wed. 9:30–8.*

⑭ Pier 21. From 1928 until 1971, refugees, returning troop ships, war brides, and more than a million immigrants arrived on Canadian soil through Pier 21, the front door to Canada. It's now a museum where the immigrant experience is re-created through live performances, multimedia presentations, and displays of photographs, documents, and artifacts. ✉ *1031 Marginal Rd.* ☎ *902/425–7770* ☞ *$6.50* ⊘ *June–Sept., daily 9–6; Oct.–May, Tues.–Sat. 10–5, Sun. noon–5.*

Point Pleasant Park. Most of the city's secondary fortifications have been turned into public parks. This one, which encompasses 186 wooded acres with walking trails and seafront paths, is popular with joggers and dog walkers and provides the perfect vantage point from which to watch ships entering and leaving the harbor. The park was leased from the British Crown by the city for 999 years, at a shilling a year. Its major military installation is a massive round martello tower dating from the late 18th century. ✉ *About 12 blocks down S. Park St. from Spring Garden Rd.*

⑩ Province House. Charles Dickens proclaimed this structure, now a National Historic Site, "a gem of Georgian architecture." Erected in 1819 to house Britain's first overseas self-government, the sandstone building still serves as the meeting place for the provincial legislature. ⊠ *1726 Hollis St.* ☎ *902/424–4661* ⊠ *Free* ⊗ *July–Aug., weekdays 9–5, weekends 10–4; Sept.–June, weekdays 8:30–4:30.*

▶ ❶ **Purdy's Wharf.** Named after a famous shipping family from the 19th century, the wharf is composed of a pier and twin office towers that stand right in the harbor. The buildings actually use ocean water to generate air-conditioning. ⊠ *Upper Water St.*

❾ **St. Paul's Church.** Opened in 1750, this is Canada's oldest Protestant church and the burial site of many colonial notables. Inside, on the north end, a piece of metal is embedded in the wall. It is a fragment of the *Mont Blanc,* one of the two ships whose collision caused the Halifax Explosion of December 6, 1917, the greatest human-caused explosion prior to that at Hiroshima. ⊠ *1749 Argyle St.* ☎ *902/429–2240* ⊗ *Sept.–May, weekdays 9–4:30; June–Aug., Mon.–Sat. 9–4:30.*

Where to Stay & Eat

$$$ ✕ **Da Maurizio Dining Room.** Subdued lighting, elegant decor, and fresh
FodorśChoice   flowers on the tables make dining a lovely experience at this Italian restau-
★   rant. Chef Maurizio's creativity and attention to detail create meals that are both impressive and satisfying and make him a local legend. Seared foie gras is covered with a wild berry–and–sauternes reduction. Brome Lake duckling is complemented with fig compote. For dessert, the zabaglione is likely to leave you weak. Connoisseurs should ask to see the specialty wine list, which tops out at $300. ⊠ *1496 Lower Water St.* ☎ *902/423–0859* ⊟ *AE, MC, V* ⊗ *Closed Sun.*

$$–$$$ ✕ **Carlton House Cafe.** Soups, sandwiches on slabs of warm bread, and delicate pastries are all made fresh on-site. If you can't get a table in this intimate 20-seat café, everything can be packed to go. Its central location makes the Carlton House the perfect spot to pick up a picnic for a short hike to Citadel Hill, the Grand Parade, or the waterfront. ⊠ *1653 Argyle St.* ☎ *902/492–0212* ⊟ *AE, MC, V* ⊗ *Closed weekends.*

$$–$$$ ✕ **Fid.** A fid is a graceful nautical tool used to splice rope. At this small, minimalist restaurant, a two-minute walk from the main gates of the Halifax Public Gardens, the chef-owner splices together unusual flavors and textures. The halibut, when available, is the most popular dish on the menu. Chocolate lovers should consider the *moelleau au chocolat,* molten chocolate-custard sauce within a shell of warm cake. ⊠ *1569 Dresden Row* ☎ *902/422–9162* ⊟ *MC, V* ⊗ *Closed Mon. No lunch.*

$$–$$$ ✕ **MacAskill's Restaurant.** Diners can experience Nova Scotian hospitality in this romantic dining room overlooking beautiful Halifax Harbour. The chefs create a variety of seafood dishes using the finest, freshest fish available. Specialties also include pepper steak, flambéed table-side. ⊠ *Dartmouth Ferry Terminal Bldg., 88 Alderney Dr.* ☎ *902/466–3100* ⊟ *AE, DC, MC, V* ⊗ *Closed Sun. Nov.–May. No lunch weekends.*

$$–$$$ ✕ **Press Gang.** Easily the hippest fine-dining establishment in Halifax, the Press Gang serves the freshest fish available. Oysters are served with freshly grated horseradish, black pepper, and lemon, or with one of the house salsas or dressings. You might try a fine muscadet from the well-stocked cellar to complement your seafood. The "Chefs Call," four courses for two ($100), rarely disappoints and is an exceptional value. Thick, cold stone walls testify to the building's era—it was built in 1759—but the restaurant is warmed by comfortable seating and intimate lighting. ⊠ *5218 Prince St.* ☎ *902/423–8816* ⌖ *Reservations essential* ⊟ *AE, MC, V.*

★ **$$–$$$** ✕ **Salty's on the Waterfront.** Overlooking Privateer's Wharf and the entire harbor, this restaurant gets the prize for the best location in the city.

Huge bowls of steaming mussels and an excellent "surf and turf" crown a menu sure to satisfy any seafood lover. Request a table with a window view and save room for the famous dessert, Cadix (chocolate mousse over praline crust). The Salty Dog Bar & Grill, on the ground level, is less expensive and serves lunch outside on the wharf in summer (it can be very windy). ⊠ *1869 Upper Water St.* ☎ *902/423–6818* ⌂ *Reservations essential* ⊟ *AE, DC, MC, V.*

★ **$$** ✕ **Economy Shoe Shop.** Variety rules at this chaotic, ever-popular place with a bar and three restaurants. Start with an imported beer in the Belgian bar, enjoy tapas in the Atrium, head to Backstage to dine among the fake trees and other theatrical decorations, and enjoy the private cave in the Diamond for after-dinner coffee or, in summer, sit on the deck, which is always packed with locals. Food at the "Shoe Shop" is adventurous—though not haute cuisine–and portions are generous. You are sure to meet some interesting people, beginning with your server, who doubles as an entertainer. ⊠ *1663 Argyle St.* ☎ *902/423–7463* ⊟ *AE, D, DC, MC, V.*

$–$$ ✕ **Cheelin Restaurant.** Some of the most flavorful and fresh dishes in the region are prepared in the open kitchen at this small and informal Chinese restaurant. Each dish receives individual attention and care, and the chef-owner personally checks with diners to make sure they are satisfied. Noodle and dumpling dishes are very popular, but if you're looking for something different, try the amazing seafood-stuffed eggplant in black-bean sauce. ⊠ *Brewery Market, 1496 Lower Water St.* ☎ *902/ 422–2252* ⊟ *AE, MC, V* ☯ *Closed Mon.*

$–$$ ✕ **Dharma Sushi.** Though the service is fast-paced here, the food doesn't suffer as a result. Tidy sushi, fresh sashimi, and feather-light tempura are artfully presented. The *chawan mushi,* a delicate egg custard with seafood, has the consistency of fine silk. ⊠ *1576 Argyle St.* ☎ *902/ 425–7785* ⊟ *AE, MC, V* ☯ *Closed Sun. No lunch Sat.*

$–$$ ✕ **Il Mercato Ristorante.** Enter this Italian eatery at your own risk: the gleaming display cases of antipasti and desserts—including the *zucotto,* a dome of chocolate and cream—are sure to tempt. In the heart of the downtown shopping district, Il Mercato is an ideal lunch stop. ⊠ *5475 Spring Garden Rd.* ☎ *902/422–2866* ⊟ *AE, MC, V.*

$–$$ ✕ **Privateer's Warehouse.** History surrounds you in this centuries-old building, where three restaurants share early-18th-century stone walls and hewn beams. The Upper Deck dining room has a nautical theme, great views of the harbor, and fresh lobsters in its holding tank. The Privateers Grill is recommended for true seafood lovers. Crawdads has a bistro-style atmosphere and specializes in crab and oysters as well as traditional cuisine. Lower Deck Good Time Pub is a boisterous bar with long trestle tables and a patio; fish-and-chips and other pub food are served. ⊠ *Historic Properties, Lower Water St.* ☎ *902/422–1289, 902/426–1500, or 902/426–1501* ⊟ *AE, DC, MC, V.*

¢–$ ✕ **Satisfaction Feast.** This small vegetarian restaurant is informal, friendly, and usually packed at lunchtime. The food is wholesome, with lots of ethnic influences—think fresh whole-wheat bread and curries. Sweet, sharp ginger beer is brewed on the premises. Enjoy an organic coffee with one of the fine cakes or desserts. ⊠ *1581 Grafton St.* ☎ *902/422– 3540* ⊟ *AE, MC, V.*

$$$–$$$$ ▦ **Cambridge Suites.** Besides the obvious convenience of being able to prepare your own food and keep a bottle of wine cold, the best feature of this all-suites hotel is its location near downtown Halifax and Citadel Hill. It is four blocks (albeit up a steep hill) from the waterfront hub and one block from Spring Garden Road's fabulous shopping and people-watching. Some suites have high-speed Internet access. ⊠ *1583 Brunswick St., B3J 3P5* ☎ *902/420–0555 or 800/565–1263* ⌂ *902/420–*

9379 ⊕ *www.cambridgesuiteshotel.com* ⇶ *200 suites* ♿ *Restaurant, room service, in-room data ports, kitchenettes, cable TV with movies, gym, hot tub, sauna, bar* ⊟ *AE, D, MC, V* ⊠ *CP.*

$$–$$$$ ▥ **Casino Nova Scotia Hotel.** Built low to match neighboring historic iron-stone buildings, this waterfront hotel varies in appearance from others in the chain. Its convenient location in the Historic Properties con-tributes to its elegance. Rooms are fairly spacious; all have desks and sitting areas. A five-minute stroll through a walkway takes you to Hal-ifax's only casino. ⊠ *1919 Upper Water St., B3J 3J5* ☎ *902/421–1700 or 800/325–3535* 🖷 *902/422–5805* ⊕ *www.casinonovascotiahotel. com* ⇶ *335 rooms, 19 suites* ♿ *Restaurant, room service, cable TV with movies and video games, indoor pool, hair salon, health club, hot tub, dock, bar, baby-sitting, dry cleaning, laundry service, concierge, Inter-net, meeting rooms, car rental, parking (fee); no smoking* ⊟ *AE, DC, MC, V.*

★ **$$–$$$$** ▥ **Prince George Hotel.** Contemporary mahogany furnishings fill the rooms at this luxurious and understated business-oriented hotel. Quiet and calm prevail in the public areas and expert staff, in starched uni-forms, wait to fulfill your every wish. Georgio's Restaurant ($$) serves eclectic cuisine in a casual setting. The hotel is connected by underground tunnel to the World Trade and Convention Centre; walkways provide access to shops, offices, and entertainment. ⊠ *1725 Market St., B3J 3N9* ☎ *902/425–1986, 800/565–1567 in Canada* ⊕ *www.princegeorgehotel. com* ⇶ *207 rooms, 9 suites* ♿ *Restaurant, cable TV, pool, gym, hot tub, sauna, bar, concierge, meeting room* ⊟ *AE, DC, MC, V.*

$$–$$$$ ▥ **Westin Nova Scotian.** An enormous brick building, this grand hotel sits solidly in downtown Halifax, next door to the VIA Rail station, with the harbor behind it and Cornwallis Park in front. Comfortable over-stuffed chairs and a warm, peachy light fill the lobby, where a nautical theme prevails. Rooms are done in green or peach; some have wicker furniture. The restaurant serves fresh fish and shellfish dishes as well as pastas and meatier fare. ⊠ *1181 Hollis St., B3H 2P6* ☎ *902/421–1000 or 800/228–3000* 🖷 *902/422–9465* ⊕ *www.westin.com* ⇶ *300 rooms, 13 suites* ♿ *Restaurant, in-room data ports, minibars, cable TV with movies, tennis court, indoor pool, gym, hot tub, sauna, bar, baby-sitting, dry cleaning, laundry service, business services, meeting rooms, no-smoking rooms* ⊟ *AE, DC, MC, V.*

$–$$$$ ▥ **Halliburton House Inn.** Three 19th-century town houses were ele-gantly renovated to create this hotel. Period antiques, goose-down du-vets, and fresh coffee await you in the comfortable rooms, lending a homey ambience. The suites have fireplaces, and there's a lovely garden. The rates here are quite varied, with some topping $300. Local game and Atlantic seafood are served in a small but elegant dining room. ⊠ *5184 Morris St., B3J 1B3* ☎ *902/420–0658* 🖷 *902/423–2324* ⊕ *www. halliburton.ns.ca* ⇶ *29 rooms, 2 suites* ♿ *Restaurant, cable TV, li-brary* ⊟ *AE, DC, MC, V* ⊠ *CP.*

$–$$$ ▥ **Inn on the Lake.** A great value in a quiet location, this small country club–style hotel sits on 5 acres of parkland on the edge of Fall River Lake, 30 minutes from Halifax and 10 minutes from the airport. Rooms are spacious and have balconies. One two-story suite has two bed-rooms, a kitchenette, and a large patio. Some rooms have whirlpool tubs. ⊠ *Box 29, 3009 Lake Thomas Dr., Waverly B0N 2S0* ☎ *902/861–3480* 🖷 *902/861–4883* ⊕ *www.innonthelake.com* ⇶ *34 rooms, 12 suites* ♿ *Restaurant, cable TV, 2 tennis courts, pool, beach, boating, basket-ball, horseshoes, shuffleboard, volleyball, lounge, Internet, business services, meeting rooms, airport shuttle, free parking* ⊟ *AE, MC, V.*

$$ ▥ **Delta Halifax.** This business-class hotel has spacious, attractive rooms, most with a panoramic harbor view. An enclosed walkway provides easy access to the Historic Properties and the Scotia Square mall. The Crown Bistro ($$–$$$) has more refined dishes as well as lighter fare. ⊠ *1990 Barrington St., B3J 1P2* ☎ *902/425–6700 or 800/441–1414* 🖷 *902/425–6214* ⊕ *www.deltahotels.com* ⇝ *279 rooms, 21 suites* ₺ *Restaurant, some in-room data ports, minibars, cable TV, indoor pool, gym, hot tub, sauna, piano bar, dry cleaning, laundry service, concierge, Internet, business services, meeting rooms, parking (fee), some pets allowed, no-smoking rooms* ▤ *AE, DC, MC, V.*

$–$$ 🏠 **Mary Queen of Scotts Inn.** Nova Scotian antiques and paintings fill this charming 19th-century Georgian house. It's just a short walk from busy Spring Garden Road, the heart of the downtown shopping district. ⊠ *1266 Queen St., B3J 2H4* ☎ *902/422–9828* ⊕ *www.premierehfx. com* ⇝ *7 rooms, 5 with bath* ₺ *Some kitchenettes, cable TV, laundry facilities, parking (fee)* ▤ *AE, MC, V.*

$ 🏠 **Garden View Bed & Breakfast.** This lovely Victorian home sits on a quiet residential street near the Halifax Commons. You can relax in the living room in front of the fire or unwind with a soak in an antique bathtub. The garden is especially charming. The living room has cable TV and a VCR. Breakfast is served in the dining room or in your room. ⊠ *6052 Williams St., B3K 1E9* ☎ *902/423–2943 or 888/737–0778* 🖷 *902/423–4355* ⊕ *www.interdesign.ca/gardenview* ⇝ *3 rooms without bath* ₺ *Dining room; no TV in some rooms, no smoking* ▤ *MC, V* ⦿I *BP.*

¢–$ 🏠 **Dalhousie University.** Most Halifax universities offer low prices for no-frills rooms from May through August. Dalhousie University rents single rooms for $36 and two-bedroom apartments for $55. Most have shared baths. A buffet breakfast is available at a minimal charge. Guests have access to the Dalplex athletic facility; ask for a schedule with pool times, court times, and classes. ⊠ *6136 University Ave., B3H 4J2* ☎ *902/494–8840* 🖷 *902/494–1219* ⊕ *www.dal.ca/mediavisit* ⇝ *420 rooms without bath, 20 apartments* ₺ *Indoor pool, gym, badminton; no a/c, no room phones, no room TVs* ▤ *MC, V.*

Nightlife & the Arts

THE ARTS Halifax has a burgeoning film industry, the product of which is presented at the **Atlantic Film Festival** (☎ 902/422–3456 ⊕ www.atlanticfilm.com), held the third week in September. The festival also showcases feature films, TV movies, and documentaries made outside Halifax. Admission to films often includes admission to a party or gala event following the screening. During the first week of September the **Atlantic Fringe Festival** (☎ 902/435–4837 or 800/565–0000 ⊕ www.atlanticfringe.com) presents numerous theatrical shows in a variety of venues scattered throughout the downtown. The **Du Maurier Atlantic Jazz Festival** (☎ 902/492–2225 ⊕ www.jazzeast.com), with an eclectic selection of jazz styles, takes place in mid-July. Some concerts are free. The internationally acclaimed **Scotia Festival of Music** (☎ 902/429–9469 ⊕ www.scotiafestival. ns.ca) presents classical musicians via concert and master classes each May and June. Pierre Boulez, Philip Glass, Maureen Forrester, and Tafelmusik are just a few of the guest artists who have attended the festival to perform, teach, coach, and lecture.

Grafton Street Dinner Theatre (⊠ 1741 Grafton St. ☎ 902/425–1961 ⊕ www.graftonstdinnertheatre.com) holds performances Wednesday through Saturday. The **Historic Feast Company** (⊠ Maritime Centre, 1505 Barrington St. ☎ 902/420–1840) presents shows set in the 19th century Thursday through Saturday evenings. The **Neptune Theatre** (⊠ 1593 Argyle St. ☎ 902/429–7300 information, 902/429–7070 box office ⊕ www.neptunetheatre.com), Canada's oldest professional repertory playhouse, has a main stage and studio theater under one roof. It stages year-round performances ranging from classics to comedy and contemporary Canadian drama. On mild July and August evenings, **Shakespeare by the Sea** (☎ 902/422–0295 ⊕ www.shakespearebythesea.ca) performs the Bard's works in Point Pleasant Park at the southern end of the Halifax peninsula. The natural setting—dark woods, rocky shore, and ruins of fortifications—serves as a dramatic backdrop.

NIGHTLIFE   Haligonians love their pubs and their music. This city has more bars per capita than any other place in Canada. At **Bearly's House of Blues and Ribs** (⊠ 1269 Barrington St. ☎ 902/423–2526), a dark, low-ceiling tavern with a couple of pool tables, you can dine on ribs, burgers, and fish-and-chips while listening to outstanding blues artists every evening except Monday and Wednesday. The trendiest spot in town, **Economy Shoe Shop Cafe and Bar, Backstage, and Diamond** (⊠ 1663 Argyle St. ☎ 902/423–7463), should be fully explored before finding the perfect place to linger: a quiet booth, a table in the middle of the action, or the gardenlike rooftop patio in summer. The eclectic decor alone is worth a visit. Food is served until 2 AM. Live jazz can be heard Monday; author readings are given Tuesday. The **Marquee Club** (⊠ 2037 Gottigen St. ☎ 902/429–3020), a cabaret-style venue with two stages and a seating capacity of 850, presents some of the hottest entertainment in town and is the main venue for big-name bands like members of the Rankin Family, Joel Plaskit, Crush, and Sloan. The club buzzes until 3:30 AM with live rock, blues, and alternative bands. Downstairs there's jazz, blues, and acoustic evenings. The bar has a good selection of locally brewed beers on tap. **Merrill's Cafe and Lounge** (⊠ 5171 George St. ☎ 902/425–5249) is a large, open bar with a DJ. The casual atmosphere is popular with the university crowd. The **Old Triangle** (⊠ 5136 Prince St. ☎ 902492–4900), a comfortable Irish pub, has traditional Irish, Scottish, and local music.

Reflections Cabaret (⊠ 5184 Sackville St. ☎ 902/422–2957), though considered a gay bar, is better described as an "anything goes" bar. Strobe lights and pounding music inspire dancing and drinking until 3:30 AM. Drag queens mingle with throngs of university students. Funky folk art hangs on the walls at the laid-back **Soho Kitchen** (⊠ 1582 Granville St. ☎ 902/423–3049). Jazz groups perform or jam Tuesday, Thursday, Friday, and Sunday nights. One of the owners might cook and serve your dinner and then join your table for a conversation. For more than 60 years patrons have been carving their initials and graffiti into the tables at the **Seahorse Tavern** (⊠ 1659 Argyle St. ☎ 902/423–7200). Cold draft beer washes down pub food. You can shoot a game of pool, contemplate the large aquarium, or sit at the bar and start a conversation with one of the many diverse regulars. **Tom's Little Havana Café** (⊠ 5428 Doyle St. ☎ 902/423–8667), a cozy pub, sells 30 types of cigars. High ceilings and a state-of-the-art air-purification system allow even nonsmokers to enjoy the comfort of a wing chair, bustling bar, or quiet booth.

Sports & the Outdoors

AUTOMOBILE   The **Moosehead Premium Dry Speedway** (⊠ 200 Prospect Rd. ☎ 902/876–
RACING   8222) hosts auto races May through October.

GOLF   Within an easy drive of downtown Halifax is **Granite Springs Golf Club** (⊠ 1441 Prospect Rd. ☎ 902/852–4653), an 18-hole, par-72 semiprivate course open to greens-fee play. Lessons and golf clinics are available. The **Sackville Golf Course** (⊠ Hwy. 1 ☎ 902/865–2179) is a 9-hole, par-29 public course. It has a driving range and a miniature golf course.

HOCKEY   The **Halifax Mooseheads** (⊠ Halifax Metro Centre, 1800 Argyle St. ☎ 902/496–5993 information, 902/421–8000 Metro Centre, 902/

451–1221 tickets), a Junior A division hockey team, play September through March.

SEA KAYAKING **Coastal Adventures Sea Kayaking** (☎ 877/404–2774) has a wide range of ocean tours for the beginner or the experienced kayaker from spring through autumn, weather permitting.

Shopping

Ambience Home Accents (✉ 5431 Doyle St. ☎ 902/423–9200) is packed to the rafters with curios and decorative functional items from all over the province and beyond. The **Art Gallery of Nova Scotia Shop** (✉ 1741 Hollis St. ☎ 902/424–7542) carries a good selection of arts and crafts; it also has a wonderful café decorated with colorful regional art. **Attica** (✉ 1652 Granville St. ☎ 902/423–2557) presents furniture, objets d'art, and housewares by Canadian and international designers.

You can find fine crafts in the **Barrington Inn Complex** (✉ 1875 Barrington St.). **Drala Books** (✉ 1567 Grafton St. ☎ 902/422–2504) stocks beautiful ceramics, handmade paper, and guides to meditation and Japanese gardening. The **Great Northern Knitters** (✉ 1870 Hollis St. ☎ 902/422–9209) sells wool and cotton sweaters, plus souvenir caps and sweatshirts and a wide range of knitted items, all at reasonable prices. In addition to being a deli and bakery with great takeout, the **Italian Gourmet** (✉ 5431 Doyle St. ☎ 902/423–7880) stocks a selection of imported gift items, including ceramics, exotic foodstuffs, and cooking gadgets.

At **Nova Scotian Crystal Ltd.** (✉ Corner of George and Lower Water Sts. ☎ 902/492–5984) watch Waterford master craftspeople blowing glass into graceful decanters and bowls, which can be purchased in the showroom. **Park Lane** (✉ 5657 Spring Garden Rd.) is a stylish indoor mall with everything from handcrafted clothing to Canadian books and bath salts. **Pewter House** (✉ 1875 Granville St. ☎ 902/423–8843) sells locally made and imported pewter goods, from knickknacks and tableware to clocks and jewelry. The **Plaid Place** (✉ 1903 Barrington Pl. ☎ 902/429–6872 or 800/563–1749) has an array of tartans and Highland accessories.

Spring Garden Road is the liveliest shopping street in town. **Atlantic Photo Supply** (✉ 5505 Spring Garden Rd., at Birmingham St. ☎ 902/423–6724) is well stocked and well staffed and can do on-site repairs. Photos by local artists are sold in the second-floor gallery. Busking musicians serenade shoppers flowing in and out of the mall at **Spring Garden Place** (✉ 5640 Spring Garden Rd.). **Jennifer's of Nova Scotia** (✉ 5635 Spring Garden Rd. ☎ 902/425–3119) sells traditional crafts from around the province, soaps, hooked mats, tartan clothing, ceramics, and pewter.

Dartmouth

🕒 *Immediately north of Halifax via the A. Murray Mackay and Angus L. Macdonald bridges.*

Suburban in demeanor, Dartmouth was first settled by Quaker whalers from Nantucket. The 23 lakes within Dartmouth's boundaries, which have given Dartmouth the moniker "City of Lakes," provided the Mi' Kmaqs with a canoe route to the province's interior and to the Bay of Fundy. A 19th-century canal system connected the lakes for a brief time, but today there are only ruins, which have been partially restored as historic sites. You can drive or take the ferry from Halifax to Dartmouth. If you walk along the water behind the modern Law Courts in Halifax, near the Historic Properties, you soon reach the Dartmouth ferry terminal, jammed with commuters during rush hour. The terminal is home to the oldest operational saltwater ferry service in North America, which began in 1732. If you do take the ferry, be sure to enjoy the sculptures by artist Dawn McNutt in the courtyard just outside the Dartmouth terminal. You may also want to head straight up the hill, along Pleasant Street, to explore funky secondhand stores, pawnbrokers, and antiques and curio shops. Visit Chez Christine for a light lunch or stop into Joe's Bar for a cold draft beer.

If you'd rather walk to Dartmouth, try the Angus L. Macdonald Bridge, which has a walkway and a bicycle path. After you come off the bridge, keep right until you can follow the wooden boardwalk for a stroll along the water. Eventually you arrive at the Dartmouth ferry terminal, where you can return to downtown Halifax or continue along the boardwalk to see remnants of the Shubenacadie Canal.

The **Black Cultural Centre for Nova Scotia,** in Westphal (a neighborhood of Dartmouth), is in the heart of the oldest black community in the area. The museum, library, and educational complex are dedicated to the preservation of the history and culture of blacks in Nova Scotia, who first arrived here in the 1600s. The center holds an annual celebration of black culture, music, and food in October. ⊠ *Hwy. 7 and Cherrybrooke Rd.* ☎ *902/434–6223* 🖃 *$5* ⊗ *Weekdays 9–5, Sat. 10–5.*

Where to Stay & Eat

$$–$$$ ✕ **La Perla.** The rich food at this northern Italian restaurant overlooking the harbor is consistently excellent, and there's a fine wine cellar. Servings are hearty. Calamari tossed with chilies and tomato has never been so tender; snails swim in a heady Gorgonzola cream sauce. Each of the three dining rooms has a distinctive character. ⊠ *73 Alderney Dr.* ☎ *902/469–3241* 🖄 *Reservations essential* 🖃 *AE, MC, V.*

$–$$$ 🏨 **Sterns Mansion B&B.** This beautifully restored century-old home is on a quiet residential street within walking distance of the Dartmouth ferry terminal. The tastefully decorated house has antique furnishings and hardwood floors. Several rooms have whirlpool tubs and gas fireplaces. Honeymoon packages are a specialty. ⊠ *17 Tulip St., B3A 2S5* ☎ *902/ 465–7414 or 800/565–3885* 🖨 *902/466–2152* ⊕ *www.sternsmansion. com* ➦ *4 rooms* ⚬ *Cable TV, in-room VCRs* 🖃 *AE, MC, V* ⭗ *BP.*

$–$$ 🏨 **Park Place Ramada Renaissance.** In Dartmouth's Burnside Industrial Park, this luxury hotel is aimed at business travelers as well as families. There is a 108-foot indoor water slide. ⊠ *240 Brownlow Ave., B3B 1X6* ☎ *902/468–8888, 800/561–3733 in Canada* 🖨 *902/468–8765* ⊕ *www. ramadans.com* ➦ *178 rooms, 30 suites* ⚬ *Restaurant, room service, some in-room data ports, minibars, cable TV with movies, indoor pool, gym, hot tub, sauna, bar, meeting room, free parking* 🖃 *AE, DC, MC, V.*

The Arts

The **Alderney Theatre** (⊠ 2 Ochterloney St., Dartmouth ☎ 902/461–4698 ⊕ www.alderneylanding.com) is home to the Eastern Front Theatre Company, which produces, presents, and hosts professional Canadian theater.

THE SOUTH SHORE & ANNAPOLIS VALLEY

Amy Pugsley Fraser

The South Shore is on the Atlantic side of the narrow Nova Scotia peninsula, the Annapolis Valley on the Bay of Fundy side; although they are less than an hour apart by car, the two seem like different worlds. The South Shore is rocky coast, island-dotted bays, fishing villages, and shipyards; the Annapolis Valley is lumberyards, farms, vineyards, and orchards. The South Shore is German, French, and Yankee; the valley, British. The sea is everywhere on the South Shore; in the valley the sea is blocked from view by a ridge of mountains.

Highway 103, Highway 3, and various secondary roads form the province's designated Lighthouse Route, which leads southwest from Halifax down the South Shore. It touches the heads of several big bays and small harbors, revealing a changing panorama of shoreline, inlet, and island. Small towns and fishing villages are spaced out every 50 km (31 mi) or so. The Lighthouse Route ends in Yarmouth, and the Evangeline Trail begins, winding along the shore of St. Mary's Bay through a succession of Acadian villages collectively known as the French Shore. Here you notice the Acadian flag, tricolor with a gold star representing *stella maris,* the star of the sea. The star has guided the French-speaking Acadians during troubled times, which have been frequent. In 1755, after residing for a century and a half in Nova Scotia, chiefly in the Annapolis Valley, the Acadians were expelled by the British—an event that inspired Henry Wadsworth Longfellow's famous poem *Evangeline.* Some eluded capture and others slowly crept back; many settled in New Brunswick and along this shore of Nova Scotia. The villages blend into one another for about 32 km (20 mi), each one, it seems, with its own wharf, fish plant, and Catholic church. The Evangeline Trail mostly focuses on the towns along Highway 1, but you follow side roads whenever the inclination strikes; the South Shore rewards slow, relaxed exploration.

The Annapolis Valley runs northeast, like a huge trench, flat on the bottom, sheltered on both sides by the North and South mountains. Occasional roads over the South Mountain lead to the South Shore; short roads over the North Mountain lead to the Fundy shore. Like the South Shore, the valley is punctuated with pleasant small towns, each with a generous supply of extravagant Victorian homes and churches. The rich soil of the valley bottom supports dairy herds, hay, grain, root vegetables, tobacco, and fruit. Apple-blossom season (late May and early June) and the fall harvest are the loveliest times to visit.

Peggy's Cove

★ ⓰ *48 km (30 mi) southwest of Halifax.*

Peggy's Cove, on Highway 333, marks the entrance to St. Margaret's Bay, which has been guarded for years by its famous octagonal lighthouse. The cove, with its houses huddled around the narrow slit in the boulders, is probably the most photographed village in Canada. A Canadian post office is in the lighthouse perched high on the rocky coast above a restless sea. Don't be tempted to venture too close—many an unwary visitor has been swept away by the mighty surf that sometimes breaks here. You can drive almost to the base of the lighthouse, but you'd do better to park in the spacious public lot below it and enjoy the village's shops and services during your three-minute walk up to the lighthouse.

A simple granite **memorial** (✉ Hwy. 333) for 1998 Swissair Flight 111, which crashed into the waters off Peggy's Cove, commemorates "those who helped and those who died"—the 229 casualties and the courageous Nova Scotia fisherfolk for their recovery work and the unstinting comfort they offered to grieving families. Another memorial stands in the town of Blandford directly across the cove.

Where to Stay & Eat

¢–$$$ ✕ **Sou'wester Restaurant.** Sou'wester, at the base of the Peggy's Cove lighthouse, serves home-style fare including a wide range of Maritime specialties—try *solomon gundy* (herring and onion with sour cream)—and fish-and-chips. There's also a large souvenir shop. ✉ *178 Peggy's Point Rd., off Hwy. 333* ☎ *902/823–2561* 🖃 *AE, DC, MC, V.*

$–$$ ✕ **Candleriggs Dining Room.** Authentic Scottish dishes, such as *Forfar bridie* (beef and potato in puff pastry), Scotch mushrooms in cream and whiskey, Scotch onion pie, and steak-and-kidney pie, share the menu with Canadian specialties at this pleasant restaurant. ✉ *8545 Peggy's Cove Rd., Indian Harbour, 3 km (2 mi) west of Peggy's Cove* ☎ *902/823–2722* 🖃 *AE, D, DC, MC, V* ⊘ *Limited hrs Nov.–mid-Mar.; call ahead.*

★ **$–$$$** 🏠 **Havenside B&B.** At this luxurious home, multilevel decks overlook a delightful seascape near Peggy's Cove. Saltwater swimming and canoeing, a serene gathering room with fireplace and library, a games room with a pool table, and a "breakfast that makes lunch redundant"—fresh homemade muffins, pancakes, French toast, eggs—enhance the package. ✉ *225 Boutillier's Cove Rd., Hackett's Cove B0J 3J0* ☎ *902/823–9322 or 800/641–8272* 🖷 *902/823–9322* ⊕ *www.havenside.com* 📞 *3 rooms, 1 suite* ⚙ *Dining room, library, Internet; no a/c, no room phones, no room TVs, no smoking* 🖃 *MC, V* ⊚ *BP.*

Shopping

Beales' Bailiwick (✉ 124 Peggy's Point Rd. ☎ 902/823–2099) carries outstanding crafts—Maritime-designed clothing, pewter, jewelry, and more. The adjoining coffee shop affords the best photo opportunity for Peggy's Cove and the lighthouse and their newest addition—a renovated red schoolhouse—provides a venue for summertime theater and concerts. **Train Station Gift Shop** (✉ 5401 St. Margaret's Bay Rd., head of St. Margaret's Bay, Upper Tantallon ☎ 902/826–7532), in a 1900 train station, is just the ticket for a selection of Maritime artists and heritage lace. The caboose is home to an array of children's toys, including Thomas & Friends. It's open seven days a week, year-round.

Chester

64 km (40 mi) west of Peggy's Cove.

Chester, a charming little town on Mahone Bay, is a popular summer retreat for an established population of well-heeled Americans and Haligonians, whose splendid homes and yachts rim the waterfront. In fact, yachting is the town's principal summer occupation, culminating each August in **Chester Race Week**, Atlantic Canada's largest regatta.

★ ☉ The **Ross Farm Living Museum of Agriculture,** a restored 19th-century farm, illustrates the evolution of agriculture from 1600 to 1925. The animals here are those found on a farm of the 1800s—draft horses, oxen, and older breeds or types of animals. Blacksmithing and other crafts are demonstrated. The Pedlar's Shop sells items made in the community. ✉ *Hwy. 12, New Ross, 29 km (18 mi) inland from Chester* ☎ *902/689–2210* 🎫 *$3* ⊘ *Mid-May–mid-Oct., daily 9:30–5:30; mid-Oct.–mid-May, Wed.–Sun. hrs vary; call ahead.*

A **passengers-only ferry** (☎ 902/275–3221) runs from the dock in Chester to the scenic **Big and Little Tancook islands,** 8 km (5 mi) out in Mahone Bay. Reflecting its part-German heritage, Big Tancook claims to make the best sauerkraut in Nova Scotia. Exploration of the island is made easy by walking trails. The boat runs four times daily weekdays and twice daily on weekends. The 45-minute ride costs $5 (round-trip ticket).

Where to Stay & Eat

$$–$$$$ ✕ **The Galley.** Decked out in nautical bric-a-brac and providing a spectacular view of the ocean, this restaurant has a pleasant, relaxed atmosphere and an outdoor dining area. The seafood chowder, lobster, and homemade desserts are recommended. Reserve ahead for summer dining. ⊠ *Hwy. 3, 115 Marina Rd., Marriot's Cove, Exit 8 off Hwy. 103, 3 km (2 mi) west of Chester* ☎ *902/275–4700* ▤ *AE, D, MC, V* ◷ *Closed Nov.–late Mar.*

¢–$ ✕ **Fo'c'sle Tavern.** This rustic midtown pub has nautical touches, including a deliciously ugly ship's figurehead, maps, displays of seamen's knots, and a ship's wheel. The mood is jolly, the food is abundant and affordable, and the potbellied woodstove exudes warmth and goodwill on chilly nights. The hearty pub fare includes hefty servings of fish-and-chips, seafood chowders, and steaks, as well as a weekend breakfast buffet. ⊠ *42 Queen St.* ☎ *902/275–3912* ▤ *V.*

¢–$ ✕ **Julien's Pastry Shop & Bakery** Grab a few delectable goodies to go along

Fodor's Choice with the deluxe sandwiches from this fabulous French bakery and then
★ take a picnic along Chester's scenic waterfront. Julien's is open from 7 to 6. ⊠ *43 Queen St.* ☎ *902/275–2324* ▤ *No credit cards* ◷ *Closed Mon. mid-Sept.–mid-June.*

★ $$$$ ✕▥ **Haddon Hall Inn.** Antiques, including some canopy beds, working fireplaces, and marble baths, fill the large rooms and suites at this luxurious resort. Each room and suite has a CD player and whirlpool bath. Outside, take advantage of the many outdoor activities or relax under trees or in the gardens, drinking in the view from the highest hill in Chester. At the restaurant ($$$$; reservations essential), which overlooks Mahone Bay, choose a seafood, meat, or vegetarian entrée for the three-course prix-fixe dinner. Rooms are in the main house; suites are spread out in four buildings. Children under 12 are welcome in two suites only. ⊠ *Box 640, 67 Haddon Hill Rd., B0J 1J0* ☎ *902/275–3577* ☒ *902/ 275–5159* ⊕ *www.haddonhallinn.com* 🛏 *4 rooms, 7 suites* ⚿ *Restaurant, minibars, cable TV, in-room VCRs, tennis court, pool, mountain bikes, lounge, Internet, meeting rooms; no smoking* ▤ *DC, MC, V* ◷ *Closed Nov.–May* ❍ *CP.*

$–$$ ✕▥ **Dauphinee Inn.** On the shore of Hubbards Cove, this charming country inn has first-class accommodations and an excellent restaurant ($–$$). The Hot Rocks is a social dining concept where guests are invited to cook fresh vegetables, seafood, beef, or chicken on a hot slab of granite. Opportunities abound for bicycling, bird-watching, and deep-sea fishing, and six golf courses are within a half-hour drive. The spacious rooms have antique beds with old-fashioned quilts and newer touches like floor-to-ceiling windows, whirlpool tubs, and CD players. ⊠ *167 Shore Club Rd., Hubbards Cove, Exit 6 off Hwy. 103, B0J 1T0, 19 km (12 mi) east of Chester* ☎ *902/857–1790 or 800/567–1790* ☒ *902/857–9555* ⊕ *www.dauphineeinn.com* 🛏 *6 rooms* ⚿ *Restaurant, cable TV, boating, fishing, lounge, meeting room; no a/c, no room phones, no smoking* ▤ *AE, D, DC, MC, V* ◷ *Closed Nov.–Apr.*

Shopping

Fiasco (⊠ *54 Queen St.* ☎ *902/275–2173*) is an eclectic shop with everything from clothing and baby gear to ships' models and hooked rugs by local artisans. It's open seven days a week year-round. The earthenware pottery at **Nova Scotia Folk Art Pottery** (⊠ *Duke St.* ☎ *902/275–3272*) is as cheerful as the bright yellow-and-green building on Chester's front harbor.

Mahone Bay

⑰ *24 km (15 mi) west of Chester.*

This quiet town perched on an idyllic bay of the same name comes alive each summer. Many of Nova Scotia's finest artists and artisans are represented in the studios and galleries that line the narrow streets. Three impressive churches stand shoulder to shoulder near the waterfront, their bells vying for attention each Sunday morning. You'll find sailing, kayaking, and walking opportunities. In July the annual **Wooden Boat Festival** celebrates the town's heritage as a shipbuilding center, and in October the hay-stuffed and pumpkin-laden street-side and storefront displays brighten up the **Scarecrow Festival.**

Where to Stay & Eat

★ **$$–$$$** ✕ **Mimi's Ocean Grill.** Inside, admire the brightly painted walls and the art by local artists (it's all for sale). Outside, the front veranda offers an unobstructed view of the bay, while the backyard courtyard offers privacy and quiet. Delectable fresh seafood and shellfish as well as chicken and lamb might be on the menu, which changes with the seasons. The famous haddock is always available. ⊠ *662 Main St.* ☎ *902/624–1342* ⊟ *MC, V.*

$–$$ ✕ **Innlet Café.** This pleasant restaurant commands a fine view of the town across the bay. A broad Canadian-style menu has poultry and meats, an understandable emphasis on chowders and seafood, and a few vegetarian options. At this writing, the café has new owners, who promise to keep the menu the same. ⊠ *249 Edgewater St.* ☎ *902/624–6363* ⊟ *MC, V.*

¢–$ ✕ **Mug & Anchor Pub.** Take in a view of the bay from inside this old British-style alehouse, or enjoy some waterside dining out on the deck. The food is basic pub fare, like fish-and-chips and hamburgers, but you can also get Lunenburg County favorites such as fish cakes and beans. Lunenburg scallops are a specialty here, as is the Standup British Pork Pie. During the summer months the pub swells with the sounds of live jazz, blues, and folk music on some Saturday nights. ⊠ *643 Main St.* ☎ *902/624–6378* ⊟ *AE, D, MC, V.*

$–$$ 🏨 **Manse at Mahone Bay Country Inn.** Classical music and fine art, a library of contemporary Canadian literature, and Mahone Bay's three handsome churches just down the hill distinguish this elegant mid-19th-century home, a former Presbyterian manse. Comfy chairs and binoculars near a broad bay window allow for the viewing of Mahone Bay. The inn has two spacious rooms in the main house; a carriage house has two huge suites. The menu is exceptional: get set for Stilton cheese–pear omelets at breakfast and a range of fresh seafood dishes at dinner (reservations essential). ⊠ *Box 475, 88 Orchard St., B0J 2E0* ☎ *902/624–1121* 🖨 *902/624–1182* ⊕ *www.bbcanada.com/manse* ⇆ *2 rooms, 2 suites* ⟡ *Dining room, in-room data ports, cable TV, meeting room; no a/c, no smoking* ⊟ *MC, V* ◯ *BP.*

$–$$ 🏨 **Countryside B&B.** Lessons in llama etiquette are part of the service at this waterfront farm with a private dock. Sheep, alpaca, and llamas (the llamas protect the sheep from coyotes) share the meadows and barns. Inside, antiques and original art share space with your host's naval memorabilia. A sumptuous breakfast might include homemade treats such as wild-blueberry crepes, baked fat-free French toast, and jams. ⊠ *28 Silver Point Rd.–R.R. 2, B0J 2E0* ☎ *902/627–1308* 🖨 *902/627–1112* ⊕ *www.countrysidebandb.com* ⇆ *3 rooms* ⟡ *Dining room, fans, in-room VCRs, dock, boating, bicycles* ⊟ *V* ◯ *BP.*

$ 🏨 **Amber Rose Inn.** All the creature comforts plus expert knowledge of this historic area are available at this 1875 inn. Each of the large suites has a whirlpool tub and handsome antiques. It's not unusual to hear your bilingual hosts chatting in Spanish around the table in the morning, where the lavish breakfast includes French toast or blueberry pancakes. Check out Carriage House Antiques, Collectibles and Gifts, next door. ⊠ *Box 450, 319 W. Main St., B0J 2E0* ☎ *902/624–1060* 🖨 *902/*

624–0997 ⊕ *www.amberroseinn.com* ➪ *3 suites* � *Refrigerators, free parking; no smoking* ⊟ *AE, MC, V* ⦿❙ *BP.*

Shopping

Amos Pewter (⊠ 589 Main St. ☎ 902/624–9547 or 800/565–3369) has been using traditional methods to make pewter for 25 years. A studio in an 1888 seaside building offers interpretive displays and demonstrations. Jewelry, sculptures, ornaments, and sand dollars are among the items available along with a new original-design Christmas ornament each year. The work of fine Atlantic Canada artists and artisans is for sale at **Moorings Gallery & Shop** (⊠ 575 Main St. ☎ 902/624–6208). The **Rags to Rugs Shoppe** (⊠ 374 Clearland Woodstock Rd. ☎ 902/624–8075) specializes in the traditional hooked rugs for which Nova Scotia is famous, beautifully crafted by senior citizens and the physically handi-
★ capped. **Suttles and Seawinds** (⊠ 466 Main St. ☎ 902/624–6177) has a worldwide reputation for its distinctively designed, quality quilts. The store, in a four-story renovated Victorian mansion, also sells unique designer clothing and home and fashion accessories. An adjacent carriage house is a gallery for stunning quilts and fabrics.

Lunenburg

⑱ *9 km (6 mi) south of Mahone Bay.*

A feast of Victorian-era architecture, wooden boats, steel draggers (a dragger is a fishing boat that operates a trawl), historic inns, and good restaurants, Lunenburg delights all the senses. The center of town, known as Old Town, is a UNESCO World Heritage Site, and the fantastic old school on the hilltop is the region's finest remaining example of Second Empire architecture, an ornate style that began in 19th-century France.

★ Lunenburg is home port to the ***Bluenose II*** (☎ 902/634–1963 or 800/ 763–1963 ⊕ www.bluenose2.ns.ca), a tall-ship ambassador for Canada sailing out of Lunenburg, Halifax, and other ports. She's a replica of the first *Bluenose,* the great racing schooner depicted on the back of the Canadian dime—a winner of four international races and the pride of Canada. When in port, the *Bluenose II* is open for tours through the Fisheries Museum of the Atlantic. Two-hour harbor sailings in summer cost $20.

☾ The **Fisheries Museum of the Atlantic,** on the Lunenburg waterfront, gives a comprehensive overview of Nova Scotia fisheries with demonstrations such as sail making, dory building, boat launching, and fish splitting. A touch tank with starfish, shellfish, and anemones; participatory demonstrations of rug hooking and quilting; and a daylong schedule of films at the theater make visiting here a busy yet rich experience. Add to that the *Bluenose* exhibit, celebrating the tall ship that won acclaim for Canada, plus a gift shop and seafood restaurant, and your day is full. ⊠ 68 *Bluenose Dr.* ☎ 902/634–4794 ⊕ *museum.gov.ns.ca/fma* ⊠ *$9 May–Oct., free Nov.–Apr.* ☾ *May–Oct., daily 9:30–5:30; Nov.–Apr., weekdays by appointment.*

Where to Stay & Eat

$$–$$$$ ✗ **Old Fish Factory Restaurant.** In the Fisheries Museum of the Atlantic, the Old Fish Factory overlooks Lunenburg Harbour. It specializes in seafood, but you can also get steaks and other dishes here. ⊠ 68 *Bluenose Dr.* ☎ 902/634–3333 or 800/533–9336 ⊟ *AE, D, MC, V* ☾ *Closed Nov.–early May.*

¢–$$$ ✗ **Grand Banker Seafood Bar & Grill.** A wide variety of seafood at modest prices is the mainstay at this bustling, big-menu establishment. You can dine on scallops, shrimp, lobster in season, or, for those with hearty appetites, a seafood platter with a combination of all of the above. ✉ *82 Montague St.* ☎ *902/634–3300* ▭ *AE, D, MC, V.*

★ **$–$$** ✕ **Magnolia's Grill.** This happening, kitschy 1950s diner is as famous for its key lime pie as for its creole peanut soup. Full of vintage collectibles, the popular and always-packed grill also serves up local fare like cod cheeks and pulled pork. ✉ *128 Montague St.* ☎ *902/634–3287* ▭ *AE, MC, V* ☉ *Closed Dec.–Jan.*

$–$$ ✕▦ **Arbor View Inn.** Lead- and stained-glass windows, extravagant wood trim, and handsome antiques enhance every room of this grand early-20th-century house. Spacious grounds invite strolls. The top-floor suite has a queen-size canopy bed, a two-person whirlpool tub, and a deck. The young chef's fresh ideas, based on a variety of ethnic influences, lend culinary sparkle to the gracious restaurant ($$–$$$; closed January–April). Though the menu changes frequently, white-chocolate crème brûlée is a fixture. ✉ *216 Dufferin St., B0J 2C0* ☎ *800/890–6650* ▤▤ *902/634–3658* ⊕ *www.arborviewinn.ns.ca* ↬ *4 rooms, 2 suites* ↺ *Restaurant; no a/c, no room phones, no room TVs, no pets, no smoking* ▭ *MC, V* ⏍ *BP.*

$ ✕▦ **Boscawen Inn and MacLachlan House.** Period antiques adorn and fireplaces warm this elegant 1888 mansion and its 1905 annex in the middle of Lunenburg's historic Old Town. Guests can take afternoon tea in one of the drawing rooms or on the balcony. Dinner is served nightly in both the casual grill and the more formal dining room (¢–$$$). Try the lobster Boscawen, a half lobster served with scallops. All rooms and suites have either water or park views. ✉ *Box 1343, 150 Cumberland St., B0J 2C0* ☎ *902/634–3325 or 800/354–5009* ▤ *902/634–9293* ⊕ *www3.ns.sympatico.ca/boscawen* ↬ *22 rooms* ↺ *2 restaurants, cable TV, some pets allowed; no smoking* ▭ *AE, D, DC, MC, V.*

★ **$** ✕▦ **Lion Inn B&B.** Original works by Lunenburg artists—for show and for sale—adorn the walls of this three-story 1835 town house where owls, from the host's collection, stare out from all sides. Three interesting guest rooms are decorated in rich greens and burgundies and have sloping ceilings, eclectic antiques, and original artwork. The inn is noted for outstanding dinners at its restaurant ($$–$$$); the star of the menu is rack of lamb, but seafood and poultry are good choices, and the mocha crème brûlée is wonderfully delicate. ✉ *Box 487, 33 Cornwallis St., B0J 2C0* ☎ *902/634–8988 or 888/634–8988* ▤ *902/634–3386* ↬ *3 rooms* ↺ *Restaurant; no a/c, no room phones, no room TVs, no pets, no smoking* ▭ *AE, MC, V* ⏍ *BP.*

$$–$$$ ▦ **Lunenburg Inn.** JFK's father, Joseph Kennedy, patronized this hostelry long before it became the gracious inn it is today. In those days it had 13 cell-size rooms sharing a single bathroom. Today its two suites and five rooms with private baths are spacious and restful and furnished with fine antiques. An elegant main-floor parlor, filled with books, adjoins the bright blue-and-white dining room. The top-floor 775-square-foot suite has a tiny kitchenette. ✉ *26 Dufferin St., B0J 2C0* ☎ *902/634–3963 or 800/565–3963* ▤ *902/634–9419* ⊕ *www.lunenburginn.com* ↬ *5 rooms, 2 suites* ↺ *Dining room, some kitchenettes, cable TV; no smoking* ▭ *MC, V* ⏍ *BP.*

$–$$ ▦ **Pelham House Bed & Breakfast.** Close to downtown, this sea captain's home, circa 1906 and decorated in the style of the era, has two friendly golden retrievers and two cats that greet guests and then return to their own quarters next door. The veranda overlooks the harbor. The rooms are large and airy, and outfitted in a homey country decor, with lots of wicker, quilts, and pine furniture. ✉ *Box 358, 224 Pelham St., B0J 2C0* ☎ *902/634–7113* ▤ *902/634–7114* ↬ *3 rooms* ↺ *Dining room, laun-*

dry facilities, Internet; no a/c, no room phones, no room TVs, no pets, no smoking ☰ *AE, MC, V* ⦿| *BP.*

$ ☷ **1826 Maple Bird House B&B.** Just steps from the Fisheries Museum and Lunenburg's fascinating waterfront, this B&B has a huge garden overlooking the harbor and a golf course. The piano in the drawing room creates a relaxing ambience that characterizes this home. The hosts know a thing or two about breakfast—crepes, omelets, cereals, and fruits appear in ample amounts. ✉ *Box 278, 36 Pelham St., B0J 2C0* 🖷🖷 *902/ 634–3863 or 888/395–3863* ⊕ *www.maplebirdhouse.ca* 🖚 *4 rooms* ⟐ *Dining room, pool; no a/c, no room phones, no room TVs, no pets, no smoking* ☰ *MC, V* ⦿| *BP.*

¢–$ ☷ **Blue Rocks Road B&B.** A bicycle shop and bike rentals are on-site at this friendly smoke-free, meat-free home. Your host is a quilter, potter, and artist, and her unique stencil designs decorate floors, walls, and ceilings in every room. An enthusiastic dog shares hosting duties. Breakfasts include homemade granola, pancakes, French toast, or a frittata with fresh herbs and vegetables from the garden. ✉ *579 Blue Rocks Rd.–R.R. 1, B0J 2C0* ☎ *902/634–8033 or 800/818–3426* 🖷 *902/634– 7147* ⊕ *www.bikelunenburg.com* 🖚 *3 rooms, 1 with bath* ⟐ *Dining room, bicycles; no room TVs, no smoking* ☰ *No credit cards* ⊘ *Closed mid-Oct.–mid-May* ⦿| *BP.*

Sports & the Outdoors

June through October **Lunenburg Whale-Watching** (☎ 902/527–7175) has three-hour trips daily at 8:30, 11:30, 2:30, and 5:30, seven days a week, from the Fisheries Museum Wharf for $35. You may spot fin, pilot, humpback, and minke whales; dolphins; seals; and myriad types of seabirds such as puffins, razorbills, and gannets. You can also arrange for bird-watching excursions and tours of Lunenburg Harbour.

Shopping

Black Duck Gallery and Gifts (✉ 8 Pelham St. ☎ 902/634–3190) sells handmade kites, local art, books, and an imaginative selection of gifts. The **Houston North Gallery** (✉ 110 Montague St. ☎ 902/634–8869) represents both trained and self-taught Nova Scotian artists as well as Inuit soapstone carvers and printmakers. It's closed in January. The **Lunenburg Forge & Metalworks Gallery** (✉ 146 Bluenose Dr. ☎ 902/634– 7125) is a traditional artist-blacksmith shop on the waterfront. One-of-a-kind handcrafted wrought-iron items and custom orders, including time-honored designs and whimsical creations, are available. Exquisite hand-chiseled sandstone carvings by a local stonemason fill the back courtyard of **Out of Hand** (✉ 135 Montague St. ☎ 902/634– 3499), a gift shop and gallery. It's open seven days a week from April to December.

Bridgewater

18 km (11 mi) west of Lunenburg.

Known as the "Main Street of the South Shore," Bridgewater is home to the South Shore's biggest mall, as well as banks, a hospital, museums, recreational facilities, and a visitor information center. Straddling the LaHave River, the town has views of the countryside, with ox farms and eagle nesting areas; the ocean, with fishing villages; historic sites (LaHave was the first area settled by the French in 1632); and magnificent sand beaches famous for windsurfing, clam digging, or just relaxing.

The **DesBrisay Museum** explores the history and people of Lunenburg County and has changing exhibits on art, science, technology, and history. The gift shop carries books by local authors and local arts and crafts. ✉ *130 Jubilee Rd.* ☎ *902/543–4033* ✆ *$2 mid-May–Sept., free Oct.–mid-May* ☉ *Mid-May–Sept., Mon.–Sat. 9–5, Sun. 1–5; Oct.–mid-May, Tues. and Thurs.–Sun. 1–5, Wed. 1–9.*

The **Wile Carding Mill,** a water-powered mill with an overshot wheel, operated from 1860 to 1968. Interpreters tell the story of Dean Wile's woolen mill. ✉ *242 Victoria Rd.* ☎ *902/543–8233* ✆ *By donation* ☉ *June–Sept., Mon.–Sat. 9:30–5:30, Sun. 1–5:30.*

Liverpool

⑲ *46 km (29 mi) south of Bridgewater.*

Nestled on the estuary of the Mersey River, Liverpool was settled around 1760 by New Englanders and is now a fishing and paper-milling town. During the American Revolution and the War of 1812, Liverpool was a privateering center; later it became an important shipping and trading port.

In a renovated Canadian National (CN) railway station, the **Hank Snow Country Music Centre Museum** commemorates the great country singer whose childhood home is nearby. A country-music archive and library and memorabilia of the singer's career are on view. ✉ *Off Hwy. 103* ☎ *902/354–4675 or 888/450–5525* ✆ *$3* ☉ *Mid-May–mid-Oct., Mon.–Sat. 9–5, Sun. noon–5.*

The **Sherman Hines Museum of Photography** contains vintage photos and cameras and the work of the noted photographer. Changing exhibits in the galleries feature top Canadian photographers, and the research center offers a good collection of photographic books and thousands of photographs. ✉ *219 Main St.* ☎ *902/354–2667* ✆ *Free* ☉ *Apr.–late Dec., Mon.–Sat. 10–5:30.*

★ **Rossignol Cultural Centre** This refurbished high school is now home to an eclectic mix of two galleries and five museums, including a trapper's cabin, an early-20th-century drugstore, 50 stuffed-wildlife exhibits, an outhouse museum, and a complete oval wood-paneled drawing room brought over from an English manor house. ✉ *205 Church St.* ☎ *902/354–3067* ⊕ *www.rossignolculturalcentre.com* ✆ *$3* ☉ *June–Aug., daily 10–5:30; Sept.–May, Mon.–Sat. 10–5:30.*

Fort Point Lighthouse Park, on the site where explorers Samuel de Champlain and Sieur de Monts landed in 1604, overlooks Liverpool Harbour. Interpretive displays and models in the 1855 lighthouse recall the area's privateering and shipbuilding heritage. Special events include a legal marriage in 1780s style, an encampment of the King's Orange Rangers (a group that reenacts the exploits of a pro-British American Revolution brigade posted to Nova Scotia 1778–83), and opportunities to meet local artisans. ✉ *End of Main St. off Hwy. 103* ☎ *902/354–5260* ✆ *By donation* ☉ *Mid-May–mid-Oct., daily 9–8.*

The **Simeon Perkins House,** built in 1766, is the historic home of privateer–turned–leading citizen Simeon Perkins, who kept a detailed diary about colonial life in Liverpool from 1760 until his death in 1812. Built by ships' carpenters, the house gives the illusion of standing in the upside-down hull of a ship. ✉ *105 Main St.* ☎ *902/354–4058* ✆ *By donation* ☉ *June–mid-Oct., Mon.–Sat. 9:30–5:30, Sun. 1–5:30.*

One of the last untouched tracts of coastline in Atlantic Canada, **Kejimkujik Seaside Adjunct** has isolated coves, broad white beaches, and imposing headlands and is protected by Kejimkujik National Park. A hike along the 6-km (4-mi) trail reveals a pristine coastline that is home to harbor seals, eider ducks, and many other species. To protect nesting areas of the endangered piping plover, parts of the St. Catherine's River beach, the main beach, are closed to the public from late April to early August. ⊠ *Off Hwy. 103, Port Joli, 25 km (16 mi) southwest of Liverpool* ☎ *902/682–2772* ⚎ *$3 May 15–Oct. 14* ☉ *Daily 24 hrs.*

Where to Stay & Eat

$–$$ ✕ **Quarterdeck Grill.** The restaurant deck at this Summerville Centre restaurant is directly over the water at high tide, giving spectacular views of surf and sand. The landmark restaurant uses seasonal fresh ingredients and is especially well known for its steamed lobster and grilled fish dishes. ⊠ *7499 Hwy. 3, 15 km (10 mi) west of Liverpool* ☎ *902/683–2998 or 800/565–1119* ⚎ *AE, DC, MC, V.*

$ ✕▥ **Lane's Privateer Inn and Bed & Breakfast.** Famed buccaneer Captain Joseph Barss once occupied this 200-year-old inn overlooking the Mersey River. Today it has comfortable guest rooms, a restaurant serving Canadian fare ($–$$$), a pub, a bookstore-café, and a specialty-food shop. Most of the 27 inn rooms have a river or harbor view. For a quieter visit, there's a two-bedroom smoke-free B&B next door, with shared bath and no air-conditioning. Nearby, there are windsurfing, golfing, deep-sea fishing, and five spectacular beaches. Lane's is within walking distance of Liverpool's major attractions and within 15 km (9 mi) of the Kejimkujik Seaside Adjunct. ⊠ *27 Bristol Ave., B0T 1K0* ☎ *902/354–3456 or 800/794–3332* 🖷 *902/354–7220* ⊕ *www3.ns.sympatico.ca/ron.lane* ☞ *29 rooms, 27 with bath* ⚐ *Dining room, cable TV, billiards, bar, no-smoking rooms; no a/c in some rooms* ⚎ *AE, D, MC, V* ☉ *B&B closed Nov.–May* ⦿ *CP.*

Sports & the Outdoors

The **Mersey River** drains Lake Rossignol, Nova Scotia's largest freshwater lake, and provides trout and salmon fishing.

Kejimkujik National Park

67 km (42 mi) northwest of Liverpool.

The gentle waterways of this 381-square-km (147-square-mi) park have been the canoe routes of the Mi'Kmaq for thousands of years. Today the routes and land trails are well marked and mapped, permitting canoeists, hikers, and campers to explore the landscape; swim in the warm lake; and glimpse white-tailed deer, beaver, owls, loons, and other wildlife. Canoes and camping equipment can be rented here. Park staffers lead interpretive hikes and canoe trips, or you can explore on your own. In late September and early October, the park's deciduous forests blaze with color. ⊠ *Hwy. 8, between Liverpool and Annapolis Royal, Maitland Bridge* ☎ *902/682–2772* ⊕ *www.pc.gc.ca* ⚎ *$3.50* ☉ *Daily 24 hrs.*

Where to Stay & Eat

¢–$ ✕▥ **Whitman Inn.** Wilderness, education, and luxurious dining are all part of the experience at this friendly inn next to Kejimkujik Park. Nature and canoeing packages are available, and weekend workshops are on topics ranging from quilting, photography, and writing to stress management and wine tasting. Antiques fill the rooms. A two-bedroom apartment has a full kitchen, a living room, and a private entrance. The small restaurant ($$; reservations essential) serves interesting full breakfasts and dinners that include seafood, poultry, pasta, and a vegetarian option. The chef whips up beautifully creative dishes with organic foods, fresh herbs, and seafood in season—a contrast to the simple pine tables and chairs. ✉ *12389 Hwy. 8, Kempt B0T 1B0* ☎ *902/682–2226 or 800/830–3855* 🖷 *902/682–3171* ⊕ *www.whitmaninn.com* ➷ *8 rooms, 1 apartment* ⟁ *Restaurant, indoor pool, hot tub, sauna, library, recreation room, meeting room* ☰ *AE, MC, V.*

★ **$$–$$$$** 🏨 **White Point Beach Resort.** Activities from kayaking and surfing to cruising, birding, and walking nature trails make for dynamic holidays at this resort. Also on-site is a beachfront grill restaurant that has outdoor buffets and barbecues. Choose a cozy room outfitted with pine furniture in one of the lodges or a one- to three-bedroom cottage with a living room and fireplace, along the beach or nestled amid mature trees. ✉ *Exit 20A off Hwy. 103, White Point B0T 1G0* ☎ *902/354–2711 or 800/565–5068* 🖷 *902/354–7278* ⊕ *www.whitepoint.com* ➷ *77 rooms, 44 cottages* ⟁ *Dining room, refrigerators, cable TV, 9-hole golf course, 4 tennis courts, indoor pool, spa, beach, boating, fishing, mountain bikes, hiking, horseback riding, recreation room, shop, playground, meeting room, no-smoking rooms* ☰ *AE, MC, V.*

★ **$$** 🏨 **Mersey River Chalets.** Barbecues, kayak-building workshops or crafts instruction, swimming in the lake, sing-alongs around the bonfire, and outdoor sports like canoeing and kayaking fill the agenda at this 375-acre wilderness resort. Seven two-bedroom chalets are nestled in dense forest and are excellent for people with mobility problems, as the chalets have exterior ramps, wide doors, and roll-in showers. From a nearly 2-km-long (1-mi-long) boardwalk, see river and waterfall scenery. For closer encounters with nature, there are tepees built on platforms on the shore of Lake Harry. ✉ *Off Hwy. 8, General Delivery, Caledonia B0T 1B0* ☎ *902/682–2443* 🖷 *902/682–2332* ⊕ *www.merseyriverchalets.ns.ca* ➷ *7 chalets, 5 tepees* ⟁ *Restaurant, outdoor hot tub, boating; no room TVs* ☰ *MC, V.*

¢ 🏨 **Old Homestead Bed & Breakfast.** Your host, "Auntie Pat," provides down-home hospitality and home-cooked food in her 150-year-old farm home near Caledonia. Sumptuous breakfasts include homemade jams, jellies, breads, muffins, and more. The sunroom overlooks hay fields and cattle, and there's a lake for swimming. Canoes can be rented nearby. A golf course and the wilderness of Kejimkujik Park are close to the inn. Pat's handmade quilts and comforters adorn the beds of the three double rooms, which share a bath. ✉ *71 Canning Rd., West Caledonia B0T 1B0* ☎ *902/682–2654* ➷ *3 rooms without bath* ⟁ *Cable TV, lake* ☰ *No credit cards* ⦿ *BP.*

CAMPING ⚠ **Kejimkujik National Park Campground.** This huge national park in the middle of the province is a haven for canoeists and hikers. Campsites are unserviced. Winter camping is available with pit toilets. A canteen in the park has basic camping supplies, take-out food, and ice cream. There are some extra-large (up to 50-foot) RV sites. Reservations are essential July 1–September 15. ⟁ *Flush toilets, pit toilets, showers, fire pits, grills* ➷ *123 tent sites, 233 RV sites* ✉ *Off Rte. 8, Maitland Bridge, 65 km (40 mi) north of Liverpool* ☎ *902/682–2772* ▣ *$18* ☰ *AE, MC, V.*

Sports & the Outdoors
Peter Rogers of **Loon Lake Outfitters** (☎ 902/682–2220) is an 18-year veteran in canoe outfitting who offers summer canoe instruction, complete and partial canoe outfitting, and recreational guiding in and around Kejimkujik Park. At Jakes Landing, within Kejimkujik Park, **Wildcat River Outfitters** (☎ 902/682–2196 or 902/682–2822), a company owned and operated by local Mi'Kmaqs, rents bicycles, food, and camping supplies, as well as kayaks and canoes.

Shelburne

⑳ *69 km (43 mi) south of Liverpool.*

The high noon of Shelburne occurred right after the American Revolution, when 16,000 Loyalists briefly made it one of the largest communities in North America—bigger than either Halifax or Montréal at the time. Today it is a fishing and shipbuilding town at the mouth of the Roseway River. Tours of some of Shelburne's historic homes are offered during periodic fund-raising endeavors. The **South Shore Tourism Association** (☎ 902/624–6466) has information.

Many of Shelburne's homes date to the late 1700s, including the **Ross-Thomson House,** now a provincial museum. Inside, the only surviving 18th-century store in Nova Scotia contains all the necessities of that period. ⊠ *9 Charlotte La.* ☎ *902/875–3141* ✆ *$2* ☉ *June–mid-Oct., daily 9:30–5:30; mid-Oct.–May, call ahead for hrs.*

Where to Stay & Eat

★ **$-$$$** ✕ **Charlotte Lane Café.** Swiss specialties, along with seafood, meats, pastas, and salads are served in this 150-year-old historic building that has a pleasant garden patio and a shop selling local crafts. ⊠ *13 Charlotte La.* ☎ *902/875–3314* ☐ *MC, V* ☉ *Closed Sun. and Mon. and Jan.–early May.*

$-$$$ ▥ **Cooper's Inn.** One of the last cooperages in North America is also a unique inn on Shelburne's historic waterfront where you can purchase one of the namesake barrels or planters. Inside the elegant 1784 inn are antiques and fine art. A specialty at breakfast is Belgian waffles with maple syrup, though there are many other choices. ⊠ *36 Dock St., B0T 1W0* ☎ *902/875–4656 or 800/688–2011* ☐ *902/875–2988* ⇄ *6 rooms, 1 suite* ⚭ *2 restaurants* ☐ *MC, V* ☉ *Closed Nov.–Mar.* ⑩ *BP.*

¢-$ ▥ **Clyde River Inn.** Queen Victoria and her pals peer down from every wall of this inn, once the main stagecoach stop between Yarmouth and Liverpool. The parlor, with a working organ, is as busy with artifacts as its Victorian forebear might have been. Unusual bric-a-brac and fine china decorate the dining room, where a breakfast of blueberry pancakes, homemade jams, and jellies is served. A golf course is a five-minute walk, and three beaches are within a 15-minute drive, including shell-strewn Round Bay Beach, which is usually deserted. ⊠ *Box 2, 10525 Hwy. 103, Clyde River B0W 1R0* ☎ *902/637–3267 or 877/262–0222* ☐ *902/637–1512* ⇄ *4 rooms* ⚭ *Dining room, some pets allowed (fee); no a/c, no room phones, no TV in some rooms* ☐ *AE, MC, V* ⑩ *BP.*

Barrington

40 km (25 mi) south of Shelburne.

Tiny Barrington has a long history reflected in a clutch of interesting museums. The **Barrington Woolen Mill Museum** represents a thriving late-19th-century industry in which the mill produced durable wool for fishermen's clothing. Today it has demonstrations of hand spinning and details about sheep raising and wool processing. ⊠ *2368 Hwy. 3* ☎ *902/637–2185* ✆ *By donation* ☉ *June–Sept., Mon.–Sat. 9:30–5:30, Sun. 1–5:30.*

The **Old Meeting House Museum** served as a church, town hall, and election center for New England settlers in the late 1700s. It's the oldest nonconformist house of worship in Canada, with a historic graveyard next door. ⊠ *2408 Hwy. 3* ☎ *902/637–2185* ✆ *By donation* ☉ *June–Sept., Mon.–Sat. 9:30–5:30, Sun. 1–5:30.*

The replica **Seal Island Lighthouse** is a lighthouse interpretation center that houses the original light and affords a fine view of the coastline. ⊠ *Hwy. 3* ☎ *902/637–2185* 💰 *By donation* ☉ *June–Sept., Mon.–Sat. 9:30–5:30, Sun. 1–5:30.*

Cape Sable Island

8 km (5 mi) south of Barrington over the causeway.

Nova Scotia's southernmost extremity is the 21-km (13-mi) road that encircles Cape Sable Island, a Yankee community with fine beaches, connected to the mainland by a bridge. On the island, the fishing village of Clark's Harbour sits on an appealing harbor sprinkled with colorful fishing boats. Hawk Point, just beyond the town, has excellent bird-watching and a fine view of the 1861 Cape Sable Island Lighthouse.

The **Archelaus Smith Museum,** named for an early New England settler, recaptures late-1700s life with household items such as quilts, toys, and cradles plus fishing gear and information about shipwrecks and sea captains. ⊠ *Hwy. 330* ☎ *902/745–3361* 💰 *Free* ☉ *Mid-June–Sept., Mon.–Sat. 9:30–5:30, Sun. 1:30–5:30.*

Pubnico

48 km (30 mi) northwest of Barrington.

Pubnico marks the beginning of the Acadian milieu; from here to Digby the communities are mostly French speaking. Favorite local fare includes *rappie* pie, made of meat or poultry with potatoes from which much of the starch has been removed. Most restaurants along the shore between Pubnico and Digby serve some variation on rappie pie.

No fewer than seven towns bear the name Pubnico: Lower West Pubnico, Middle West Pubnico, and West Pubnico, all on the west shore of Pubnico Harbour; three East Pubnicos on the eastern shore; and just plain Pubnico, at the top of none other than Pubnico Harbour. These towns were founded by Phillipe Muis D'Entremont, and they once constituted the only barony in French Acadia. D'Entremont was a prodigious progenitor: to this day, many people in the Pubnicos are D'Entremonts, and most of the rest are D'Eons or Amiraults.

Where to Eat

¢–$$　✕ **Red Cap Restaurant.** This venerable 1946 establishment that seats 140 overlooks Pubnico Harbour and includes a six-unit motel and a café that serves an acclaimed version of a favorite Acadian dish, rappie pie. The menu also lists lobster and other seafood, chowder, and bread pudding. ⊠ *Exit 31 off Rte. 335 S, Middle West Pubnico B0W 2M0* ☎ *902/762–2112* 🖷 *902/762–2887* ⊕ *www.tusket.com/present/rest/redcap* ▭ *MC, V.*

Yarmouth

㉑　*41 km (25 mi) north of Pubnico.*

Visitors have been arriving in Yarmouth for nearly three centuries, and they're still pouring in, chiefly by car ferry from Bar Harbor, Maine, and cruise ferry from Portland, Maine. In fact, the town's status as a large port city and its proximity to New England accounted for its early prosperity, and its great shipping heritage is reflected in its fine harbor, its two marinas, and its museums. Handsome Victorian architecture, a pleasantly old-fashioned main street lined with friendly shops, and easy access to the Acadian villages to the north or the Lighthouse Trail to the south make Yarmouth much more than just a ferry dock.

The **Yarmouth County Museum** presents one of the largest collections of ship paintings in Canada; artifacts associated with the *Titanic*; exhibits of household items displayed in period rooms; musical instruments, including rare mechanical pianos and music boxes; and items that richly evoke centuries past. The museum has a preservation wing and an archival research area, where local history and genealogy are documented. Next door is the **Pelton–Fuller House,** summer home of the original Fuller Brush Man; it's maintained and furnished much as the family left it. ✉ *22 Collins St.* ☎ *902/742–5539* ⊕ *yarmouthcountymuseum.ednet.ns.ca* 🖾 *Museum $2.50, museum and Pelton–Fuller House $4, archives $5* ⊙ *Museum June–mid-Oct., Mon.–Sat. 9–5, Sun. 2–5; mid-Oct.–May, Tues.–Sun. 2–5. Pelton–Fuller House June–mid-Oct., Mon.–Sat. 9–5.*

😊 The **Firefighters Museum of Nova Scotia** recounts Nova Scotia's fire-fighting history through photographs and artifacts, including vintage pumpers, hose wagons, ladder trucks, and an 1863 Amoskeag steamer. Kids can don a fire helmet and take the wheel of a 1933 Bickle pumper. ✉ *451 Main St.* ☎ *902/742–5525* 🖾 *$2* ⊙ *June and Sept., Mon.–Sat. 9–5; July–Aug., Mon.–Sat. 9–9, Sun. 10–5; Oct.–May, weekdays 9–4, Sat. 1–4.*

Where to Stay & Eat

¢–$$ ✕ **Harris' Quick 'n Tasty.** Laminated tables, vinyl banquettes, and bright
Fodor'sChoice lights greet you at this venerable, no-nonsense '50s-style diner. Dishes
★ include fresh seafood and old standbys like turkey burgers and club sandwiches. Haligonians are known to make the three-hour trek for the famed hot-lobster sandwich. Best of all is the rappie pie, a baked and crisply refried potato-and-chicken casserole. ✉ *Hwy. 1, Dayton, 4 km (2 mi) northeast of Yarmouth* ☎.*902/742–3467* ▤ *AE, MC, V* ⊙ *Closed mid-Dec.–mid-Jan.*

¢ ✕ **Ceilidh Desserts Plus.** Homemade soups, breads, and desserts—all free of additives and preservatives—have won a loyal clientele locally and beyond for this cinnamon-scented café in the heart of Yarmouth. The owner starts at dawn to whip up the day's baked goods and tasty lunches, which are modestly priced and served at simple wooden tables. ✉ *276 Main St.* ☎ *902/742–0031* ▤ *AE, V* ⊙ *Closed Sun. mid-Oct.–mid-May.*

$ ✕🏨 **Manor Inn.** A circular rose garden is the highlight of this 9-acre waterfront property near Yarmouth. Rooms are spread throughout the inn, coach house, and handsome, white main lodge. Dinner specialties at the restaurant ($$–$$$) are fresh Nova Scotia seafood, prime rib, chicken, and pasta. ✉ *Box 56, Hwy. 1, Hebron B0W 1X0* ☎ *902/742–2487 or 888/626–6746* 🖷 *902/742–8094* ⊕ *www.manorinn.com* 🛏 *53 rooms* ☖ *2 restaurants, café, cable TV, tennis court, pool, boating, bicycles, badminton, croquet, horseshoes, 2 bars, car rental* ▤ *AE, DC, MC, V* ⦿| *CP.*

★ $$$–$$$$ 🏨 **Trout Point Lodge.** On 200 acres of protected wilderness and built of massive spruce logs with chiseled granite walls, Trout Point has many outdoor activities, including swimming, canoeing, kayaking, fishing, hiking, and wildlife watching. La Ferme d'Acadie, a seaside farm at Cheboque Point, provides culinary instruction as part of its three- to five-day Food Learning Vacations package. The lodge, with its sturdy construction, high ceilings, and twig furnishings, is a nature lover's getaway. Transportation is provided from Yarmouth Airport or the ferry terminal. ✉ *East Branch Rd., off Hwy. 203, East Kemptville, 40 km (25 mi) northeast of Yarmouth* ⧉ *R.R. 2, Box 2690, Yarmouth B5A 4A6* ☎ *902/742–0980 or 877/812–0112* 🖷 *902/742–1057* ⊕ *www. troutpoint.com* 🛏 *8 rooms, 2 suites* ☖ *Dining room, fishing, moun-*

tain bikes, hiking, meeting room; no room TVs ▭ *AE, MC, V* ⊘ *Closed Jan.–Mar.*

★ **$$–$$$** ⌂ **Charles C. Richards House B&B.** One of Nova Scotia's most distinctive B&Bs, this grand, old Queen Anne–style structure was built as a wealthy industrialist's residence in 1893, using the finest imported materials. It later served time as a Women's Army Corps barracks, the town library, and finally an apartment building. Most recently, it was rescued by energetic young owners who are performing every step in the restoration process themselves. The rooms are spacious. An orchid conservatory opens onto a wide veranda and a patio. Breakfast is an elegant affair. ⊠ *17 Collins St., B5A 3C7* ☏☏ *902/742–0042 or 866/798–0929* ⊕ *www. charlesrichardshouse.ns.ca* ⌥ *4 rooms* ⌂ *No smoking* ▭ *AE, MC, V* ⦿ *BP.*

$–$$ ⌂ **Harbour's Edge B&B.** The spacious rooms in this serene 1864 home, with its spectacular view of Yarmouth Harbour, are named for women who lived in the town. Ornate wrought-iron fireplaces dominate the parlor and dining room, which open onto a veranda overlooking the harbor. At high tide the water laps against the lawn; at low tide myriad birds pay frequent visits. Harbour's Edge was reclaimed by new owners after a fire in 1990, and they are landscaping the vast 2-acre garden with its century-old rhododendrons, quince, laburnum, and Japanese cherry trees. ⊠ *12 Vancouver St., B5A 2N8* ☏ *902/742–2387* ☐ *902/742– 5484* ⊕ *www.harboursedge.ns.ca* ⌥ *3 rooms* ⌂ *Dining room; no room phones, no room TVs, no smoking* ▭ *MC, V.*

$ ⌂ **Murray Manor B&B.** The distinctive pointed windows of this handsome 1825 Gothic-style house are reminiscent of a church. Century-old rhododendrons bloom in the garden and decorate the long dining-room table, where guests share a hearty breakfast of fresh fruit, eggs with fresh garden herbs, and maple sausages. The ferry terminal is a block away. The rooms share one bathroom. ⊠ *225 Main St., B5A 1C6* ☏ *902/742– 9625 or 877/742–9629* ☐ *902/742–9625* ⊕ *www.murraymanor.com* ⌥ *4 rooms without bath* ⌂ *Cable TV; no room phones, no smoking* ▭ *MC, V* ⦿ *BP.*

Shopping

Professional potters Michael and Frances Morris, tired of crafts shows, opened a crafts shop, **At the Sign of the Whale** (⊠ 543 Hwy. 1, R.R. 1, Dayton ☏ 902/742–8895), in their home on the outskirts of Yarmouth. Antique furniture forms a handsome backdrop for the work of 150 artisans. Wood, textiles, pewter, clothing, and the Morrises' own excellent stoneware can be found here.

Point de l'Église

㉒ *70 km (43 mi) north of Yarmouth.*

Point de l'Église (Church Point) is the site of **Université Ste-Anne** (⊠ 1695 Hwy. 1 ☏ 888/338–8337), the only French-language institution among Nova Scotia's 17 degree-granting colleges and universities. Founded in 1891, this small university off Highway 1 is a focus of Acadian studies and culture in the province. The university offers five-week immersion French courses in summer.

St. Mary's Church, along the main road that runs through Point de l'Église, is the tallest and largest wooden church in North America. Completed in 1905, it is 190 feet long and 185 feet high. The steeple, which requires 40 tons of rock ballast to keep it steady in the ocean winds, can be seen for miles on the approach. Inside the church is a small museum with an excellent collection of vestments, furnishings, and photographs. Tours are given by appointment. ✉ *Main road* ☎ *902/769–2832* 💲 *$2* ⊙ *Mid-June–mid-Oct., daily 9–5.*

Nightlife & the Arts

Evangeline, Longfellow's famous epic poem about the Acadian expulsion, comes to life in a very visual musical drama presented in Acadian French with English translation. Performances are held at 8 PM Tuesday and Friday. There are outdoor English performances (weather permitting) Wednesday at 8 PM behind St. Mary's Church, next to the Université Sainte-Anne. ✉ *Marc Lescarbot Theatre, Université Sainte-Anne* ☎ *902/769–2114* 💲 *$15* ⊙ *July 11–Aug. 16.*

> **en route**
>
> **St. Bernard Church,** a few miles north of Point de l'Église, marks the end of the French Shore. Thanks to magnificent acoustics, internationally acclaimed choirs sometimes perform in the town's impressive granite Gothic church, which seats 1,000. ✉ *Rte. 1, St. Bernard* ☎ *902/837–5687* ⊙ *Mid-June–mid-Sept., daily 8–5; mid-Sept.–mid-June, call ahead.*

Digby

㉓ *35 km (22 mi) northeast of Point de l'Église.*

Digby is an underappreciated city—people tend to race to or from the ferry service connecting the town with Saint John, New Brunswick. But there's much more to Digby, including a rich history that dates to the arrival in 1783 of Loyalist refugees from New England; a famous scallop fleet that anchors in colorful profusion at the waterfront; and the plump, sweet scallops that are served everywhere. The waterfront begs leisurely strolls to view the Annapolis Basin and the boats; here you can buy ultrafresh halibut, cod, scallops, and lobsters—some merchants will even cook them up for you on the spot. You can also sample Digby chicks—salty smoked herring—in pubs or buy them from fish markets. **Digby Scallop Days** is a four-day festival replete with parades, fireworks, and food in early August.

The **Admiral Digby Museum** relates the history of Digby through interesting collections of furnishings, artifacts, paintings, and maps. ✉ *95 Montague Row* ☎ *902/245–6322* 💲 *Free* ⊙ *June–Aug., daily 9–5.*

Where to Stay & Eat

★ **$$–$$$** ✕▥ **Pines Resort Hotel.** Complete with fireplaces, sitting rooms, walking trails, and a view of the Annapolis Basin, this casually elegant property offers myriad comforts. It contains a Norman château–style hotel, 30 cottages, and lavish gardens. Local seafood with a French touch is served daily in the restaurant ($$$–$$$$), and the lounge is perfect for quiet relaxation. ✉ *Box 70, 103 Shore Rd., B0V 1A0* ☎ *902/245–2511 or 800/667–4637* 🖷 *902/245–6133* ⊕ *www.signatureresorts.com/pines* ⇨ *144 rooms* ⚘ *Restaurant, cable TV, 18-hole golf course, 2 tennis courts, pool, health club, sauna, bar; no smoking* 🖃 *AE, D, DC, MC* ⊙ *Closed mid-Oct.–May.*

$ ▥ **Thistle Down Country Inn.** A flowery haven overlooks the Annapolis Basin and Digby's fishing fleet at this historic 1904 home where wicker and antiques furnish the rooms. An annex is decorated with colonial furniture. For breakfast, consider ordering the scallop omelet. Fresh local seafood is served at the 6:30 dinner (reservations essential), followed by rich desserts. ✉ *Box 508, 98 Montague Row, B0V 1A0* ☎ *902/245–4490 or 800/565–8081* 🖷 *902/245–6717* ⊕ *www.thistledown.ns.ca* ⇨ *12 rooms* ⚘ *Dining room, some refrigerators, library, shop; no* *room phones, no room TVs, no smoking* ⊟ *AE, DC, MC, V* ⊙ *Closed Nov.–Apr.* †◎† *BP.*

¢–$ ▦ **Coastal Inn Kingfisher.** Your affable host's encyclopedic knowledge and contagious enthusiasm for his adopted province open the door to little-known sights and adventures. This traditional strip motel handy to all Digby's features has wheelchair-accessible rooms. The dining room has one of the widest arrays of scallops in Digby, including scallops l'Acadie (with tomatoes, brandy, and black olives) and "southern scallops" (with peaches and peach schnapps). Try the creamed scallops on toast for breakfast. ⊠ *Box 280, 111 Warwick St., B0V 1A0* ☎ *902/245–4747 or 800/401–1155* 🖷 *902/245–4866* ⊕ *www.coastalinns.com* ⇝ *36 rooms* ⧉ *Dining room, cable TV* ⊟ *AE, DC, MC, V.*

Bear River

16 km (10 mi) southeast of Digby.

A thriving arts-and-crafts center in summer, and almost a ghost town in winter, Bear River is called the Switzerland of Nova Scotia for the delightful vista of its deep valley, dissected by a tidal river. Some buildings have been built on stilts to stay above the tides. Crafts and coffee shops line the main street, and the community center, **Oakdene Centre** (⊠ 1913 Clementsvale Rd. ☎ 902/467–3939), contains an artist-run gallery, crafts workshops, and live theater and music. The **Riverview Ethnographic Museum** houses a collection of folk costumes and artifacts from around the world. ⊠ *18 Chute Rd.* ☎ *902/467–4321* ⧉ *$2* ⊙ *Nov.–Sept., Tues.–Sat. 10–5.*

Annapolis Royal

❷❹ *29 km (18 mi) northeast of Digby.*

Annapolis Royal's history spans nearly four centuries, and gracious and fascinating remnants of that history abound. The town's quaint and quiet appearance belies its turbulent past. One of Canada's oldest settlements, it was founded as Port Royal by the French in 1605, destroyed by the British in 1613, rebuilt by the French as the main town of French Acadia, and fought over for a century. Finally, in 1710, New England colonists claimed the town and renamed it in honor of Queen Anne. There are approximately 150 historic sites and heritage buildings here, including the privately owned 1708 De-Gannes–Cosby House, the oldest wooden house in Canada, on St. George Street, the oldest town street in Canada. A lively **market** with fresh produce, home baking, local artists, and street musicians takes place every Saturday mid-May through mid-October on St. George Street, next to Ye Olde Town Pub.

Fort Anne National Historic Site, first fortified in 1629, holds the remains of the fourth fort to be erected here and garrisoned by the British as late as 1854. Earthwork fortifications, an early-18th-century gunpowder magazine, and officers' quarters have been preserved. Four hundred years of history are depicted on the Fort Anne Heritage Tapestry. A guided candlelight tour of the historic Garrison Graveyard is a summer specialty Tuesday, Thursday, and Sunday nights. ⊠ *St. George St.* ☎ *902/532–2397 or 902/532–2321* ⊕ *www.pc.gc.ca* ⧉ *Grounds free, museum $3.50* ⊙ *Mid-May–mid-Oct., daily 9–6; mid-Oct.–mid-May, by appointment.*

The **Annapolis Royal Historic Gardens** are 10 acres of magnificent theme gardens, including a Victorian garden and a knot garden, connected to a wildlife sanctuary. ⊠ *441 Upper St. George St.* ☎ *902/532–7018* ⧉ *$5* ⊙ *Mid-May–mid-Oct., daily 8–dusk.*

The **Annapolis Royal Tidal Power Project,** ½ km (¼ mi) from Annapolis Royal, was designed to test the feasibility of generating electricity from tidal energy. This pilot project is the only tidal generating station in North America and one of only three operational sites in the world. The interpretive center explains the process with guided tours. ⊠ *Annapolis River Causeway* ☎ *902/532–5454* ☑ *Free* ☉ *Mid-May–mid-June and Sept.–mid-Oct., daily 9–5:30; mid-June–Aug., daily 9–8.*

Apple orchards, green lawns, and beautiful trees of the Annapolis Valley cover **Upper Clements Park,** which has 26 rides and attractions. Brave the Tree Topper Roller Coaster, the highest ride in Atlantic Canada, or take a dip on the 302-foot Fundy Splash Water Slide. For a tamer time, there are also a train ride, an old-fashioned carousel, and indoor-outdoor golf. Bring your lunch and eat at one of the picnic tables in the apple orchard. Admission includes entry to the nearby wildlife park. ⊠ *Exit 22 off Hwy. 101* ☎ *902/532–7577* ☑ *$5.75* ☉ *Mid-June–mid-Oct., daily 11–7.*

Where to Stay & Eat

★ **$$–$$$** ✕ **Secret Garden Restaurant.** Light lunches (soups and sandwiches), snacks, afternoon tea, and desserts are served in a garden that overlooks the Annapolis Royal Historic Gardens. ⊠ *441 St. George St.* ☎ *902/532–2200* ▤ *MC, V* ☉ *Closed Oct.–May.*

★ **$–$$$** ✕ **Newman's Restaurant.** Fresh flowers, fine art, and the host's handmade pottery give this quality establishment a homey air. The excellent cuisine is made with ultrafresh seafood and produce and the menu changes daily. Try the New York strip loin, scallop linguine, or the catch of the day. The owners are famous for their shortcake, which is made with whatever fruits are in season (strawberries, blueberries, raspberries, and peaches), served with their own homemade ice cream. ⊠ *218 St. George St.* ☎ *902/532–5502* ▤ *MC, V* ☉ *Closed Oct.–mid-Apr.*

$–$$$ ✕ **Charlie's Place.** Fresh local seafood with a Chinese flavor is served at this pleasant restaurant on the edge of town. Lobster, shrimp, scallops, meat dishes, and vegetarian fare are prepared in Cantonese or Szechuan style. ⊠ *38 Prince Albert Rd. (Hwy. 1)* ☎ *902/532–2111* ▤ *AE, D, MC, V.*

¢–$$ ✕ **Ye Olde Town Pub.** Down-home lunches and dinners are served at this merry, low-key pub popular with locals. Many dishes are prepared with regional blueberries. Diners sometimes spill out onto the patio, which is adjacent to a square where markets and music take place in summer. ⊠ *11 Church St.* ☎ *902/532–2244* ▤ *MC, V.*

¢–$ ✕▥ **Garrison House Inn.** Opened in 1854, when Annapolis Royal was the capital of Nova Scotia, this inn facing Fort Anne and its extensive parkland has been carefully restored with period furniture and Victorian-era decor. It comes complete with a friendly ghost, called Emily, whose playful presence is made known only to women. Three intimate dining rooms ($$$–$$$$) and a dining deck are the settings for dinners that favor fresh seafood, especially scallops and lobster. Breakfast is included in the room rate during summer months. ⊠ *350 St. George St., B0S 1A0* ☎ *902/532–5750* 🖷 *902/532–5501* ⊕ *www.garrisonhouse.ca* ⇶ *7 rooms, 1 suite* ⚂ *3 restaurants* ▤ *AE, MC, V* ☉ *Closed Jan.–Mar.*

$$–$$$ ▥ **Queen Anne Inn.** This lovely old Victorian mansion is surrounded by a 5-acre garden. Large guest rooms are handsomely decorated with period furniture and Victorian accessories and have extra touches like handmade soaps. The owners pride themselves on their four-course breakfast affair. Rooms have DVD players. ⊠ *Box 218, 494 Upper St. George St., B0S 1A0* ☎ *902/532–7850 or 877/536–0403* 🖷 *902/532–2078* ⊕ *www.queenanneinn.ns.ca* ⇶ *10 rooms* ⚂ *Restaurant,* *cable TV, croquet, Internet; no a/c in some rooms, no smoking* 💳 *MC, V* 🍽 *BP.*

★ $–$$ 🏨 **Bread and Roses Country Inn.** Rivalry between a doctor and a dentist gave Annapolis Royal this interesting hostelry. After the town doctor built a fine house in 1880, the dentist, in the spirit of competition, set out to build a better one. Today this Queen Anne–style inn is replete with exquisite architectural details and wood trim made with mahogany, black walnut, black cherry, and other woods. A traditional fountain is centered on the front lawn, and the garden invites sitting and strolling. The lavish breakfast may include homemade scones or muffins and the popular "three-cheese egg," a delectable quiche made with a variety of cheeses. ✉ *82 Victoria St., B0S 1A0* ☎ *902/532–5727 or 888/899–0551* 🌐 *www.breadandroses.ns.ca* *9 rooms* *Dining room; no room TVs, no smoking* 💳 *AE, MC, V* 🍽 *BP.*

$–$$ 🏨 **Hillsdale House.** Princes, kings, and prime ministers have all visited this historic 1849 property, which is furnished with antiques and paintings and is on 15 acres of lawns and gardens. The renovated coach house has added two bright and spacious rooms to the original 11 bedrooms. The large breakfast includes homemade breads and jams. ✉ *Box 148, 519 George St., B0S 1A0* ☎ *902/532–2345 or 877/839–2821* 📠 *905/532–2345* *13 rooms* 💳 *MC, V* 🍽 *BP.*

¢ 🏨 **Moorings Bed & Breakfast.** Built in 1881, this tall, beautiful home overlooking Annapolis Basin has a fireplace, tin ceilings, antiques, and contemporary art. One room has a half bath; three rooms share one bathroom. ✉ *Box 118, 5287 Granville St., Granville Ferry B0S 1K0* ☎📠 *902/532–2146* 🌐 *www.bbcanada.com/1000.html* *3 rooms without bath* *Dining room, bicycles, library; no room TVs* 💳 *V* 🍽 *BP.*

Port Royal

8 km (5 mi) west (downriver) from Annapolis Royal on the opposite bank.

One of the oldest settlements in Canada, Port Royal was Nova Scotia's first capital (for both French and English) until 1749, and the province's first military base. The **Port Royal National Historic Site** is a reconstruction of a French fur-trading post originally built by Sieur de Monts and Samuel de Champlain in 1605. Here, amid the hardships of the New World, North America's first social club—the Order of Good Cheer—was founded, and Canada's first theatrical presentation was written and produced by Marc Lescarbot. ✉ *Hwy. 1 to Granville Ferry, then left 12 km (7 mi) on Port Royal Rd.* ☎ *902/532–2898 or 902/532–5589* 🌐 *www.pc.gc.ca* *$3.50* ⏲ *Mid-May–mid-Oct., daily 9–6.*

Long Island & Brier Island

25 *Tiverton, Long Island is a 5-minute ferry ride from East Ferry at the end of Digby Neck. Brier Island is an 8-minute ferry ride from Freeport, Long Island.*

Digby Neck is extended seaward by two narrow islands, Long Island and Brier Island. Because the surrounding waters are rich in plankton, the islands attract a variety of whales, including finbacks, humpbacks, minkes, and right whales, as well as harbor porpoises. Wild orchids and other wildflowers abound here, and the islands are also an excellent spot for bird-watching.

Brier Island Ferry (☎ 902/839–2302) links the islands. Ferries must scuttle sideways to fight the ferocious Fundy tidal streams coursing through the narrow gaps. Ferries operate hourly, at a cost of $4 each way for car and passengers. One of the boats is the *Joshua Slocum*, named for Westport's most famous native, the first man to circumnavigate the world single-handedly. A cairn at the southern tip of Brier Island commemorates his voyage.

Where to Stay & Eat

$–$$ ✕⊞ **Olde Village Inn.** The restored 19th-century buildings that make up this property—the main inn, an annex, and various cottages—are furnished with antiques, wicker, quilts, and local art. Dinners ($$–$$$; reservations essential) emphasize fresh seafood and steaks. Quaint Sandy Cove, population 100, snuggles the shore halfway along Digby Neck. The town has one of Nova Scotia's highest waterfalls and a lookout affording panoramic views of the water and sometimes whales. ⊠ *387 Sandy Cove Rd., just off Hwy. 217, Sandy Cove B0V 1E0* ☎ *902/834–2202 or 800/834–2206* ⊟ *902/834–2927* ⊕ *www.oldevillageinn.com* ⥽ *13 rooms, 1 cabin, 3 cottages* ⚭ *Restaurant, cable TV* ⊟ *AE, MC, V* ⊘ *Closed mid-Oct.–mid-May* ⦿ *BP.*

¢–$$ ✕⊞ **Brier Island Lodge and Restaurant.** Atop a bluff at Nova Scotia's most westerly point, this rustic lodge commands a panoramic view of the Bay of Fundy. Most rooms have ocean and lighthouse views. Whale- and bird-watching and coastal hiking are the most popular activities here; closer to home there are hens, a flock of sheep, a pig, and some friendly dogs to delight children. Seafood chowder, lobster-stuffed haddock, and solomon gundy (marinated herring with sour cream and onion) are dinner specialties in the attractive restaurant ($–$$), which also serves breakfast and packs box lunches for day-trippers. ⊠ *Water St., Westport, Brier Island B0V 1H0* ☎ *902/839–2300 or 800/662–8355* ⊟ *902/839–2006* ⊕ *www.brierisland.com* ⥽ *39 rooms* ⚭ *Restaurant, cable TV, lounge; no smoking* ⊟ *MC, V* ⊘ *Closed Nov.–Apr.*

Sports & the Outdoors

Brier Island Whale & Seabird Cruises (☎ 902/839–2995 or 800/656–3660 ⊕ www.brierislandwhalewatch.com) offers whale-watching and seabird tours May–October. Onboard researchers and naturalists collect data for international research organizations. The fare is $40, and a portion of the fee is used to fund the research. **Mariner Cruises** (☎ 902/839–2346 or 800/239–2189 ⊕ www.marinercruises.ns.ca) provides whale and seabird tours with an onboard photographer and a naturalist. The three- to five-hour cruises ($35) run from June to October and include a light lunch.

Wolfville

㉖ *60 km (37 mi) east of Annapolis Royal.*

Settled in the 1760s by New Englanders, Wolfville is a charming college town with stately trees and ornate Victorian homes. Dikes, built by the Acadians in the early 1700s to reclaim fertile land from the unusually high tides, can still be viewed in Wolfville at the harbor and along many of the area's back roads.

Chimney swifts—aerobatic birds that fly in spectacular formation at dusk—are so abundant in the Wolfville area that an interpretive display is devoted to them at the **Robie Tufts Nature Centre** (⊠ Front St. ☎ No phone ⊕ www.wolfville.com/centre.htm). The **Grand Pré National Historic Site** commemorates the expulsion of the Acadians by the British in 1755. A statue of the eponymous heroine of Longfellow's epic poem *Evangeline* stands outside a memorial stone church that contains Acadian genealogical records. ⊠ *Hwy. 1, Grand Pré, 5 km (3 mi) east of*

Wolfville ☎ *902/542–3631* ⊕ *www.pc.gc.ca* ✉ *Free* ⊙ *Mid-May–mid-Oct., daily 9–6.*

Get spectacular views of the Bay of Fundy on the 45-minute tour of 10-acre **Domaine de Grand Pré** vineyard. Tours are offered twice daily from mid-May through mid-October. Call ahead to arrange a wine tasting or try the wines at the restaurant (Le Caveau), open for lunch and dinner March through December. Buy the wine or the estate's fruity hard apple cider at the on-site shop. ✉ *11611 Hwy. 1, 3 km (2 mi) east of Wolfville* ☎ *902/542–1753 or 866/479–4637* ⊕ *www.grandprewines.ns.ca* ✉ *$6* ⊙ *Mar.–Dec., Wed.–Sun. 11–5; call to schedule a tour.*

off the beaten path

HALLS HARBOUR – One of the best natural harbors on the upper Bay of Fundy can be reached via Highway 359. Go for a walk on a gravel beach bordered by cliffs; try sea kayaking or wilderness camping; or seek out the intaglio printmaking studio and other artists' studios, open during summer months. **CAPE BLOMIDON** – At Greenwich, take Highway 358 to Cape Blomidon via Port Williams and Canning for a spectacular view of the valley and the Bay of Fundy from the 600-foot Lookoff.

Where to Stay & Eat

$$–$$$ ✕ **Acton's Grill & Café.** Restaurateurs from Toronto, where their Fenton's
FodorsChoice Restaurant was *the* place to dine, have created an equally appealing din-
★ ing establishment here, with an interesting and eclectic menu. Consider rabbit pie, Digby scallops in fresh herbed pasta, or Fundy lobster. ✉ *406 Main St.* ☎ *902/542–7525* ☰ *AE, MC, V* ⊙ *Closed Jan.*

$$–$$$ ✕ **Tempest.** The muted, subdued tones and Zen-like waterfall here re-flect the owner's wish to offer a "refuge from the storm." Authentically prepared ethnic food like tandoori chicken or Bahamian cracked conch is served at lunch; dinner is loaded with world fusion cuisine, like Osaka halibut and lobster with ginger and wine. There's an intermezzo sorbet between courses and, if you still have room, a hazelnut chocolate torte or passion-fruit ice cream for dessert. The patio, which seats 40, is open on fine days. ✉ *117 Front St.* ☎ *902/542–0588* ☰ *MC, V.*

★ **$–$$$** ✕🏠 **Blomidon Inn.** Ramble through this inn's 3-acre English country gar-den, with its fish-stocked ponds, roses, cacti, azaleas, and rhododendrons, and a terraced vegetable garden that serves as a restaurant. Built by a shipbuilder in 1887, the inn is filled with teak and mahogany and has marble fireplaces and a painted ceiling mural. A two-story gift shop is packed with Maritime crafts. Intimate meals are expertly prepared at the restaurant ($$–$$$$; reservations essential), where fresh Atlantic salmon is a specialty. It's a family affair at the inn: the owners' sons are the chef and sommelier. ✉ *Box 839, 195 Main St., B0P 1X0* ☎ *902/ 542–2291 or 800/565–2291* 🖶 *902/542–7461* ⊕ *www.blomidon.ns.ca* 🛏 *28 rooms* ⚴ *Restaurant, some in-room hot tubs, cable TV, tennis court, croquet, horseshoes, shuffleboard, meeting room* ☰ *MC, V* ⊦○⫙ *CP.*

★ **$–$$$** 🏠 **Victoria's Historic Inn and Carriage House B&B.** An 8-foot-high stained-glass window imported from Britain over a century ago sets the tone for this fine Victorian home. Richly carved Nova Scotian furniture adds to the ambience. Rooms are spacious and have CD players; suites have double whirlpool tubs. The lavish breakfast celebrates the bounty of the Annapolis Valley. Expect plenty of blueberries and a wide selection of breakfast staples. ✉ *Box 308, 600 Main St., B0P 1X0* ☎ *902/542–5744 or 800/556–5744* ⊕ *www.victoriashistoricinn.com* 🛏 *14 rooms, 2 suites* ⚴ *Dining room, cable TV, in-room VCRs* ☰ *AE, D, DC, MC, V* ⊦○⫙ *BP.*

$$ ⊡ **Fundy Bay Holiday Homes B&B.** The trek to this seaside resort is amply rewarded by the spectacular view of the Bay of Fundy and the North Shore beyond. On 265 rolling wooded acres, this family-owned property has two two-bedroom houses with comfy living rooms, woodstoves, and kitchens. Stays at the three-room B&B include a hearty German breakfast of deli meats and sausages, European cheeses, German breads, and copious amounts of good German coffee. Groomed walking trails traverse the wooded property. ⊠ *2165 McNally Rd., Victoria Harbour, Aylesford B0P 1C0, 40 km (25 mi) northwest of Wolfville* ☎ *902/847–1114* 🖶 *902/847–1032* ⊕ *www.fundyhomes.com* ➲ *3 rooms, 2 houses* ⅄ *Dining room, some kitchens, cable TV, beach, laundry facilities* ▭ *V.*

¢–$ ⊡ **Farmhouse Inn B&B.** This 1860 B&B has cozy accommodations, most
Fodor's Choice   with a two-person whirlpool tub and/or propane fireplace and all with
★   whimsical dolls and stuffed animals warming the beds. Afternoon tea is complimentary. The knowledgeable hosts may suggest day trips to nearby Blomidon Provincial Park and Cape Split, for hiking, or to the 600-foot Lookoff, which affords panoramic views of five counties. Birdwatchers are likely to enjoy the maneuvers of the chimney swifts on summer evenings. ⊠ *Box 38, 9757 Main St., Canning B0P 1H0, 15 km (10 mi) north of Wolfville* ☎ *902/582–7900 or 800/928–4346* ⊕ *www.farmhouseinn.ns.ca* ➲ *1 room, 4 suites* ⅄ *Dining room, cable TV, in-room VCRs* ▭ *AE, MC, V* ⊪ *BP.*

Nightlife & the Arts

★   The **Atlantic Theatre Festival** (⊠ 502 Main St. ☎ 902/542–4242 or 800/337–6661) stages classical plays mid-June through September; tickets are $21–$28.

Sports & the Outdoors

A popular series of **hiking trails,** 25 km (16 mi) north of Wolfville, leads from the end of Highway 358 to the dramatic cliffs of Cape Split, a 13-km (8-mi) round-trip.

Shopping

The **Carriage House Gallery** (⊠ 386 Main St. ☎ 902/542–3500) displays artwork from Nova Scotia in several media, including oils, acrylics, watercolors, sculpture, and quilting. **Edgemere Gallery and Crafts** (⊠ 395 Main St. ☎ 902/542–1046) carries the work of Nova Scotia artists in all media, with exhibits changing monthly. Artisans from the Atlantic provinces are also represented by unique quality crafts. **Weave Shed Crafts** (⊠ 360 Main St. ☎ 902/542–5504) is a cooperative crafts shop selling quality work by local artisans in stained glass, pottery, wood, metal, and textiles.

Windsor

㉗ *25 km (16 mi) southeast of Wolfville.*

Windsor claims to be the birthplace of modern hockey: the game was first played here around 1800 by students of King's-Edgehill School, the first independent school in the British Commonwealth and Canada's oldest private residential school. But the town's history dates further back—to 1703 when it was settled as an Acadian community. **Fort Edward,** an assembly point for the Acadian expulsion, is the only remaining colonial blockhouse in Nova Scotia. ⊠ *Exit 6 off Hwy. 1; take the 1st left at King St., then another left up street facing fire station* ☎ *902/542–3631* 🎫 *Free* ⊙ *Mid-June–early Sept., daily 10–6.*

The **Evangeline Express** train makes a 55-km (34-mi), three-hour round-trip from Windsor to Wolfville Sunday in summer, weather permitting.

The train stops at the Grand Pré National Historic Site in Wolfville and affords views of the Minas Basin and the Annapolis Valley. ⊠ 2 *Water St.* ☎ *902/798–5667* 🖼 *$18.50* ⊙ *Late June–early Sept.; train departs at 11.*

The **Windsor Hockey Heritage Centre** takes a fond look at Canada's favorite winter sport with photographs and antique equipment and skates. ⊠ *128 Gerrish St.* ☎ *902/798–1800* 🖼 *Free* ⊙ *Daily 10–4, plus early evening hrs in summer.*

🖑 The **Mermaid Theatre** uses puppets and performers to retell traditional and contemporary children's classics. Props and puppets are on display. ⊠ *132 Gerrish St.* ☎ *902/798–5841* 🖼 *By donation* ⊙ *Jan.–Nov., weekdays 9–4:30.*

The **Haliburton House Museum,** a provincial museum on a manicured 25-acre estate, was the home of Judge Thomas Chandler Haliburton (1796–1865), a lawyer, politician, historian, and humorist. His best-known work, *The Clockmaker,* pillories Nova Scotian follies from the viewpoint of a Yankee clock peddler, Sam Slick, whose witty sayings are still commonly used. ⊠ *414 Clifton Ave.* ☎ *902/798–2915* 🖼 *Free* ⊙ *June–mid-Oct., Mon.–Sat. 9:30–5:30, Sun. 1–5:30.*

Tours at the family-owned **Sainte Famille Winery** in Falmouth, 5 km (3 mi) west of Windsor, combine ecological history with the intricacies of growing grapes and aging wine. Tasting is done in the gift shop, where bottles are sold at a steal. ⊠ *Dyke Rd. and Dudley Park La.* ☎ *902/798–8311 or 800/565–0993* 🖼 *$3* ⊙ *Apr.–Dec., Mon.–Sat. 9–5, Sun. 12–5; Jan.–Mar., Mon.–Sat. 9–5.*

off the beaten path

UNIACKE MUSEUM PARK – This country mansion was built around 1815 for Richard John Uniacke, attorney general and advocate general to the Admiralty court during the War of 1812. Now a provincial museum, the house is preserved in its original condition with authentic furnishings. The spacious lakeside grounds are surrounded by walking trails. ⊠ *758 Main Rd., off Hwy. 1, Mount Uniacke, 30 km (19 mi) east of Windsor* ☎ *902/866–2560* 🖼 *Free* ⊙ *June–mid-Oct., Mon.–Sat. 9:30–5:30, Sun. 11–5:30.*

Where to Stay & Eat

¢–$$ ✕ **Kingsway Gardens Restaurant.** From the Bavarian decor to the home-made sauerkraut to the Black Forest cheesecake, this establishment declares its owner's German origins. Lunch and dinner specialties include German and Canadian variations on seafood, turkey, and chicken. ⊠ *Wentworth Rd., Exit 5A off Hwy. 101* ☎ *902/798–5075* 🖃 *AE, D, DC, MC, V.*

¢–$ ✕ **Rose Arbour Café.** True to its name, the Rose Arbour has a flowery, bright interior, with posy-covered handmade wreaths plastering the walls. Tasty food, a smiling staff, and reasonable prices make this a pleasant find. Try the fish-and-chips or fresh clams in season, and one of their homemade desserts, like the popular rice pudding or cheesecake. ⊠ *109 Garrish St.* ☎ *902/798–2322* 🖃 *V.*

Fodor'sChoice ★

¢–$ 🏨 **Hampshire Court Motel and Cottages.** Once an elegant estate, this property retains its splendid 1762 home. Spacious rooms are furnished with antiques and are undergoing renovations at this writing. The two-bedroom cottages are suitable for a family or two couples. Rooms in the strip motel are very basic. ⊠ *1081 King St., B0N 2T0* ☎ *902/798–3133* 🖨 *902/798–2499* 🛏 *11 rooms, 4 cottages* ♢ *Cable TV, tennis court* 🖃 *AE, MC, V* ⊙ *Closed mid-Oct.–mid-May.*

THE EASTERN SHORE & NORTHERN NOVA SCOTIA

Updated by
Shelley
Cameron-
McCarron

From the rugged coastline of the Atlantic to the formidable tides of the Bay of Fundy to the gentle shores of the Northumberland Strait, the area east and north of Halifax presents remarkable contrasts within a relatively small area. The road toward Cape Breton meanders past fishing villages, forests, and remote cranberry barrens. The Northumberland Strait is bordered by sandy beaches, hiking trails, and is rich with the heritage of its early Scottish settlers. The Bay of Fundy serves up spectacular scenery—dense forests and steep cliffs that harbor prehistoric fossils and semiprecious stones. The mighty Fundy tides—swift and dangerous—can reach 40 feet. When they recede, you can walk on the bottom of the sea.

There are two excellent driving tours you can follow here. The Sunrise Trail Heritage Tour leads to unusual and historic sights along the Northumberland Strait, from the Tantramar Marsh in Amherst to the Heritage Museum at Antigonish and on to the still-active St. Augustine Monastery. The Fundy Shore Ecotour traces 100 million years of geology, the arrival of Samuel de Champlain, the legends of the Mi'Kmaq, the Acadians, and the shipbuilders. Tour details are available at visitor information centers or from Nova Scotia Tourism.

This region takes in parts of three of the official Scenic Trails, including the 315-km (195-mi) Marine Drive, the 316-km (196-mi) Sunrise Trail, and the 365-km (226-mi) Glooscap Trail. Any one leg of the routes could be done comfortably as an overnight trip from Halifax.

Musquodoboit Harbour

28 *45 km (28 mi) east of Dartmouth.*

Musquodoboit Harbour (locals pronounce it *must-go-dob-bit*) is a substantial village with about 2,500 residents at the mouth of the Musquodoboit River. The river offers good trout fishing, and the village touches on two slender and lovely harbors.

A 1916 train station, five railcars, and a fine collection of railway artifacts, including a legion of lanterns dating from the late 1800s, make the volunteer-run **Musquodoboit Railway Museum** a must for rail buffs. A library is rich in both railway and local historical documentation and photos. It also houses the visitor information center. ⊠ *Main St. (Hwy. 7)* ☎ *902/889–2689* ✉ *By donation* ☉ *Late May–mid-Oct., daily 9–5.*

One of the Eastern Shore's best beaches, **Martinique Beach,** is about 12 km (7 mi) south of Musquodoboit Harbour, at the end of East Petpeswick Road. Clam Bay and Clam Harbour, several miles east of Martinique, are also fine beaches.

off the
beaten
path

MOOSE RIVER GOLD MINES AND MUSEUM – On-the-spot radio coverage of a mine disaster put Moose River on the map in 1936. Today the town is quiet; a provincial park marks the site of the 12-day effort to rescue three miners trapped far underground (two of the men survived). The museum completes the story with displays, photographs, and artifacts. ⊠ *Moose River Rd. off Hwy. 224, 15 km (9 mi) east of Middle Musquodoboit* ☎ *902/384–2006* ✉ *Donations accepted* ☉ *June–Aug., daily 10–5.*

Where to Stay & Eat

$–$$ ✕🖃 **Salmon River House Country Inn.** Views of the water and country-side are glorious from the inn's guest rooms and cottages. Two cottages are on the ocean and are intended for stays of a week or more. Some rooms have whirlpool tubs, and one cottage allows pets. At the inn, you can fish from the floating dock; hike the trails of the 30-acre property; or make use of the inn's canoe, kayak, or rowboat. The Lobster Shack restaurant (¢–$$) serves lunch, dinner, and a breakfast buffet on its screened deck. ⊠ *9931 Hwy. 7, Salmon River Bridge, Jeddore B0J 1P0, 10 km (6 mi) east of Musquodoboit Harbour* ☎ *902/889–3353 or 800/ 565–3353* 🖷 *902/889–3653* ⊕ *www.salmonriverhouse.com* ⇌ *7 rooms, 3 cottages* ⚱ *Restaurant, fans, some kitchens, cable TV, boating, fishing* ▭ *AE, DC, MC, V.*

en route | As you travel through **Ship Harbour** on Highway 7, take note of the strings of colorful buoys, marking one of North America's largest cultivated mussel farms. Vistas of restless seas and wooded shorelines make for excellent photo opportunities.

Sherbrooke Village

㉙ *166 km (103 mi) northeast of Musquodoboit Harbour.*

Fodor'sChoice
★

A living-history museum set within the contemporary town of Sherbrooke, Sherbrooke Village contains 30 restored 19th-century buildings that present life during the town's heyday, from 1860 to 1914. Back then this was a prime shipbuilding, lumbering, and gold-rush center. Arti-sans demonstrate weaving; wood turning; and pottery-, candle-, and soap making daily. A working water-powered sawmill is down the road. Special events, like old-fashioned Christmas and courthouse concerts, are held through the year. ⊠ *Hwy. 7, Sherbrooke* ☎ *902/522–2400 or 888/743–7845* ⊕ *sherbrookevillage.museum.gov.ns.ca* ⊡ *$8.25* ⊘ *June–mid-Oct., daily 9:30–5:30.*

off the
beaten
path | **PORT BICKERTON LIGHTHOUSE BEACH PARK –** Two lighthouses share a lofty bluff about 20 km (12 mi) east of Sherbrooke on Highway 211. One lighthouse is still working; the other, built in 1910, houses the Nova Scotia Lighthouse Interpretive Centre, which recounts the history, lore, and vital importance of these lifesaving lights. Hiking trails and a boardwalk lead to a sandy beach. ⊠ *630 Lighthouse Rd., Port Bickerton* ☎ *902/364–2000* ⊡ *$3* ⊘ *July–Aug., daily 9–6; June 15–30 and Sept., daily 9–5.*

Where to Stay & Eat

$–$$ ✕🖃 **Black Duck Seaside Inn.** From a third-floor picture window, equipped with binoculars and a telescope provided by the inn, you can observe birds, sea life, and maybe a star or two over Beaver Harbour. Expect lavish breakfasts of blueberry pancakes and fruit in the airy dining room ($–$$); for dinner, try the fisherman's lasagna (seafood and pasta in a cream sauce) or another seafood dish. ⊠ *25245 Hwy. 7, Port Duf-ferin, 90 km (56 mi) west of Sherbrooke Village* 🖅 *Box 26, Sheet Har-bour B0J 3B0* 🖷🖷 *902/654–2237* ⇌ *2 rooms, 2 suites* ⚱ *Restaurant, dock, bicycles* ▭ *MC, V.*

¢–$ ✕🖃 **Sherbrooke Village Inn & Cabins.** This comfy hostelry with rooms and woodsy cabins is a five-minute walk from St. Mary's River (open for trout- and sometimes salmon fishing). Take part in nature walks and enjoy a spectacular view. The pleasant dining room ($–$$) serves up homemade meals—full Canadian breakfasts, lunches, and dinners heavy on the seafood. The restaurant is closed from November to mid-April. The inn rooms are wheelchair accessible. ⊠ *Box 40, 7975 Hwy. 7, Sherbrooke B0J 3C0* ☎*902/522–2235* ᗺ*902/522–2716* ⊕*www.sherbrookevillageinn. ca* ⇨ *15 rooms, 3 chalets* ♿ *Dining room, cable TV; no smoking* ▬ *AE, D, DC, MC, V.*

¢–$ 🏨 **St. Mary's River Lodge.** Sherbrooke Village is steps away from this lodge with immaculate rooms. The Swiss owners, in love with their adopted countryside, are helpful in planning day trips and tours. You can also rent houses in nearby Port Hilford for weeklong stays. The views are notable, looking out onto the river and ocean bay frontage. ⊠ *21 Main St., Sherbrooke B0J 3C0* ☎ *902/522–2177* ᗺ *902/522–2515* ⊕ *www. riverlodge.ca* ⇨ *5 rooms, 1 suite, 1 house* ♿ *Some kitchens, cable TV, in-room VCRs; no a/c in some rooms* ▬ *MC, V* ❙❙❙ *BP.*

Canso

③⓪ *123 km (76 mi) east of Sherbrooke Village.*

Canso is one of Nova Scotia's oldest settlements, founded in 1605. Each July the town hosts the **Stan Rogers Folk Festival** (⊕ www.stanfest. com), which commemorates the much-loved Canadian folk singer and composer.

The **Canso Island National Historic Site** recounts early struggles to control the lucrative fishing industry. A free boat ride takes you to the island for an interpretive tour of what remains of a once-thriving community, a 1744 casualty of the war between France and England. Graphics, models, and audiovisuals set the scene. ⊠ *Canso Waterfront, off Union St.* ☎ *902/ 295–2069* 🎟 *$2.50* ☉ *June–mid-Sept., daily 10–6.*

Where to Stay & Eat

¢ ✕ **Last Port Restaurant** Fish-and-chips is a popular menu item at this fast-food restaurant with friendly service. For breakfast you have your choice of eggs any way you like them with bacon, ham, sausage, or bologna; white or wheat toast; hash browns; and hot or cold cereal. ⊠ *R.R. 1, B0H 1H0* ☎ *902/366–2400 or 877/366–2400* ▬ *AE, MC, V.*

$–$$ 🏨 **SeaWind Landing Country Inn.** On a 20-acre coastal estate, this restored sea captain's home—with bird-watching, interpretive nature walks, and sandy beaches—is a luxurious escape. Short boat tours to offshore islands, where seals bask and bald eagles soar, include white-linen lunches served with fine wines. Home-cooked dinners favor fresh seafood. The inn is furnished with antiques, quilts, and fine art. The comfortable rooms, close to the seaside, have ocean or garden views. Most rooms have whirlpool baths, balconies, and private entrances. You must request a room TV. ⊠ *1 Wharf Rd., Charlos Cove B0H 1T0, just south of Canso* ☎☎ *902/525–2108* ⊕ *www.seawindlanding.com* ⇨ *12 rooms* ♿ *Dining room, beach, boating, mountain bikes, Internet; no room TVs* ▬ *AE, MC, V* ☉ *Closed mid-Oct.–mid-May.*

Antigonish

★ ③① *85 km (53 mi) northwest of Canso.*

Antigonish, on the main route to Cape Breton Island, is home to **St. Francis Xavier University** (⊠ West St. off Hwy. 104 ☎ 902/863–3300 ⊕ www. stfx.ca), a center for Gaelic studies and the first coeducational Catholic institution to graduate women. The university **art gallery** (☎ 902/867–2303) has changing exhibits year-round. A drama program is presented all summer at the **Festival Antigonish** (☎ 902/867–3333 or 800/563–7529 ⊕ www.festivalantigonish.com). Matinees for kids, evening performances for adults, and theater camps take place in the 226-seat theater.

The **Antigonish Heritage Museum,** in a 1908 rail station, depicts the town's early history. ✉ *20 E. Main St.* ☎ *902/863–6160* 🎫 *Free* ⏲ *July–Aug., Mon.–Sat. 10–5; Sept.–June, weekdays 10–noon and 1–5.* The biggest and oldest **Highland Games** (☎ 902/863–4275 🌐 www.antigonishhighlandgames.com) outside Scotland are held here each July, complete with caber tossing, highland flinging, and pipe skirling.

Where to Stay & Eat

$–$$$ Fodor'sChoice ★ ✕ **Gabrieau's Bistro Restaurant.** Gabrieau's has earned a place in Antigonish hearts with its pleasant interior and its epicurean yet affordable menu of Continental cuisine. Seafood, gourmet pizzas, luscious desserts, and several vegetarian selections are available. ✉ *350 Main St.* ☎ *902/863–1925* 🌐 *www.gabrieaus.com* 💳 *AE, D, MC, V* ⏲ *Closed Sun.*

$–$$$ ✕ **Lobster Treat Restaurant.** This cozily decorated brick, pine, and stained-glass restaurant was once a two-room schoolhouse. The varied menu includes fresh seafood, chicken, pastas, stir-fries, and bread and pies baked on the premises. This is a good choice for families as there is a children's menu and the atmosphere is quite relaxed. ✉ *241 Post Rd. (Trans-Canada Hwy.)* ☎ *902/863–5465* 💳 *AE, DC, MC, V* ⏲ *Closed mid-Nov.–mid-Apr.*

$–$$ ✕🏨 **Maritime Inn.** The Main Street Café ($$–$$$) at this inn serves breakfast, lunch, and a tempting dinner menu with lots of seafood options. Try the haddock glazed with apricot and ginger or the baby back ribs. One of five in a Maritime chain, this property has two sizes of rooms and one two-bedroom suite with a whirlpool bath. ✉ *158 Main St., B2G 2B7* ☎ *902/863–4001 or 888/662–7484* 📠 *902/863–2672* 🌐 *www.maritimeinns.com* *31 rooms, 1 suite* *Restaurant, room service, some in-room data ports, cable TV, some in-room VCRs, some pets allowed, no-smoking rooms* 💳 *AE, D, DC, MC, V.*

$–$$ 🏨 **Antigonish Victorian Inn.** A mansion fit for politicians and bishops that has, in fact, been occupied by both at various phases of its life, this luxurious establishment is a gateway to many Antigonish attractions. Rooms are commodious and handsomely appointed with Victorian-style furniture. The dining room serves a breakfast of cereal, fruit, French toast, and bacon and eggs. ✉ *149 Main St., B2G 2B6* ☎ *800/706–5558* ☎📠 *902/863–1103* *12 rooms* *Dining room, cable TV, Internet; no smoking* 💳 *AE, DC, MC, V* 🍽 *BP.*

Sports & the Outdoors

A 3-km (2-mi) **walking trail** along the shoreline of Antigonish Harbour borders a large tidal marsh teeming with ospreys, bald eagles, and other birds.

Shopping

Lyncharm Pottery (✉ 9 Pottery La. ☎ 902/863–6970 🌐 www.lyncharm.com) produces handsome functional stoneware that's sold in its own shop and exported worldwide. The **Lyghtesome Gallery** (✉ 166 Main St. ☎ 902/863–5804 🌐 www.lyghtesome.ns.ca) has a good variety of Nova Scotian art at reasonable prices.

en route

The **Sunrise Trail** (✉ Hwy. 337 from Antigonish to Cape George, then Hwy. 245 to New Glasgow) runs north from Antigonish for a glorious drive along St. George's Bay with its many good swimming beaches. After you've passed through this area, the road abruptly climbs 1,000 feet to Cape George. High above the sea, the road runs west along Northumberland Strait through farmlands and tiny villages such as **Arisaig,** where you can search for fossils on the shore. **Lismore,** just a few miles west of Arisaig, affirms the Scottish origin of its people with a stone cairn commemorating Bonnie Prince Charlie's Highland rebels, slaughtered by the English at Culloden in 1746. Lobster is landed and processed in shoreside factories here, making the town a great place to buy fresh lobster.

Stellarton

② *60 km (37 mi) west of Antigonish.*

The **Nova Scotia Museum of Industry** brings industrial heritage to life. Like factory and mine workers of old and even today, you punch in with a time card. Hands-on exhibits show how to hook a rag mat, print a bookmark, work a steam engine, or assemble a World War II artillery shell. Interactive computer exhibits explore multimedia as a tool of industry. Canada's oldest steam locomotives and a historic model railway layout are also displayed, and there's a restaurant. ⊠ *147 N. Foord St., Exit 24 off Hwy. 104* ☎ *902/755–5425* ⊕ *www.industry.museum.gov.ns.ca* 🎫 *$7* ☉ *Year-round Mon.–Sat. 9–5; May–June, Sun. 1–5; July–Oct., Sun. 10–5.*

Pictou

★ **③** *20 km (12 mi) north of Stellarton.*

First occupied by the Mi'Kmaqs, this well-developed town became a Scottish settlement in 1773 when the first boat of Scottish Highlanders landed, giving the town the distinction of being "the birthplace of New Scotland." Thirty-three families and 25 unmarried men arrived aboard the *Hector,* an aging cargo ship that was years later reproduced in minute detail and launched in the harbor. The **Hector Heritage Quay,** where the new 110-foot fully rigged *Hector* can be toured, recounts the story of the hardy Scottish pioneers and the flood of Scots who followed them. Working blacksmith and carpentry shops are on display, along with an interpretive center. ⊠ *33 Caladh Ave.* ☎ *902/485–4371 or 877/574–2868* 🎫 *$5* ☉ *Mid-May–late Oct., Mon.–Sat. 9–5, Sun. 12–5.*

A lively **weekend crafts market** at the waterfront, from June to September, showcases crafts and craftspeople from the area and across the province. **Melmerby Beach,** one of the warmest beaches in the province, is about 23 km (14 mi) east of Pictou. To get here, follow the shore road from Highway 104.

Where to Stay & Eat

¢–$$ ✕🏨 **Braeside Inn.** Every nook and cranny has collectible treasures on display at this handsome 1938 inn perched on a 5-acre hillside. China, crystal, silver, statuary, inlaid lacquer, and gadgets invite hours of browsing. You can stroll to the historic waterfront or watch your ship come into Pictou Harbour from the picture window in the dining room ($$–$$$). Prime rib and seafood are specialties here. ⊠ *Box 1810, 126 Front St., B0K 1H0* ☎ *902/485–5046 or 800/613–7701* 🖷 *902/485–1701* ⊕ *www.braesideinn.com* ⊅ *18 rooms* ⌂ *Restaurant, in-room data ports, some refrigerators, cable TV, some in-room VCRs, meeting room; no smoking* ▭ *AE, DC, MC, V.*

$–$$ 🏨 **Auberge Walker Inn.** A registered Heritage Property, this friendly inn is a block from the historic Pictou waterfront. The compact 1865 town house has one wheelchair-accessible suite with a kitchenette, a whirlpool bath, and a patio. Twelve-foot ceilings grace the inn's rooms. ⊠ *34 Coleraine St., B0K 1H0* ☎ *902/485–1433 or 800/370–5553* 🖷 *902/485–1222* ⊕ *www.townofpictou.com/walkerinn* ⊅ *10 rooms,*

1 suite ⟂ *Dining room, fans, cable TV; no room phones, no smoking* ⊟ *AE, MC, V* ⦿ *CP.*

$–$$ ▣ **Customs House Inn.** A former customs house on Pictou's waterfront is now a nifty inn, with spacious high-ceiling rooms overlooking the water. All have hardwood floors, and most have the original although non-working fireplaces. A basement pub has Celtic entertainment and serves Sunday brunch. ⊠ *Box 1542, 38 Depot St., B0K 1H0* ☎ *902/485–4546* 🖷 *902/485–1657* ⊕ *www.customshouseinn.ca* ⇌ *8 rooms* ⟂ *In-room data ports, in-room hot tubs, some kitchenettes, cable TV, pub, library, business services, meeting room* ⊟ *AE, DC, MC, V* ⦿ *CP.*

$–$$ ▣ **Stonehame Lodge & Chalets.** Handmade quilts and welcoming bottles
FodorsChoice   of homemade jam await, along with lots of peace and quiet at these log
★   chalets and lodge rooms atop Fitzpatrick Mountain. In season you can swim in the heated outdoor pool, hike or ski nearby woodland trails, visit a neighboring dairy farm, take a sleigh ride, see crop harvesting, or just relax before the chalet's woodstove. Accommodations are wheelchair accessible. ⊠ *R.R. 3, Scotsburn B0K 1R0, 12 km (7½ mi) west of Pictou, Exit 19 or 21 off TCH 104* ☎ *902/485–3468 or 877/646–3468* ⊕ *www.stonehamechalets.com* ⇌ *5 rooms, 9 chalets* ⟂ *Some kitchens, cable TV, some in-room VCRs, some pets allowed* ⊟ *AE, D, MC, V.*

¢–$$ ▣ **Consulate Inn.** From 1836 to 1896 this was the U.S. Consulate, and from 1810 to 1836 it was a private home. Today the inn is a showplace for the innkeepers' creativity: she's a skilled quilter and painter; he's an artist in the kitchen. Colorful quilted hangings and original art decorate the spacious rooms in the main house. Rooms in the next-door annex have private patios or balconies, and the two-bedroom cottage has a full kitchen and a deck overlooking Pictou Harbour. Continental breakfast and afternoon tea are served. There are cats on the premises. ⊠ *Box 1642, 157 Water St., B0K 1H0* ☎ *902/485–4554 or 800/424–8283* 🖷 *902/485–1532* ⊕ *www.consulateinn.com* ⇌ *10 rooms, 1 cottage* ⟂ *Some refrigerators, cable TV with movies, in-room VCRs* ⊟ *AE, MC, V* ⦿ *CP.*

Nightlife & the Arts
The **DeCoste Entertainment Centre** (⊠ Water St. ☎ 902/485–8848 or 800/353–5338 ⊕ www.decostecentre.ca) is a handsome theater that presents a summerlong program of concerts, pipe bands, highland dancing, and *ceilidhs* (Gaelic music and dance).

Shopping
The artisans' cooperative **Water Street Studio** (⊠ 110 Water St. ☎ 902/485–8398) sells hand-dyed and natural yarns, felted woolen items, and knit items such as hats, socks, shawls, and scarves, plus weaving, blankets, pottery, stained glass, jewelry, and woodwork.

New Glasgow

22 km (14 mi) southwest of Pictou.

The largest community along the Sunrise Trail has a rich Scottish heritage. From the 1820s to the 1920s, New Glasgow was a major shipbuilding center and port. The town's prosperity has always been linked to the East River, so the ongoing redevelopment of the riverfront seems appropriate. New Glasgow is the setting in early August of the **Riverfront Music Jubilee,** which attracts local and national performers. In mid-July New Glasgow hosts the **Festival of the Tartans,** which includes highland dancing, the Pictou County Pipes and Drums on Parade, a kilted golf tournament, concerts, beer gardens, and much more.

Tatamagouche

34 *50 km (31 mi) west of Pictou.*

Despite the size of its population—all of 600 souls—Tatamagouche is a force to be reckoned with. Canada's second-largest Oktoberfest and a major quilt show are held here each fall. Summer brings strawberry and blueberry festivals, lobster and chowder suppers, and a lively farmer's market each Saturday morning. This charming town on Highway 6 on the North Shore is at the juncture of two rivers, and Tatamagouche is a Mi'Kmaq name meaning "meeting place of the waters." An old rail bed along the river's edge, part of the Trans-Canada Trail, is ideal for hiking, cycling, walking, and bird-watching.

The **Sunrise Trail Museum** traces the town's Mi'Kmaq, Acadian, French, and Scottish roots and its shipbuilding heritage. ☒ *216 Main St.* ☎ *902/657–3007* ☜ *$1* ☺ *Late June–early Sept., daily 9–5.*

Local artists' works are shown at the **Fraser Cultural Centre,** which promotes arts, crafts, and cultural activities through demonstrations and exhibits. The building also houses the Tatamagouche visitor information center, North Shore archives, and a display about the giantess Anna Swan, who was born near Tatamagouche and earned fame in P.T. Barnum's American Museum in New York. ☒ *Main St.* ☎ *902/657–3285* ☜ *Free* ☺ *June–Aug., daily 10–5; Sept., daily 1–4.*

off the beaten path

BALMORAL GRIST MILL MUSEUM – A water-powered gristmill, built in 1874, serves as the centerpiece of this museum near Tatamagouche. It's one of the few operating mills in Nova Scotia. You can observe milling demonstrations, stroll the 1-km (½-mi) walking trail, and buy freshly ground flour in the shop. ☒ *660 Matheson Brook Rd., Balmoral Mills* ☎ *902/657–3016* ⊕ *museum. gov.ns.ca/bgm* ☜ *$3* ☺ *June–mid-Oct., Mon.–Sat. 9:30–5:30, Sun. 1–5:30; demonstrations daily 10–noon and 2–4.*

Where to Stay & Eat

¢–$$ ✕ **Big Al's Acadian Restaurant and Lounge.** The likenesses of local giantess Anna Swan and her husband are on display here in murals and wooden statues depicting the village's history. Overlooking Tatamagouche Bay, Big Al's serves steaks, seafood, and chicken wings, as well as pizza from Papa Al's Pizza, which is in the same building. ☒ *9 Station Rd.* ☎☎ *902/657–3341* ☎ *902/657–0335* ▤ *AE, V.*

¢–$ ✕ **Villager Restaurant.** This homey low-key place serves steaks, seafood, and salads. Try the popular fish-and-chips and haddock dinners. The dining room has a tin ceiling and a painted picture of the village of Tatamagouche from years ago. Downtown shops are a two-minute walk. ☒ *Main St.* ☎ *902/657–2029* ▤ *V.*

$$$$ ✕▥ **Fox Harb'r Resort.** Manor-style houses have suites with views of the Northumberland Strait, plus luxuries like heated marble bathroom floors, propane fireplaces, and terrace access at this 1,000-acre gated complex with a manicured garden. A sprawling, 18-hole traditional Scottish golf course on the jagged ocean coastline is the resort's crown jewel—a round of golf is $200 ($250 for nonguests). Trap- and skeet shooting can be done on-site. Cuisine ($$$$) is classic French and European; frequent requests are halibut, lobster, rack of lamb, and filet mignon. The wine cellar is well stocked. Arrive by car, private plane, or boat. ☒ *1337 Fox Harbour Rd., B0K 1Y0, 22 km (13½ mi) west of Tatamagouche and 8 km (5 mi) north of Wallace* ☎ *902/257–1801 or 866/257–1801* 🖷 *902/257–1852* ⊕ *www.foxharbr.com* ⬖ *72 suites*

&phase; 2 *restaurants, in-room data ports, in-room hot tubs, kitchenettes, mini-bars, cable TV, 18-hole golf course, 9-hole golf course, 2 tennis courts, pro shop, indoor pool, spa, marina, convention center, airstrip; no smoking ⊟ AE; D, DC, MC, V ⊙ Closed late Oct.–May.*

★ ¢–$$ 🚉 **Train Station Inn.** Railway history lives on in Tatamagouche, where this unique inn has B&B accommodations in a century-old station and in seven cabooses parked nearby. The stationmaster's quarters include three rooms, a guest parlor, and a kitchen and laundry for guest use. Downstairs, a main-floor café, where tasty breakfasts are served, is decorated with authentic railroad memorabilia. The caboose suites have all the creature comforts, plus touches of railroad life—signal switches and elevated conductors' cupolas with their revolving chairs. Lobster or steak dinners are served in the dining car ($$$), by reservation only. ✉ *21 Station Rd., B0K 1V0* 🕿 *902/657–3222 or 888/724–5233* 📠 *902/657–9091* ⊕ *www.trainstation.ns.ca* ⟲ *3 rooms, 7 suites* &phase; *Dining room, café, in-room data ports, cable TV in some rooms, laundry facilities, Internet; no TVs in some rooms* ⊟ *AE, MC, V.*

$ 🚉 **Balmoral Motel.** This small motel overlooks Tatamagouche Bay and offers water views from all rooms. There are a large grassy play area and direct access to walking, cross-country skiing, and snowmobiling on the nearby Trans-Canada Trail. German and Canadian dishes are served in the Mill Dining Room. ✉ *Box 178, Main St., B0K 1V0* 🕿 *902/657–2000 or 888/383–9357* 📠 *902/657–2205* ⊕ *www.balmoralmotel.ca* ⟲ *18 rooms* &phase; *Dining room, fans, cable TV, Internet, some pets allowed (fee), no-smoking rooms* ⊟ *AE, MC, V.*

Shopping

At **Sara Bonnyman Pottery** (✉ Hwy. 246, 1½ km [1 mi] uphill from post office 🕿 902/657–3215), watch the well-known potter at work each morning produce handsome stoneware pieces bearing sunflower and blueberry motifs and her one-of-a-kind plates and bowls. She also makes wool hand-hooked rugs in colorful primitive designs. The studio is open Monday–Saturday 10–4, June–mid-September, and by appointment off-season. Maritime crafts sold at the **Sunflower Crafts Shop** (✉ 249 Main St. 🕿 902/657–3276) include pewter, wood, baskets, wrought iron, quilts, candles, Chéticamp hooking, the work of noted local potter Sara Bonnyman, and unusual framed pictures made of caribou tufting. The shop is open June 15–December 24, Monday–Saturday 10–4:30.

Malagash

35 *17 km (11 mi) west of Tatamagouche.*

Malagash is best known for its winery, **Jost Vineyards,** which flourishes in the warm climate moderated by the Northumberland Strait. A surprisingly wide range of award-winning wines is produced here, including a notable ice wine (a sweet wine made after frost has iced the grapes). There's a well-stocked wine shop. ✉ *Hwy. 6 off Hwy. 104* 🕿 *902/257–2636 or 800/565–4567* ⊕ *www.jostwine.com* ⊙ *Mid-June–mid-Sept., Mon.–Sat. 9–6, Sun. noon–6; mid-Sept.–mid-June, Mon.–Sat. 10–5, Sun. noon–5; tours mid-June–mid-Sept., daily at noon and 3.*

Springhill

36 *40 km (25 mi) west of Malagash.*

The coal-mining town of Springhill, on Highway 2, was the site of the famous mine disaster of the 1950s immortalized in the folk song "The Ballad of Springhill," by Peggy Seeger and Ewen McColl. You can tour a real coal mine at the **Springhill Miners Museum.** Retired miners act as guides and recount firsthand memories of mining disasters. ⊠ *145 Black River Rd., off Hwy. 2* ☎ *902/597–3449* ☒ *$4.50* ☉ *Mid-May–mid-Oct., daily 10–6.*

Springhill is the hometown of internationally acclaimed singer Anne Murray, whose career is celebrated at the **Anne Murray Centre.** ⊠ *36 Main St.* ☎ *902/597–8614* ☒ *$5.50* ☉ *Mid-May–mid-Oct., daily 9–5.*

off the beaten path	**WILD BLUEBERRY & MAPLE CENTRE –** This center in Oxford, about 10 km (6 mi) outside Springhill, details the history of two tasty industries—75% of Nova Scotia's blueberry and maple-syrup production occurs in surrounding Cumberland County. Self-guided tours, interactive displays, and a beehive tell the story. ⊠ *105 Lower Main St., Oxford* ☎ *902/447–2908* ⊕ *www.town.oxford.ns.ca* ☒ *Free* ☉ *Apr.–Oct., daily (call or check Web site for hrs).*

Amherst

37 *28 km (17 mi) northwest of Springhill.*

Near the New Brunswick border, this now-quiet town was a bustling center of industry and influence from the mid-1800s to early 1900s. Four of Canada's Fathers of Confederation hailed from Amherst, including Sir Charles Tupper, who later became prime minister. In contrast with tame Amherst is the **Tantramar Marsh,** alive with incredible birds and wildlife. It was originally called Tintamarre (literally "din," in French) because of the racket made by vast flocks of wildfowl. Said to be the world's largest marsh, the marsh is a migratory route for hundreds of thousands of birds, and a breeding ground for more than 100 species.

From Amherst the Sunrise Trail heads toward the Northumberland Strait, while the Glooscap Trail runs west through fossil country. The **Fundy Shore Ecotour** (☎ 902/893–8782, 800/895–1177 in Canada), which mainly follows near the Glooscap Trail, has been developed by the local tourism authority to highlight the region's six distinct ecozones. Brochures are available at information centers; call for locations.

Where to Stay & Eat

$$–$$$ ✕ **David A.'s Cafe and Catering** A Cordon Bleu–certified owner-chef presides over this intimate yet informal dining room. Everything is made from scratch. The seafood chowder draws a crowd as do the delectable desserts. ⊠ *125 Victoria St. E* ☎ *902/661–0760* ☰ *MC, V* ☉ *Closed Sun. No dinner Mon.–Wed. Oct.–June.*

★ **$–$$** ✕▦ **Amherst Shore Country Inn.** This seaside country inn, with a beautiful view of Northumberland Strait and acres of lawns and gardens, has rooms, suites, and a cottage fronting 600 feet of private beach. Relax in comfort surrounded by antique furnishings and handmade quilts. Some suites have double whirlpool baths, propane fireplaces, and small decks. The two-bedroom rustic seaside cottage has kitchen facilities. Well-prepared four-course, prix-fixe dinners incorporating homegrown produce are served at one daily seating ($$$$; reservations essential). Look for themed gourmet or romantic packages. ⊠ *Hwy. 366–R.R. 2, Lorneville B4H 3X9, 32 km (20 mi) northeast of Amherst* ☎ *800/661–2724* ⊞⊞ *902/661–4800* ⊕ *www.ascinn.ns.ca* ➷ *4 rooms, 4 suites, 1 cottage* ⌂ *Restaurant, some in-room hot tubs, cable TV, beach; no smoking* ☰ *AE, MC, V* ☉ *Closed weekdays Nov.–Apr.*

$–$$ ▦ **Wandlyn Inn.** Just inside the Nova Scotia–New Brunswick border, this dependable inn offers a slew of amenities. Rooms are comfortable and convenient, and the attached Legend's Lounge with entertainment is a good place to unwind. ⊠ *Box 275, Victoria St.–Trans-Canada Hwy.,*

B4H 3Z2 ☎902/667–3331 or 800/561–0000 📠902/667–0475 ⊕*www. wandlyninns.com* 🛏*88 rooms* ⚑*Restaurant, indoor pool, hot tub, sauna, laundry facilities, convention center* ▭ *AE, DC, MC, V.*

Joggins

38 *35 km (22 mi) southwest of Amherst.*

Joggins's main draw is the coal-age fossils embedded in its 150-foot sand-stone cliffs. At the **Joggins Fossil Centre** you can view a large collection of 300-million-year-old fossils and learn about the region's geological and archaeological history. Maps are issued for independent fossil hunters. ✉ *30 Main St.* ☎ *902/251–2727* 💲 *$3.50* ⊙ *June–Sept., daily 9–5:30.*

Cape Chignecto & Cape d'Or

70 km (43 mi) southwest of Joggins.

Fodor'sChoice
★

Two imposing promontories—Cape Chignecto and Cape d'Or—reach into the Bay of Fundy near Chignecto Bay. Cape Chignecto, home to the newest provincial park, **Cape Chignecto Provincial Park,** is an untouched wilderness of 10,000 acres of old-growth forest harboring deer, moose, and eagles. It's circumnavigated by a 50-km (31-mi) hiking trail along rugged cliffs that rise to 600 feet above the bay. Wilderness cabins and campsites are available. ✉ *Off Hwy. 209, West Advocate* ☎ *902/392–2085 or 902/254–3241* ⊕ *www.capechignecto.net* 💲 *$3* ⊙ *Late May–Oct., weekdays 8–5, weekends 8–8.*

Fodor'sChoice
★

South of Cape Chignecto is **Cape d'Or** (Cape of Gold), named by Samuel de Champlain for its glittering veins of copper. The region was actively mined a century ago, and at nearby Horseshoe Cove you may still find nuggets of almost pure copper on the beach as well as amethysts and other semiprecious stones. Cape d'Or's hiking trails border the cliff edge above the Dory Rips, a turbulent meeting of currents from the Minas Basin and the Bay of Fundy punctuated by a fine lighthouse.

A delightful beach walk at **Advocate Harbour,** named by Samuel de Champlain for a lawyer friend, follows the top of an Acadian dike that was built by settlers in the 1700s to reclaim farmland from the sea. Advocate Beach, noted for its tide-cast driftwood, stretches 5 km (3 mi) from Cape Chignecto to Cape d'Or.

The **Age of Sail Museum Heritage Centre** traces the history of the area's shipbuilding and lumbering industries. You can also see a restored 1857 Methodist church, a blacksmith shop, and a lighthouse. ✉ *Hwy. 209, Port Greville* ☎ *902/348–2030* 💲 *$2* ⊙ *June–Sept., daily 10–6.*

Where to Stay & Eat

$–$$ ✕ **Harbour Lite Restaurant.** Every bite you eat in this unpretentious road-side diner is home-cooked by the friendly owner, who is on the job 12 hours a day all summer. Clam chowder, lobster (in season) and other fresh seafood, plus sandwiches and sweets like featherlight cinnamon buns, muffins, pies, and cakes, round out the menu. ✉ *4160 Main St., Advocate* ☎ *902/392–2277* ▭ *MC, V* ⊙ *Closed Dec.–Feb.*

¢–$ ✕ **Fundy Tides Campground Restaurant.** This small restaurant is large on hospitality. In the campground's main building, the 18-seat restaurant serves diner-type food that ranges from hamburgers to seafood. Everything is made from scratch, from the fries to the fish batter. It's eat in or take out. Breakfast is also served. ✉ *95 Mills Rd., Advocate Harbour* ☎ *902/392–2584 or 800/395–7085* ▭ *V* ⊙ *Closed mid-Nov.–mid-Apr.*

$$ ⊞ **Driftwood Park Retreat.** Five mist-blue cottages face the Fundy shore and its powerful tides. Four of the two-story, two-bedroom units have cathedral ceilings, pine floors, gas fireplaces, well-equipped kitchens, and upstairs living rooms with fine views of the bay. The fifth cottage is an open-plan ranch unit with living room, dining room, and kitchen area. It is wheelchair-accessible and has one bedroom. The living room has a propane fireplace. The cottages are close to a driftwood beach, hiking trails, and clam digging and mineral hunting areas. ⊠ *47 Driftwood La., West Advocate B0M 1A0* ☎ *902/392–2008 or 866/810–0110* 🖴 *902/392–2041* ⊕ *www.driftwoodparkretreat.com* ⬅ *5 cottages* ⟁ *Kitchens, laundry service; no room TVs, no smoking* ▭ *MC, V.*

$ ⊞ **Lightkeeper's Kitchen and Guest House.** Before automation, two light keepers manned the crucial light on the rocky Cape d'Or shore, and their cottages have been transformed—one to an excellent restaurant and the other to a small inn with a comfortable lounge and picture windows overlooking the Minas Basin. This wild and lovely place offers hiking, bird-watching, seal sightings, outdoor lobster boils and clambakes, and exceptional young hosts whose warmth and gourmet cooking make leaving difficult. A common area has a breakfast bar, books and games, an old TV, and a small refrigerator. Getting here is a bit challenging: a 5½-km-long (3-mi-long) road off Highway 209 from Advocate, then a steep gravel path down to the shore. ⊠ *Cape d'Or off Hwy. 209* ⓓ *Box 122, Advocate B0M 1A0* ☎ *902/670–0534* ⊕ *www.capedor.ca* ⬅ *4 rooms, 1 with bath* ⟁ *Restaurant, in-room VCRs; no smoking* ▭ *V* ⊗ *Closed end Oct.–mid-May.*

¢ ⊞ **Reid's Tourist Home.** Nestled between Cape d'Or and Cape Chignecto, this cattle farm is a working operation where you can enjoy the bucolic pleasures of country life or take a short walk to the Fundy shore. The suites occupy a separate building near the picturesque farmhouse. Chignecto Park is just over 1 km (½ mi) away. ⊠ *1391 W. Advocate Rd., West Advocate* ⓓ *R.R. 3, Parrsboro B0M 1S0* ☎ *902/392–2592* 🖴 *902/392–2523* ⬅ *4 suites* ⟁ *Refrigerators* ▭ *No credit cards* ⊗ *Closed Oct.–May.*

¢ ⊞ **Spencer's Island B&B.** Once home to Captain Bigelow, who built the mysterious ship *Mary Celeste,* whose crew vanished at sea, the house today is a modest and friendly B&B with cozy rooms and an antiques-furnished parlor. Wood-burning fireplaces and a vintage woodstove in the kitchen add to the ambience. Blueberry waffles and the cheese soufflé are breakfast favorites. The inn is just uphill from the Spencer's Island lighthouse and the Fundy shore, and it's a 10-minute drive from the wilderness of Cape Chignecto. ⊠ *Off Hwy. 209, Spencer's Island* ⓓ *R.R. 3, Parrsboro B0M 1S0* ☎ *902/392–2721* ⬅ *3 rooms, 1 with bath* ⟁ *In-room VCRs* ▭ *No credit cards* ⊗ *Closed Sept.–May* ⦿ *BP.*

---

en route   A cairn at **Spencer's Island Beach** on Highway 209 commemorates the *Mary Celeste,* a ship built here in 1861 that in 1872 was found abandoned at sea, all sails set, undamaged, but without a trace of the crew and passengers.

Parrsboro

㊴ *55 km (34 mi) east of Cape d'Or.*

A center for rock hounds and fossil hunters, Parrsboro is the main town on this shore and hosts the **Nova Scotia Gem and Mineral Show** every third weekend of August. The fossil-laden cliffs that rim the **Minas Basin** are washed by the world's highest tides twice daily. The result is a wealth of plant and animal fossils revealed in the rocks or washed down to the shore. Semiprecious stones such as amethyst, quartz, and stilbite can be found at **Partridge Island**, 1 km (½ mi) offshore and connected to the mainland by an isthmus.

The **Fundy Geological Museum** isn't far from the Minas Basin area, where some of the oldest dinosaur fossils in Canada have been found. Two-hundred-million-year-old dinosaur fossils are showcased here alongside other mineral, plant, and animal relics. ⊠ *162 Two Island Rd.* ☎ *902/ 254–3814* ⊕ *fundygeo.museum.gov.ns.ca* ⊠ *$5* ☉ *June–mid-Oct., daily 9:30–5:30; mid-Oct.–June, Tues.–Sat. 9–5.*

The world's smallest dinosaur footprints, along with rare minerals, rocks, and fossils, are displayed at Eldon George's **Parrsboro Rock and Mineral Shop and Museum.** Mr. George, a goldsmith, lapidary, and woodcarver, sells his work in his shop and has tours for fossil and mineral collectors. ⊠ *349 Whitehall Rd.* ☎ *902/254–2981* ⊠ *Donations accepted* ☉ *May–Oct., daily 10–6.*

Although fossils have become Parrsboro's claim to fame, this harbor town was also a major shipping and shipbuilding port, and its history is described at the **Ottawa House Museum-by-the-Sea.** This house, which overlooks the Bay of Fundy, is the only surviving building from a 1700s settlement. It was later the summer home of Sir Charles Tupper (1821–1915), a former premier of Nova Scotia who was briefly prime minister of Canada. ⊠ *Whitehall Rd., 3 km (2 mi) east of downtown* ☎ *902/254–2376* ⊠ *$2* ☉ *Mid-June–mid-Sept., daily 10–6.*

Where to Stay & Eat

$-$$ ✕ **Stowaway Restaurant.** The menu is rich in seafood—thick chowder, fish-and-chips, and scallops—but includes chicken and meat dishes. Interesting antiques, which are for sale, fill the deep window wells at this friendly and spacious place. In one wing a bakery ruins diets with its fresh apple pies, doughnuts, and bread. There's a takeout counter, too. Breakfast is served. ⊠ *69 Main St.* ☎ *902/254–3371* ⊟ *AE, DC, MC, V.*

¢-$$ ✕ **Harbour View Restaurant.** The owners maintain their own boats to fish for scallops and lobster, which, along with clams, flounder, and other seafood, are menu staples at this beachfront restaurant. The dining room, with windows overlooking the water and the lighthouse, displays paintings and photos of Parrsboro's past. Breakfast is also served. ⊠ *476 Pier Rd.* ☎ *902/254–3507* ⊟ *MC, V* ☉ *Closed mid-Oct.–Apr.*

¢-$$ ✕ **John's Café.** This funky café serves healthful salads, sandwiches, and soups, plus decadent desserts. Seventies music plays indoors or on a pleasant patio. Breakfast is also served. Call before heading to the café in winter—it may be closed. ⊠ *151 Main St.* ☎ *902/254–3255* ⊟ *No credit cards.*

$$$$ ⊞ **Beach House on Hatfield Road.** Fourteen picture windows provide panoramic views of the Bay of Fundy and a saltwater marsh. The two-story house can sleep six to eight and has access to two beaches and all the attractions of the Glooscap Trail. Fully equipped, from beach towels to fax machine, fondue pots to fireplace, it includes two bedrooms, two bathrooms, a sunroom, balconies, a dining room, and a sitting room with fireplace. The house is rented in one-week increments for summer and forshorter breaks in winter. ⊠ *Fox River, 19 km (12 mi) west of Parrsboro* ⊕ *Reservations: 96 Sherwood Ave., Toronto, ON M4P 2A7* ☎ *416/481–4096* 🖶 *416/487–4048* ⊕ *www.lizyorke.com* ⇔ *1 house* ⚙ *Kitchen, cable TV, beach, laundry facility, business services, some pets allowed; no smoking* ⊟ *No credit cards.*

¢-$$ ⊞ **Maple Inn, Parrsboro.** Local residents often reserve Room 1 in this Italianate-style home built in 1860–90 because many of them were born here when the building was a hospital and this was the delivery room.

All the rooms, however, are dramatic, including one that's painted black with lush, flowery touches. Parrsboro's center and the Bay of Fundy are within walking distance. ⊠ *Box 457, 2358 Western Ave., B0M 1S0* ☎ *877/627–5346* 🖷 *902/254–3735* ⊕ *www3.ns.sympatico.ca/ mapleinn* ⇆ *8 rooms, 1 suite* ⚘ *Fans, cable TV in some rooms; no smoking* ▭ *AE, MC, V* ⦿⬤ *BP.*

$ 🏠 **Gillespie House B&B.** Wild roses border the driveway leading up to this handsome home. Yoga and spa weekends can be arranged for groups. A lavish vegetarian breakfast and tons of visitor information are part of the service. Antique furnishings, hardwood floors, fireplaces, and comfy down duvets provide a pleasant ambience in this 1890s home. ⊠ *358 Main St., B0M 1S0* ☎ *902/254–3196 or 877/901–3196* ⊕ *www.gillespiehouseinn.com* ⇆ *4 rooms* ⚘ *Bicycles; no room TVs* ▭ *AE, MC, V* ⊙ *Closed Nov.–Apr.* ⦿⬤ *BP.*

$ 🏠 **Parrsboro Mansion.** This 1880 home, set far back on a 4-acre lawn, presents an imposing face; inside it's brightly modern, with contemporary European art and furnishings. The owners invite guests to join them in a morning jog and, later, to learn about regeneration and relaxation through magnetic-field therapy. The quiet ground-floor rooms are spacious and have big windows and sitting areas. Each room is decorated in a particular theme: Nova Scotia, Italian, and romantic. ⊠ *Box 579, 15 Eastern Ave., B0M 1S0* ☎ *866/354–2585* 🖷 *902/254–2585* ⊕ *www.parrsboromansion.com* ⇆ *3 rooms* ⚘ *Fans, cable TV, gym, sauna, laundry facilities, business services; no smoking* ▭ *AE, MC, V* ⊙ *Closed Nov.–June* ⦿⬤ *CP.*

Nightlife & the Arts

Ship's Company Theatre (⊠ 198 Main St. ☎ 902/254–2003 or 800/565–7469 ⊕ www.shipscompany.com) presents top-notch plays, comedy, and a concert series aboard the M. V. *Kipawo,* a former Minas Basin ferry, early July through early September. **Joy Laking Studio Gallery** (⊠ 6730 Hwy. 2, Portaupique, 5 km [3 mi] east of Bass River ☎ 902/647–2816 or 800/565–5899 ⊕ www.joylakinggallery.com), midway between Truro and Parrsboro, is owned by one of Nova Scotia's best-known painters.

Five Islands

④⓪ *24 km (15 mi) east of Parrsboro.*

Among the most scenic areas along Highway 2 is Five Islands, which, according to Mi'Kmaq legend, was created when the god Glooscap threw handfuls of sod at Beaver, who had mocked and betrayed him. **Five Islands Provincial Park,** on the shore of Minas Basin, has a campground ($18 a night), a beach, and hiking trails. Interpretive displays reveal the area's interesting geology: semiprecious stones, Jurassic-age dinosaur bones, and fossils. The Five Islands Lighthouse, at Sand Point Campground, has access to good swimming and clamming; you can "walk on the ocean floor" at low tide, when the water recedes nearly a mile, but beware the awesome return of the tides, which can outrun man or beast. ⊠ *Hwy. 2, 32 km (20 mi) east of Parrsboro and 57 km (35 mi) west of Truro* ☎ *902/254–2980* 🖻 *Free* ⊙ *Mid-May–Aug., daily dawn–dusk.*

Cobequid Interpretation Centre highlights the geology, history, and culture of the area with pictures, videos, and interpretive panels. Get a sweeping view of the countryside and the impressive tides from the World War II observation tower. The center is home base for **Kenomee Hiking and Walking Trails,** which allow one to explore the area's varied landscapes—the coast itself plus cliffs, waterfalls, and forested valleys. ⊠ *3248 Hwy. 2, Central Economy* ☎ *902/647–2600* 🖻 *By donation* ⊙ *Mid-Oct.–June, daily dawn–dusk.*

Where to Stay

$ ▦ **Gemstow B&B.** At this B&B, breakfast is served on an airy sunporch that overlooks flowery perennial beds and has a fine vista of Five Islands beyond. Photographers nab their best shots of the windswept islands from the front deck. Inside, the rooms and the lounge are tastefully furnished. Your host leads hikes to a hidden waterfall or clamming on the shore. ⊠ *463 Hwy. 2, Lower Five Islands B0M 1N0, 20 km (12 mi) east of Parrsboro* ☎ *902/254–2924* ⊕ *www3.ns.sympatico.ca/ gemstow* ⇆ *2 rooms* ♦ *No a/c, no room phones, no room TVs* ⊟ *MC, V* ⦿⦿ *BP.*

$ ▦ **MacLellans Cottages.** Midway between Parrsboro and Truro are four modest seaside units equipped with everything from hair dryers to rolling pins to clam-digging gear. The large property has direct access to the Minas Basin Beach. ⊠ *3120 Hwy. 2, Economy B0M 1J0* ☎ *902/ 647–2592 or 877/647–2209* 🖷 *902/647–2592* ⇆ *4 cottages* ♦ *Fishing, basketball, horseshoes, volleyball, laundry facilities* ⊟ *AE, MC, V* ⊘ *Closed Oct.–May.*

Truro

㊶ *67 km (42 mi) east of Five Islands.*

Truro's central location places it on many travelers' routes. Throughout Truro, watch for the Truro Tree Sculptures—a creative tribute to trees killed by the dreaded Dutch elm disease. Artists Albert Deveau, Ralph Bigney, and Bruce Wood have been transforming the dead trees into handsome sculptures of historical figures, wildlife, and cultural icons. An international tulip festival takes place in May.

Truro's least-known asset is also its biggest—the 1,000-acre **Victoria Park** where, smack in the middle of town, you can find hiking trails, a winding stream flowing through a deep gorge with a 200-step climb to the top, and two picturesque waterfalls. ⊠ *Park Rd.* ☎ *902/893–6078* 🎟 *Free* ⊘ *Daily dawn–dusk.*

Where to Stay & Eat

$–$$ ✕ **Frank & Gino's Grill and Pasta House.** A comfortable, family atmosphere and cool decor greet you at this restaurant. Enjoy the popular pasta or ribs, or choose something else from its full menu. Each of the restaurant's corners is filled with memorabilia focusing on one of four themes: Marilyn Monroe, antique sports, local lore, and traveling by ship. Portions are generous—pasta is accompanied by salad and bread—so Frank & Gino's Teeny Weeny Cheesecake is just the right size for a taste of heaven dessert. ⊠ *286 Robie St.* ☎ *902/895–2165* ⊕ *www.frankandginos. com* ⊟ *D, DC, MC, V.*

¢–$ ✕ **Sugar Moon Farm Maple Products and Pancake House.** Nova Scotia's
FodorsChoice only year-round maple destination is this log sugar camp and pancake
★ house nestled in the Cobequid Mountains about 30 km (19 mi) north of Truro. Enjoy whole-grain buttermilk pancakes and waffles, maple syrup, local sausage, fresh biscuits, maple baked beans, and organic coffee. One night each month a guest chef prepares a gourmet meal ($50). From 9 to 5 daily, you can tour the working maple farm, hike the sugar woods, and see demos (spring only). At this writing, the restaurant plans to expand its meal service for 2004; call ahead. ⊠ *Alex MacDonald Rd., Earltown* ☎ *902/657–3348 or 866/816–2753* ⊕ *www.sugarmoon.ca* ⊟ *MC, V* ⊘ *Closed Tues.–Wed. and weekdays Sept.–June.*

★ $$–$$$$ ✕▦ **John Stanfield Inn.** Rescued from demolition and moved to this site, the John Stanfield Inn has been restored to its original Queen Anne glory, with delicate wood carvings, elaborate fireplaces, bow windows, and fine antique furniture. The restaurant ($–$$) serves unusual seafood specialties, including a fisherman's plate with half a dozen seafood varieties; desserts such as berries Romanoff; and a lavish Sunday brunch in summer. ☒ *437 Prince St., B2N 1E6* ☏ *902/895–1505, 902/895–1651, or 800/561–7666* 🖷 *902/893–4427* ⊕ *www.johnstanfieldinn.com* ➪ *10 rooms, 2 suites* ♿ *Restaurant, in-room data ports, some kitchenettes, cable TV, lounge, laundry service, business services, meeting rooms; no smoking* ▭ *AE, D, DC, MC, V* ⫶❍⫶ *CP.*

¢ ⊡ **Suncatcher B&B.** Call this modest B&B 10 minutes outside Truro a "glass act": stained glass adorns every available window, wall, and cranny. Two-day workshops in crafting stained glass are available (reservations required). The breakfast menu includes homemade breads, jams, muffins, fruits (in season), and eggs. The hosts, longtime B&B providers, know their province from stem to stern and cheerfully advise on itineraries and attractions. The four rooms share two bathrooms. ☒ *25 Wile Crest Ave.–R.R. 6, B2N 5B4* ☏☏ *902/893–7169 or 877/203–6032* ⊕ *www.bbcanada.com/1853.html* ➪ *4 rooms without bath* ♿ *Fans; no room TVs, no smoking* ▭ *V* ⫶❍⫶ *BP.*

Sports & the Outdoors

Riding the rushing tide aboard a 16-foot self-bailing Zodiac with **Shubenacadie River Runners** (☒ 8681 Hwy. 215, Maitland ☏ 902/261–2770 or 800/856–5061 ⊕www.tidalborerafting.com) is an adventure you won't soon forget. Tide conditions and time of day let you choose a mildly turbulent ride or an ultrawild one. A 3½-hour excursion costs $65, including gear and a barbecue. The **Truro Raceway** (☒ Main St. ☏ 902/893–8075) holds year-round harness racing.

CAPE BRETON ISLAND

Fodor'sChoice
★

The highways and byways of the island of Cape Breton, including those on the **Cabot Trail,** make up one of the most spectacular drives in North America. As you wind through the rugged coastal headlands of Cape Breton Highlands National Park, you can climb mountains and plunge back down to the sea in a matter of minutes. The Margaree River is a cultural dividing line: south of the river the settlements are Scottish, up the river they are largely Irish, and north of the river they are Acadian French. Visit villages where ancient dialects can still be heard and explore a fortress where period players bring the past to life. This is a place where cultural heritage is alive, where the atmosphere is maritime, and where inventors Marconi and Bell share the spotlight with coal miners and singers like Rita MacNeil. Wherever you go in Cape Breton, you are sure to experience warmth and hospitality.

Bras d'Or Lake, a vast, warm, almost-landlocked inlet of the sea, occupies the entire center of Cape Breton. The coastline of the lake is more than 967 km (600 mi) long, and people sail yachts from all over the world to cruise its serene, unspoiled coves and islands. Bald eagles have become so plentiful around the lake that they are now exported to the United States to restock natural habitats. Four of the largest communities along the shore are native Mi'Kmaq communities.

If Halifax is the heart of Nova Scotia, Cape Breton is its soul, complete with soul music—flying fiddles, boisterous rock, velvet ballads. Cape Breton musicians—weaned on Scottish jigs and reels—are among the world's finest, and in summer you can hear them at dozens of local festivals and concerts. In summer every community in the southern end of Inverness County takes a different night of the week to offer a square dance. Propelled by driving piano and virtuoso fiddling, locals of every age whirl through "square sets," the best of them step dancing and square

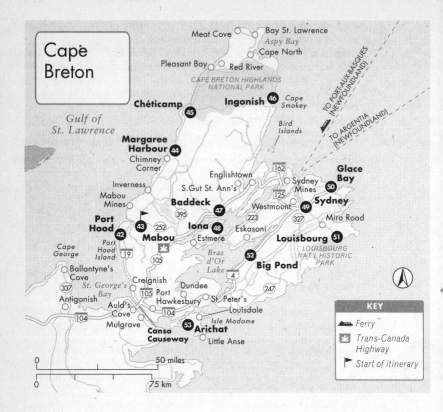

Cape Breton

Gulf of St. Lawrence

Meat Cove   Bay St. Lawrence
Aspy Bay
Cape North
Pleasant Bay   Red River
CAPE BRETON HIGHLANDS
NATIONAL PARK

Chéticamp 45

Ingonish 46   Cape Smokey

Bird Islands

Margaree Harbour 44
Chimney Corner

Inverness
Mabou Mines   S.Gut St. Ann's   Englishtown   162

Sydney Mines   **Glace Bay** 50

Baddeck 47   125

Westmount 49   **Sydney**

Port Hood 42   43   252   **Iona** 48   395   223   327   Mira Road

Mabou   Estmere   Eskasoni   **Louisbourg** 51

Cape George   Port Hood Island   19   Bras d'Or Lake   52   LOUISBOURG NAT'L HISTORIC PARK

Ballantyne's Cove   105   **Big Pond**

337   St. George's Bay   Creignish   4

Antigonish   105   Dundee   247

Auld's Cove   Port Hawkesbury   St. Peter's

104   Mulgrave   Louisdale

Canso Causeway 53 **Arichat**   Isle Madame

Little Anse

0   50 miles
0   75 km

KEY
⚓ *Ferry*
⬇ *Trans-Canada Highway*
▶ *Start of itinerary*

dancing simultaneously. Local bulletin boards and newspapers list square dance times and locations.

Allow five days for a meandering tour of approximately 710 km (440 mi) that begins by entering the island via the Canso Causeway on Highway 104. Turn left at the rotary and take Highway 19, the Ceilidh Trail, which winds for 129 km (80 mi) along the mountainside through glens and farms, with fine views across St. George's Bay to Cape George. This western shoreline of Cape Breton faces the Gulf of St. Lawrence and is famous for its sandy beaches and warm saltwater.

Port Hood

42 *45 km (28 mi) northwest of the Canso Causeway on Hwy. 19; 103 km (64 mi) northwest of Antigonish.*

At this fishing village you can buy lobster and snow crab fresh off the wharf as the boats return in midafternoon. With a little persuasion, one of the fisherfolk might give you a lift to **Port Hood Island**, a mile across the harbor. It's a 10-minute walk from the island's wharf to the pastel-color cliffs of wave-mottled alabaster on the seaward shore. Both the village and the island have sandy beaches ideal for swimming.

Mabou

▶ 43 *13 km (8 mi) northeast of Port Hood on Hwy. 19.*

The pretty village of Mabou is very Scottish, with its Gaelic signs and traditions of Scottish music and dancing. Most Saturday nights offer a helping of local culture in the form of a dance or kitchen party, which is an informal and intimate gathering that usually involves music and dance. Check bulletin boards at local businesses for information about these events. This is the hometown of national recording and performing artists such as John Allan Cameron, Jimmy Rankin, and the Rankin Family (now disbanded). Stop at a local gift shop and buy tapes to play as you drive down the long fjord of Mabou Harbour.

Where to Stay & Eat

¢–$$ ✕ **Mull Café and Deli.** You can hardly drive by this informal restaurant on Mabou's main thoroughfare without seeing a parking lot full of cars. One of the most popular establishments on western Cape Breton, its pasta, seafood chowder, fish-and-chips, steaks, and homemade desserts are particular draws. The restaurant has a deli counter and is fully licensed. Local artwork is on display. The café closes at 9 PM in summer and 7 PM in winter. ✉ *11630 Rte. 19* ☎ *902/945–2244* ⊕ *www.auracom. com/~mulldci/* ☰ *AE, MC, V.*

$–$$ ✕🖭 **Duncreigan Country Inn.** Though they were built in the 1990s, the buildings that make up this inn on the shore of Mabou Harbour suggest the early 1900s in design and furnishings. Several decks afford beautiful views and are ideal for relaxing, reading, and leaving your cares behind. The restaurant ($$–$$$), open for dinner from late June to mid-October, has an enviable reputation. Continental breakfast is included in the room rate in summer. ✉ *Box 59, Rte. 19, B0E 1X0* ☎ *902/945– 2207, 800/840–2207 for reservations* 🖶 *902/945–2206* ⊕ *www. auracom.com/~mulldci* ↩ *7 rooms, 1 suite* ♿ *Restaurant, bicycles* ☰ *MC, V.*

$–$$ ✕🖭 **Mabou River Inn.** Hospitality, tasty home-cooked meals, and clean, comfortable rooms are staples of the Mabou River Inn, which has been undergoing constant renovations since its current owner took over in 1997. Most recently a hostel, it has also been a boys' boarding school. A common room has a bay window, a fireplace, and a TV and VCR. You can use the inn's sea kayaks. Friendly hosts provide information on the local area. The two-bedroom apartments have separate entrances, kitchens, and pull-out sofas. The dining room serves dinner and lobster suppers. ✉ *Box 255, off Rte. 19 B0E 1X0* ☎ *902/945–2356 or 888/ 627–9744* 🖶 *902/945–2605* ⊕ *www.mabouriverinn.com* ↩ *9 rooms, 2 apartments* ♿ *Restaurant, some kitchens, cable TV, some in-room VCRs, hair salon, mountain bikes, billiards, recreation room, laundry facilities, Internet, business services, meeting room* ☰ *MC, V* 🍽 *BP.*

$–$$$ 🖭 **Glenora Inn & Distillery.** North America's only single-malt-whiskey distillery adjoins this friendly inn. Here you can sample a "wee dram" of the inn's own whiskey—Glen Breton Rare. Even if you don't stay overnight, you can take a tour of the distillery and museum, enjoy fine cuisine and traditional Cape Breton music, and tour the courtyard gardens. MacLellan's Brook runs through the property. Rooms in the inn overlook the courtyard; chalets have two-person whirlpool baths, woodstoves, and kitchens. ✉ *Box 181, Hwy. 19, Glenville B0E 1X0* ☎ *902/ 258–2662 or 800/839–0491* 🖶 *902/258–3572* ⊕ *www.glenoradistillery. com* ↩ *9 rooms, 6 chalets* ♿ *Restaurant, some kitchens, cable TV, pub, shop, convention center* ☰ *AE, D, MC, V* ⊘ *Closed Nov.–June.*

Nightlife

To sample Cape Breton's famous music scene and grab a quick bite or a cool ale, drop into the **Red Shoe Pub** (✉ Main St. [Rte. 19] ☎ 902/ 945–2626 ⊕ www.redshoepub.com). Once home to dry goods and groceries, it's music and conversation you find now in this former general store. Musicians sometimes make impromptu visits; there's scheduled talent as well.

Mabou Coal Mines

10 km (6 mi) northwest of Mabou.

This quiet area is a place so hauntingly exquisite that you expect to meet the *sidhe,* the Scottish fairies, capering on the hillsides. Within the hills of Mabou Mines is some of the finest hiking in the province, and above the land fly bald eagles, plentiful in this region. Inquire locally or at the tourist office in Margaree Forks for information about trails.

Outdoors & Sports

FodorsChoice
★
Gaelic and English names on wooden signs mark the way for 15 **hiking trails** on more than 20 square km (7.5 square mi) of coastal wilderness in Cape Mabou. All are as natural as possible. Some follow old cart tracks that connected pioneer settlements. Gaelic-speaking immigrants from Scotland settled this region of plunging cliffs, isolated beaches, rising mountains, glens, meadows and hardwood forests. Trail maps are available by mail from the **Cape Mabou Trail Club** (⊠ Inverness, B0E 1N0). Include $2 and a self-addressed, stamped envelope.

en route
Take Highway 19 to Highway 219 and follow the coast to the rural area of **Chimney Corner.** A nearby beach has "sonorous sands"—when you step on or drag a foot through it the sand, it squeaks and moans.

Margaree Harbour

④④ *33 km (20 mi) north of Mabou.*

The Ceilidh Trail joins the Cabot Trail at Margaree Harbour at the mouth of the Margaree River, a famous salmon-fishing and fly-fishing stream and a favorite canoe route. Exhibits at the **Margaree Salmon Museum,** in a former schoolhouse, include fishing tackle, photographs, and other memorabilia related to salmon angling on the Margaree River. ⊠ *60 E. Big Intervale Rd., North East Margaree* ☎ *902/248–2848* ✉ *$1* ☉ *Mid-June–mid-Oct., daily 9–5.*

Where to Stay & Eat

$–$$$ ✕⊞ **Normaway Inn.** Nestled on 250 acres in the hills of the Margaree Valley at the beginning of the Cabot Trail, this secluded 1920s inn has distinctive rooms and cabins, most with woodstoves and screened porches. Nightly entertainment might be a film or traditional music, and there are weekly square dances in the Barn. The restaurant ($$$$) is known for its country cuisine, particularly the vegetable chowders and fresh seafood ragout. Cabins and the dining room are available off-season by arrangement. ⊠ *Box 101, 691 Egypt Rd., 3 km (2 mi) off Cabot Trail, B0E 2C0* ☎ *902/248–2987 or 800/565–9463* ⊟ *902/248–2600* ⊕ *www. normaway.com* ✎ *12 rooms, 17 cabins* ⚫ *Restaurant, some in-room hot tubs, tennis court, hiking; no room TVs* ⊟ *MC, V* ☉ *Closed mid-Oct.–mid-June.*

Chéticamp

④⑤ *26 km (16 mi) north of Margaree Harbour.*

This Acadian community has the best harbor and the largest settlement on this shore. Even after 200 years of history, Chéticamp's Acadian culture and traditions are still very much a way of life in the region. Nestled on one side by the mountains and on the other by the sea, the community offers the pride, traditions, and warmth of Acadian hospitality. Its tall silver steeple towers over the village, which stands exposed on a wide lip of flat land below a range of bald green hills. Behind these hills lies the high plateau of the Cape Breton Highlands. The area is known for its *suêtes,* strong southeast winds of 120 km–130 km (75 mi–80 mi) per hour that may develop into a force of up to 200 km (125 mi) per hour. They have been known to blow the roofs off buildings.

Chéticamp is famous for its hooked rugs, available at many local gift shops. The **Dr. Elizabeth LeFort Gallery and Museum: Les Trois Pignons** displays artifacts, fine hooked rugs, and tapestries. Dr. LeFort created more than 300 tapestries, several of which have been hung in such well-known places as the Vatican, the White House, and Buckingham Palace. The museum is also an Acadian cultural and genealogical information center. ⊠ *Box 430, 15584 Cabot Trail, B0E 1H0* ☎ *902/224–2642* 🖷 *902/224–1579* ⊕ *www.cheticampns.com* 🎟 *$3.50* ☉ *July–Aug., daily 8–7; Sept.–June, daily 9–5.*

La Pirogue Museum. A dazzling collection of Gilbert van Ryekevorsel's underwater photography, traditional rag rugs, an Acadian homestead replica, fishery displays, and artifacts from the Charles Robin store are found in the Chéticamp Development Commission's three-level waterfront museum. This is an ideal place to learn about the community's ties to fishing. A geothermal heat pump extracts saltwater from the sea to heat and cool the building. ⊠ *15359 Cabot Trail* ☎ *902/224–3349* 🖷 *902/224–2801* ⊕ *cbmuseums.tripod.com/cape_breton_museums/ id27.html* 🎟 *$5* ☉ *May–Sept., daily 9–9; Oct.–Apr., daily 9–5.*

Where to Stay & Eat

$$–$$$ ✕ **Le Gabriel.** You can't miss Le Gabriel, with its large lighthouse entranceway. The casual tavern offers simple but good fresh fish dinners and traditional Acadian dishes, such as meat pie, potato pancakes, fish cakes, or *fricot* (a hearty stew with potatoes, pork bits, chives, and beef or chicken). Snow crab and lobster specials are available in season. At night things heat up with live music and dancing in the lounge. The dining room is smoke-free and wheelchair-accessible. ⊠ *15424 Cabot Trail* ☎ *902/224–3685* ⊕ *www.legabriel.com* 🚻 *AE, MC, V* ☉ *Dining room closed late Oct.–Apr.*

$–$$ ✕ **Harbour Restaurant and Bar.** An enviable ocean view adds to the ambience at this popular restaurant where you can sample seafood, pasta, "sterling silver" beef, and homemade desserts. The bar serves a variety of cocktails, single-malt scotches, and wines. For a little exercise after your meal, stroll on the boardwalk behind the restaurant. It's a pleasant walk, connecting shops, a tourist information booth, and whale-watching excursions. ⊠ *15299 Cabot Trail* ☎ *902/224–2042* 🖷 *902/224– 1515* 🚻 *AE, MC, V* ☉ *Closed mid-Oct.–mid-May.*

$$–$$$$ 🏨 **Cabot Trail Sea & Golf Chalets.** Next to Le Portage Golf Course and overlooking the ocean, these chalets are ideal for families and golfers. One- and two-bedroom chalets have covered decks with gas barbecues. Some units have fireplaces. There is a play area for children, and cribs, cots, and high chairs are available. The three-bedroom country suite has a washer, dryer, and dishwasher. ⊠ *Box 8, 71 Fraser Doucet La., B0E 1H0* ☎ *902/224–1777 or 877/224–1777* 🖷 *902/224–1999* ⊕ *www. seagolfchalets.com* 🛏 *13 chalets* ⚅ *Some in-room hot tubs, some kitchens, cable TV, 18-hole golf course, playground, business services* 🚻 *AE, D, MC, V* ☉ *Closed mid-Oct.–mid-May.*

¢–$ 🏨 **Chéticamp Outfitters' Inn B&B.** The clean and cozy rooms at this homey inn, operated by a bilingual family, overlook the ocean, mountains, and valley. The furniture includes homemade wooden pieces, paintings by the innkeeper, and quilts. Fantastic blueberry muffins are a highlight of the home-cooked breakfast. Guide and outfitting services are available.

✉ *13938 Cabot Trail, B0E 1H0* 🖷🖷 *902/224–2776* ⊕ *www.cheticampns. com/cheticampoutfitters* ⛵ *6 rooms, 3 with bath* ♿ *Some microwaves, some refrigerators, some in-room VCRs, fishing* ▤ *AE, MC, V* ⊗ *Closed mid-Dec.–Apr. 1* ⅋ *BP.*

Sports & the Outdoors

Chéticamp is known for its whale-watching cruises, which depart from the government wharf twice daily in May and June, increasing in July and August to three times daily. **Whale Cruisers Ltd.** (☎ 902/224–3376 or 800/813–3376 ⊕ www.whalecruises.com) is a reliable charter company and was the first whale-watching company in Nova Scotia. Tours run two or three times daily, May 15–October 15, and are $29. Expect to see minke, pilot, and fin whales in their natural environment; seabird and bald-eagle sightings are also common.

Cape Breton Highlands National Park

Fodor'sChoice
★

5 km (3 mi) north of Chéticamp; 108 km (67 mi) north of Ingonish.

A 950-square-km (366-square-mi) wilderness of wooded valleys, plateau barrens, and steep cliffs, this park stretches across northern Cape Breton from the gulf shore to the Atlantic. The highway through the park (world-renowned Cabot Trail) is magnificent. It rises to the tops of the coastal mountains and descends through scenic switchbacks to the sea. In fact, the road has been compared to a 298-km (185-mi) roller-coaster ride, stretching from Chéticamp to Ingonish. Good brakes and attentive driving are advised. Pull-offs provide photo opportunities, and exhibits explain the land and history. For wildlife watchers there's much to see, including moose, eagles, deer, bears, foxes, and bobcats. Your chances of seeing wildlife are better if you venture off the main road and hike one of the trails at dusk or dawn. Note that it is illegal to feed or approach any animal in the park. Always take care to observe the animals from a safe distance; in particular, you should exercise caution driving in the moose zones, marked by signs on the highway. Moose sometimes claim the road as their own by standing in the middle of it. Hitting one can be damaging to both you and the animal.

High-altitude bogs are home to delightful wild orchids and other unique flora and fauna. If you plan to hike or camp in the park, stop at the Chéticamp Information Centre for advice and necessary permits. Inside the center you can buy *Walking in the Highlands,* a guide to the park's 25 hiking trails, from the nature bookstore Les Amis du Plein Air. Trails range from easy 20-minute strolls to tough overnight treks. Five hundred fifty campsites in six spectacular locations provide a variety of facilities and services—some are even equipped with showers, cooking shelters, and full hookups. A park permit or pass is required for sightseeing along sections of the Cabot Trail highway when within the national park and for use of such facilities as exhibits, hiking trails, picnic areas, and washrooms. Seasonal and national park passes are available; there are additional fees for camping and fishing. ✉ *Entrances on Cabot Trail near Chéticamp and Ingonish* ☎ *902/224–2306, 902/224–3814 bookstore* ⊕ *www.pc. gc.ca* 🎫 *$3.50* ⊗ *May–Oct., daily dawn–dusk.*

For those who prefer to stay on dry land to observe sea life, stop by the **Whale Interpretive Centre.** Using zoom scopes on the whale-spotting deck, you may catch a close-up glimpse of many different species of whales that are often frolicking just off shore from the center. Inside the modern structure, exhibits and models explain the unique world of whales. ✉ *104 Harbour Rd., Pleasant Bay* ☎ *902/224–1411* 🖷 *902/224–1751* ⊕ *www.whalecentre.ca* 🎫 *$4.50* ⊗ *Mid-May–Oct.*

GAMPO ABBEY – The most northerly tip of the island is not part of the national park; a spur road (take a left at Pleasant Bay) creeps along the cliffs to Red River, beyond which, on a broad flat bench of land high above the sea, is this Tibetan Buddhist monastery. It's the only residential monastery in North America. It's possible to tour the abbey when it's not in retreat. The only way to know whether a tour is available is to drive to the abbey and check the sign at the gate. If the abbey is closed, you can continue down the road for about a ½ km (¼ mi) to visit the Stupa, a large and elaborate shrine.

Sports & the Outdoors

All whale-watching tours have a money-back guarantee if you don't see a whale. You may see pilot, finback, humpback, or minke whales on **Captain Mark's Whale and Seal Cruise** (☎ 902/224–1316 or 888/754–5112 ⊕ www.whaleandsealcruise.com). If you don't see them, you may at least be able to hear them with the help of an onboard hydrophone. It's also possible to catch sight of dolphins, seals, bald eagles, moose, black bears, and numerous seabirds. Cruises allow for exploration of sea caves, waterfalls, and rock and cliff formations along a remote stretch of unspoiled Cape Breton coastline. Tours are May 15 through October 15 and cost $25. With **Highland Coastal Nature Tours** (☎ 902/224–1816) you set sail aboard a Cape Islander fishing vessel. The owner and captain earned his living as a lobster, crab, cod, and mackeral fisherman. Tours ($25) are August 1–September 30. **Pleasant Bay Fiddlin' Whale Tours** (☎ 902/224–2424 or 866/688–2424) throws a "kitchen party" on the water. Enjoy live traditional Cape Breton fiddling on a covered boat while cruising the seas. Tours ($30) are June 1 through October 1. **Wesley's Whale Watching** (☎ 902/224–1919 or 866/999–4253) leads two-hour trips in Cape Island boats or Zodiacs May 15–October 15 to see whales, dolphins, seals, and scenery. Tours are $24.

Bay St. Lawrence

76 km (47 mi) north of Chéticamp.

The charming fishing village of Bay St. Lawrence is nestled in a bowl-shape valley around a harbor pond. You can hike along the shore to the east and the Money Point Lighthouse, or find a quiet corner of the shoreline for a wilderness campsite. A "feed of lobster" can be purchased from the fisher who brought it up from the sea an hour before.

Cabot's Landing Provincial Park (✉ Bay St. Lawrence Rd., 2 km [1 mi] north of Four Mile Beach Inn ☎ no phone) is a must-visit for views, walking, and a sandy beach enclosed by rugged mountains. It's a perfect spot for a picnic. Admission to the park is free. The park is open daily 9–9 mid-May–mid-October. On-site is a National Historic Site cairn of Italian explorer John Cabot.

MEAT COVE – Named for the moose and (now absent) caribou that roamed the highlands and once supplied protein for passing sailing vessels, Meat Cove feels like the end of the earth. It lies at the end of a daunting 12-km (7-mi) mostly unpaved road along a precipitous cliff marked by sudden switchbacks. It's spectacular. To get here, leave the Cabot Trail at Cape North on the Bay St. Lawrence Road. At the foot of the hill leading into St. Margaret's, turn left and follow the sign to Capstick; that road leads to Meat Cove.

Where to Stay

Four Mile Beach Inn. The view of Aspy Bay and the ridge of the high-land mountains is spectacular from this large, white historic house near Cabot's Landing. The hosts know the Cabot Trail and can provide personalized day planning. Canoeing and kayaking are possible from the small dock on the property, and bike rentals are available. Rooms are clean and have a simple country look. The suites have a private entrance and a deck. An old-fashioned general store sells ice cream and souvenirs. ⊠ *R.R. 1, Cape North B0C 1G0* ☎ *902/383–2282 or 888/503–5551* 🖷 *902/564–5877* ⊕ *www.fourmilebeachinn.com* ➥ *5 rooms, 2 suites* ⚴ *Some kitchens, dock, boating, bicycles* ⊟ *MC, V* ☉ *Closed mid-Oct.–May* ⫙ *CP.*

CAMPING ⚠ **Meat Cove Campground.** High on a cliff overlooking the ocean, this campground attracts an adventurous crowd and is ideal for hiking, mountain biking, ocean swimming, whale-watching, and nature walks. The campground has a boat launch. Whale-watching tours are available. ⚴ *Flush toilets, showers, fire pits, swimming (ocean)* ⊠ *Take Bay St. Lawrence Rd. to foot of hill leading into St. Margaret's, turn left, and follow sign to Capstick; that road leads to Meat Cove* ⫐ *Meat Cove, Cape Breton B0C 1E0* ☎ *902/383–2379* ➥ *25 tent sites* ⛁ *$18* ⊟ *No credit cards* ☉ *Open June–Oct.*

Sports & the Outdoors

Capt. Cox's Whale Watch (☎ 902/383–2981 or 888/346–5556 ⊕ www.aco.ca/captcox) gives several tours daily—weather permitting—July through August. The cost is $25. If you don't see a whale, you get another free trip.

Ingonish

46 *113 km (70 mi) northeast of Chéticamp; 37 km (23 mi) south of Bay St. Lawrence.*

Ingonish, one of the leading holiday destinations on the island, is actually several villages—Ingonish Centre, Ingonish Beach, South Ingonish Harbour, and Ingonish Ferry—on two bays, divided by a long narrow peninsula called Middle Head. Each bay has a sandy beach.

off the
beaten
path

BIRD ISLANDS – The small islands on the far side of the mouth of St. Ann's Bay are the Bird Islands, breeding grounds for Atlantic puffins, black guillemots, razor-billed auks, and cormorants. From Baddeck, take Highway 105 east 35 km (22 mi) to Exit 14, then left 6 km (4 mi) to the Bird Island Boat Tour. These tours are offered several times daily mid-May–mid-September from **Bird Island Boat Tour** (⊠ 1672 Old Rte. 5, Big Bras d'Or ☎ 902/674–2384 or 800/661–6680 ⊕ www.birdisland.net). Landing by private boat is forbidden.

Where to Stay & Eat

✕ **Keltic Lodge.** Spread across cliffs overlooking the ocean, the provincially owned Keltic Lodge is on the Cabot Trail in Cape Breton Highlands National Park and has stunning views of Cape Smokey and the surrounding highlands. Rooms in the main lodge have charm and character, while rooms at the Inn at Keltic are larger and air-conditioned. Cottages and suites are also available. Activities include golfing on the world-class Highlands Links. Seafood stars in the Purple Thistle Dining Room ($$$). Three public tennis courts are within walking distance. ⊠ *Middle Head Peninsula, Ingonish Beach B0C 1L0* ☎ *902/285–2880 or 800/565–0444* ⊕ *www.signatureresorts.com* ➥ *72 rooms, 2 suites,*

10 cottages ♿ 2 restaurants, fans, golf privileges, pro shop, pool, beach, bicycles, hiking, shop, laundry service, meeting rooms; no a/c in some rooms ⊟ AE, D, DC, MC, V ☉ Closed late Oct.–mid-May ⦿ MAP.

$–$$$$ ⊡ **Glenghorm Beach Resort.** Swim in the ocean, hike, bike, and kayak while staying at this resort's motor inn, cottages, or beach-house suites. Pick up locally made souvenirs and handicrafts at the gift shop. ⊠ Box 39, Cabot Trail, B0C 1K0 ☎ 902/285–2049 or 800/565–5660 🖷 902/285–2395 ⊕ www.capebretonresorts.com ⇨ 70 rooms, 10 suites, 10 cottages ♿ Restaurant, pool, gym, beach, pub, shop, meeting rooms ⊟ D, DC, MC, V ☉ Closed Nov.–Apr.

$–$$ ⊡ **Castle Rock Country Inn.** Surrounded by an idyllic setting of mountains and ocean and offering the tranquillity of a lounge area, the Castle Rock provides an excellent environment for contemplation and relaxation. The spacious guest rooms have queen beds, and most have an additional sofa bed; some have ocean views. The Georgian-style inn is right on the Cabot Trail in Ingonish Ferry. ⊠ 39339 Cabot Trail, B0C 1L0 ☎ 902/285–2700 or 888/884–7625 🖷 902/285–2525 ⊕ www.ingonish.com/castlerock ⇨ 16 rooms ♿ Dining room, cable TV ⊟ AE, MC, V.

Outdoors & Sports

Perennially ranked as one of Canada's top courses, **Highland Links** (⊠ Cape Breton Highlands National Park ☎ 902/285-2600 or 800/441-1118) has abundant natural scenery in the form of mountains and sea, not to mention great golfing. It's open daily, from mid-May until the end of October 6 AM–8 PM, weather-permitting. A round of 18 holes is $83.

Englishtown

65 km (40 mi) south of Ingonish on Hwy. 312.

A short (five-minute) ferry ride heads from Jersey Cove across St. Ann's Bay to Englishtown, home of the celebrated Cape Breton Giant, Angus MacAskill. Ferries run 24 hours a day; the fare is $5 per car.

The **Giant MacAskill Museum** holds artifacts of the 7-foot, 9-inch man who traveled with P. T. Barnum's troupe in the 1800s. His remains are buried in the local cemetery nearby. ⊠ Hwy. 312 ☎ 902/929–2875 ⊡ $2 ☉ Mid-June–mid-Sept., daily 9–6.

South Gut St. Ann's

10 km (6 mi) west of Englishtown.

Settled by the Highland Scots, South Gut St. Ann's is home to North America's only Gaelic College, called—Gaelic College. From it you can follow the Cabot Trail as it meanders along the hills that rim St. Ann's Bay. The 30-km (19-mi) stretch between St. Ann's and Indian Brook is home to a collection of fine crafts shops.

The **Great Hall of the Clans** depicts Scottish history and has an account of the Great Migration, the exodus of Scottish people for the New World in the late 18th and early 19th centuries. The college offers courses in Gaelic language and literature, Scottish music and dancing, weaving, and other Scottish arts. There's also a Scottish gift shop. ⊠ Gaelic College, 51779 Cabot Trail, Exit 11 off Hwy. 105 ☎ 902/295–3411 ⊕ www.gaeliccollege.edu ⊡ $2.50 ☉ Mid-June–late Sept., daily 9–5.

Baddeck

47 20 km (12 mi) south of South Gut St. Ann's.

Baddeck, the most highly developed tourist center on Cape Breton, has more than 1,000 motel beds, a golf course, fine gift shops, and many restaurants. This was also the summer home of Alexander Graham Bell until he died here at the age of 75. The annual **regatta** of the Bras d'Or Yacht Club is held the first week of August. Sailing tours and charters are available, as are bus tours along the Cabot Trail. On the waterfront, check out the **Water's Edge Gallery,** a treasure trove of original works from Cape Breton and Maritime artists.

In summer a free passenger ferry shuttles between the government wharf and the sandy **Kidston Island Beach,** by the lighthouse.

The **Celtic Colours International Festival** (☎ 902/562–6700 or 877/285–2321 ⊕ www.celtic-colours.com) takes place during 10 days spanning the second and third weekends in October. It draws the world's best Celtic performers at the height of autumn splendor. International artists travel from Celtic countries around the world, and homegrown talent shines in 44-plus performances in over 30 communities scattered around the island. The cost for each performance is $15–$25. Workshops and seminars covering all aspects of Gaelic language, lore, history, crafts, and culture fill the festival days.

★ ℭ The **Alexander Graham Bell National Historic Site of Canada** explores Bell's inventions. Experiments, kite making, and other hands-on activities are designed for children. From films, artifacts, and photographs, you learn how ideas led Bell to create man-carrying kites, airplanes, and a marine record-setting hydrofoil boat. The site has reduced services from the end of October through May. ✉ *Chebucto St.* ☎ *902/295–2069* ⊕*www.pc.gc.ca* ✑*$5.75* ☉ *July–mid-Oct., daily 8:30–6; mid-Oct.–May, daily 9–5; June, daily 9–6.*

At the **Wagmatcook Culture & Heritage Centre** the ancient history and rich traditions of the native Mi'Kmaq are demonstrated. Mi'Kmaq guides provide interpretations and cultural entertainment. The on-site restaurant highlights traditional foods like moose and eel, as well as more contemporary choices. The crafts shop has local native products. ✉ *Wagmatcook First Nation, Rte. 105, 16 km (10 mi) west of Baddeck* ☎ *902/295–2999* ✑ *$2* ☉ *Mid-May–Oct.*

Where to Stay & Eat

$$–$$$ ✕**Baddeck Lobster Suppers.** For lobsters cooked fresh right as you come in the door, try this restaurant in a former legion hall. During busy times you may have to wait for a table. Your entrée options are ham salad plate, cold poached salmon, hot planked salmon, and lobster. Each comes with mussels, chowder, dessert, beverage, and homemade buns and biscuits. At lunch the menu is considerably cheaper and includes a lobster roll platter, chowder, mussels, and homemade beef soup. There are a bar and a gift shop. ✉ *17 Ross St.* ☎ *902/295–3307, 902/295–3424 mid-Oct.–mid-June* ☒ *902/295–3424* ▤ *MC, V* ☉ *Closed mid-Oct.–mid-June.*

$–$$$$ ✕▦ **Inverary Resort.** On the shores of the magnificent Bras d'Or Lake, this resort has stunning views and lots of activities. You can choose from cottage suites, modern hotel units, or the elegant 100-year-old main lodge; some rooms have fireplaces. There are boating and swimming in close proximity to the village, but the resort remains tranquil. Dining choices are the casual Lakeside Café and the elegant main dining room ($$–$$$). ✉ *Box 190, Hwy. 205 and Shore Rd., B0E 1B0* ☎ *902/295–3500 or 800/565–5660* ☒ *902/295–3527* ⊕ *www.capebretonresorts.com/ inverary.asp* ⇌ *129 rooms, 9 cottages* ♻*Restaurant, café, 2 tennis courts, indoor pool, gym, sauna, spa, snorkeling, boating, bicycles, fishing, pub, playground* ▤ *AE, D, DC, MC, V.*

$$–$$$$ ▦ **Auberge Gisele's Inn.** An inn and motel share lovely landscaped flower gardens and overlook the Bras d'Or Lake. The atmosphere is one of taste-

ful hospitality. Some rooms have fireplaces. The chef prepares breakfast, lunch by reservation, and dinner in the dining room. Deal a hand in the card-playing room or enjoy a cocktail in the smoke-free lounge, outdoor patio, and art gallery. The executive suites have whirlpool tubs and gas fireplaces. Rooms are modern and deluxe. Language assistance is available in French, German, and Ukrainian. ⊠ *387 Shore Rd., B0E 1B0* ☎ *902/295–2849* 🖷 *902/295–2033* ⊕ *www.giseles.com* ⇆ *75 rooms, 3 suites* ♨ *Dining room, in-room data ports, sauna, bicycles, laundry facilities* ▤ *D, MC, V* ☉ *Closed late Oct.–early May.*

$–$$ 🏨 **Duffus House.** Facing the harbor, this quiet inn is furnished with antiques and has cozy sitting rooms and a secluded, well-tended garden. The Continental breakfast is substantial. An extensive library, English gardens, verandas, and a private waterfront and dock add to the charm. The inn is close to all village amenities. ⊠ *Box 427, 108 Water St., B0E 1B0* ☎ *902/295–2172* ⊕ *www.baddeck.com/duffushouse* ⇆ *4 rooms, 3 suites* ♨ *Dock, library; no smoking* ▤ *V* ☉ *Closed mid-Oct.–end of May* ⦿ *CP.*

¢–$ 🏨 **Bain's Heritage House B&B.** In the center of Baddeck sits this tastefully appointed historic home built in the 1850s. On cooler evenings you can relax in front of the fire in the sitting room. ⊠ *121 Twining St., B0E 1B0* ☎ *902/295–1069* ⇆ *3 rooms, 1 with bath* ♨ *Cable TV* ▤ *MC, V* ⦿ *BP.*

Sports & the Outdoors

The **Bell Bay Golf Club** (⊠ Shore Rd. ☎ 902/295–1333 or 800/565–3077 ⊕ www.bellbaygolfclub.com) has panoramic views from almost every hole on its par-72, 18-hole course. Bell Bay has the largest practice facilities in Atlantic Canada. The greens fee is $79.

Iona

48 *56 km (35 mi) south of Baddeck.*

Iona, where some residents still speak Gaelic, is the site of a living-history museum. To get here from Baddeck, take Trans-Canada Highway 105 to Exit 6, which leads to Little Narrows, where you can take a ferry Fodor'sChoice to the Washabuck Peninsula. The **Highland Village Museum** is set high ★ on a mountainside, with a spectacular view of Bras d'Or Lake and the narrow Barra Strait. The village's 10 historic buildings were assembled from all over Cape Breton to depict the Highland Scots' way of life from their origins in the Hebrides to the present day. Among the staff at this museum are a smith in the blacksmith shop and a clerk in the store. The complex also houses Roots Cape Breton, a genealogy and family-history center for Cape Breton Island. ⊠ *Hwy. 223* ☎ *902/725–2272* ⊕ *www.highlandvillage.museum.gov.ns.ca* 🎟 *$7* ☉ *Mid-May–mid-Oct., daily 9–6.*

Where to Stay & Eat

$ ✕🏨 **Highland Heights Inn.** The rural surroundings, the Scottish home-style cooking served near the restaurant's huge stone fireplace, and the view of the lake substitute nicely for the Scottish Highlands. The inn is on a hillside beside the Nova Scotia Highland Village, overlooking Iona. The salmon (or any fish in season), fresh-baked oatcakes, and homemade desserts at the restaurant ($–$$) are good choices. The staff at the inn, part of Cape Breton Resorts, plans adventures such as whale-watching, golf, and sailing. ⊠ *4115 Hwy. 223, B2C 1A3* ☎ *902/ 725–2360 or 800/660–8122* 🖷 *902/725–2800* ⊕ *www. highlandheightsinn.com* ⇆ *32 rooms* ♨ *Restaurant, no-smoking rooms* ▤ *D, MC, V* ☉ *Closed mid-Oct.–mid-May.*

en route The Barra Strait Bridge joins Iona to Grand Narrows. The East Bay route runs through the Mi'Kmaq village of **Eskasoni**, the largest native community in the province. This friendly village has a fascinating cultural heritage.

Sydney

④ *60 km (37 mi) northeast of Iona.*

The heart of Nova Scotia's second-largest urban cluster, this city encompasses villages, unorganized districts, and a half-dozen towns—most of which sprang up around the coal mines, which fed the steel plant at Sydney. These are warmhearted, interesting communities with a diverse ethnic population that includes Ukrainians, Welsh, Poles, Lebanese, West Indians, and Italians. Most residents are descendants of the miners and steelworkers who arrived a century ago, when the area was booming.

Sydney has the island's only real airport, its only university, and a lively entertainment scene that specializes in Cape Breton music. It is also a departure point—fast ferries leave from North Sydney for Newfoundland, and scheduled air service to Newfoundland and the French islands of St-Pierre and Miquelon departs from Sydney Airport. Cruise ships have been a familiar sight since 1962.

Where to Stay & Eat

$$–$$$ ✕ **Governor's Restaurant.** Sydney's first mayor, Walter Crowe, once lived in this Victorian home, built in the late 1800s. The restaurant, with hardwood floors, a fireplace, and high ceilings, is known for its seafood and steaks, though it has a full menu. Both the restaurant and Bunker's Peanut Bar upstairs have two large patios that overlook Sydney Harbour. Desserts are homemade. ✉ *233 Esplanade B1P 1A6* ☎ *902/562–7646* ☐ *AE, D, MC, V.*

$$–$$$$ ✕▥ **Gowrie House.** This unexpected jewel between North Sydney and
Fodor'sChoice Sydney Mines, minutes from the Newfoundland ferry, is shaded by
★ towering trees on grounds filled with gardens and flowering shrubs. Cherry trees supply the main ingredient for chilled black-cherry soup served in what some consider Nova Scotia's finest restaurant ($$$$). Antiques, fine art, and exquisite china add to the elegance. The main house has six rooms; the secluded garden house four more; and the caretaker's cottage provides deluxe private accommodation. Whether you stay overnight or are a guest for dinner only, dinner reservations are essential. ✉ *840 Shore Rd., Sydney Mines B1V 1A6* ☎ *902/544–1050 or 800/372–1115* ⊕ *www.gowriehouse.com* ➲ *11 rooms* ⚘ *Restaurant, cable TV* ☐ *AE, MC, V* ⦿ *BP.*

$$ ▥ **Delta Sydney.** This hotel is on the harbor, beside the yacht club and close to the center of town. Guest rooms are attractive and have harbor views. The restaurant specializes in seafood and Continental cuisine. ✉ *300 Esplanade, B1P 1A7* ☎ *902/562–7500 or 800/565–1001* ☐ *902/562–3023* ⊕ *www.deltasydney.com* ➲ *152 rooms* ⚘ *Restaurant, cable TV with movies and video games, indoor pool, gym, sauna, lounge* ☐ *AE, DC, MC, V.*

Nightlife & the Arts

Many fiddlers appear at the weeklong **Big Pond Festival** (✉ Rte. 4, 1 km [½ mi] east of Rita's Tea Room ☎ 902/828–2667) in mid-July. At the **Casino Nova Scotia** (✉ 525 George St. ☎ 902/563–7777) you can try the slot machines, roulette, or gaming tables or enjoy live entertainment. The **University College of Cape Breton** (✉ 1250 Grand Lake Rd. ☎ 902/ 539–5300) has facilities open to the public, such as the Boardmore Playhouse and the island's only public art gallery.

Glace Bay

50 *21 km (13 mi) east of Sydney.*

★ A coal-mining town and fishing port, Glace Bay has a rich history of industrial struggle. The **Glace Bay Miners' Museum** houses exhibits and artifacts illustrating the hard life of early miners in Cape Breton's undersea collieries (mines). Former miners guide you down into the damp recesses of the mine and tell stories of working all day where the sun never shines. ✉ *42 Birkley St., Quarry Point* ☏ *902/849–4522* ⊕ *www.minersmuseum. com* ⌨ *Museum $4.50, museum and mine tour $8* ⊗ *June 2–Sept. 1, Wed.–Mon. 10–6, Tues. 10–7; Sept. 2–June 1, weekdays 9–4.*

The **Marconi National Historic Site of Canada** commemorates the site at Table Head where in 1902 Guglielmo Marconi built four tall wooden towers and beamed the first official wireless messages across the Atlantic Ocean. An interpretive trail leads to the foundations of the original towers and transmitter buildings. The visitor center has large models of the towers as well as artifacts and photographs chronicling the radio pioneer's life and work. ✉ *Timmerman St. (Hwy. 255)* ☏ *902/842–2530* ⊕ *www.pc.gc.ca* ⌨ *Free* ⊗ *June–mid-Sept., daily 10–6.*

Nightlife & the Arts

Glace Bay's grand Victorian-style **Savoy Theatre** (✉ 116 Commercial St. ☏ 902/842–1577 ⊕ www.savoytheatre.com), built in 1927, is home to a variety of live drama, comedy, and music performances.

Louisbourg

51 *55 km (34 mi) south of Glace Bay.*

★ ♺ Though best known as the home of the largest historical reconstruction in North America, Louisbourg is also an important fishing community with a lovely harbor front. The **Fortress of Louisbourg National Historic Site of Canada** may be the most remarkable site in Cape Breton. After the French were forced out of mainland Nova Scotia in 1713, they established their headquarters here in a walled and fortified town on a low point of land at the mouth of Louisbourg Harbour. The fortress was twice captured, once by New Englanders and once by the British; after the second siege, in 1758, it was razed. Its capture was critical in ending the French empire in America. A quarter of the town has been rebuilt on its original foundations to look just as it did in 1744, before the first siege. Costumed actors re-create the activities of the original inhabitants; you can watch a military drill, see nails and lace being made, and eat food prepared from 18th-century recipes in the town's three inns. Plan on spending at least a day. Louisbourg tends to be chilly, so pack a warm sweater or windbreaker. Walking tours are given only October 16–31 and in May. ✉ *259 Parks Service Rd.* ☏ *902/733–2280 or 888/ 773–8888* ⊕ *www.pc.gc.ca* ⌨ *$13.50* ⊗ *June and Sept., daily 9:30–5; July–Aug., daily 9–6; Oct. 1–15 limited service.*

At the **Sydney and Louisbourg Railway Museum** a restored 1895 railroad station exhibits the history of the S&L Railway, railroad technology, and marine shipping. The rolling stock includes a baggage car, coach, and caboose. ✉ *7336 Main St.* ☏ *902/733–2720* ⌨ *Free* ⊗ *Mid-May–June and Sept.–mid-Oct., daily 9–5; July–Aug., daily 8–8.*

Both live theater performances and traditional Cape Breton music are served up at the **Louisbourg Playhouse,** a 17th-century–style theater, which was originally constructed as part of a Disney movie set. ✉ *11 Aberdeen St.* ☏ *902/733–2996 or 888/733–2787* ⊕ *www.gdlewis. ednet.ns.ca/lsbrg/playentr.html* ⊗ *Mid-June–Oct.*

Where to Stay & Eat

$$–$$$$ ✕ **Grubstake Restaurant.** Coquilles St. Jacques, chateaubriand, and stuffed sole are popular menu items at this 120-seat restaurant where elegant, family, and country cuisine are all wrapped into one. One part of the building is more than 100 years old and houses some antiques. Desserts are made on-site. ✉ 7499 Main St., B1C 1H8 ☎ 902/733–2308 ⊕ www. c-level.com/grubstake ☱ AE, MC, V ✹ Closed Nov.–mid-June.

$–$$ ▥ **Cranberry Cove Inn.** This fully renovated home from the early 1900s is within walking distance of the Fortress of Louisbourg National Historic Park. Inquire about the theme guest rooms, some of which have gas fireplaces. Each room has a different theme, ranging from the captain's den to the secret garden. The inn has many antiques and a Victorian decor. Rooms are available off-season by arrangement. ✉ 12 Wolfe St., B1C 2J2 ☎ 902/733–2171 or 800/929–0222 ☐ 902/733–2171 ⊕ www.louisbourg.com/cranberrycove ➴ 7 rooms ⌕ Some in-room hot tubs; no room phones, no smoking ☱ MC, V ⑩ CP.

$–$$ ▥ **Louisbourg Harbour Inn.** In the center of the community, overlooking a fishing wharf, this renovated century-old sea captain's house affords ocean views from most rooms and balconies. All rooms have hardwood floors, high ceilings, and a queen-size bed. Most rooms and balconies have views of the ocean and Fortress Louisbourg. ✉ 9 Lower Warren St., B1C 1G6 ☎ 902/733–3222 or 888/888–8466 ⊕ www.louisbourg. com/louisbourgharbourinn ➴ 8 rooms ⌕ Some in-room hot tubs ☱ MC, V ✹ Closed mid-Oct.–May ⑩ CP.

$–$$ ▥ **Louisbourg Heritage House B&B.** Built in 1887, this former Victorian rectory also housed a museum–art gallery and then town offices before opening as a B&B in July 2002. Original wood floors, high ceilings, and private balconies in each room add charm. In the town's center, the inn is nestled between two churches and is close to restaurants and the Louisbourg Playhouse. Some rooms have views of Fortress Louisbourg or the harbor. ✉ 7544 Main St., B1C 1J5 ☎ 902/733–3222 or 888/888–8466 ⊕ www.louisbourg.com/louisbourgheritagehouse ➴ 6 rooms ⌕ Some refrigerators, cable TV in 1 room ☱ MC, V ✹ Closed Nov.–June ⑩ BP.

Big Pond

⑤² 50 km (31 mi) west of Louisbourg.

This little town comprises just a few houses, and one of them is the home of singer-songwriter Rita MacNeil, who operates **Rita's Tea Room.** Originally a one-room schoolhouse, the building has been expanded to accommodate the multitude of visitors who come to sample Rita's Tea Room Blend Tea, which is served along with a fine selection of sandwiches and baked goods. You can visit a display room of Rita's awards and photographs and browse through her gift shop. ✉ Hwy. 4 ☎ 902/828–2667 ✹ June–mid-Oct., daily 9–7.

en route Highway 4 rolls along Bras d'Or Lake, sometimes by the shore and sometimes in the hills. At **St. Peter's** the Atlantic Ocean is connected with the Bras d'Or Lake by the century-old St. Peter's Canal, still used by pleasure craft and fishing vessels. From St. Peter's to Port Hawkesbury the population is largely Acadian French.

Arichat

⑤³ 62 km (38 mi) southwest of Big Pond.

The principal town of Isle Madame, Arichat is a 27-square-km (10-square-mi) island named for Madame de Maintenon, second wife of Louis

XIV. It was an important shipbuilding and trading center during the 19th century, and some fine old houses from that period still remain. The two cannons overlooking the harbor were installed after the town was sacked by John Paul Jones during the American Revolution.

To get here from Big Pond, take Highway 247 to Highway 320, which leads through Poulamon and D'Escousse and overlooks Lennox Passage, with its spangle of islands. Highway 206 meanders through the low hills to a maze of land and water at West Arichat. Together, the two routes encircle the island, meeting at Arichat. The island lends itself to biking, as most roads glide gently along the shore. A good half-day hike leads to Gros Nez, the "large nose" that juts into the sea.

One of the best ways to experience Isle Madame is by foot. Try Cape Auguet Eco-Trail, an 8-km (5-mi) hiking trail that extends from Boudreauville to Mackeral Cove on Isle Madame and follows the rocky coastline overlooking Chedabucto Bay.

Arichat was once the seat of the local Catholic diocese. **Notre Dame de l'Assumption** Church, built in 1837, still retains the grandeur of its former cathedral status. Its bishop's palace is now a law office. ✉ *2316 High Rd.* ☎ *902/226–2109* ✉ *Free* ⊗ *Dawn–dusk. Mass June–Sept., Sat. 7:30 PM and Sun. 9:30 AM.* **LeNoir Forge** (✉ Hwy. 206 off Hwy. 4 via Exit 46 to Isle Madame ☎ 902/226–9364) is a restored, French, 18th-century stone blacksmith shop open June–August, daily 9–5.

off the
beaten
path

LITTLE ANSE – With its red bluffs, cobble shores, tiny harbor, and brightly painted houses, Little Anse can be particularly attractive for artists and photographers. The town is at the southeastern tip of Isle Madame.

NOVA SCOTIA A TO Z

To research prices, get advice from other travelers, and book travel arrangements, visit www.fodors.com.

AIR TRAVEL

Air Canada, Tango (owned by Air Canada), American, Continental, Delta, and Northwest provide service to Halifax and Sydney from various cities. Air travel within the area is very limited. Air Canada provides regional service to other provinces and to Sydney, Nova Scotia. Provincial Airlines, a regional Air Canada carrier, flies between Newfoundland and Labrador and Halifax. Pan Am has service to Halifax from Bangor, Maine; Martha's Vineyard, Massachusetts; and Manchester, New Hampshire. 🛧 Airlines & Contacts **American Airlines** ☎ 800/433–7300 ⊕ www.aa.com. **Air Canada** ☎ 888/247–2262 ⊕ www.aircanada.ca. **Continental** ☎ 800/523–3273 ⊕ www. continental.com. **Delta Airlines** ☎ 800/221–1212 ⊕ www.delta.com. **Northwest** ☎ 800/ 225–2525 ⊕ www.nwa.com. **Pan Am** ☎ 800/359–7262 ⊕ www.flypanam.com. **Provincial Airlines** ☎ 709/576–1666, 800/563–2800 in Atlantic Canada ⊕ www.provair.com. **Tango Air** ☎ 514/369–1386 or 800/315–1390 ⊕ www.flytango.ca.

AIRPORTS

The Halifax International Airport is 40 km (25 mi) northeast of downtown Halifax. Sydney Airport is 13 km (8 mi) east of Sydney. 🛧 Airport Information **Halifax International Airport** ✉ 1 Bell Blvd., off Hwy. 102, Elmsdale ☎ 902/873–1223. **Sydney Airport** ✉ 280 Airport Rd. ☎ 902/564–7720.

AIRPORT
TRANSFERS

Limousine and taxi services, as well as car rentals, are available at the Halifax and Sydney airports. Airport bus service to Halifax and Dartmouth hotels from Halifax International Airport costs $20 round-trip,

$12 one-way. Airbus has regular bus service from the Halifax airport to most major hotels in Halifax. Regular taxi fare to Halifax from Halifax International is $40 each way. If you book ahead with Share-A-Cab, the fare is $24, but you must share your car with another passenger. The trip takes 30–40 minutes.

🚹 **Airbus** ☎ 902/873-2091. **Share-A-Cab** ☎ 902/429-5555.

BOAT & FERRY TRAVEL

Car ferries connect Nova Scotia with Maine and New Brunswick: Prince of Fundy Cruises sails from Portland, Maine, to Yarmouth, Nova Scotia, twice daily July–August and once a day May–June and September–October. Bay Ferries Ltd. sails from Bar Harbor, Maine, to Yarmouth, and from Saint John, New Brunswick, to Digby, Nova Scotia, twice daily July–August and once daily May–June and September–October. Bay Ferries' Bar Harbor–Yarmouth service uses a high-speed catamaran, cutting the trip from 6 to 2¾ hours. Known as the *Cat,* this catamaran is very popular for both its convenience and its speed, so reserve ahead.

Weather permitting, from May through December, Northumberland Ferries operates between Caribou, Nova Scotia, and Wood Islands, Prince Edward Island, making the trip once a day. Marine Atlantic operates year-round between North Sydney and Port aux Basques, on the west coast of Newfoundland, and June through September between North Sydney and Argentia, on Newfoundland's east coast. Marine Atlantic makes one trip per day.

Metro Transit runs passenger ferries from the Halifax ferry terminal at Lower Water Street to Alderney Gate in downtown Dartmouth and to Woodside Terminal (near Dartmouth Hospital) on the hour and half hour from 6:30 AM to 11:57 PM. Ferries are more frequent during weekday rush hours; they also operate on Sunday in summer (June through September). Free transfers are available from the ferry to the bus system (and vice versa). A single crossing costs $1.65 and is worth it for the up-close view of both waterfronts.

🚹 Boat & Ferry Information **Bay Ferries Ltd.** ☎ 902/566-3838 or 888/249-7245 ⊕ www. nfl-bay.com. **Marine Atlantic** ☎ 902/794-5254, 709/772-7701, or 800/341-7981 ⊕ www. marine-atlantic.ca. **Metro Transit** ☎ 902/421-6600. **Northumberland Ferries** ☎ 902/ 566-3838 or 800/565-0201. **Prince of Fundy Cruises** ☎ 800/341-7540 in Canada, 800/ 482-0955 in Maine.

BUS TRAVEL

Because of conflicting schedules, getting to Nova Scotia by bus can be problematic. Greyhound Lines from New York, and Voyageur from Montréal, connect with Scotia Motor Tours (SMT) through New Brunswick. SMT links—inconveniently, due to scheduling—with Acadian Lines and provides service between urban centers within Nova Scotia. Airbus runs between the Halifax International Airport and major hotels in Halifax and Dartmouth. Shuttle van services with convenient transportation between Halifax and Sydney include Cape Shuttle Service and Scotia Shuttle Service.

A number of small companies provide regional bus service; however, connections are not always convenient. Outside Halifax there is no inner-city bus services. For information call Nova Scotia Tourism.

Metro Transit provides bus service throughout Halifax and Dartmouth, the town of Bedford, and (to a limited extent) the county of Halifax. The fare is $1.65; only exact change is accepted.

🚹 Bus Information **Acadian Lines** ☎ 902/454-9321. **Airbus** ☎ 902/873-2091. **Cape Shuttle Service** ☎ 800/349-1698. **Greyhound Lines** ☎ 800/231-2222. **Metro Transit**

☏ 902/490–4000. **Nova Scotia Tourism** ☏ 902/424–5000 or 800/565–0000 ⊕ www. novascotia.com. **Scotia Motor Tours** ☏ 506/458–6000. **Scotia Shuttle Service** ☏ 877/ 898–5883. **Voyageur Inc.** ☏ 514/842–2281.

CAR RENTAL

Halifax is the most convenient place from which to begin a driving tour of Nova Scotia or Atlantic Canada. Avis, Budget, Hertz, National, and Thrifty have locations in Halifax.

🚩 Major Agencies **Avis** ✉ 5600 Sackville St., Halifax ☏ 902/492–2847, 902/429– 0963 airport. **Budget** ✉ 1558 Hollis St., Halifax ☏ 902/492–7500 or 800/268–8900. **Hertz** ✉ Sheraton Halifax, 1919 Upper Water St., Halifax ☏ 902/421–1763, 902/873–3700 airport. **National** ✉ 3484 Kempt Rd., Halifax ☏ 902/422–4439, 902/873–3505 airport. **Thrifty** ✉ 6419 Lady Hammond, Halifax ☏ 902/422–4455, 902/873–3527 airport.

CAR TRAVEL

Most highways in the province lead to Halifax and Dartmouth. Highways 3/103, 7, 2/102, and 1/101 terminate in the twin cities. Many of the roads in rural Nova Scotia require attentive driving, as they are not well signed, are narrow, and do not always have a paved shoulder. But they are generally well surfaced and offer exquisite scenery.

Motorists can enter Nova Scotia through the narrow neck of land that connects the province to New Brunswick and the mainland. The Trans-Canada Highway (Highway 2 in New Brunswick) becomes Highway 104 on crossing the Nova Scotia border at Amherst. It is possible to drive over the Confederation Bridge from Prince Edward Island into New Brunswick near the Nova Scotia border. Otherwise, car ferries dock at Yarmouth (from Maine), Digby (from New Brunswick), Caribou (from Prince Edward Island), and North Sydney (from Newfoundland).

ROAD MAPS   The province has 11 designated "Scenic Travelways," five in Cape Breton and six on the mainland, which are identified by roadside signs with icons that correspond with trail names. These lovely routes are also shown on tourist literature from Nova Scotia Tourism and on maps that are available at gas stations and tourist information centers.

RULES OF   Highways numbered from 100 to 199 are all-weather, limited-access
THE ROAD   roads, with speed limits between 100 kph and 110 kph (between 62 mph and 68 mph). The last two digits usually match the number of an older trunk highway along the same route, numbered from 1 to 99. Thus, Highway 102, between Halifax and Truro, matches the older Highway 2, between the same towns. Roads numbered from 200 to 399 are secondary roads that usually link villages. Unless otherwise posted, the speed limit on these and any roads other than the 100-series highways is 80 kph (50 mph).

EMERGENCIES

🚩 Emergency Services **Ambulance, fire, and police** ☏ 911.
🚩 Hospitals **Cape Breton Regional Hospital** ✉ 1482 George St., Sydney ☏ 902/567– 8000. **Queen Elizabeth II Health Sciences Centre** ✉ 5909 Jubilee Rd., Halifax ☏ 902/ 473–2700 switchboard, 902/473–2043 emergencies.

SPORTS & THE OUTDOORS

BIKING   *Bicycle Tours in Nova Scotia* ($7) is published by Bicycle Nova Scotia. Atlantic Canada Cycling can provide information on tours and rentals.
🚩 **Atlantic Canada Cycling** ☏ 902/423–2453. **Bicycle Nova Scotia** ✉ Box 3010, 5516 Spring Garden Rd., Halifax B3J 3G6 ☏ 902/425–5450.

BIRD-WATCHING   Nova Scotia is on the Atlantic flyway and is an important staging point for migratory species. A fine illustrated book, *Birds of Nova Scotia,* by Robie Tufts, is a must on every ornithologist's reading list. The Nova

Scotia Museum of Natural History organizes walks and lectures for people interested in viewing local bird life in the Halifax area.

🚩 **Nova Scotia Museum of Natural History** ✉ 1747 Summer St. ☎ 902/424-6475.

CANOEING   Especially good canoe routes are within Kejimkujik National Park. Canoeing information is available from Canoe NS. The publication *Canoe Routes of Nova Scotia* and route maps are available from Service Nova Scotia.

🚩 **Canoe NS** ☎ 902/425-5450 Ext. 316. **Service Nova Scotia** ☎ 902/424-7580 ⊕ www.gov.ns.ca.

FISHING   You are required by law to have a valid Nova Scotia fishing license for freshwater fishing. A seven-day nonresident license costs $23. For information about obtaining licenses, contact the Department of Natural Resources. Fishing charters are plentiful; contact the Nova Scotia Department of Fisheries and Aquaculture for information.

🚩 **Department of Natural Resources** ☎ 902/424-4467. **Nova Scotia Department of Fisheries and Aquaculture** ☎ 902/485-5056.

GOLF   The province offers golfers many well-manicured courses that are both panoramic and challenging. Contact Golf Nova Scotia for information on individual courses and tournaments.

🚩 **Golf Nova Scotia** ☎ 800/565-0001 ⊕ www.golfnovascotia.com.

HIKING   The province has a wide variety of trails along the rugged coastline and inland through forest glades, which enable you to experience otherwise inaccessible scenery, wildlife, and vegetation. *Hiking Trails of Nova Scotia,* published by Gooselane Editions, is available at most local bookstores.

🚩 **Gooselane Editions** ✉ 469 King St., Fredericton, NB E3R 1E5 ☎ 506/450-4251.

SKIING   The Nova Scotia Ski Area Association is a veritable fountain of skiing knowledge. Employees bend over backward to give you information on schedules, snow conditions, trail conditions, prices, and more.

🚩 **Nova Scotia Ski Area Association** ☎ 902/828-2804.

TAXIS

In Halifax, rates begin at about $2.50 and increase based on mileage and time. A crosstown trip should cost $6 to $7, depending on traffic. There are taxi stands at major hotels and shopping malls or you can usually hail a cab in the downtown area. Most Haligonians simply phone for taxi service.

🚩 Taxi Companies **Casino Taxi** ☎ 902/429-6666. **Yellow Cab** ☎ 902/420-0000 or 902/422-1551.

TOURS

VIA Rail's *Bras d'Or* land cruise, a 10-hour train trip between Sydney and Halifax (June–October only), has fine regional cuisine, an onboard tour guide, and a singer strolling the aisles. Enjoy scenery from two dome cars and a 45-minute stop in Port Hawkesbury. VIA and partners Tourism Nova Scotia, Tourism Cape Breton, and Enterprise Cape Breton offer discounts with hotels and rental-car companies. Tickets are $232. The *Bras d'Or* leaves Halifax and Sydney once a week, June–mid-October.

🚩 Tour Companies **VIA Rail *Bras d'Or* land cruise** ☎ 888/VIA-RAIL ⊕ www.viarail.ca.

BOAT TOURS   Boat tours have become very popular in all regions of the province. Murphy's on the Water sails various vessels: *Harbour Queen I,* a paddle wheeler; *Haligonian III,* an enclosed motor launch; *Stormy Weather I,* a 40-foot Cape Islander (fishing boat); and *Mar II,* a 75-foot sailing ketch. All operate from mid-May to late October from berths at 1751 Lower Water Street on Cable Wharf next to the Historic Properties in Halifax.

Some tours include lunch, dinner, or entertainment. A cash bar may also be available. Costs vary, but a basic tour of the Halifax Harbour ranges from $15 to $25. Tours vary from two hours to all day in length.

Harbour Hopper Tours offers a unique amphibious tour of historic downtown Halifax and the Halifax Harbour. Tours are approximately one hour long (half on land, half on water) and run hourly from the early morning until late evening. The cost is $22.50 for adults or $55.95 for a family of four.

🔒Harbour Hopper Tours ☎ 902/490-8687. Murphy's on the Water ☎ 902/420-1015.

BUS & RICKSHAW TOURS Gray Line Sightseeing and Cabana Tours run coach tours through Halifax, Dartmouth, and Peggy's Cove. Halifax Double Decker Tours offers two-hour tours on double-decker buses that leave daily from the Historic Properties in Halifax.Virtually every cab company in Halifax gives custom tours. Yellow Cab provides clean, comfortable cars with eloquent, amicable drivers who are well versed in local history and lore. Cab tours to locations such as Wolfville or Peggy's Cove are possible with prior arrangement. Prices vary, but be sure to set a fee with the tour guide before you begin. Greater Halifax Rickshaw Service has intimate narrated tours of downtown Halifax.

🔒 Cabana Tours ☎ 902/455-8111. Gray Line Sightseeing ☎ 902/423-6242. Greater Halifax Rickshaw Service ☎ 902/455-6677. Halifax Double Decker Tours ☎ 902/420-1155. Yellow Cab ☎ 902/420-0000 or 902/422-1551.

TRAIN TOURS VIA Rail conducts weekly first-class guided rail tours between Halifax and Sydney from May through mid-October.

🔒 VIA Rail ☎ 800/561-3952.

WALKING TOURS Explore Halifax's rich tradition of stories of pirates, haunted houses, buried treasure, and ghosts with Halifax Ghost Walk. Tours begin at the Old Town Clock at 8:30 PM on any scheduled night.

🔒 Halifax Ghost Walk ☎ 902/469-6716.

VISITOR INFORMATION

Nova Scotia Tourism publishes a wide range of literature, including an annual (free) travel guide called the *Nova Scotia Doers and Dreamers Guide*. Call to have it mailed to you.

Visiting pilots can obtain aviation-related information for the flying tourist from the Aviation Council of Nova Scotia.

🔒 Tourist Information Aviation Council of Nova Scotia ⫏ Box 100, Debert B0M 1G0 ☎ 902/895-1143. Nova Scotia Tourism ⫏ Box 130, Halifax B3J 2M7 ☎ 902/424-5000 or 800/565-0000. Nova Scotia Tourism Information Centre ⊠ Old Red Store at Historic Properties, Halifax ☎ 902/424-4248. Tourism Cape Breton ☎ 902/563-4636 ⊕ www.cbisland.com. Tourism Halifax & Nova Scotia Tourism ⊠ International Visitors Centre, 1595 Barrington St., Halifax ☎ 902/490-5946.

NEW BRUNSWICK

2

FODOR'S CHOICE

Fundy National Park, *Alma*

Fundy Park to Hopewell Rocks drive

Hopewell Rocks, *Hopewell Cape*

Kings Landing Historical Settlement, *near Fredericton*

Kingsbrae Arms, *St. Andrews by-the-Sea*

Kingsbrae Garden, *St. Andrews by-the-Sea*

La Fine Grobe-Sur-Mer, *near Caraquet*

Little Shemogue Country Inn, *near Shediac*

Morrisey Rock, *near Campbellton*

Pump House Brewery, *Moncton*

St. John River Valley drive

Swallowtail, *Grand Manan Island*

HIGHLY RECOMMENDED

SIGHTS Acadian Historical Village, *Caraquet*

Beaverbrook Art Gallery, *Fredericton*

Campobello Island

Christ Church Cathedral, *Fredericton*

Irving Eco-Centre, *Bouctouche*

Kouchibouguac National Park, *Kouchibouguac*

New Brunswick Museum, *Saint John*

Parlee Beach, *Shediac*

Reversing Falls, *Saint John*

Many other great hotels and restaurants enliven New Brunswick.
For other favorites, look for the black stars as you read this chapter.

By Ana Watts   **THE GREAT CANADIAN FOREST MEETS THE SEA** in New Brunswick, where it is sliced by sweeping river valleys and modern highways. The province is an old place in New World terms, and the remains of a turbulent past are still evident in some of its quiet nooks. Near Moncton, for instance, wild strawberries perfume the air of the grassy slopes of Fort Beauséjour, where, in 1755, one of the last battles for possession of Acadia took place—the English finally overcoming the French. The dual heritage of New Brunswick (33% of its population is Acadian French) provides added spice. Today New Brunswick is Canada's only officially bilingual province. Other areas of the province were settled by the British and by Loyalists, American colonists who chose to live under British rule after the American Revolution. If you stay in both Acadian and Loyalist regions, a trip to New Brunswick can seem like two vacations in one.

For every gesture as grand as the giant rock formations carved by the Bay of Fundy tides, there is one as subtle as the gifted touch of a sculptor in her studio. For every experience as colorful as salmon and fiddleheads served at a church supper, there is another as low-key as the gentle waves of the Baie des Chaleurs. New Brunswick is the luxury of an inn with five stars or the tranquillity of camping under a million of them.

At the heart of New Brunswick is the forest, which covers 85% of the province's entire area—nearly all its interior. The forest drives the economy, defines the landscape, and delights hikers, anglers, campers, and bird-watchers. But New Brunswick's soul is the sea. The largest of Canada's three Maritime provinces, New Brunswick has 2,000 km (1,243 mi) of coastline. The warm waters of the Baie des Chaleurs, Gulf of St. Lawrence, and Northumberland Strait lure swimmers to their sandy beaches. The chilly Bay of Fundy, with its monumental tides, draws breaching whales, whale-watchers, and kayakers.

About the Restaurants

Good things often come in small packages in this province. Watch for little restaurants, where the owner is apt to be the chef or waiter or even both. These places are closely tied to the community.

About the Hotels

Among its more interesting options, New Brunswick has a number of officially designated Heritage Inns. These historically significant establishments run the gamut from elegant to homey; many have antique china and furnishings. Cottage clusters are springing up in coastal communities, and Saint John, Moncton, and Fredericton each have a link in first-rate hotel chains. Accommodations are at a premium in summer, so reserve ahead.

WHAT IT COSTS In Canadian Dollars				
$$$$	**$$$**	**$$**	**$**	**¢**
RESTAURANTS over $30	$20–$30	$12–$20	$8–$12	under $8
HOTELS over $250	$175–$250	$125–$175	$75–$125	under $75

Restaurant prices are per-person for a main course at dinner. Hotel prices are for two people in a standard double room in high season, excluding 15% harmonized sales tax (HST).

Exploring New Brunswick

Rivers and ocean are the original highways of New Brunswick, and the St. John River in the west and the Fundy and Acadian coasts in the south and east essentially encompass the province. A well-designed and marked system of provincial scenic drives takes you to most of the places you want to go. Begin in the south, on the phenomenal Fundy Coastal Drive (watch for the lighthouse-on-a-cliff logo). At the upper end of the bay it connects with the Acadian Coastal Drive (the logo is a setting sun and fishing boat), which hugs the gentle eastern shore. In the middle of the Acadian Drive is a bit of a detour for the Miramichi River Route (trees and a jumping salmon logo). The Acadian Drive eventually meets the Appalachian Range Route (mountains and cliffs logo). It takes you across the rugged northern part of the province where the hardwood ridges ignite in a blaze of color in fall and connects with the River Valley Scenic Drive (rolling green hills and wide blue river logo), which takes you down the entire western side of the province and back to Saint John, on the Fundy Coastal Drive, where the adventure began.

Timing

Late spring through fall are lovely times to visit, when festivals celebrate everything from jazz to salmon. Many communities have festivities for Canada Day (July 1), and on the Acadian Peninsula many festivals, including the unique Blessing of the Fleet, are clustered around the August 15 Acadian national holiday. Fall colors are at their peak from mid-September through mid- or late October. The **Autumn Colours Line** (☎ 800/268–3255) provides daily information on where fall foliage is at its best. Winter sports lovers have plenty of options from December to March. Whales are more plentiful in the Bay of Fundy after the first of August.

SAINT JOHN

Like any seaport worth its salt, Saint John is a welcoming place. The natives welcomed Samuel de Champlain and Sieur de Monts when they landed here on St. John the Baptist Day in 1604. Nearly two centuries later, in May 1783, 3,000 British Loyalists—fleeing the aftermath of the American Revolutionary War—poured off a fleet of ships to make a home amid the rocks and forests. Two years later the city of Saint John became the first in Canada to be incorporated.

Although most of the Loyalists were English, there were some Irish among them. Following the Napoleonic Wars in 1815, thousands more Irish workers found their way to Saint John. It was the potato famine that spawned the largest influx of Irish immigrants, though; a 20-foot Celtic cross on Partridge Island at the entrance to Saint John Harbour stands as a reminder of the hardships and suffering they endured. Their descendants make Saint John Canada's most Irish city, an undisputed fact that is celebrated in grand style each March with a weeklong St. Patrick's festival.

All the comings and goings over the centuries have exposed Saint Johners to a wide variety of cultures and ideas and made it a sophisticated city in a friendly Maritime way. Major provincial artists like Jack Humphrey, Millar Brittain, Fred Ross, and Herzl Kashetsky were born here, and Hollywood notables like Louis B. Mayer, Donald Sutherland, and Walter Pidgeon grew up here.

Saint John remains a welcoming place—just ask the thousands of visitors who stream ashore from the dozens of cruise ships that dock at downtown Pugsley Wharf each year. They are greeted with music, flowers, and cheerful people ready and willing to help in any way they can.

Industry and salt air have combined to give parts of this city a weather-beaten quality, but you also find lovingly restored 19th-century wooden and redbrick homes as well as modern office buildings, hotels, and shops.

Numbers in the text correspond to numbers in the margin and on the New Brunswick, Downtown Saint John, and Fredericton maps.

2

If you have
4 days

If you have only a short time, concentrate on one region, like the Fundy Coast. Art, history, nature, and seafood abound in the resort community of ⊠ **St. Andrews by-the-Sea** ⑭ ▶. Whale-watching tours leave from the town wharf, there's an outstanding garden, and some of the province's finest crafts are found in its shops. Spend a day and a night. Just an hour's drive east of St. Andrews is the venerable city of ⊠ **Saint John** ❶ – ⑫. It's steeped in English and Irish traditions, rich in history and art. Spend a day and a night here as well, then take Route 1 past Sussex to Route 114 and **Fundy National Park** ⑲. Route 915 above the park hugs the coast. Watch for **Cape Enrage** ⑳, which is as dramatic as it sounds. There are lots of things to do around ⊠ **Riverside-Albert** and ⊠ **Hopewell Cape** ㉑, where the Fundy tides have sculpted gigantic flower-pot rocks that turn into islands at high tide. Finish the trip with ⊠ **Moncton** ㉒, a microcosm of New Brunswick culture and less than an hour's drive from Riverside-Albert.

If you have
7 days

Add an Acadian coastal experience to the four-day tour above. Head north from **Moncton** ㉒ ▶ and explore the area around **Shediac** ㉔, famous for its lobsters and Parlee Beach. ⊠ **Bouctouche** ㉕ is just beyond that, with its wonderful dunes and the make-believe land of La Sagouine. Another 50 km (31 mi) north is unspoiled **Kouchibouguac National Park** ㉖, which protects beaches, forests, and peat bogs. The coastal drive from Kouchibouguac Park to ⊠ **Miramichi City** ㉗, about 75 km (47 mi), passes through several bustling fishing villages. Most of the communities are Acadian, but as you approach Miramichi City, the English language dominates again. A stopover here positions you perfectly to begin your exploration of the Acadian Peninsula. It's only about 120 km (74 mi) from Miramichi City to ⊠ **Caraquet** ㉘. The entire peninsula is so different from the rest of the province it's like a trip to a foreign country. The Acadian Historical Village is a careful re-creation of the traditional Acadian way of life.

If you have
**10
days**

Follow the seven-day itinerary above. From **Caraquet** ㉘ plan at least half a day to drive across the top of New Brunswick (Route 134 along the coast and Route 17 inland through the forest) to the St. John River valley. Begin your explorations among the flowers and the music of the New Brunswick Botanical Gardens in St-Jacques, just outside ⊠ **Edmundston** ㉙. The drive from here to Fredericton is about 275 km (171 mi) of panoramic pastoral and river scenery, including a dramatic gorge and waterfall at **Grand Falls** ㉚ and the longest covered bridge in the world at Hartland. **Kings Landing Historical Settlement** ㉛, near Fredericton, provides a faithful depiction of life on the river in the 19th century. With its Gothic cathedral, Victorian architecture, museums, and riverfront pathways, ⊠ **Fredericton** ㉝ – ㊴ is a beautiful, historic, and cultural stopping place. The drive from Fredericton to Saint John on Route 102 is just over 100 km (62 mi); about halfway between the two is the village of **Gagetown** ㊵, a must-see for its art and history.

Downtown Saint John

An ambitious urban renewal program undertaken in the early 1980s spruced up the waterfront and converted old warehouses into trendy restaurants and shops. Underground and overhead walkways connect several attractions and shops in the area.

A Good Walk

Saint John is a city on hills, and **King Street** ❶, its main street, slopes steeply to the harbor. A system of escalators, elevators, and skywalks inside buildings allows you to climb to the top and take in some of the more memorable spots without effort, though you can also walk outside. Start at the foot of King Street, **Market Slip** ❷. This is where the Loyalists landed in 1783 and is the site of **Barbour's General Store** ❸ and the Little Red Schoolhouse. At Market Square, restored waterfront buildings house historic exhibits, shops, restaurants, and cafés. Also here are the Saint John Regional Library, a year-round visitor information center, and the fine **New Brunswick Museum** ❹.

From the second level of Market Square a skywalk crosses St. Patrick Street, and an escalator takes you up into the City Hall shopping concourse. Here you can branch off to Harbour Station, with its busy schedule of concerts, sporting events, and trade shows. Once you are through City Hall, another skywalk takes you across Chipman Hill and into the Brunswick Square Complex of shops, offices, and a hotel. To visit historic **Loyalist House** ❺, exit onto Germain Street and turn left; it's on the corner at the top of the hill. Continue on for a block to see the venerable **St. John's (Stone) Church** ❻. In the flavorful **Old City Market** ❼, across from Brunswick Square, make your way past fish- and cheesemongers, butchers, greengrocers, sandwich makers, and craftspeople. This is a great place to stop for lunch. When you leave by the door at the top of the market, you're near the head of King Street and right across Charlotte Street from **King's Square** ❽. Take a walk through the square, past the statues and bandstand, to Sydney Street. Cross Sydney Street, and you're in the **Old Burial Ground** ❾. Make your way back to Sydney Street and then cross King Street East to the **Old Courthouse** ❿ with its spiral staircase. Head south on Sydney Street; turn right on King's Square South, and you're at the handsome Imperial Theatre. Follow King's Square South and cross Charlotte Street to reach the back door of historic **Trinity Church** ⓫.

To end your walk, make your way back to King Street and walk down the hill toward the water. **Prince William Street** ⓬ is at the foot of the hill, just steps from where you began at Market Slip. Turn left for antiques shops, galleries, and historic architecture.

TIMING   Allow the better part of a day for this walk if you include a few hours for the New Brunswick Museum and some time for shopping. If you don't stop, the route takes a couple of hours. On Sunday the indoor walkways are open, but the City Market is closed.

Sights to See

❸ **Barbour's General Store.** This 19th-century shop, now a museum, is filled with the aromas of tobacco, smoked fish, peppermint sticks, and dulse, an edible seaweed. There are an old post office and a barbershop, too. ⊠ *Market Slip* ☎ *506/658–2939* ⊡ *Free* ☉ *Mid-June–mid-Sept., daily 9–6.*

❶ **King Street.** The steep main street of the city is lined with solid Victorian redbrick buildings filled with a variety of shops.

❽ **King's Square.** Laid out in a Union Jack pattern, this green refuge has a two-story bandstand and a number of monuments. The mass of metal

2

Beaches

There are two kinds of saltwater beaches in New Brunswick: warm and c-c-c-cold. The warm beaches are along the east coast. At Parlee it's sand castles, sunscreen, and beach volleyball on the side. For solitude try Kouchibouguac National Park and its 26 km (16 mi) of beaches and dunes. The cold beaches are on the Bay of Fundy, on the province's southern coast. The highest tides in the world (a *vertical* difference of as much as 48 feet) have carved some spectacular caves, crevices, and cliffs. There are some sandy beaches, and hardy souls swim in the "invigorating" saltwater. Extreme tides make it possible to explore rich tidal pools and walk on the flats at low tide. Beaches like Cape Enrage combine salt air and opportunities for thrilling adventures such as rappelling. Others, like the beach at Marys Point, where thousands of semipalmated plovers take flight, allow you to observe awesome natural sights.

Fishing

Dotted with freshwater lakes, crisscrossed with fish-laden rivers, and bordered by 1,129 km (700 mi) of seacoast, this province is one of Canada's natural treasures. Anglers are drawn by the bass fishing and such world-famous salmon rivers as the Miramichi. Commercial fishers often take visitors line fishing for groundfish.

Tastes of New Brunswick

Cast your line just about anywhere in New Brunswick, and you catch some kind of fish-and-chips. Nearly every restaurant has its own chowder, but for fresh seafood, head to a better restaurant. New Brunswick's oysters, scallops, clams, crabs, mussels, lobsters, and salmon are worth it. Some seafood is available seasonally, but salmon is available any time of year. A spring delicacy is fiddleheads—emerging ostrich ferns that look like the curl at the end of a violin neck. These emerald gems are picked along riverbanks, then boiled and sprinkled with lemon juice or vinegar and butter, salt, and pepper. Summer ends with wild blueberries—delicately flavored dark pearls—sprinkled on cereal, baked in muffins, or stewed with dumplings in a grunt. Try snacking on dulse, a dried purple seaweed as salty as potato chips and as compelling as peanuts. Find it on Grand Manan Island, in the Old Saint John City Market, and at some seafood restaurants. What New Brunswick serves most often is comfort food: staples like ham and scalloped potatoes, turkey dinners, pork chops, and liver and onions. The beer of choice is Moosehead, brewed in Saint John.

Whale-Watching

One unforgettable New Brunswick experience is the sighting of a huge humpback, right whale, finback, or minke. Outfitters along the Bay of Fundy take people to see a variety of whales. Most trips run from May through September.

Winter Sports

New Brunswick can get as much as 16 feet of snow each year, so winter fun often lasts well into spring. Dogsledding is taking off, ice-fishing communities pop up on many rivers, and tobogganing, skating, and snowshoeing are popular. Groomed cross-country skiing trails abound at Mactaquac Provincial Park near Fredericton, Fundy National Park in Alma, and Kouchibouguac National Park between Moncton and Miramichi. Many communities and small hotels have groomed trails, but skiers can also set off on their own. New Brunswick downhill ski areas usually operate mid-December through April.

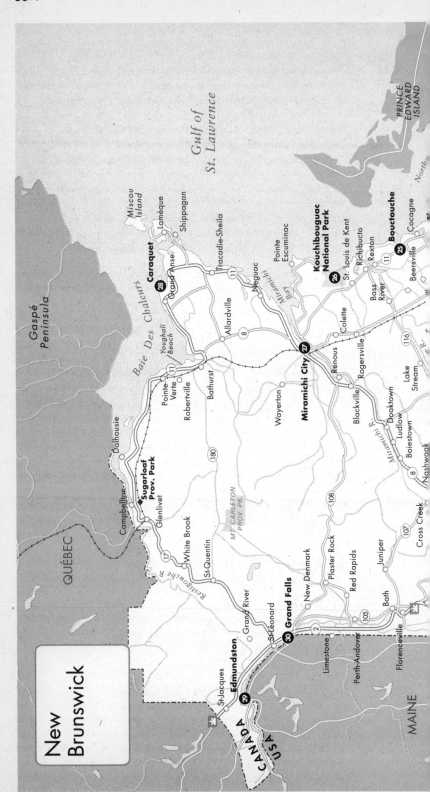

New
Brunswick

Barbour's
General
Store **3**

King Street. . . . **1**

King's
Square. **8**

Loyalist
House **5**

Market Slip . . . **2**

New
Brunswick
Museum **4**

Old Burial
Ground **9**

Old City
Market. **7**

Old
Courthouse . . **10**

Prince
William
Street. **12**

St. John's
(Stone)
Church **6**

Trinity
Church. **11**

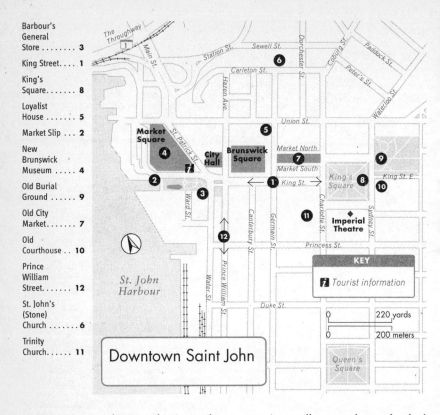

Downtown Saint John

on the ground in its northeast corner is actually a great lump of melted stock from a neighboring hardware store that burned down in Saint John's Great Fire of 1877, in which hundreds of buildings were destroyed. ⊠ *Between Charlotte and Sydney Sts.*

❺ Loyalist House. David Daniel Merritt, a wealthy Loyalist merchant, built this imposing Georgian structure in 1810. It is distinguished by its authentic period furniture and eight fireplaces. July through August the mayor hosts a tea party here each Wednesday afternoon, when admission to the house is free. ⊠ *120 Union St.* ☎ *506/652-3590* ⊠ *$3* ⏱ *June, weekdays 10–5; July–Aug., daily 10–5; Sept.–May, by appointment.*

❷ Market Slip. The waterfront area at the foot of King Street is where the Loyalists landed in 1783. Today it's the site of Market Square, the Hilton Saint John, an amphitheater, and restaurants, but it still conveys a sense of the city's Maritime heritage. A floating wharf accommodates boating visitors to the city and those waiting for the tides to be right to sail up the St. John River.

★ ☝ ❹ New Brunswick Museum. Delilah, a suspended, full-size young right-whale skeleton, is on display at this fine museum. Hike along a geologic trail and watch the phenomenal Bay of Fundy tides rise and fall in a glass tube. Creative exhibits trace the province's industrial, social, and artistic history, and outstanding artwork hangs in the galleries. The Family Discovery Gallery has fun and educational games. ⊠ *Market Sq.* ☎ *506/643-2300* ⊕ *www.gov.nb.ca/0130* ⊠ *$6* ⏱ *Mid-May–Oct., Mon.–Wed. and Fri. 9–5, Thurs. 9–9, weekends noon–5; Nov.–mid-May, Tues., Wed., and Fri. 9–5, Thurs. 9–9, weekends noon–5.*

❾ Old Burial Ground. This Loyalist cemetery, now a landscaped park, is like a history book published in stone. Brick walkways, gardens, and a beaver-pond fountain make it a delightful spot. ⊠ *Off Sydney St. between King and E. Union Sts.* ⌐ *Free* ⊙ *Daily 24 hrs.*

❼ Old City Market. The 1876 inverted ship's-hull ceiling of this handsome market occupies a city block between Germain and Charlotte streets. Its temptations include live and fresh-cooked lobsters, great cheeses, dulse, and tasty, inexpensive snacks, along with plenty of souvenir and craft items. ⊠ *47 Charlotte St.* ☎ *506/658–2820* ⊙ *Mon.–Thurs. 7:30–6, Fri. 7:30–7, Sat. 7:30–5.*

❾ Old Courthouse. This 1829 neoclassical building has a three-story spiral staircase built of tons of unsupported stones. The staircase can be seen year-round during business hours, except when court is in session. Hours sometimes vary, so call ahead. ⊠ *King St. E and Sydney St.* ⌐ *Free* ⊙ *Weekdays 9–5.*

⑫ Prince William Street. South of King Street near Market Slip, this street is full of historic bank and business buildings that now hold shops, galleries, and restaurants. The lamp known as the Three Sisters, at the foot of Prince William Street, was erected in 1848 to guide ships into the harbor. Next to it is a replica of the Celtic cross on nearby Partridge Island, where many immigrants landed and were quarantined.

❻ St. John's (Stone) Church. The first stone building in the city, this church was built for the garrison posted at nearby Fort Howe. The stone was brought from England as ships' ballast. ⊠ *87 Carleton St.* ☎ *506/634–1474* ⌐ *By donation* ⊙ *Guided tours July–Aug., weekdays 10–4.*

⑪ Trinity Church. The present church dates from 1880, when it was rebuilt after the Great Fire. Inside, over the west door, there's a coat of arms— a symbol of the monarchy—rescued from the council chamber in Boston by a British colonel during the American Revolution. It was deemed a worthy refugee and given a place of honor in the church. ⊠ *115 Charlotte St.* ☎ *506/693–8558* ⌐ *Free* ⊙ *Hrs vary; call ahead.*

Greater Saint John

Relax on a secluded beach while talking to the harbor seals and listening to the birds, all within 10 minutes of downtown. The St. John River, its Reversing Falls, and St. John Harbour divide the city into eastern and western districts. The historic downtown area is on the east side. The venerable brick homes (like New York's and Boston's brownstones) near mercantile King Street enjoy the summer shade of mature trees. On the lower west side, painted-wood homes with flat roofs—characteristic of Atlantic Canadian seaports—slope to the harbor. Industrial activity is prominent on the west side, which has stately older homes on huge lots. Since World War II subdivisions have pushed the city boundaries out to meet the rambling summer homes and cottages on the St. John River and the mansions of the town of Rothesay.

A Good Drive

From Market Square in downtown Saint John, head west in your car (or on any westbound bus) to see the **Reversing Falls.** Go up St. Patrick Street and cross the viaduct to Main Street. Drive to the top of the hill and turn left on Douglas Avenue, with its grand old homes. A right off Douglas Avenue onto Fallsview Drive takes you to a Reversing Falls lookout and the Reversing Falls Jet Boat ride. Return to Douglas Avenue, turn right, and keep right to cross the Reversing Falls Bridge. At the end of the bridge, on your left, is the Falls Restaurant and a city visitor information center with a falls interpretation center. The west side is also home to **Carleton Martello Tower.** Turn left from the Reversing Falls

Tourist Bureau, past the Simms Brush Factory, and bear left when the road splits. The rest of the way is well marked. You're near **Irving Nature Park** (off Route 1, Exit 9A, if you're on the highway), 600 acres of volcanic rock and forest that are a haven for wildlife and hikers. There's more exotic wildlife at **Cherry Brook Zoo**, northeast of downtown. The zoo is part of **Rockwood Park**, the largest in-city park in Canada.

•TIMING To appreciate fully the Reversing Falls takes time; you need to visit at high, slack, and low tides. Check with any visitor information office for these times to help you plan a visit.

Sights to See

Carleton Martello Tower. The tower, a great place from which to survey the harbor and Partridge Island, was built during the War of 1812 as a precaution against an American attack. Guides tell you about the spartan life of a soldier living in the stone fort, and an audiovisual presentation outlines its role in the defense of Saint John during World War II. ⊠ *Whipple St. at Fundy Dr.* ☎ *506/636–4011* ✆ *$4* ☉ *June–early Sept., daily 10–6; early Sept.–mid-Oct., by appointment.*

☺ **Cherry Brook Zoo.** Wildebeests and other exotic species are highlights of this small zoo. There are a monkey house and a trail with extinct-animal exhibits. ⊠ *901 Foster Thurston Dr.* ☎ *506/634–1440* ✆ *$6.50* ☉ *May–Oct., daily 10–dusk; Nov.–Apr., weekends 10–dusk.*

Irving Nature Park. The ecosystems of the southern New Brunswick coast are preserved in this lovely 600-acre park on a peninsula close to downtown. Roads and eight walking trails (up to several kilometers long) make bird- and nature-watching easy. Many shorebirds breed here, and it's a staging site on the flight path of birds migrating to and from the Arctic and South America. Stop at the entrance for a naturalist's notebook, a guide to what you'll find in the park season by season. ⊠ *Sand Cove Rd.; from downtown take Rte. 1 west to Exit 9A (Catherwood Rd.) south; follow Sand Cove Rd. 4½ km (3 mi)* ☎ *506/653–7367* ✆ *Free* ☉ *May–mid-Nov., daily dawn–dusk.*

★ **Reversing Falls.** The strong Fundy tides rise faster than the river can empty, so twice daily at the Reversing Falls rapids, the tide water pushes the river water back upstream. When the tide ebbs, the river once again pours over the rock ledges and the rapids appear to reverse themselves. To learn more about the phenomenon, watch the film shown at the Reversing Falls Tourist Bureau. There's a restaurant here, too. Jet boat tours provide a closer (and wetter) look. A pulp mill on the bank is less scenic, and the smell it occasionally emits is a less charming part of a visit. ⊠ *Rte. 100, Reversing Falls Bridge* ☎ *506/658–2937* ✆ *Free* ☉ *Daily dawn–dusk; jet boat tours June–mid-Oct., daily 10 AM–dusk.*

☺ **Rockwood Park.** Encompassing 2,000 acres, this is the largest in-city park in Canada. There are hiking trails through the forest, 13 lakes, several sandy beaches, a campground, a golf course with an aquatic driving range, the Cherry Brook Zoo, horseback riding, and a unique play park for people of all ages. ⊠ *Main entrance off Crown St.* ☎ *506/658–2883* ✆ *Free* ☉ *Daily 10 AM–dusk.*

Where to Stay & Eat

$$–$$$$ ✗ **Billy's Seafood Company.** It's a restaurant, it's an oyster bar, it's a fish market—and it's lots of fun, too, with jazzy background music and funny, fishy paintings. The oysters Rockefeller are served with a hint of Pernod. Billy's Seafood Splash is a lobster surrounded by sautéed scallops, steamed clams, and mussels. Live and cooked lobsters can be packed to

go. ⊠ *Old City Market, Charlotte St. entrance* ☎ *506/672–3474 or 888/933–3474* ▤ *AE, DC, MC, V.*

$–$$$$ ✕ **Grannan's.** Seafood brochette with scallops, shrimp, and lobster tail, sautéed at your table in a white wine–and–mushroom sauce, is a favorite in this nautical-theme restaurant. The desserts, including bananas Foster, flambéed while you watch, are memorable. Dining spills onto the sidewalk in summer. ⊠ *1 Market Sq.* ☎ *506/634–1555* ▤ *AE, DC, MC, V.*

$–$$$$ ✕ **Steamer's Lobster Company and Water Street Dinner Theatre.** Fishnets and lobster traps decorate this rustic spot, where a meal feels like part of a Maritime kitchen party. Lobsters, mussels, and clams are steamed outside on the patio. Dinner theater, mostly musical comedy, happens upstairs Thursday, Friday, and Saturday all year at 6:30. Cruise ships dock at Pugsley Terminal, across the street. ⊠ *110 Water St., just off Market Sq.* ☎ *506/648–2325* ▤ *AE, DC, MC, V.*

★ $$$ ✕ **Beatty and the Beastro.** Quaint and quirky (check out the specially made plates), this place next to the Imperial Theatre hops at lunchtime and during pre- and posttheater dinners. The frequently changing menu, with its distinctive European accent, takes advantage of local and seasonal meat, seafood, and produce. Breads and soups are specialties; there are lines when Scotch broth is on the menu (the last stop for the local spring lamb). ⊠ *60 Charlotte St., at King's Sq.* ☎ *506/652–3888* ▤ *AE, DC, MC, V* ⊘ *Closed Sun.*

$–$$$ ✕ **Incredibles.** International cuisine is the focus of this reinvented restaurant. At each of its weekly Passport Weekends food from a different country is presented. The mussels, curries, and chicken paprika are good every day. The service is attentive, the recipes are authentic, and with several small dining rooms, the experience is intimate and cozy. ⊠ *42 Princess St.* ☎ *506/633–7554* ▤ *AE, DC, MC, V.*

$$–$$$ ✕ **Suwanna Restaurant.** The Thai duck at this authentic Thai restaurant is outstanding, but if you want it, you need to order it in advance. The wine cellar is excellent, and green and yellow curries are always available. The signature dish, Suwanna chicken, is a stir-fry of chicken, sweet peppers, and hot peppers drizzled with a dark sauce. The flavor is delicate and unique (and not too spicy, unless you actually eat one of the hot peppers). ⊠ *325 Lancaster Ave.* ☎ *506/637–9015* ▤ *MC, V* ⊘ *Closed Sun. No lunch.*

$–$$ ✕ **Taco Pica.** This modest place is a slice of home for the Guatemalan refugees who run it as a workers' co-op. The atmosphere is colorful—ornamental parrots rule in the dining room—and the recipes are authentic, seasoned with garlic, mint, coriander seeds, and cilantro. Frequently, a guitarist entertains on Friday and Saturday evenings. ⊠ *96 Germain St.* ☎ *506/633–8492* ▤ *AE, DC, MC, V.*

$$$ ✕▥ **Delta Brunswick Hotel.** Part of Brunswick Square, this hotel is in the heart of downtown Saint John. MRA's, a venerable department store that presided over the mercantile life of generations of Saint Johners, used to stand here. The hotel honors the old store in the names of some of its rooms and in its courtly service. Rooms are large, modern, and comfortable. Shucker's Restaurant ($$–$$$$) specializes in New Brunswick's best, including dishes made with local seafood, fiddleheads, and blueberries. This property is connected by a walkway to shopping and entertainment facilities. ⊠ *39 King St., E2L 4W3* ☎ *506/648–1981* ⊟ *506/658–0914* ⊕ *www.deltahotels.com* ◄⫸ *255 rooms* ⟐ *Restaurant, some microwaves, cable TV with movies and video games, pool, gym, bar, meeting rooms, parking (fee), some pets allowed* ▤ *AE, D, DC, MC, V.*

$$–$$$ ✕▥ **Hilton Saint John.** In this Hilton, furnished in Loyalist decor, guest rooms overlook the harbor or the town. A pedestrian walkway system connects the 10-story property to uptown shops, restaurants, a library, a museum, an aquatic center, and a civic center. The large restaurant ($$$–$$$$) has terrific views of the harbor. ✉ *1 Market Sq., E2L 4Z6* ☎ *506/693–8484, 800/561–8282 in Canada* 🖶 *506/657–6610* ⊕ *www. hilton.com* 🖙 *197 rooms* ⚭ *Restaurant, cable TV with movies, pool, gym, bar, parking (fee)* 🖿 *AE, D, DC, MC, V.*

★ $–$$$ ✕🖾 **Shadow Lawn Inn.** In an affluent suburb with tree-lined streets, palatial homes, tennis, golf, and a yacht club, this inn fits right in with its clapboards, columns, and antiques. Some bedrooms have fireplaces; one suite has a whirlpool bath. The chef honed his skills in some of the finest upper-Canadian kitchens. His creative ideas are reflected in the dining room's ($$$–$$$$) Continental and seafood dishes. ✉*3180 Rothesay Rd., Rothesay E2E 5V7, 12 km (7 mi) northeast of Saint John* ☎ *506/847–7539 or 800/561–4166* 🖶 *506/849–9238* ⊕ *www.shadowlawninn. com* 🖙 *9 rooms, 2 suites* ⚭ *Restaurant, some microwaves, Internet, meeting rooms, free parking, some pets allowed; no a/c in some rooms* 🖿 *AE, DC, MC, V* ⦿ *CP.*

$–$$ 🖾 **Homeport Historic Inn c1858.** Graceful arches, fine antiques, Italian marble fireplaces, Oriental carpets, and a Maritime theme are at home in these 19th-century twin mansions built by a prominent Saint John shipbuilding family. The two buildings make a large inn that commands stunning harbor views and is close to downtown and to the Reversing Falls. Each oversize room is elegant, unique, and equipped with modern amenities. One has a ghost named Beatrice. The breakfast is hearty. ✉ *60–80 Douglas Ave., E2K 1E4* ☎ *506/672–7255 or 888/678–7678* 🖶 *506/672–7250* ⊕ *www.homeport.nb.ca* 🖙 *6 rooms, 4 suites* ⚭ *Some microwaves, in-room VCRs, meeting rooms, free parking, some pets allowed; no smoking* 🖿 *AE, MC, V* ⦿ *BP.*

★ $ 🖾 **Inn on the Cove and Day Spa.** With its back lawn terraced down to the ocean, this inn near Irving Nature Park has as much character as its owners, who used to tape their delightful cooking show in the kitchen. Bedrooms are furnished with local antiques, several have balconies overlooking the ocean. A three-course dinner ($40 per person; reservations essential) is served Tuesday–Saturday in a dining room with a view of the Bay of Fundy. Guests and nonguests can, with reservations, get treatments at the spa. ✉ *Box 3113, Station B, 1371 Sand Cove Rd., E2M 4Z9* ☎*506/672–7799 or 877/257–8080* 🖶*506/635–5455* ⊕*www. innonthecove.com* 🖙 *1 room, 3 suites, 1 apartment* ⚭ *Dining room, some microwaves, some cable TV, spa, meeting rooms, free parking; no a/c in some rooms, no phones in some rooms, no kids under 12, no smoking* 🖿 *MC, V* ⦿ *BP.*

¢ 🖾 **Earle of Leinster B&B.** This 1877 three-story brick home in the heart of one of the city's oldest residential areas is within easy walking distance of theaters, restaurants, and more. The rooms in the main house are Victorian; rooms in the coach house in the courtyard have kitchenettes. The video library has a wide selection. ✉ *96 Leinster St., E2L 1J3* ☎ *506/652–3275* 🖙 *7 rooms* ⚭ *Some kitchenettes, some microwaves, refrigerators, in-room VCRs, billiards, recreation room, laundry facilities; no smoking* 🖿 *AE, MC, V* ⦿ *BP.*

Nightlife & the Arts

The Arts

Saint John Arts Centre (✉ 20 Hazen Ave. ☎ 506/633–4870), in a former Carnegie library, has several galleries displaying the work of local artists and artisans. Performance art pieces are occasionally presented here. Saint John's theater, opera, ballet, and symphony productions

★ take place at the **Imperial Theatre** (✉King's Sq. ☎ 506/633–9494), a beautifully restored 1913 vaudeville arena. Tours ($2) are available in July, Monday–Saturday 10–6; winter tours must be arranged in advance.

Nightlife

D'Arcy Farrow's Pub (✉ 43 Princess St. ☎ 506/657–8939) has five rooms and a main stage area that features live Celtic, jazz, and blues music. Top musical groups and other performers appear at **Harbour Station** (✉ 99 Station St. ☎ 506/657–1234 or 800/267–2800 ⊕ www. ★ harbourstation.nb.ca). **O'Leary's Pub** (✉ 46 Princess St. ☎ 506/634–7135), in the middle of the Trinity Royal Preservation Area, specializes in old-time Irish fun complete with Celtic performers; on Wednesday Brent Mason, a well-known neofolk artist, starts the evening and then turns the mike over to the audience. **Tapps Brew Pub and Steak House** (✉ 78 King St. ☎ 506/634–1957) pleases the over-30 crowd. Watch the action in the microbrewery, play cards at a big wooden table, or hide out in a secluded booth.

Sports & the Outdoors

Eastern Outdoors (✉ Brunswick Sq. at King and Germain Sts. ☎ 506/634–1530 or 800/565–2925 ⊕ www.easternoutdoors.com) has single and double kayaks and lessons, tours, and white-water kayaking. Make arrangements over the phone or at the Eastern Outdoors retail store in Brunswick Square in downtown Saint John. The **Reversing Falls Jet Boat** (✉ Fallsview Park off Fallsview Dr. ☎ 506/634–8987 or 888/634–8987 ⊕ www.jetboatrides.com ☉ June–mid-Oct.) has 20-minute thrill rides in the heart of the Reversing Falls or more sedate sightseeing tours along the falls. Age and size restrictions apply on certain rides. Tours depart June–mid-October 10 AM–dark and cost $30. The **Rockwood Park Golf Course** (✉ 1255 Sandy Point Rd. ☎ 506/634–0090) is an 18-hole course with an aquatic driving range as well. The course is 300 yards past the Saint John Regional Hospital entrance; follow the signs to the hospital off Route 1 in Saint John.

Shopping

Brunswick Square (✉ King and Germain Sts. ☎ 506/658–1000), a verti-★ cal mall, has many top-quality boutiques. **Handworks Gallery** (✉ 12 King St. ☎ 506/652–9787) carries the best of professional crafts and fine art made in New Brunswick. **House of Tara** (✉ 72 Prince William St. ☎ 506/634–8272) is wonderful for fine Irish linens and woolens. **Peter Buckland Gallery** (✉ 80 Prince William St. ☎ 506/693–9721), open Tuesday through Saturday or by appointment, is an exceptionally fine gallery that carries prints, photos, paintings, drawings, and sculpture by Canadian artists including Saint John native Jack Humphrey. **Tim Isaac Antiques** (✉ 97 Prince William St. ☎ 506/652–3222) has fine furniture, glass, china, Oriental rugs, and a well-informed staff. Unique sales are often advertised in local papers. **Trinity Galleries** (✉ 128 Germain St. ☎ 506/634–1611) represents fine Maritime and Canadian artists.

en route Unlike most Bay of Fundy beaches, **New River Beach** (✉ Off Hwy. 1, 50 km [30 mi] west of Saint John) is sandy and great for swimming, especially if you wait until the tide is coming in. The sun warms the sand at low tide, and the sand warms the water as it comes in. It is part of a provincial park ($5 admission) that offers interpretive programs. There are hiking trails and kayak rentals, too.

THE FUNDY COAST

Bordering the chilly and powerful tidal Bay of Fundy is some of New Brunswick's most dramatic coastline. This area extends from the border town of St. Stephen and the lovely resort village of St. Andrews, past tiny fishing villages and rocky coves, through Saint John, and on to Fundy National Park, where the world's most extreme tides rise and fall twice daily. The Fundy Isles—Grand Manan Island, Deer Island, and Campobello—are havens of peace that have lured harried mainlanders for generations. Some of the impressive 50-km (31-mi) stretch of coastline between St. Martins and Fundy National Park is accessible. The **Fundy Trail Parkway** (⊕ www.fundytrailparkway.com) is 11 km (7 mi) of coastal roadway with a 16-km (10-mi) network of walking, hiking, and biking trails that lead to an interpretation center and suspension bridge at Big Salmon River. On the other side of the bridge is the Fundy Footpath, for serious hikers. Vehicle access to the parkway ($5 per car) is mid-May through mid-October. Trail access for hikers, bikers, and skiers is free year-round.

St. Stephen

⑬ *107 km (66 mi) west of Saint John.*

St. Stephen is across the St. Croix River from Calais, Maine. The small town is a mecca for chocoholics: the chocolate bar was invented here; an elegant factory-outlet chocolate-candy store dominates the main street; and in early August "Choctails," chocolate puddings and cakes and even complete chocolate meals, are served during the Chocolate Festival. There's a provincial **visitor information center** (⊠ 5 King St. ☎ 506/466–7390) on King Street.

Ganong's famed hand-dipped chocolates and other candies are available at the factory store, **Ganong Chocolatier.** ⊠ 73 Milltown Blvd. ☎ 506/465–5611 ☉ Jan.–Apr., Mon.–Sat. 10–5; May, daily 9–5; June–Aug., weekdays 8–8, Sat. 9–5, Sun. noon–5; Sept.–Dec., Mon.–Sat. 9–5.

ⓒ The **Chocolate Museum,** behind Ganong Chocolatier, explores the sweet history of candy making with hand-dipping videos and hands-on exhibits. ⊠ 73 Milltown Blvd. ☎ 506/466–7848 ⊕ www.chocolatemuseum. ca ⊠ $5 ☉ Mar.–mid-June and Sept.–Nov., weekdays 9–5; mid-June–Aug., daily 9–6:30.

> [en route] **St. Croix Island** can be seen from an interpretive park on Route 127, between St. Stephen and St. Andrews. An International Historic Site, St. Croix is where explorers Samuel de Champlain and Sieur de Monts spent their first harsh winter in North America in 1604. Commemorative events planned for June 21–July 4 2004 include pow-wows, concerts, reenactments, art exhibits, a culinary festival, and more. Check for updates at www.stecroix2004.org.

St. Andrews by-the-Sea

▶ ★ ⑭ *29 km (18 mi) southeast of St. Stephen.*

On Passamaquoddy Bay, St. Andrews by-the-Sea, a designated National Historic District, is one of North America's prettiest resort towns. It has long been a summer retreat of the affluent (mansions ring the town). Of the town's 550 buildings, 280 were erected before 1880, and 14 of those have survived from the 1700s. Some Loyalists even brought their homes with them piece by piece from Castile, Maine, across the bay, when the American Revolution didn't go their way. If you'd like to take a self-guided tour, pick up a walking-tour map at the visitor information center at 46 Reed Avenue (next to the arena) and follow it through the pleasant streets. Water Street, by the harbor, has eateries, gift and crafts shops, and artists' studios. Knowledgeable costumed guides from **Heritage Discovery Tours** (☎ 506/529–4011) conduct historical walking tours of St. Andrews. There are nighttime ghost walks in summer.

A particular gem is the **Court House** (✉ 123 Frederick St. ☎ 506/529–4248), which has been active since 1840.

Directly adjacent to the Court House is the stone-walled **Old Gaol,** which functioned as the town jail from 1834 to 1979. Today it houses the Charlotte County archives. Tours are given May through August. ✉ *123 Frederick St.* ☎ *506/529–4248* ✉ *Free* ☉ *Weekdays 9–noon and 1–5.*

Greenock Church (✉ Montague and Edward Sts. ☎ no phone) owes its existence to a remark someone made at an 1822 dinner party about the "poor" Presbyterians not having a church of their own. Captain Christopher Scott, who took exception to the slur, spared no expense on the building, which is decorated with a carving of a green oak tree in honor of Scott's birthplace, Greenock, Scotland.

The **Ross Memorial Museum** was established by an American couple who had a summer home in St. Andrews for 40 years. The Rosses donated the trappings of that home—and an extensive collection of 19th-century New Brunswick furniture and decorative artwork—to the town and purchased this 1824 Georgian mansion to house them. ✉ *188 Montague St.* ☎ *506/529–5124* ✉ *By donation* ☉ *Late June–Aug., Mon.–Sat. 10–4:30; Sept.–mid-Oct., Tues.–Sat. 10–4:30.*

Nearly 2,000 varieties of trees, shrubs, and plants cover the 27 acres of **Kingsbrae Horticultural Garden,** one of Canada's most spectacular public gardens. Mature cedar hedges and rare Acadian old-growth forest coupled with innovative new plantings (some experimental) create an attractive mishmash of old and new gardening styles. Unusual and exotic flowers border the pathways, and towering trees line the woodland trail. Each garden has a purpose or theme: one attracts butterflies; another is designed for children. Among the unconventional displays are the Touch and Feel Garden, a garden maze, and the Therapy Garden, designed for people with disabilities. Demonstration gardens reveal the secrets of successful horticulture. Kingsbrae also has an art gallery and a café that serves light meals and decadent desserts. ✉ *220 King St.* ☎ *506/529–3335* ✉ *$7.50* ☉ *May–Oct., daily 9–6.*

FodorsChoice ★

The Huntsman Marine Science Centre provides educational displays at its **Huntsman Aquarium and Museum.** Marine life includes a teeming touch tank and some very entertaining seals, which are fed at 11 and 4 daily. ✉ *1 Lower Campus Rd.* ☎ *506/529–1202* ⊕ *www.huntsmanmarine.ca* ✉ *$5.25* ☉ *May and June, daily 10–4:30; July and Aug., daily 10–6; Sept.–Oct., Mon. and Tues. noon–4:30, Wed.–Sun. 10–4:30.*

off the beaten path

MINISTERS ISLAND – This huge island estate, once completely self-sufficient, was the summer home of Sir William Van Horne, chairman of the Canadian Pacific Railway from 1899 to 1915. Touring the island is a two-hour adventure and requires a car. Line up on Bar Road at low tide (check local schedules) and be prepared to drive across the sandbar. On the island are the Covenhoven Mansion, where just a few artifacts are on display; a tidal swimming pool; a *livestock barn; a cottage; an old windmill; and the 1790 Minister's House, from which the island takes its name. ⊠ Bar Rd. off Rte. 127, 5 km (3 mi) north of St. Andrews ☎ 506/529–5081 for tour information ≋ $5 ⊘ June–Oct., sunrise–sunset at low tide.*

Where to Stay & Eat

¢–$$ ✕ **The Gables.** Salads, fish, and seafood as well as fresh-made desserts are served in this casual harborside eatery. The owner's art decorates the walls, and there's a deck for alfresco dining in summer. ⊠ 143 Water St. ☎ 506/529–3440 ▭ MC, V.

¢–$$ ✕ **Ossie's Seafood Take-Out.** The gaudy billboard outside this unassuming take-out joint reads THE BEST SEAFOOD IN NORTH AMERICA. Those who have tried it tend to agree. A local institution since 1957, Ossie's seafood is deep-fried and served with a famous "house" tartar sauce. Apart from fried seafood, Ossie's also turns out fish chowder, turkey soup, rolls, and pies and other desserts. There is no dining room, but there are lots of picnic tables. ⊠ 3222 Hwy. 1, Bethel ☎ 506/755–2758 ▭ No credit cards ⊘ Closed late Oct.–early Apr.

¢–$ ✕ **Sweet Harvest Market.** Known for its natural products and made-on-site breads, cookies, cakes, cheesecakes, and preserves, this casual bakery-deli is always experimenting. ⊠ 182 Water St. ☎ 506/529–6249 ▭ V.

$$$–$$$$ ✕▣ **Windsor House.** The rooms in this restored 1798 Georgian home are exquisite, with mahogany furnishings, four-poster beds, working fireplaces, and antiques and fabrics true to the period. Note the fine-art collection, unusual lighting fixtures, and attention to detail as you wander about the house. Menus at the fine restaurant ($$–$$$) are built around locally grown produce and freshly baked goods. The rack of lamb is excellent. A good wine cellar, two quiet dining rooms, and a garden courtyard complete the experience. ⊠ 132 Water St., E5B 1A8 ☎ 506/529–3330 or 888/890–9463 ⊟ 506/529–4063 ⊕ www.townsearch.com/ windsorhouse ⇄ 4 rooms, 2 suites ⌂ Dining room, billiards, bar ▭ AE, D, DC, MC, V ⦿| BP.

★ $$–$$$$ ✕▣ **Pansy Patch.** A visit to this B&B, a 1912 Normandy-style farmhouse with an art gallery, is a bit like a close encounter with landed gentry who are patrons of the arts and who like their gardens as rich and formal as their meals. Four rooms are in the Corey Cottage next door. All rooms have period furniture and are individually decorated. Afternoon tea and cookies are served wherever you like—in the dining room, in your room, in the garden, or on the deck overlooking the water. The restaurant ($$$) serves lunch and dinner. Entrées include seafood paella, beef tenderloin, and lobster. Guests can use the pool and tennis courts of the Fairmont Algonquin Hotel next door. ⊠ 59 Carleton St., E5B 1M8 ☎ 506/529–3834 or 888/726–7972 ⊟ 506/529–9042 ⊕ www. pansypatch.com ⇄9 rooms ⌂ Restaurant, concierge ▭MC, V ⊘ Closed mid-Oct.–mid-May ⦿| BP.

$$$$ ▣ **A. Hiram Walker Estate Heritage Inn.** This restored mansion, built for the Hiram Walker Distillery family in 1912, is gracious, elegant, and welcoming. It sprawls across manicured grounds, with Passamaquoddy Bay in the distance. All rooms have fireplaces; most have four-poster beds and oversize whirlpool baths. The owner is well informed about everything from the mustard served with your breakfast ham to the chandelier over the dining table. A converted carriage house has two additional rooms and an apartment. ⊠ 109 Reed Ave., E5B 2J6 ☎ 506/529–4210 or 800/470–4088 ⊟ 506/529–4311 ⊕ www.walkerestate.com ⇄ 13 rooms ⌂ Dining room, cable TV, pool, library ▭ AE, MC, V.

$$$$ ▣ **Kingsbrae Arms.** An experience as much as a property, this restored
FodorśChoice 1897 estate is a member of Relais & Châteaux. Eclectic antiques fill the
★ rooms and pampering touches are plentiful—roses and Belgian choco-

lates in the rooms, plush robes, a pantry stocked with biscotti, and daily afternoon tea. Expect excellent service from the gregarious owners and staff. Celebrate a honeymoon or anniversary here and get champagne and red roses. Each evening brings a meal made with the freshest local ingredients. The two-story carriage house has a private entrance, patio, and balcony, plus a kitchen (minus stove). All rooms have CD players and high-speed Internet access. ⊠ *219 King St., E5B 1Y1* ☎ *506/529– 1897* 🖷 *506/529–1197* ⊕ *www.kingsbrae.com* ➶ *6 rooms, 1 suite, 1 carriage house* ♿ *Dining room, in-room data ports, some minibars, cable TV, in-room VCRs, golf privileges, pool, library, piano, some pets allowed; no smoking* 🖃 *AE, MC, V* ⊙ *Closed Nov.–Feb.* ⧈❮ *MAP.*

★ **$$$–$$$$** 🍴 **Fairmont Algonquin.** This grand old resort, where the bellhops wear kilts and dinner is served on the wraparound veranda in fine weather, presides like an elegant dowager on a hill above the town. The rooms have a feeling of relaxed refinement; those in the newer Prince of Wales wing are especially comfortable. The Passamaquoddy Dining Room, open for breakfast and dinner (summer only), is noted for its seafood and regional dishes. Other options are the casual Right Whale Pub and the cozy Library Lounge and Bistro. Sign up for a beachfront lobster boil in summer. Concierge service and children's programs are available in summer. ⊠ *184 Adolphus St., E0G 2X0* ☎ *506/529–8823 or 800/ 257-7544* 🖷 *506/529–7162* ⊕ *www.fairmont.com/algonquin* ➶ *234 rooms* ♿ *3 restaurants, room service, in-room data ports, some microwaves, some refrigerators, cable TV with movies and games, 18-hole golf course, putting green, 2 tennis courts, pro shop, pool, gym, hot tub, sauna, spa, beach, bicycles, croquet, racquetball, shuffleboard, squash, 2 bars, shop, playground, dry cleaning, laundry service, meeting rooms, business services, some pets allowed (fee)* 🖃 *AE, DC, MC, V.*

$$–$$$$ 🍴 **Treadwell Inn.** Gardens, a huge deck, and balconies all overlook the ocean at this gracious old inn. Built by a ship chandler about 1820, the inn has been faithfully restored and furnished to reflect the era. All the rooms are lovely, though the less expensive ones overlook the street. A healthful, hearty breakfast is served in the big kitchen, which also has an ocean view. ⊠ *129 Water St., E5B 1A7* ☎ *506/529–1011 or 888/529– 1011* 🖷 *506/529–4826* ⊕ *www.townsearch.com/treadwell* ➶ *6 rooms* ♿ *Some kitchenettes, cable TV, laundry service* 🖃 *AE, MC, V* ⧈❮ *BP.*

$ 🍴 **Seaside Beach Resort.** If the click of a closing screen door sounds like summer at the beach to you, this waterfront cluster of cottages is your kind of place. At one end of the town's main street, the cabins, cottages, and apartments are close to all the action and a beach. Units are simple but comfortable and well equipped, right down to big pots for boiling lobsters. This is a terrific casual choice for kids and dogs. ⊠ *339 Water St., E5B 2R2* ☎ *506/529–3846 or 800/506–8677* 🖷 *506/529– 4479* ⊕ *www.seaside.nb.ca* ➶ *24 cottages* ♿ *Picnic area, some kitchens, some kitchenettes, cable TV, laundry facilities, some pets allowed; no smoking* 🖃 *AE, MC, V.*

Sports & the Outdoors

🎠 **St. Andrews Creative Playground** (⊠ 168 Frederick St.) is an amazing wooden structure for climbing, swinging, performing, making music, and playing games. The **Sunbury Shores Arts & Nature Centre** (⊠ 139 Water St. ☎ 506/529–3386) offers art workshops in drawing, etching, painting, pottery, and many other techniques and media in conjunction with environmental excursions.

GOLF The **Algonquin Golf Club** (⊠ Off Rte. 127 ☎ 506/529–7124 ⊕ www. algonquingolf.com) has a beautifully landscaped 18-hole, par-71 signature course, designed by Thomas McBroom. The holes on the back 9—especially the 12th—have beautiful views of Passamaquoddy Bay.

WATER SPORTS   The **Day Adventure Centre** (☎ 506/529–2600), open May through early
September, can arrange explorations of Passamaquoddy Bay on various
kinds of boats. **Fundy Tide Runners** (☎ 506/529–4481 ⊕ www.
fundytiderunners.com) uses a 24-foot Zodiac to search for whales,
seals, and marine birds. The clipper **M. V. Corey** (☎ 506/529–8116) is
an elegant vessel for whale-watching. **Seascape Kayak Tours** (☎ 506/529–
4866) provides instruction as well as trips around the area that last from
a half day to a week.

Shopping

Cottage Craft (⊠ Town Sq. ☎ 506/529–3190) employs knitters year-round
to make mittens, sweaters, blankets, and woolen crafts from its specially
dyed wool. The **Crocker Hill Store/Steven Smith Designs** (⊠ 45 King St.
☎ 506/529–4303) has art and other items for those who love gardens
and birds. **Garden by the Sea** (⊠ 217 Water St. ☎ 506/529–8905) is an
aromatic shop whose owners made a name for themselves with natural, vegetarian soap. Buy the soap, along with herbal shampoos, rinses,
masks, and bath fragrances. Attached to the store is the Garden Party
herbal tearoom. **Jon Sawyer Glass** (⊠ 719 Mowat Dr. ☎ 506/529–
3012) has exquisite handblown decorative glass objects. Observe the process of smoking some of New Brunswick's best salmon at **Oven Head
Salmon Smokers** (⊠ 101 Oven Head Rd., off Hwy. 1, Bethel ☎ 506/755–
2507 or 877/955–2507). Buy the smoked salmon at the on-site store or
in local grocery stores—or try it off the menu in many fine dining rooms
in the region. The **Seacoast Gallery** (⊠ 174 Water St. ☎ 506/529–0005)
★   carries fine arts and crafts by eminent New Brunswick artists. **Serendipin'
Art** (⊠ 168 Water St. ☎ 506/529–3327) sells handblown glass, hand-
painted silks, jewelry, and other crafts by New Brunswick artists.Top-
notch Canadian, American, and English antiques—including furniture,
rugs, silver, china, paintings, and drawings—can be found at **Windsor
House Art & Antiques** (⊠ 136 Water St., next to Windsor House ☎ 506/
529–3026).

Grand Manan Island

⑮   *35 km (22 mi) east of St. Andrews by-the-Sea to Black's Harbour, 2 hrs
by car ferry from Black's Harbour.*

Grand Manan, the largest of the three Fundy Islands, is also the farthest
from the mainland; you might see whales, seals, or a rare puffin on the
way over. Circular herring weirs dot the island's coastal waters, and fish
sheds and smokehouses lie beside long wharfs that reach out to bob-
bing fishing boats. Place-names are evocative: Swallowtail, Southern Head,
Seven Days Work, and Dark Harbour. It's easy to get around; only about
32 km (20 mi) of road lead from the lighthouse at Southern Head to
the one at North Head. John James Audubon, that human encyclope-
dia of birds, visited the island in 1831, attracted by the more than 240
species of seabirds that nest here. The puffin may be the island's symbol, but whales are the stars here. Giant finbacks, right whales, minkes,
and humpbacks feed in the rich waters. A day trip is possible, but your
car might not make the infrequent ferry both ways. It's this limited access that keeps the island authentic and relaxing, so you might as well
plan to stay a while. Ferry service is provided by **Coastal Transport**
(☎ 506/662–3724), which leaves the mainland from Black's Harbour,
off Route 1, and docks at North Head on Grand Manan Island.

Where to Stay & Eat

$ ✕▨ **Inn at Whale Cove Cottages.** Rustic surroundings join with elegant
furnishings at this secluded waterfront compound. Full breakfast is included for guests in rooms (not cottages). The dining room ($$–$$$;

reservations essential) serves everything from local seafood to chicken Oscar (breaded chicken breast stuffed with lobster and cheese) from 6 to 8:30 daily. An on-site food shop offers meals and snacks to go. Cottages are available by the week only. ⊠ *26 Whale Cove Cottage Rd., E5G 2B5* ☎ *506/662–3181* ⊕ *www.holidayjunction.com/whalecove* ⇆ *3 rooms, 3 cottages* ⚬ *Dining room, some microwaves, beach, library, some pets allowed; no a/c in some rooms, no room phones, no room TVs, no smoking* ═ *MC, V* ⊘ *Closed Nov.–Apr.*

$–$$ ⊡ **Compass Rose.** Two old houses on the water combine to give this small, English-style country inn a cottage atmosphere. The floral-theme guest rooms are bright and comfortable. Afternoon tea has evolved to include cappuccino, café au lait, and desserts. A wall of windows in the dining room overlooks the busy fishing wharf. A full English breakfast is served each day, and all rooms overlook the water. ⊠ *65 Rte. 776, E5G 1A2* ☎☎ *506/662–8570* ⊕ *www.compassroseinn.com* ⇆ *6 rooms* ⚬ *Restaurant; no a/c, no room phones, no kids under 12, no smoking* ═ *MC, V* ⦿ *BP.*

$ ⊡ **Marathon Inn.** This mansion built by a sea captain sits on a hill overlooking the harbor. The Marathon has been an inn since 1871, and many of its original furnishings can still be found in the guest rooms. The dining room specializes in seafood; it does not serve lunch but can pack lunches for guests. ⊠ *19 Marathon La., North Head E0G 2M0* ☎ *506/ 662–8488* ⊕ *www.angelfire.com/biz2/marathon* ⇆ *28 rooms, 15 with bath* ⚬ *Restaurant, tennis court, pool, 2 lounges, meeting rooms, some pets allowed (fee); no a/c* ═ *MC, V.*

Sports & the Outdoors

A whale-watching cruise from Grand Manan takes you well out into the bay. Dress warmly; some boats have winter jackets, hats, and mittens on board for those who don't heed this advice. Most operators give refunds if no whales are sighted. **Island Coast Boat Tours** (☎ 506/662–8181, 877/662–9393 in Canada and the U.S.) has been around for many years and has a great whale-watching reputation. The four- to five-hour tours ($48) run July–mid-September. **Sea Land Adventure** (☎ 506/ 662–8997) has the only whale-watching schooner in the Bay of Fundy. Seven-hour trips ($75) take place mid-June–September. The trip includes an on-board biologist, sailing instruction, lunch, and snacks. Interpreters on **Sea Watch Tours** (☎ 877/662–8552) are very knowledgeable about the birds you might encounter on your cruise, as well as the whales. Trips ($48) last 4–5 hours, July–September. For complete information on bird-watching, nature photography, hiking, cycling, horseback riding, sea kayaking, and whale-watching, contact **Tourism New Brunswick** (⊕ Box 12345, Fredericton E3B 5C3 ☎ 800/561–0123 ⊕ www.tourismnewbrunswick.ca).

Deer Island

⑯ *50 km (31 mi) east of St. Andrews by-the-Sea to Letete, 40 min by free ferry from Letete.*

One of the pleasures of Deer Island is walking around the fishing wharves like those at Chocolate Cove. Exploring the island takes only a few hours; it's 12 km (7 mi) long, varying in width from almost 5 km (3 mi) to a few hundred feet at some points. At **Deer Point,** walk through a small nature park while waiting for the ferry to Campobello Island. If you listen carefully, you may be able to hear the sighing and snorting of the **Old Sow,** the second-largest whirlpool in the world. If you can't hear it, you'll be able to see it, just a few feet offshore in the Western Passage off Point Park.

Where to Stay & Eat

$–$$$ ✕ **45th Parallel Restaurant.** Seafood is an integral part of home cooking on this island and at this restaurant. So are lasagna, hamburgers, and chicken dinners, and they're all on the menu, too. Flowers surround this casual and friendly place with red-and-white awnings. A dining terrace overlooks Passamaquoddy Bay. ✉ *941 Hwy. 772, Fairhaven* ☎ *506/ 747–2222 year-round, 506/747–2231 May–Oct.* ▭ *AE, MC, V* ⊘ *Closed weekdays Nov.–Mar.*

$ ▥ **West Isles World B&B.** This white frame house overlooks the cove and has two snug rooms with an informal country feel—the big upstairs suite has a water view. The owners can arrange whale-watching cruises and kayaking. Reserve ahead for a lobster dinner. ✉ *3 Mountain Side Dr., Lambert's Cove E5V 1G3* ☎ *877/744–2946* 🖷 *506/747–2946* ⊕ *www.westislesworld.nb.ca* ⥱ *2 rooms* ⌂ *Dining room, kitchenettes, microwaves; no room phones, no smoking* ▭ *V* ⧀ *BP.*

¢–$ ▥ **Sunset Beach Cottage & Suites.** A modern property surrounded by natural beauty, this complex is right on a secluded cove. Watch the porpoises and bald eagles during the day, and in the evening enjoy a rare east-coast treat—an ocean sunset. ✉ *21 Cedar Grove Rd., Fairhaven E5V 1N3* ☎ *506/747–2972 or 888/576–9990* ⊕ *www.cottageandsuites. com* ⥱ *5 suites, 1 cottage* ⌂ *Microwaves, cable TV with videos, inroom VCRs, pool; no a/c in some rooms, no smoking* ▭ *V.*

Sports & the Outdoors

Cline Marine Tours (✉ Richardson Wharf, 91 Richardson Rd., Richardson ☎ 506/747–0114 or 800/567–5880 ⊕ www.clinemarine.com) offers scenic and whale-watching tours. Kayaking along the Fundy coast is popular. **Eastern Outdoors** (☎ 506/529–4662 or 800/565–2925 ⊕ www. easternoutdoors.com) has single and double kayaks and offers lessons, tours, and white-water trips.

Campobello Island

★ **⑰** *40 min by ferry (June and July only) from Deer Island; 90 km (56 mi) southeast of St. Stephen via bridge from Lubec, Maine.*

Neatly manicured, preening itself in the bay, Campobello Island has always had a special appeal to the wealthy and the famous. It was here that the Roosevelt family spent its summers. The 34-room rustic summer cottage of the family of President Franklin Delano Roosevelt is now part of a nature preserve, **Roosevelt Campobello International Park,** a joint project of the Canadian and U.S. governments. The miles of trails here make for pleasant strolling. President Roosevelt's boyhood home was also the setting for the movie *Sunrise at Campobello*. To drive here from St. Stephen, cross the border to Maine, drive about 80 km (50 mi) down Route 1, take Route 189 to Lubec, Maine, and then cross a bridge to the island. ✉ *Roosevelt Park Rd.* ☎ *506/752–2922* 🎫 *Free* ⊘ *House late May–mid-Oct., daily 10–6; grounds daily year-round.*

The island's **Herring Cove Provincial Park** (✉ Welshpool ☎ 506/752–7010) has camping facilities, a restaurant, a 9-hole, par-36 Geoffrey Cornish golf course, a sandy beach, and miles of hiking trails.

Where to Stay & Eat

¢–$ ✕▥ **Lupine Lodge.** Originally a vacation home built by the Adams family (friends of the Roosevelts) in the early 1900s, these three attractive log cabins on a bluff overlooking the Bay of Fundy are now a modern guest lodge. Nature trails connect Lupine Lodge to Herring Cove Provincial Park. Two of the cabins contain the guest rooms, which are rustic, with modern furniture and homemade quilts. The third cabin houses the dining room ($–$$), which specializes in simple but well-prepared local seafood. A deck overlooking the bay connects the three buildings. ✉ *610 Rte. 774, Welshpool E5E 1A5* ☎ *506/752–2555 or 888/912–8880* ⊕ *www.lupinelodge.com* ⤳ *10 rooms, 1 suite* ⚙ *Restaurant, lounge, some pets allowed (fee)* ▤ *MC, V.*

$$$ ▦ **Water's Edge Villas.** Watch the sun set over the water from the deck of a modern two-bedroom cottage with all the comforts of home, including a lobster pot and a barbecue. The kitchen appliances are full size, and the living room couch is a pullout, so six can sleep comfortably. The water is just across the road, and the rocky beach is great for explorers. ✉ *37 Hutchins Rd., Welshpool E5E 1H1* ☎ *506/752–2359 or 800/836–7648* ⊕ *www.campobello.com/waedge/wateredg.html* ⤳ *3 villas* ⚙ *Microwaves, cable TV, in-room VCRs, laundry service, some pets allowed (fee); no room phones* ▤ *MC, V.*

St. Martins

⑱ *45 km (28 mi) east of Saint John.*

The fishing village of St. Martins has a rich shipbuilding heritage, whispering caves, miles of lovely beaches, spectacular tides, and a cluster of covered bridges, as well as several Heritage Inns and a couple of restaurants right on the beach. It's also the gateway to the Fundy Trail Parkway. The scenic drive portion of the linear **Fundy Trail Parkway** extends to an interpretation center at Salmon River. The road closely parallels the cycling-walking Fundy Trail along the shore. There are lots of places to park and many accessible scenic lookouts. The Fundy Footpath, for expert hikers, continues through to Fundy National Park. The parkway portion operates mid-May through mid-October at $5 per car. Trail access is free and open year-round.

Some of New Brunswick's finest artists and craftspeople welcome visitors to their galleries and studios. Amid the green and rolling hills between St. Martins and Sussex is **Powning Design** (✉ 610 Markhamville Rd. ☎ 506/433–1188 ⊕ www.powning.com), a studio-gallery operated by Peter and Beth Powning. Peter has won many awards for his work in clay, cast bronze, and other media. Beth is a writer and photographer whose work is found in galleries and books throughout North America. Call ahead to arrange a visit.

Where to Stay & Eat

$–$$$ ✕ **Broadway Cafe.** On a quiet and colorful street in "downtown" Sussex, this charming café sits across from a defunct but well-maintained train station, now an ice-cream parlor and tourist center. Dine at a streetside table or in the shaded garden. Inside, the café is a jumble of Christmas lights, wooden booths, and artwork. Breakfasts (10 AM–11:30 AM), lunches, and dinners are hearty. Sandwiches, pizzas, and salads fill the lunch menu; eclectic dinner choices include curries, chicken paprika, quiches, and plenty of seafood. ✉ *73 Broad St., Sussex, 60 km (37 mi) northeast of St. Martins* ☎ *506/433–5414* ⊕ *www.broadwaycafe.ca* ▤ *MC, V* ⊘ *Closed Sun. No dinner Mon.–Thurs.*

$$ ✕ **Adair's Wilderness Lodge.** All the food at this cedar lodge in the woods is made in the kitchen from scratch. You are served hearty portions of just about anything you like, including scallops, rainbow trout, and sirloin steak. If you want fresh lobster, call ahead. ✉ *Creek Rd., 12 km (7 mi) past Poley Mountain* ☎ *506/432–6687* ▤ *AE, DC, MC, V.*

$ ✕▦ **Weslan Inn.** Fireplaces, antiques, and lots of floral prints give the rooms in this Heritage Inn an English country feel. Breakfast is served in your room. The dining room ($$–$$$; reservations essential) specializes

in seafood; lobster pie is a hot item. ✉ *45 Main St., E5R 1B4* ☎ *506/
833–2351* ⊕ *www.weslaninn.com* ⇴ *3 rooms* ⚲ *Restaurant* ☰ *MC,
V* ⑩ *BP.*

$–$$ ✕⊡ **St. Martins Country Inn.** High on a hill overlooking the Bay of Fundy,
this restored sea captain's home is furnished with Victorian antiques.
The adjacent carriage house has four rooms. Formal dinners ($$–$$$)
in the Candlelight Dining Room are excellent. Children are welcome to
stay in the carriage house, though not in the main inn. ✉ *303 Main St.,
E5R 1C1* ☎ *506/833–4534 or 800/565–5257* 🖷 *506/833–4725* ⊕ *www.
stmartinscountryinn.com* ⇴ *16 rooms* ⚲ *Restaurant* ☰ *MC, V.*

Sports & the Outdoors

SKIING   **Poley Mountain Resort** (✉ Waterford Rd., 10 km [6 mi] southeast of Sussex ☎ 506/433–7653 ⊕ www.poleymountain.com) has 23 trails, a
snowboard park, a 660-foot vertical drop, and a tubing park with four
trails and its own lift.

Fundy National Park

⑲ *135 km (84 mi) northeast of Saint John*

FodorsChoice
★   Fundy National Park is an awesome 206-square-km (80-square-mi) microcosm of New Brunswick's inland and coastal climates. Park naturalists offer several programs each day, including beach walks and hikes
to explore the park's unique climatic conditions and the fascinating bi-
ological evolution evident in the forests. The park has 100 km (60 mi)
of varied hiking and mountain-biking trails, some gravel-surface auto
trails, year-round camping, golf, tennis, a heated Bay of Fundy saltwater pool, and a restaurant. In the evening there are interactive programs
in the amphitheater and campfires. Its more than 600 campsites range
from full-service to wilderness. ✉ *Rte. 114, Alma E4H 1B4* ☎ *506/887–
6000* ⊕ *www.pc.gc.ca* ✉ *$6 late May–mid-Oct., free mid-Oct.–late May*
☉ *Daily 24 hrs.*

The small seaside town of **Alma** services Fundy National Park with motels, restaurants that serve good lobster, and a bakery that sells sublime
sticky buns. Around this area, much of it in Albert County, there's
plenty to do outdoors—from bird-watching to spelunking. The **Albert
County Tourism Association** (✉ Hopewell Cape E0A 1Y0 ☎ 888/228–0444
or 506/882–2004) can provide information by phone or mail.

Salem & Hillsborough Railroad Inc. offers one-hour train excursions. Occasional three-hour dinner trains run through mid-October. The train
skirts the Petitcodiac River, travels near scenic marshlands and wooded
areas, and crosses a high trestle. A gift shop and museum on-site are
open daily 10–6. ✉ *2847 Main St., Hillsborough E4H 2X7* ☎ *506/734–
3195 seasonal* ⊕ *www.shrr.ca* ✉ *$10, $30 dinner train* ☉ *Mid-June–early
Sept., Tues., Wed., and weekends.*

Sports & the Outdoors

BIRD-WATCHING   The bit of shoreline at **Marys Point** (✉ follow signs off Rte. 915) draws
tens of thousands of migrating birds, including semipalmated sand-
pipers and other shorebirds, each summer. The area, now a bird sanctuary and interpretive center, is near Riverside-Albert.

GOLF   The **Fundy National Park Golf Club** (✉ Fundy National Park near the Alma
entrance ☎ 506/887–2970) is near cliffs overlooking the restless Bay
of Fundy; it's one of the province's most beautiful and challenging 9-
hole courses.

HORSEBACK   **Broadleaf Guest Ranch** (✉ 5526 Rte. 114, Hopewell Hill ☎ 506/882–
RIDING   2349 or 800/226–5405 ⊕ www.broadleafranch.com) can provide an

overnight adventure in the forest or a short trail ride through lowland marshes or along a beach. The Ranch Restaurant has themed evenings— for example, line dancing or roping instruction; reservations are required. Stay a while in a two-bedroom log cottage with all the comforts of home for $150 a night.

SEA KAYAKING **Baymount Outdoor Adventures** (⊠ Hillsborough ☎ 506/734–2660) offers sea kayaking around the Hopewell Rocks. **Fresh Air Adventure** (⊠ 16 Fundy View Dr., Alma ☎ 506/887–2249 or 800/545–0020 ⊕ www. freshairadventure.com) conducts Bay of Fundy sea-kayaking excursions that last from two hours to three days. Guides, instruction, and equipment are provided.

SPELUNKING **Baymount Outdoor Adventures** (⊠ Hillsborough ☎ 506/734–2660 ⊕ www. baymountadventures.com) has interpreters who lead expeditions into the White Caves near the Bay of Fundy. Caving is fun, but not for the faint of heart, as it requires crawling on cave floors and slithering through narrow openings. Baymount also arranges hikes and sea kayaking at Hopewell Rocks. Make reservations for all activities.

en route Along Routes 915 and 114 from Alma to Moncton are dozens of talented artists and craftspeople, many of whom open their studios and galleries to visitors. Visitor information centers have more information and a map. **Cornucopia Great Gifts and Fine Art** (⊠ 2816 Main St., Hillsborough ☎ 506/734–1118) stocks New Brunswick's finest crafts, including pottery, glass, wood, metal, and jewelry. Lynne Saintonge, an owner of **Joie de Vivre Contemporary Art & Craft** (⊠ Rte. 114, Riverside-Albert ☎ 506/882–2276 or 877/ 595–2276), is a painter–visual artist who uses computer and sound to enhance her images. Her fascinating work is created in a studio upstairs from the gallery. **Kindred Spirits Stained Glass Studio** (⊠ 2831 Main St., Hillsborough ☎ 506/734–2342) is where Diana Boudreau creates unique patterns with glass carefully chosen for its color and texture. Brian Blakney, of **Lonesome Rose Pottery** (⊠ Waterside Rd., east of Fundy National Park ☎ 506/882–2770) has over 20 years of experience in stoneware, porcelain, and raku clay, which influences the form and design of the pieces here. **Samphire Casuals** (⊠ Albert Mines Rd. off Rte. 114 near Hopewell ☎ 506/734–2851) is a converted one-room schoolhouse where Judy Tait silk-screens her unique designs on T-shirts, sweatshirts, and even mugs. Lars Larsen's **Studio on the Marsh** (⊠ Mary's Point Rd. off Rte. 915 ☎ 506/882–2917) is the perfect setting for his wildlife art. Many of **Tim Isaac and Karin Bach's** (⊠ Rte. 915 between Alma and Riverside-Albert ☎ 506/882–2166) wildlife clay sculptures and fountains are on display in a garden outside their studio. **Wendy Johnston's Pottery** (⊠ Behind the post office on Main St., Hillsborough ☎ 506/734–2046) is contemporary, functional, and brightly colored with abstract designs.

Cape Enrage

20 *15 km (9 mi) east of Alma.*

Route 915 takes you to the wild driftwood–cluttered beach at Cape Enrage, which juts out into the bay. A lighthouse, restaurant, gift shop, and some spectacular views can be found here.

Sports & the Outdoors

Cape Enrage Adventures (⊠ Off Rte. 915 ☎ 506/887–2273 ⊕ www. capenrage.com) has rappelling and rock climbing ($50; 2½ hours), kayaking ($55; 2½ hours), a ropes obstacle course ($10; 2 hours), and hiking. The five-day coastal hike is particularly challenging. Make reservations in advance.

Hopewell Cape

㉑ *40 km (25 mi) north of Alma.*

The coastal road (Route 114) from Alma to Moncton winds through covered bridges and along rocky coasts. **Hopewell Rocks** is home to the famous Giant Flowerpots—rock formations carved by the Bay of Fundy tides. They're topped with vegetation and are uncovered only at low tide, when you can climb down for a closer study. There are also trails, an interactive visitor center, a restaurant, a gift shop, and a children's play area. But be careful—there are big cliffs at low tide, and you must exit the beach quickly when tide comes in. ⊠ *131 Discovery Rd.* ☎ *877/ 734–3429* ⊕ *www.thehopewellrocks.ca* ⊡ *$5* ⊙ *Late May–June and Sept.–Oct, daily 8–5; July–Aug., daily 8–8; closing hrs vary slightly, so call ahead.*

Where to Stay & Eat

$ ✕⊡ **Aubergine & Spa.** Within this 1854 converted country home are cozy rooms, a cedar sauna, and an intimate restaurant ($–$$) that specializes in Indonesian food with some Thai and Indian choices as well. The furniture is antique, and many of the paintings are by young Acadian artists; the combination works amazingly well. ⊠ *5 Maple St., Riverside-Albert E4H 3X1, 24 km (15 mi) southwest of Hopewell Cape* ☎ *506/882–1800 or 877/873–1800* ⊟ *506/882–1801* ⊕ *www.auberginespa.com* ⊅ *4 rooms* ⚭ *Restaurant, sauna, spa, laundry service, meeting room; no a/c, no room phones, no smoking* ⊟ *AE, DC, MC, V* ⊙| *CP.*

$ ⊡ **Florentine Manor Heritage Inn.** With silver candlesticks on the dining-room table and handmade quilts on the beds, this restored old shipbuilder's house is a haven for honeymooners and romantics. All the rooms have at least two windows, the better to hear the birds in the trees outside. Two rooms have fireplaces and two have whirlpool baths. Dinner is served by request. ⊠ *356 Rte. 915, Harvey on the Bay E4H 2M2* ☎ *506/882– 2271 or 800/665–2271* ⊟ *506/882–2936* ⊅ *9 rooms* ⚭ *Dining room, bicycles; no a/c, no room phones, no kids under 8, no smoking* ⊟ *MC, V* ⊙| *BP.*

Moncton

▶ **㉒** *80 km (50 mi) north of Alma.*

A friendly city, often called the Gateway to Acadia because of its mix of English and French and its proximity to the Acadian shore, Moncton has a renovated downtown with unique shops and restaurants. Its twin city Dieppe is home to wisely placed malls that do a booming business. A water-theme park and nearby beaches make Moncton a cool summer spot. The World Wine Festival in November and the HubCap Comedy Festival in February warm up winter. A walking-tour brochure, available at the tourist information centers at both Magnetic Hill on Route 126 and in Bore Park on Main Street, indicates the city's historic highlights.

This city has long touted two natural attractions: the Tidal Bore and the Magnetic Hill. You may be disappointed if you've read too much tourist hype, though. In days gone by, before the harbor mouth filled with silt, the **Tidal Bore** was an incredible sight, a high wall of water that surged in through the narrow opening of the river to fill red mud banks to the brim. It still moves up the river, and is worth seeing, but it's no longer a raging torrent. Bore Park on Main Street is the best vantage point; viewing times are posted there.

☽ **Magnetic Hill** creates a bizarre optical illusion. If you park your car in neutral at the designated spot, you seem to be coasting uphill without power. Shops, a water-theme park, a restaurant, a zoo, a golf course, and a small railroad are part of the larger complex here; there are extra charges for the attractions. ⊠ *North of Moncton off Trans-Canada Hwy.; watch for signs* 🖾 *$3* ☽ *May–early Sept., daily 8–8.*

☽ An excellent family water-theme park, **Magic Mountain** is adjacent to Magnetic Hill. ⊠ *Off Trans-Canada Hwy. on the outskirts of Moncton* 🕾 *506/857–9283, 800/331–9283 in Canada* 🖾 *$20.95* ☽ *Mid–late June and mid-Aug.–early Sept., daily 10–6; July–mid-Aug., daily 10–8.*

☽ The **Magnetic Hill Zoo,** the largest zoo in Atlantic Canada, has no shortage of exotic species: lemurs, lions, and muntjacs. There's a tropical house with reptiles, amphibians, birds, and primates. At Old MacDonald's Barnyard children can pet domestic animals or ride a pony in summer. ⊠ *Off Trans-Canada Hwy. on the outskirts of Moncton* 🕾 *506/384–0303* 🖾 *$6* ☽ *July–mid-Aug., daily 8–8; mid-Aug.–June, hrs of operation vary with funding, so call ahead.*

★ A restored 1920s vaudeville stage, the opulent **Capitol Theatre** is a beautiful attraction in itself as well as a venue for plays, musicals, ballets, and concerts. Free tours are given when guides are available. ⊠ *811 Main St.* 🕾 *506/856–4379, 800/567–1922 in Canada* ☽ *Tour times vary according to performances and availability; call ahead.*

The 1821 **Free Meeting House,** a simple and austere National Historic Site operated by the Moncton Museum, is Moncton's oldest standing building. It was built as a gathering place for all religious denominations without their own places of worship. ⊠ *100 Steadman St.* 🕾 *506/856–4383* 🖾 *By donation* ☽ *Mon.–Sat. 9–4:30, Sun. 1–5.*

Comprehensive exhibits trace the city's history from the days of the Mi' Kmaq people to the present at the **Moncton Museum.** ⊠ *20 Mountain Rd.* 🕾 *506/856–4383* 🖾 *By donation* ☽ *Mon.–Sat. 9–4:30, Sun. 1–5.*

The halls of the **Aberdeen Cultural Centre,** a converted schoolhouse, ring with music and chatter. This is home to theater and dance companies, a framing shop, and several galleries. **Galerie 12** represents leading contemporary Acadian artists. **Galerie Sans Nom** is an artist-run co-op supporting avant-garde artists from throughout Canada. The English, artist-run **IMAGO Inc.** is the only print production shop in the province. Guided tours are available by appointment. ⊠ *140 Botsford St.* 🕾 *506/857–9597* 🖾 *Free* ☽ *Weekdays 10–4.*

The **Acadian Museum,** at the University of Moncton, has a remarkable collection of artifacts reflecting 300 years of Acadian life in the Maritimes. There's also a fine gallery showcasing contemporary art by local and Canadian artists. ⊠ *Clement Cormier Bldg., Université Ave.* 🕾 *506/858–4088* ⊕ *www.umoncton.ca/maum* 🖾 *$3* ☽ *July–Aug., daily 9:30–7; Sept.–June, weekdays 9:30–5, Sun. 1–4.*

Where to Stay & Eat

$$–$$$$ ✕ **Fisherman's Paradise.** The enormous dining area in this restaurant seats more than 350 people. Memorable à la carte seafood dishes are served in an atmosphere of candlelight and wood furnishings. ⊠ *375 Dieppe Blvd.* 🕾 *506/859–4388* 🞸 *AE, DC, MC, V.*

★ $$–$$$ ✕ **Le Château à Pape.** This riverside restaurant in an old Victorian home has it all—crisp white linen, romantic atmosphere, and a well-stocked wine cellar (you go down and select your own). The chef is third generation in the French-Acadian tradition. He prepares everything from steak to seafood with an Acadian flare. Traditional Acadian dishes include *fricot* (stew) and *poutine à trou* (apple pastry). ✉ *2 Steadman St.* ☎ *506/855–7273* ▤ *AE, DC, MC, V* ⊘ *No lunch.*

¢–$$ ✕ **Pump House Brewery.** The pub fare here goes above and beyond, with
FodorśChoice   wood-oven pizzas—the veggie version is particularly hearty—a custom
★   veggie burger, hamburgers, chicken burgers, steaks, club sandwiches, and snack food. Beer is brewed on site, and there's even beer bread, made with grains left over from the brewing process. With metal fermentation tanks and bags of hops as part of the decor, this place is anything but formal. ✉ *5 Orange La.* ☎ *506/855–2337* ▤ *AE, MC, V.*

¢–$ ✕ **Vito's.** This restaurant is the original of what is now a small but successful family chain. The pizza toppings are fresh and generous. Pasta, chicken dishes, seafood, and veal round out the selection. The Mediterranean decor completes the mood. Vito's can be busy on weekends, so reserve ahead. ✉ *726 Mountain Rd.* ☎ *506/858–5000* ▤ *AE, DC, MC, V.*

★ **$$–$$$**   ✕▦ **Delta Beauséjour.** Moncton's finest hotel is conveniently located downtown and has friendly service. The decor of the guest rooms echoes the city's Loyalist and Acadian roots. L'Auberge, the main hotel restaurant ($$–$$$$), has a distinct Acadian flavor. The more formal Windjammer dining room ($$$$) is modeled after the opulent luxury liners of the early 1900s. ✉ *750 Main St., E1C 1E6* ☎ *506/854–4344* ☐ *506/858–0957* ⊕ *www.deltahotels.com* ⟲ *299 rooms, 11 suites* ⟲ *2 restaurants, café, cable TV with movies and video games, indoor pool, gym, bar, Internet, meeting rooms, some pets allowed* ▤ *AE, D, DC, MC, V.*

$$ ▦ **Château Moncton Hotel & Suites.** This modern châteaulike hotel stretches along the Petitcodiac River. The decor is European with custom-made cherrywood furniture. It's close to downtown businesses, large shopping malls, restaurants, theaters, and an amusement park. ✉ *100 Main St., E1C 1B9* ☎ *506/870–4444 or 800/576–4040* ☐ *506/870–4445* ⊕ *www.chateau-moncton.nb.ca* ⟲ *106 rooms, 12 suites* ⟲ *In-room data ports, minibars, cable TV with movies, gym, lounge, meeting rooms* ▤ *AE, DC, MC, V* ⊠ *CP.*

$$ ▦ **Ramada Plaza Crystal Palace.** Part of an amusement complex, this hotel keeps the fun coming with theme rooms devoted to rock and roll, the Victorian era, and more. The hotel also has movie theaters, a giant bookstore, an indoor pool, and an indoor amusement park. Champlain Mall is just across the parking lot. ✉ *499 Paul St., Dieppe E1A 6S5* ☎ *506/858–8584 or 800/561–7108* ☐ *506/858–5486* ⊕ *www.crystalpalacehotel.com* ⟲ *92 rooms, 23 suites* ⟲ *Restaurant, minibars, cable TV with movies, indoor pool, gym, meeting rooms, some pets allowed* ▤ *AE, D, DC, MC, V.*

Nightlife & the Arts

Top musicians and other big acts appear at the **Coliseum Arena Complex** (✉ 377 Killam Dr. ☎ 506/857–4100 ⊕ www.monctoncoliseum.com). **Club Cosmopolitan** (✉ 700 Main St. ☎ 506/857–9117) is open Wednesday through Sunday for rock, jazz, or blues, and dancing. Live bands play Sunday. **Club Mystique** (✉ 939 Mountain Rd. ☎ 506/858–5861) features major Canadian rock and alternative artists a couple of times
FodorśChoice   a month. Fermentation tanks are in plain view at the **Pump House Brew-**
★   **ery** (✉ 5 Orange La. ☎ 506/855–2337), where seasonal ales, such as pumpkin for Halloween, are served, along with house brews like blueberry ale—complete with floating blueberries. There's live Celtic music Saturday night, and the pub is a venue for the HubCap Comedy Festival in February. **Rockin Rodeo** (✉ 415 Elmwood Dr. ☎ 506/384–4324)

is the biggest country-and-western bar in the province. **Voodoo** (✉ 938 Mountain Rd. ☎ 506/858–8844) has lots of room for dancing and caters to the 25-plus crowd.

Sports & the Outdoors

The **All World Super Play Park** (✉ Cleveland Ave., Riverview), across the river from Moncton, is a giant wooden structure with plenty of room for children to exercise their bodies and imaginations. **Royal Oaks Golf Club** (✉ 1746 Elmwood Dr. ☎ 506/388–6257, 866/769–6257 in Canada ⊕ www.royaloaks.ca) is an 18-hole, par-72 PGA Championship course, the first Canadian course designed by Rees Jones.

Shopping

Five spacious malls, retail stores, and numerous pockets of shops make Moncton and nearby Dieppe two of the best places to shop in New Brunswick. This city is also the province's fashion trendsetter. Moncton has its share of fine crafts as well.

AMS Fashions (✉ Highfield Sq., 1100 Main St. ☎ 506/854–4475) is one of the few women's clothing shops in Moncton that isn't part of a chain. **Harlequin** (✉ 297 Mountain Rd. ☎ 506/854–1137) has a selection of power suits for women. **La Difference Fine Craft and Art** (✉ 823 Main St. ☎ 506/861–1800) specializes in Atlantic Canadian woodwork, jewelry, and pottery and also features paintings and photographs. The **Moncton Market** (✉ 120 Westmorland St. ☎ 506/383–1749) brims with fresh produce, baked goods, ethnic cuisine, and crafts every Saturday morning 7–1.

TANTRAMAR REGION

History and nature meet on the Tantramar salt marshes east of Moncton. Bounded by the upper reaches of the Bay of Fundy, the province of Nova Scotia, and the Northumberland Strait, the region is rich in history and culture and is teeming with birds. The marshes provide a highly productive wetland habitat, and this region is along one of North America's major migratory bird routes.

Dorchester & Memramcook

Memramcook is 20 km (12 mi) southeast of Moncton. Dorchester is another 10 km (6 mi) south of Memramcook.

Acadian roots run deep in Memramcook; on the other side of a marsh, Dorchester was a center of British culture and industry long before the Loyalists landed. Dorchester is home to some of the province's oldest buildings. The **Bell Inn Restaurant** (✉ 3515 Cape Rd., off Rte. 106 ☎ 506/379–2580), on the village square in Dorchester, was built in 1811 as a stagecoach stop. It is reputed to be the oldest stone structure in New Brunswick. Wander through the three dining rooms to get a good sense of what it used to be.

Keillor House & Coach House Museum and Saint James Church is a cluster of historic properties turned into museums. The restored 1813 Keillor House has 16 rooms and nine fireplaces. Saint James Church is home to the Beachkirk textile collection and is a working textile museum. *✉ 4974 Main St., Dorchester ☎ 506/379–6633 June–mid-Sept. ⊕ www.keillorhousemuseum.com ☑ $2 each property ☉ June–mid-Sept., Mon.–Sat. 10–5, Sun. 1–5.*

The **Monument Lefebvre National Historic Site** explores the turbulent history of the Acadian people in passionate detail. *✉ 480 Central St.,*

Memramcook ☎ *506/758–9808* ⊕ *www.pc.gc.ca* ✉ *$3.50* ☉ *June–mid-Oct., daily 9–5; mid-Oct.–May, by appointment.*

Sports & the Outdoors

Along the beaches at **Johnson's Mills** (✉ Rte. 935, about 8 km [5 mi] south of Dorchester) is part of the internationally recognized staging area for migratory shorebirds like semipalmated sandpipers. The numbers are most impressive in July and August.

Sackville

㉓ *22 km (14 mi) southeast of Dorchester and Memramcook.*

Sackville is an idyllic university town complete with a swan-filled pond. Its stately homes and ivy-clad university buildings are all shaded by venerable trees, and there's a waterfowl park right in the town. It makes for a rich blend of history, culture, and nature. The **Sackville Waterfowl Park,** in the heart of the town, has more than 3 km (2 mi) of boardwalk and trails. The area is dotted with viewing areas and interpretive signs throughout the marsh that reveal the rare waterfowl species that nest here. There's an interpretation center, and guided tours ($5) are available in French and English June through August. ✉ *Main St.* ☎ *506/364–4968* ⊕ *www.sackvillewaterfowlpark.com* ✉ *Free* ☉ *Daily 24 hrs.*

The sophisticated **Owens Art Gallery** is on the Mt. Allison University campus. One of the oldest and largest university art galleries in the country, it houses 19th- and 20th-century European, American, and Canadian artwork. ✉ *61 York St.* ☎ *506/364–2574* ⊕ *www.mta.ca/owens* ✉ *Free* ☉ *Mon. and Wed.–Fri. 10–5, Tues. 10–9, weekends 1–5.*

Near the Nova Scotia border in Aulac and 12 km (7 mi) east of Sackville, the **Fort Beauséjour National Historic Site** holds the ruins of a star-shape fort that played a part in the 18th-century struggle between the French and English. The fort has indoor and outdoor exhibits as well as fine views of the marshes at the head of the Bay of Fundy. ✉ *Rte. 106* ☎ *506/364–5080 June–mid-Oct., 506/876–2443 mid-Oct.–May* ⊕ *www. pc.gc.ca* ✉ *$3.50* ☉ *June–mid-Oct., daily 9–5.*

Where to Stay & Eat

¢–$$ ✕ **Schnitzel Haus.** This unpretentious roadside restaurant is refreshingly authentic. The German owners make schnitzel, bratwurst, spaetzle, and other traditional dishes. ✉ *153 Aulac Rd., Aulac, 12 km (7 mi) east of Sackville* ☎ *506/364–0888* ▤ *MC, V* ☉ *Closed Jan.*

★ $ ✕▦ **Marshlands Inn.** In this white-clapboard inn with a carriage-house annex, a welcoming double parlor with fireplace sets the comfortable country atmosphere. Bedrooms are furnished with sleigh beds or four-posters. The chefs offer traditional and modern dishes; seafood, pork, and lamb are specialties ($$–$$$). In summer most of the vegetables come from the organic garden in the backyard. ✉ *55 Bridge St., E4L 3N8* ☎ *506/536–0170 or 800/561–1266* ▤ *506/536–0721* ⊕ *www. marshlands.nb.ca* ⇨ *20 rooms* ♨ *Restaurant, Internet; no a/c in some rooms, no smoking* ▤ *AE, DC, MC, V.*

Sports & the Outdoors

Without a doubt, bird-watching is the pastime of choice in this region. For information contact the **Canadian Wildlife Service** (✉ 17 Waterfowl La. ☎ 506/364–5044). **Cape Jourimain Nature Centre** (✉ Exit 51 off Rte. 16 at foot of Confederation Bridge, Bayfield ☎ 866/538–2220 or 506/538–2220 ⊕ www.capejourimain.ca), at the Cape Jourimain National Wildlife Area, covers 1,800 acres of salt and brackish marshes. Large numbers of waterfowl, shorebirds, and other species can be seen here. It includes a fine nature interpretation center, a nature store, a restaurant, a viewing tower, and a 13-km (8-mi) trail network. **Goodwin's Pond** (⊠ Off Rte. 970), near the Red-Wing Blackbird Trail in Baie Verte, allows for easy viewing of wetland birds and boasts more birds per acre than anywhere else in the province. The **Port Elgin Rotary Pond and Fort Gaspereaux Trail** (⊠ 30 km [19 mi] northeast of Sackville via Rte. 16) have diverse coastal landscapes that attract migrating waterfowl, bald eagles, and osprey. At the **Tantramar Marshes** (⊠ High Marsh Rd. between Sackville and Point de Bute) you may be able to spot marsh hawks. The **Tintamarre National Wildlife Area** (⊠ Goose Lake Rd. off High Marsh Rd. ☎ 506/364–5044) consists of 5,000 acres of protected land ideal for sighting several species of ducks, rails, pied-billed grebes, and American bitterns.

Shopping

Fog Forest Gallery (⊠ 14 Bridge St. ☎ 506/536–9000 ⊕ www. fogforestgallery.ca) is a small, friendly, and reputable commercial gallery representing Atlantic Canadian artists. The **Sackville Harness Shop** (⊠ 110 Main St. ☎ 506/536–0642) still makes harnesses for horses and is the only place in North America that makes horse collars by hand. Pick up fine leather belts, wallets, bags, and jewelry. **Tidewater Books** (⊠ 4 Bridge St. ☎ 506/536–0404) has old-fashioned service and all the latest titles.

THE ACADIAN COAST & PENINSULA

The white sands and gentle tides of the Northumberland Strait and Baie des Chaleurs are as different from the rocky cliffs and powerful tides of the Bay of Fundy as the Acadians are from the Loyalists. Along the Acadian Coast the water is warm, the sand is fine, and the accent is French—except in the middle. Where the Miramichi River meets the sea, there is an island of First Nations, English, Irish, and Scottish tradition that is unto itself, rich in folklore and legend. Many people here find their livelihood in the forests, in the mines, and on the sea. In the Acadian Peninsula, fishing boats and churches define a land where a French-language culture survives. You're not likely to run into any language barriers in stores, restaurants, and attractions along the beaten path, but down the side roads it's a different story altogether.

Shediac

㉔ *25 km (16 mi) east of Moncton.*

Shediac is the self-proclaimed Lobster Capital of the World. It even has a giant lobster sculpture to prove it. But it is beautiful Parlee Beach that draws people to this fishing village–resort town. A 3-km (2-mi) stretch ★ of glistening sand, **Parlee Beach** has been named the best beach in Canada by several surveys. It is a popular vacation spot for families and plays host to beach-volleyball and touch-football tournaments; an annual sand-sculpture contest and a triathlon are held here as well. Services include canteens and a restaurant. ⊠ *Off Rte. 133* ☎ *506/533–3363* ⊠ *$5 per vehicle* ☉ *Mid-May–mid-Sept., 7 AM–9 PM.*

Parc de l'Aboiteau, on the western end of Cap-Pelé, has a fine sandy beach as well as a boardwalk that runs through salt marshes where waterfowl nest. The beach complex includes a restaurant and lounge with live music in the evening. Cottages are available for rent year-round. ⊠ *Exit 53 off Rte. 15* ☎ *506/577–2005 or 888/366–5555* ⊠ *$4 per vehicle* ☉ *Beach June–Sept., daily dawn–dusk.*

Where to Stay & Eat

$–$$$ ✕ **Paturel Shorehouse Restaurant.** This big "cottage" on the beach is quite cozy, and because it's right next door to a fish-processing plant, you can get nearly anything you want—even a 5-pound lobster. The chef has a way with salmon and sole. ✉ *46 Cap Bimet, at Legere St.* ☎ *506/532–4774* 🖃 *AE, DC, MC, V* ⊙ *Closed mid-Sept.–mid-May. No lunch.*

$ ✕🏠 **Little Shemogue Country Inn.** The unusual name (pronounced shim-o-*gwee*) is Mi'Kmaq for "good feed for geese." More surprising is the inn itself, a jewel hidden along a rough country road. The main inn is an exquisitely restored country home. A three-story wall of windows in the common area of the modern Log Point annex overlooks the ocean; the rooms here are large and have ocean views and whirlpool tubs. The outdoor hot tub is full of saltwater. The 200-acre property has its own white-sand beach, canoes, and trails along a salt marsh. Breakfast and a five-course prix-fixe dinner ($$$$) are served in four dining rooms by reservation. ✉ *2361 Rte. 955, Little Shemogue E4M 3K4, 40 km (25 mi) east of Shediac* ☎ *506/538–2320* 🖷 *506/538–7494* ⊕ *www.little-inn.nb.ca* ⇨ *9 rooms* ⇘ *Dining room, spa, beach, boating, bicycles, Internet, meeting rooms; no a/c in some rooms, no kids under 10, no smoking* 🖃 *AE, MC, V.*

Fodor'sChoice
★

$ ✕🏠 **Auberge Belcourt Inn.** This elegant Heritage Inn was built around 1912 and has been carefully restored and furnished with lovely period furniture. In summer the front veranda is an ideal spot for a drink before dinner at the Lobster Deck restaurant next door. The inn's restaurant is closed June–August and December and January but serves authentic Chinese dinners ($$$$) the rest of the year. ✉ *310 Main St., E4P 2E3* ☎ *506/532–6098* 🖷 *506/533–9398* ⊕ *www.sn2000.nb.ca/comp/auberge-belcourt* ⇨ *7 rooms* ⇘ *Restaurant, laundry service* 🖃 *AE, DC, MC, V* ⊙ *Closed Dec.–Jan.* ⏍ *BP.*

Bouctouche

㉕ *35 km (22 mi) north of Shediac.*

Le Pays de la Sagouine is a theme park with a make-believe island community that comes to life in French in daylong musical and theatrical performances and dinner theater–musical evenings July through September. There are some English-language tours, and the Friday-night jam sessions are accessible for English-speaking visitors, too. La Sagouine is an old charwoman-philosopher created by award-winning author Antonine Maillet. ✉ *Exit 32 off Hwy. 11* ☎ *506/743–1400 or 800/561–9188* ⊕ *www.sagouine.com* ⊡ *$14* ⊙ *Mid-June–Aug., daily 9:30–5:30; Sept., daily 10–3.*

★ **Irving Eco-Centre: La Dune de Bouctouche** is a superb example of a coastal ecosystem that protects the exceptionally fertile oyster beds in Bouctouche Bay. Hiking trails and boardwalks to the beach make it possible to explore sensitive areas without disrupting the environment of one of the few remaining great dunes on the northwest coast of North America. An outstanding interpretive center puts the ecosystem in perspective. The staff regularly conducts educational programs for visitors. Swimming and clam digging are allowed. ✉ *1932 Rte. 475* ☎ *888/640–3300 or 506/743–2600* ⊕ *www.irvingecocentre.com* ⊡ *Free* ⊙ *Hiking trails and boardwalk daily dawn–dusk. Visitor center May–June, daily noon–8; July–Aug., daily 10–8; Sept.–Oct., weekdays noon–5, weekends 10–6.*

Where to Stay & Eat

$ ✕🏠 **Auberge le Vieux Presbytère de Bouctouche.** This inn, formerly a rectory and then a retreat house complete with chapel (now a conference room), has a courtly staff and is brimming with wonderful New Brunswick art and fascinating collections of antiques and books. The restaurant ($$–$$$) serves seafood and Acadian fare and is supported by a substantial wine cellar. ⊠ *157 chemin du Couvent, E4S 3B8* ☎ *506/743–5568* 🖶 *506/743–5566* ⊕ *www.sn2000.nb.ca/comp/ presbytere* 🛏 *19 rooms, 3 suites* ♿ *Restaurant* ⊟ *AE, MC, V* ⊘ *Closed Oct.–June* ⫶○⫶ *CP.*

Kouchibouguac National Park

★ ➁⑥ *40 km (25 mi) north of Bouctouche, 100 km (62 mi) north of Moncton.*

The park's white dune-edged beaches, some of the finest on the continent, are preserved here. Kellys Beach is supervised and has facilities. The cycling is great here, with more than 35 km (22 mi) of virtually flat biking trails. In winter the trails are great for cross-country skiing, snowshoeing, snow walking, and kick sledding. The park also protects forests and peat bogs, which can be explored along its 10 nature trails. There are lots of nature interpretation programs, and you can canoe, kayak, and picnic, too. Bikes and boats can be rented. Reserve ahead for one of the 311 campsites. ⊠ *186 Rte. 117, Kouchibouguac* ☎ *506/ 876–2443* ⊕ *www.pc.gc.ca* ✉ *$6 late May–mid-Sept., free mid-Sept.–late May* ⊘ *Daily 24 hrs.*

Sports & the Outdoors

Kouchibouguac National Park conducts **Voyager Canoe Day Adventures** (☎ 506/876–2443), which take you to offshore sandbars to meet gray seals and common terns. You also learn about the area's Mi'Kmaq and Acadian culture. The cost is $30, and outings take place in English and French. Call for days and times. **Kayakouch, Inc.** (☎ 506/876–1199 ⊕ www.kayakouch.com), offers guided interpretive tours ranging anywhere from four hours to five days through the waters of Kouchibouguac National Park.

Miramichi City

➁⑦ *40 km (25 mi) north of Kouchibouguac, 150 km (93 mi) north of Moncton.*

The fabled Miramichi region is one of lumberjacks and fisherfolk. Celebrated for salmon rivers that reach into some of the province's richest forests and for the ebullient nature of its residents (Scottish, English, Irish, and a smattering of First Nations and French), this is a land of lumber kings, ghost stories, folklore, and festivals—celebrating the Irish in July and folk songs in August. Sturdy wood homes dot the banks of Miramichi Bay at Miramichi City, which incorporates the former towns of Chatham and Newcastle and several small villages. This is also where the politician and British media mogul Lord Beaverbrook grew up and is buried.

The **Atlantic Salmon Museum and Aquarium** provides a look at the endangered Atlantic salmon and at life in noted fishing camps along the rivers. ⊠ *263 Main St., Doaktown, 80 km (50 mi) southwest of Miramichi City* ☎ *506/365–7787* ⊕ *www.atlanticsalmonmuseum.com* ✉ *$5* ⊘ *June–early Oct., daily 9–5.*

♨ **Ritchie Wharf Park** has a nautical-theme playground complete with a "splash pad" that sprays water from below and dumps it from buckets above. Shops sell local crafts, and there are several restaurants and docking facilities. An amphitheater showcases local entertainers on Sunday afternoon in summer. ⊠ *Norton's La., Newcastle waterfront* *off King George Hwy.* ✉ *Free* ⊘ *Park daily dawn–dusk. Shops June–early Sept., daily 9–9.*

Dare the Dark for the Headless Nun! is a tragic tale told in the dark while being led to the city's most infamous haunts by costumed guides. ✉ *French Fort Cove; watch for signs along the King George Hwy. through the city* ☎ *800/459-3131* ✉ *$5* ⊘ *July–Aug., Mon., Wed., Fri. at dark.* The **Central New Brunswick Woodmen's Museum**, with artifacts that date from the 1700s, is in what looks like two giant logs, set on more than 60 acres of land. The museum portrays a lumberjack's life through displays, but its tranquil grounds are excuse enough to visit. A 10-passenger amusement train ($2) is a 1½-km (1-mi) woodland adventure. ✉ *6342 Rte. 8, Boiestown, 110 km (68 mi) southwest of Miramichi City* ☎ *506/369-7214* ⊕ *www.woodsmenmuseum.com* ✉ *$5* ⊘ *May–Sept., daily 9–5.*

Where to Stay & Eat

¢–$ ✕ **Cunard Restaurant.** With its Irish accent and lumberjack history, Miramichi is an unlikely place to find a great Chinese restaurant. The Cunard, however, has what it takes to make it anywhere. It is renowned for its Szechuan chicken and beef. Steaks and seafood are on the menu, too. ✉ *32 Cunard St* ☎ *506/773-7107* ▭ *AE, DC, MC, V.*

$–$$ ✕▥ **Rodd Miramichi River.** This grand riverside hotel, with warm natural wood and an earth-tone interior, manages to feel like a fishing lodge. The rooms are comfortable, with lots of fishing prints on the walls. Four rooms are specially equipped for guests with disabilities, and have wheelchair-accessible shower stalls. The Angler's Reel Restaurant ($$–$$$) is dedicated to fresh salmon. ✉ *1809 Water St., E1N 1B2* ☎ *506/773-3111* ▤ *506/773-3110* ⊕ *www.rodd-hotels.ca* ⇜ *76 rooms, 4 suites* ⌂ *Restaurant, cable TV with movies, indoor pool, gym, hot tub, bar, Internet, meeting rooms, some pets allowed (fee)* ▭ *AE, DC, MC, V.*

$$ ▦ **Pond's Chalet Resort.** Parts of this property are now more luxurious than rustic, after a 2002 fire made it necessary to rebuild. But you still get a traditional fishing-camp experience in the lodge and chalets along the Miramichi River. Surrounded by trees and overlooking a salmon river, the resort is ideal for outdoor recreation. There's a golf course nearby. ✉ *91 Porter Cove Rd., Ludlow E9C 2J3, 100 km (62 mi) southwest of Miramichi City; follow signs on Rte. 8* ☎ *506/369-2612* ▤ *506/369-2293* ⊕ *www.pondsresort.com* ⇜ *8 suites, 1 5-bedroom lodge, 14 cabins* ⌂ *Dining room, tennis court, volleyball, cross-country skiing, snowmobiling, bar, meeting rooms, some pets allowed; no a/c in some rooms* ▭ *AE, D, DC, MC, V.*

Shippagan

37 km (23 mi) north of Tracadie-Sheila.

Shippagan is an important commercial fishing and marine education center as well as a bustling, modern town with lots of amenities. It's also the gateway to the idyllic islands of Lamèque and Miscou. The wonderful **Aquarium and Marine Centre** has a serious and a fun side. The labs here are the backbone of marine research in the province, and the marine museum houses more than 3,000 specimens. A family of seals in the aquarium puts on a great show in the pool at feeding time. There's a touch tank for making the acquaintance of various sea creatures, and during the fisheries and aquaculture festival in July there are fish races in a special tank with numbered racing lanes. Place a bet on your favorite fish, and you could win a prize. ✉ *100 rue de l'Aquarium* ☎ *506/336-3013* ✉ *$6* ⊘ *May–Sept., daily 10–6.*

Across a causeway from Shippagan is Île Lamèque and the **Sainte-Cécile church** (⊠ Rte. 113 at Petite-Rivière-de-l'Île). Although the church is plain on the outside, every inch of it is decorated on the inside. Each July the **International Festival of Baroque Music** (☎ 506/344–5846) takes place here. **Île Miscou,** accessible by bridge from Île Lamèque, has white sandy beaches.

Caraquet

28 *40 km (25 mi) west of Shippagan.*

Perched along the Baie des Chaleurs, with Québec's Gaspé Peninsula beckoning across the inlet, Caraquet is rich in French flavor and is the acknowledged Acadian capital. Beaches are another draw. The two-week **Acadian Festival** (☎ 506/727–6515) held here in August includes the Tintamarre, in which costumed participants noisily parade through the streets, and the Blessing of the Fleet, a colorful and moving ceremony that eloquently expresses the importance of fishing to the Acadian economy and way of life.

★ ☺ A highlight of the Acadian Peninsula is **Acadian Historical Village.** The more than 40 restored buildings re-create Acadian communities between 1770 and 1939. There are modest homes, a church, a school, and a village shop, as well as an industrial area that includes a working hotel, a bar and restaurant, a lobster hatchery, a cooper, and tinsmith shops. Guided tours are given year-round at any time of day. ⊠ *Rte. 11, 10 km (6 mi) west of Caraquet* ☎ *506/726–2600 or 877/721–2200* ⊕ *www.villagehistoriqueacadien.com* ☜ *$14* ☉ *June–early-Sept., daily 10–6; mid-Sept., daily 10–5 with only 6 homes open; late Sept.–mid-Oct., daily 10–5.*

With 86 figures in 23 scenes, the **Acadian Wax Museum** traces the history of the Acadians between 1604 and 1761. ⊠ *Rte. 11 outside Acadian Historical Village* ☎ *506/727–6424* ⊕ *www.museedecire.com* ☜ *$7* ☉ *June and Sept., daily 9–6; July–Aug., daily 9–7.*

The **Pope's Museum,** 7 km (4 mi) outside Caraquet, is the only museum in North America dedicated to papal history. It celebrates the church's artistic and spiritual heritage with replicas of buildings like St. Peter's Basilica and the Florence Cathedral. ⊠ *184 Acadie St., Grand-Anse* ☎ *506/732–3003* ⊕ *www.museedespapes.com* ☜ *$5* ☉ *Mid-June–Aug., daily 10–6.*

Where to Stay & Eat

$$$–$$$$ ✕ **La Fine Grobe-Sur-Mer.** North of Bathurst in Nigadoo, about 80 km
Fodor'sChoice (50 mi) outside of Caraquet, is one of New Brunswick's finest restau-
★ rants. The French cuisine, seafood, and wine are outstanding because the chef-owner never compromises. Sample dishes include seafood crepes, bouillabaisse, and roast leg of lamb. The dining room is small but has a cozy fireplace and three walls of windows overlooking the ocean. ⊠ *289 rue Principal, Nigadoo* ☎ *506/783–3138* ⊕ *www.finegrobe.com* ☽ *Reservations essential* ⊟ *AE, DC, MC, V* ☉ *Lunch by special arrangement only.*

$ ✕▦ **Hotel Paulin.** Each pretty room of this quaint property has its own unique look, with old pine dressers and brass beds. The third-floor suites have spectacular water views. An excellent small restaurant ($$–$$$) offers traditional Acadian dishes, like *palourds* (Cohog clam pie) and *morue salée à la crème* (salt cod baked in cream), in addition to its other fine fare. ⊠ *143 blvd. St-Pierre W, E1W 1B6* ☎ *506/727–9981 or 866/727–9981* 🖷 *506/727–4808* ➥ *6 rooms, 6 suites* ☼ *Restaurant, in-room data ports* ⊟ *MC, V* ❢◻ *BP.*

CloseUp

ACADIAN CULTURE

CULTURE IS OFTEN DEFINED by geographical boundaries. Acadian culture, however, defines Acadia, because it isn't so much a place as it is an enduring French society. In New Brunswick it abides (although not exclusively) above an imaginary line drawn from Edmundston to Moncton. In the heartland you hear remnants of Norman-French. Around Moncton you're just as apt to hear a melodious Acadian dialect called Chiac, a tweedy kind of French with flecks of English.

French settlers arrived in the early 1600s and brought with them an efficient system of dikes called aboiteaux that allowed them to farm the salt marshes. In the 1700s they were joined by Jesuit missionaries who brought the music of Bach, Vivaldi, and Scarlatti along with their zeal. In 1713 England took possession of the region, and authorities demanded Acadians swear an oath to the English crown. Some did, others didn't. By 1755 it didn't seem to matter. Only those who fled into the forests escaped Le Grand Dérangement—the Expulsion of the Acadians—which dispersed them to Québec, the eastern seaboard, Louisiana (where they became known as Cajuns), France, and even as far as the Falkland Islands. It was a devastating event that probably should have eradicated French language and culture in the Maritimes. It didn't. It did, however, profoundly affect Acadian expression—mobility remains a pervasive theme in the art, literature, and music of the Acadian people.

Whether they were hiding deep in Maritime forests or living in exile, Acadians clung tenaciously to their language and traditions. Within 10 years of their deportation, Acadians began to return. They built new communities along coasts and waterways remote from English settlement. In the 1850s Acadians began to think "nationally." By 1884 there was an Acadian national anthem and a flag.

The Acadian national holiday on August 15 provides an official reason to celebrate Acadian culture. Le Festival Acadien de Caraquet stretches the celebration out for two weeks. Caraquet is also home to Théâtre Populaire d'Acadie, which mounts original productions for French communities throughout the Maritimes and encourages contemporary Acadian playwrights. Books by Acadian authors, including internationally renowned Antonine Maillet, circulate in Québec, France, and Belgium. Conceptual artist Herménégilde Chiasson pushes the envelope with his poetry and painting, and Paulette Foulem Lanteigne's palate contains the bright colors that have traditionally defined the Acadian spirit.

The earliest Acadian settlers made pine furniture that was elegant in its simplicity. Modern Acadian artisans continue to make functional things such as pottery and baskets into things of beauty. Handmade wooden spoons are doubly beautiful—in pairs they keep time to the music at kitchen parties, where Acadian families have traditionally sung their history around the kitchen fire. But it isn't necessary to have a party to enjoy "music de cuisine." Today folk singer Edith Butler of Paquetville takes some of that history back to her French cousins in Paris. A lively pop band called Mechants Maquereaux (roughly translated that's "Naughty Mackerel") carries the same messages with a modern spin.

Clearly, the love of music endures here: it rings clear in churches, the cotillion and quadrille are danced at Saturday-night soirees, Acadian sopranos and jazz artists enjoy international renown, and a world-class Baroque music festival in Lamèque still celebrates Bach, Vivaldi, and Scarlatti.

— Ana Watts

Sports & the Outdoors

The eight trails on the 507-foot drop at **Sugarloaf Provincial Park** (✉ 596 Val d'Amour Rd., Atholville E3N 4C9, 180 km (112 mi) north of Caraquet ☎ 506/789–2366) accommodate skiers of all levels. There are also 25 km (16 mi) of cross-country ski trails. Instruction and equipment rentals are available. In summer an alpine slide offers fun on the ski hill, and there's lots of space for camping and hiking. The park has a lounge and cafeteria.

ST. JOHN RIVER VALLEY

The scenery of the St. John River valley is panoramic—gently rolling hills and sweeping forests, with just enough rocky gorges to keep it interesting. And the native peoples—those of French, English, Scottish, and Danish heritage who live along the river—ensure that the area's culture is equally intriguing. The St. John River forms 120 km (74 mi) of the border with Maine, then swings inland. Eventually it cuts through the heart of Fredericton and rolls down to Saint John. Gentle hills of rich farmland and the blue sweep of the water make this a lovely area in which to drive. The Trans-Canada Highway (Route 2) follows the banks of the river for most of its winding 403-km (250-mi) course. New highway construction has left Route 102 (the old Route 2) above Fredericton as a quiet scenic drive. In the early 1800s the narrow wedge of land at the northern end of the valley was coveted by Québec and New Brunswick; the United States claimed it as well. To settle the issue, New Brunswick governor Sir Thomas Carleton rolled dice with the governor of British North America at Québec. Sir Thomas won—by one point. Settling the border with the Americans was more difficult; even the lumberjacks engaged in combat. Finally, in 1842, the British flag was hoisted over Madawaska County. One old-timer, tired of being asked to which country he belonged, replied, "I am a citizen of the Republic of Madawaska." So began the mythical republic, which exists today with its own flag (an eagle on a field of white) and a coat of arms.

Edmundston

29 *275 km (171 mi) northwest of Fredericton.*

Edmundston, the unofficial capital of Madawaska, has always depended on the wealth of the deep forest around it. Even today the town looks to the Fraser Papers pulp mills as its major source of employment. In these woods the legend of Paul Bunyan was born, and then tales about Bunyan spread to Maine and beyond. **St-Jacques,** a suburb 5 km (3 mi) north of Edmundston, has Les Jardins de la République Provincial Park, plus recreational facilities, the Antique Auto Museum, and a botanical garden. The annual **Foire Brayonne** (☎ 506/739–6608), held in Edmundston over the long weekend surrounding New Brunswick Day (first Monday in August), is the biggest Francophone festival outside Québec. It's also one of the liveliest and most vibrant cultural events in New Brunswick, with concerts by acclaimed artists as well as local musicians and entertainers.

At the **New Brunswick Botanical Garden** roses, rhododendrons, alpine flowers, and dozens of other annuals and perennials bloom in eight gardens. The music of Mozart, Handel, Bach, or Vivaldi often plays in the background. Two arboretums have coniferous and deciduous trees and shrubs. ✉ *Main St., St-Jacques* ☎ *506/737–5383* 💲 *$4.75* 🕙 *June and Sept., daily 9–6; July and Aug., daily 9–8.*

Where to Stay & Eat

$$ ✕⌂ **Auberge Les Jardins Inn.** Fine French cuisine ($$–$$$$) is the major attraction at this modern inn with a motel-like annex. The five "inn" rooms are superior and decorated in maple, cedar, aspen, oak, and pine. Paintings and fabrics in the annex rooms are decorated with provincial and territorial flowers. Some rooms have whirlpool baths, and others have fireplaces. There's lovely terrace dining in summer, a walking trail runs past the front door, and the New Brunswick Botanical Garden is nearby. The restaurant serves breakfast and dinner. ⊠ *60 rue Principal, St-Jacques E7V 1B7* ☎ *506/739–5514 or 800/630–8011* ⊕ *www. auberge-lesjardins-inn.com* ⇔ *17 rooms* ⌂ *Restaurant, cable TV, in-room VCRs, pool, meeting rooms* ⊟ *AE, MC, V.*

$ ⌂ **Howard Johnson Hotel & Convention Centre.** The downtown location of this chain hotel—within a shopping complex near the town's river-side walking trail—makes it worth visiting. The small restaurant has talented chefs. ⊠ *100 Rice St., E3V 1T4* ☎ *506/739–7321 or 800/576–4656* ⊟ *506/735–9101* ⇔ *99 rooms, 4 suites* ⌂ *Restaurant, cable TV with movies, indoor pool, hot tub, sauna, meeting rooms, some pets allowed* ⊟ *AE, D, DC, MC, V.*

Sports & the Outdoors

Mont Farlagne (⊠ 360 Mont Farlagne Rd., St-Jacques ☎ 506/735–8401) has 20 trails for downhill skiing on a vertical drop of 600 feet. Its four lifts can handle 4,000 skiers per hour, and there's night skiing on eight trails. Snowboarding and tube sliding add to the fun. Equipment rentals are available, and it has a cafeteria and a bar. At this writing, the future of Farlagne is uncertain as it is set to be auctioned; call ahead.

Grand Falls

③⓪ *50 km (31 mi) south of Edmundston.*

The St. John River rushes itself over a high cliff, squeezes through a narrow rocky gorge, and emerges as a wider river at the town of Grand Falls. The result is a magnificent cascade, whose force has worn strange round wells in the rocky bed, some as large as 16 feet in circumference and 30 feet deep.

A **pontoon boat** operates June through early September at the lower end of the gorge and offers an entirely different perspective on the cliffs and the wells. Boat tickets are available at the **La Rochelle Tourist Information Centre** (⊠ 1 Chapel St. ☎ 877/475–7769 or 506/475–7766 ⊕ www. grandfalls.com). ⊠ *2 Chapel St.* ☎ *506/475–7760* ⊠ *$10* ☾ *Boat trips June–early Sept., daily 10–7 on the hr.*

The Gorge Walk, which starts at the **Malabeam Tourist Information Center** and covers the full length of the gorge, is dotted with interpretation panels and monuments. There's no charge for the walk, unless you descend to the wells ($3), which are holes worn in the rocks by the swirling water. Guided walking tours ($6) are also available. According to native legend, a young maiden named Malabeam led her Iroquois captors to their deaths over the foaming cataract rather than guide them to her village. ⊠ *24 Madawaska Rd.* ☎ *506/475–7788* ⊠ *Free* ☾ *Daily dawn–dusk.*

The **Grand Falls Historical Museum** has pioneer and early Victorian artifacts as well as the balance beam used by a daredevil who crossed the falls on a tightrope. ⊠ *142 Court St., Suite 103* ☎ *506/473–5265* ⊠ *Free* ☾ *July–Aug., weekdays 9–5.*

en route

About 75 km (47 mi) south of Grand Falls, stop in Florenceville for a look at the small but reputable **Andrew and Laura McCain Gallery** (✉ McCain St., Florenceville ☎ 506/392-6769), which has launched the career of many New Brunswick artists. The Trans-Canada Highway is intriguingly scenic, but if you're looking for less crowded highways and typical small communities, cross the river to Route 105 at Hartland—about 20 km (12 mi) south of Florenceville—via the longest **covered bridge** in the world: 1,282 feet in length.

Kings Landing Historical Settlement

🕐 ③① 210 km (130 mi) south of Grand Falls. 30 km (19 mi) west of Fredericton.

Fodor'sChoice
★

The Kings Landing Historical Settlement was built by moving period buildings to a new shore. The drive from Fredericton takes less than a half hour; to appreciate the museum, plan to spend at least a half day. Route 102 passes through some spectacular river and hill scenery on the way, including the Mactaquac Dam—turn off here if you want to visit Mactaquac Provincial Park.

This excellent outdoor living-history museum on the St. John River evokes the sights, sounds, and society of rural New Brunswick between 1790 and 1900. The winding country lanes and meticulously restored homes pull you back a century or more, and programs are available that allow you to cane a chair at the carpenter shop or to bake bread on an open hearth. There are daily dramas in the theater, barn dances, and strolling minstrels. See how the wealthy owner of the sawmill lived and just how different things were for the immigrant farmer. Hearty meals are served at the Kings Head Inn. ✉ *Exit 253 off Trans-Canada Hwy., near Prince William* ☎ *506/363-4999* ⊕ *www.kingslanding.nb.ca* 🎟 *$14* ⊙ *June–mid-Oct., daily 10–5.*

Mactaquac Provincial Park

🕐 ③② 12 km (7 mi) north of Mactaquac Park. 25 km (16 mi) west of Fredericton.

Surrounding the giant pond created by the Mactaquac Hydroelectric Dam on the St. John River is Mactaquac Provincial Park. Its facilities include an 18-hole championship golf course, two beaches with lifeguards, two marinas (one for powerboats and the other for sailboats), supervised crafts activities, myriad nature and hiking trails, and a restaurant. Reservations are advised for the 300 campsites in summer. Winter is fun, too: there are lots of trails for cross-country skiing, and snowshoeing and sleigh rides are available by appointment. The toboggan hills and the ponds for skating and ice hockey are even lighted in the evening. ✉ *Rte. 105 at Mactaquac Dam* ☎ *506/363-4747* 🎟 *$6 per vehicle June–Aug., free Sept.–May* ⊙ *Daily dawn–dusk; overnight camping mid-May–mid-Oct.*

en route

Oromocto, along Route 102 from Mactaquac Provincial Park, is the site of the Canadian Armed Forces Base, **Camp Gagetown,** the largest military base in Canada (not to be confused with the pretty village of Gagetown farther downriver). Prince Charles completed his helicopter training here. The base has an interesting military museum. ✉ *Museum: Bldg. A5 off Tilley St.* ☎ *506/422-1304* 🎟 *Museum free* ⊙ *June–Aug., weekdays 8–4, weekends noon–4; Sept.–May, weekdays 8–4.*

FREDERICTON

The small inland city of Fredericton spreads itself on a broad point of land jutting into the St. John River. Its predecessor, the early French settlement of St. Anne's Point, was established in 1642 during the reign of the French governor Villebon, who made his headquarters at the junction of the Nashwaak and St. John rivers. Settled by Loyalists and named for Frederick, second son of George III, the city serves as the seat of government for New Brunswick's 753,000 residents. Wealthy and scholarly Loyalists set out to create a gracious and beautiful place, and thus even before the establishment of the University of New Brunswick, in 1785, the town served as a center for liberal arts and sciences. It remains a gracious and beautiful place as well as a center of education, arts, and culture. St. John River, once the only highway to Fredericton, is now a focus of recreation.

Exploring Fredericton

Downtown Queen Street runs parallel to the river, and its blocks enclose historic sights and attractions. Most major sights are within walking distance of one another. An excursion to Kings Landing Historical Settlement, a reconstructed village, can bring alive the province's history.

Dressed in 18th-century costume, actors from the **Calithumpians Theater Company** (☎ 506/457–1975) bring Fredericton history to life from Canada Day (July 1) to Labor Day. They conduct free historical walks several times a day. In the evening they offer Time Travellers Tours ($8) during which you meet famous characters from Fredericton's past, including Benedict Arnold, J. J. Audubon, Lord Beaverbrook, and Bliss Carmen. After dark, actors lead a Haunted Hike ($13) through historic neighborhoods and ghostly graveyards. The Haunted Hikes continue into the fall on weekends. Check at the **City Hall Visitor Information Centre** (✉ 397 Queen St. ☎ 506/460–2020) for details.

A Good Walk

Start at City Hall, formerly a farmer's market and opera house, on Phoenix Square, at the corner of York and Queen streets. Its modern council chambers are decorated with tapestries that illustrate Fredericton's history. Walk down (as the river flows) Queen Street to Carleton Street to the **Historic Garrison District** ㉝, a military compound that includes the New Brunswick Sports Hall of Fame and the **York-Sunbury Museum** ㉞, the latter occupying what used to be the Officers' Quarters in Officers' Square. Here the Calithumpians offer outdoor comedy theater at lunchtime. The next stop down the river side of Queen Street is the **Beaverbrook Art Gallery** ㉟, with its sculpture garden outside. Turn right on Church Street and walk to **Christ Church Cathedral** ㊱. Once you have had your fill of its exquisite architecture and stained glass, turn right and walk back up Queen Street. The **Provincial Legislature** ㊲ is on your left. Restaurants and cafés along Queen Street provide opportunities for refreshments. Turn left on St. John Street and then take the second right onto Brunswick Street, where the wonders of **Science East** ㊳ await. If you make your way back to York Street (across from where you started at City Hall), turn left to visit a chic block of shops. One variation to this walk: if you're touring on Saturday, start in the morning with the **Boyce Farmers' Market** ㊴, off George and Brunswick streets, to get a real taste of the city.

TIMING The distances are not great, so the time you spend depends on how much you like history, science, art, and churches. You could do it all

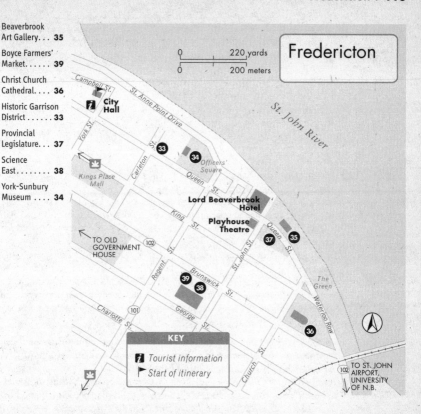

Beaverbrook
Art Gallery... **35**

Boyce Farmers'
Market...... **39**

Christ Church
Cathedral.... **36**

Historic Garrison
District...... **33**

Provincial
Legislature... **37**

Science
East........ **38**

York-Sunbury
Museum.... **34**

in an afternoon, but start at the Boyce Farmers' Market on a Saturday morning.

Sights to See

★ ③⑤ **Beaverbrook Art Gallery.** A lasting gift of the late Lord Beaverbrook, this gallery could hold its head high in the company of some smaller European galleries. Salvador Dali's gigantic *Santiago el Grande* has always been the star, but a rotation of avant-garde Canadian paintings now shares pride of place. The McCain "gallery-within-a-gallery" is devoted to the finest Atlantic Canadian artists. ⊠ *703 Queen St.* ☎ *506/458–8545* 🖅 *$5* ☾ *June–Sept., Mon. and Wed.–Fri. 9–6, Tues. 9–8, weekends 10–6; Oct.–May, Tues.–Fri. 9–5, Sat. 11–5, Sun. noon–5.*

③⑨ **Boyce Farmers' Market.** It's hard to miss this Saturday-morning market because of the crowds. You'll find lots of local meat and produce, baked goods, crafts, and seasonal items like wreaths and maple syrup. The market sells good ready-to-eat food, from German sausages to tasty sandwiches. ⊠ *Bounded by Regent, Brunswick, and George Sts.*

★ ③⑥ **Christ Church Cathedral.** One of Fredericton's prides, this gray-stone building, completed in 1853, is an excellent example of decorated neo-Gothic architecture. The cathedral's design was based on an actual medieval prototype in England, and it became a model for many American churches. Inside is a clock known as "Big Ben's little brother," the test run for London's famous timepiece, designed by Lord Grimthorpe. ⊠ *Church St.* ☎ *506/450–8500* 🖅 *Free* ☾ *Self-guided tours daily 9–4, except during services. Guided tours mid-June–Aug., weekdays 9–6, Sat. 10–5, Sun. 1–5.*

off the
beaten
path

MARYSVILLE – A National Historic District, Marysville is one of Canada's best-preserved examples of a 19th-century mill town. Its architecture and social history are amazing and can be appreciated with the help of a self-guided walking-tour booklet available at the York-Sunbury Museum and at Westminster Books on King Street. Marysville itself is on the north side of the St. John River, about 10 km (6 mi) from downtown via Route 8. **Knobb Hill Gallery** (⊠ 285 Canada St. ☎ 506/450–1986), home of the Catherine Karns Munn Collection, is a sentimental stop, with paintings and crafts depicting the local area and Victorian scenes.

33 Historic Garrison District. The restored buildings of this British and Canadian post, which extends two blocks along Queen Street, include soldiers' barracks, a guardhouse, and a cell block. Local artisans operate studios in the casemates below the soldiers' barracks. In July and August free guided tours run throughout the day, and there are outdoor concerts in Officers' Square Tuesday and Thursday evenings. Redcoat soldiers have long stood guard in Officers' Square, and a formal changing-of-the-guard ceremony takes place July–August at 11 and 7. It's even possible for children of all ages to live a soldier's life for a while: each summer afternoon at 3, would-be redcoats get their own uniforms and practice drilling ($12 per person, $40 per family). ⊠ *Queen St. at Carleton St.* ☎ *506/460–2129* ▨ *Free* ⊙ *Daily 24 hrs.*

Old Government House. This imposing 1828 Palladian mansion has been restored as the official seat of office for the province's lieutenant governor. A hands-on interpretation center spans 12,000 years of history. Guided tours take in elegantly restored state rooms and art galleries. The 11-acre grounds include a 17th-century Acadian settlement and border an early Maliseet burial ground. ⊠ *51 Woodstock Rd.* ☎ *506/ 453–2505* ▨ *Free* ⊙ *June–early Sept., daily 10–5 (last hourly tour begins at 4); early Sept.–May, by chance or appointment.*

37 Provincial Legislature. The interior chamber of the legislature, where the premier and elected members govern the province, reflects the taste of the late Victorians. The chandeliers are brass, and the prisms are Waterford. Replicas of portraits by Sir Joshua Reynolds of King George III and Queen Charlotte hang here. There's a freestanding circular staircase, and a volume of Audubon's *Birds of America* is on display. Call ahead to arrange a tour. ⊠ *Queen St.* ☎ *506/453–2527* ▨ *Free* ⊙ *Legislature tours June–Aug., daily 9–6; Sept.–May, weekdays 9–4. Library weekdays 8:15–5.*

38 Science East. This hands-on science center, in the former York County Jail, has family fun locked up. Walk into a giant kaleidoscope, see a pattern-making laser beam, create a minitornado, or experience one of the other 70 exhibits. ⊠ *668 Brunswick St.* ☎ *506/457–2340* ⊕ *www. scienceeast.nb.ca* ▨ *$5* ⊙ *June–Sept., Mon.–Sat. 10–5, Sun. 1–4; Oct.–May, Tues.–Fri. noon–5, Sat. 10–5.*

York Street. Here is the city's high-fashion block, with designer shops, an incense-burning boutique, a general store with an eclectic assortment of gifts and housewares, and a newsstand–cigar store. At the middle of the upriver side of the block is Mazucca's Alley, the gateway to the pubs and restaurants in Piper's Lane. King and Queen streets, at either end of the block, have some fun shops, too.

34 York–Sunbury Museum. The Officers' Quarters in the Historic Garrison District houses a museum that offers a living picture of the community from the time when only First Nations peoples inhabited the area, through the Acadian and Loyalist days, to the immediate past. Its World

War I trench puts you in the thick of battle, and the shellacked remains of the giant Coleman Frog, a Fredericton legend, still inspire controversy. ⊠ *Officers' Sq., Queen St.* ☎ *506/455–6041* ☞ *$3* ☉ *Mid-Apr.–June, Tues.–Sat. 1–4; July and Aug., daily 10–5; Sept.–mid-Dec., Tues.–Sat. 1–4.*

Where to Stay & Eat

$–$$$ ✕ **Brewbaker's.** With an old-world Italian atmosphere, California and eclectic cuisine, and a rooftop garden patio, Brewbaker's is downtown's most popular casual lunch and dinner spot. Dishes include fabulous salads, authentic pastas, and thin-crust pizzas baked in a wood-fired brick oven. ⊠ *546 King St.* ☎ *506/459–0067* ▤ *AE, DC, MC, V.*

$–$$$ ✕ **El Burrito Loco.** With cooking experience on his hands and family recipes in his head, Perez Huerta moved to his wife's home in Fredericton from his home in Puerto Vallarta, Mexico. His authentic Mexican dishes—even huevos rancheros for breakfast—caught on like wildfire up north. Everything is made on the spot, from the burritos and tacos to the guacamole and salsa. There's a patio for summer, and occasionally local Spanish guitarists or mariachi players from Montréal entertain. ⊠ *304 King St.* ☎ *506/459–5626* ▤ *AE, DC, MC, V.*

$–$$$ ✕ **Lobster Hut.** A 125-gallon tank stocked with 1- to 2-pound lobsters adds the finishing touch to the nautical decor of this popular spot, despite its location at a busy intersection next to a highway ramp. In season, the vegetables come from the backyard garden. Prices for most entrées are reasonable, but a few are in the $30–$40 range. ⊠ *City Motel, 1216 Regent St.* ☎ *506/454–7376* ▤ *AE, DC, MC, V* ☉ *Closed Sun. and Mon. No lunch.*

★ $$ ✕ **Piper's Palate.** It's small but mighty—mighty fine. The chef leans toward Mediterranean and western European dishes, but isn't afraid to experiment. Even lunches, which are a real bargain, are creative. There are Canadian dishes, too, including lots of seafood. ⊠ *462 Queen St.* ☎ *506/450–7911* ▤ *MC, V* ☉ *Closed Sun.–Mon.*

$–$$ ✕ **Dimitri Souvlaki.** Chicken souvlaki reigns supreme in this downtown authentic Greek eatery, but lots of people make a meal of the appetizers, especially the *pikilia* (hors d'oeuvres) platters and *saganaki* (sautéed goat's milk cheese with lemon juice). ⊠ *349 King St., at Piper's La.* ☎ *506/ 452–8882* ▤ *AE, DC, MC, V.*

$$$ ▥ **Delta Fredericton.** This stately riverside property is within walking distance of downtown. The elegant country decor is almost as delightful as the sunset views over the river from the patio restaurant and many of the modern rooms. The gift shop carries top-notch crafts. Bruno's serves legendary buffets, seafood on Friday evening, and brunch on Sunday. ⊠ *225 Woodstock Rd., E3B 2H8* ☎ *506/457–7000* ☎ *506/457– 4000* ⊕ *www.sheraton.com/fredericton* ☞ *208 rooms, 14 suites* ⌂ *Restaurant, cable TV with movies, pool, indoor pool, gym, hair salon, hot tub, sauna, spa, bar, Internet, meeting rooms, some pets allowed* ▤ *AE, DC, MC, V.*

$$ ▥ **Holiday Inn Hotel and Resort Fredericton.** Overlooking the Mactaquac Headpond, this modern hotel has a luxurious look but a relaxed country atmosphere. There's a fireplace in the lobby, and the suites have electric fireplaces. Some of the rooms with water views have cathedral ceilings. The cottages are ideal for boating and skiing families. ⊠ *35 Mactaquac Rd., E3E 1L2, off Rte. 102, 20 km (12 mi) west of Fredericton* ☎ *506/363–5111 or 800/561–5111* ☎ *506/363–3000* ⊕ *www. holidayinnfredericton.com* ☞ *72 rooms, 4 suites, 6 cottages* ⌂ *Dining room, in-room data ports, cable TV with movies and video games, tennis court, indoor pool, gym, hot tub, dock, lounge, Internet, meeting rooms, some pets allowed* ▤ *AE, D, DC, MC, V.*

$$ 🏨 **Lord Beaverbrook Hotel.** The downtown waterfront location of this hotel is its most attractive feature. It's directly across the street from the Playhouse, next door to the Beaverbrook Art Gallery, and the riverfront walking trail runs directly behind it. ⊠ *659 Queen St., E3B 5A6* ☎ *506/455–3371 or 866/444–1946* 🖷 *506/455–1441* 🛏 *155 rooms, 13 suites* ⚴ *2 restaurants, cable TV with movies and video games, indoor pool, hot tub, sauna, bar, Internet, meeting rooms, some pets allowed, nosmoking rooms* 🗏 *AE, DC, MC, V.*

$$ 🏨 **On the Pond Lodge.** This woodland European-style lodge near the river offers several opportunities for relaxation and rejuvenation, including spa packages, canoeing, kayaking, hiking, and biking. There are an 18-hole golf course and a sandy beach next door at Mactaquac Provincial Park. Everything about the place is elegant yet substantial, from the big stone fireplace and exposed beams in the great room to the well-appointed bedrooms. Dinner in the dining room can be as decadent or as nutritious as you like. ⊠ *20 Rte. 615, Mactaquac E6L 1M2* ☎ *506/363–3420, 800/984–2555 in Canada and the U.S.* 🖷 *506/363–3479* ⊕ *www.onthepond.com* 🛏 *8 rooms* ⚴ *Dining room, cable TV, in-room VCRs, hot tub, sauna, boating, bicycles, Internet, meeting rooms; no kids under 12, no smoking* 🗏 *MC, V.*

$ 🏨 **Carriage House Inn.** The lovely bedrooms in this venerable mansion are furnished with Victorian antiques. Breakfast, complete with homemade maple syrup for the fluffy pancakes, is served in the solarium. ⊠*230 University Ave., E3B 4H7* ☎ *506/452–9924 or 800/267–6068* 🖷 *506/458–0799* ⊕ *www.bbcanada.com/carriagehouse* 🛏 *11 rooms* ⚴ *Meeting room, some pets allowed; no smoking* 🗏 *AE, DC, MC, V* ⦿| *BP.*

$ 🏨 **The Very Best—A Victorian B&B.** This elegant home, with its fine antiques and original artwork, is in the downtown Heritage Preservation Area. The smoked-salmon omelet is an outstanding breakfast choice. ⊠ *806 George St., E3B 1K7* ☎ *506/451–1499* 🖷 *506/454–1454* ⊕ *www.bbcanada.com/2330.html* 🛏 *3 rooms* ⚴ *Dining room, pool, sauna, billiards, laundry facilities, Internet, meeting room; no smoking* 🗏 *AE, MC, V* ⦿| *BP.*

Nightlife & the Arts

The Arts

The **Calithumpians Theater Company** (☎ 506/457–1975) has free outdoor performances daily in summer (12:15 weekdays, 2 weekends) in Officers' Square and an evening Haunted Hike ($15) through a historic haunted neighborhood and ghostly graveyards. The annual **Harvest Jazz and Blues Festival** (⊠ 65 York St. ☎ 506/454–2583 or 888/622–5837 ⊕ www.harvestjazzblues.nb.ca) takes place in late summer or early fall. The **Playhouse** (⊠ 686 Queen St. ☎ 506/458–8344) is the venue for theater and most other cultural performances, including Symphony New Brunswick, Theatre New Brunswick, and traveling ballet and dance companies.

Nightlife

Fredericton has a lively nightlife, with lots of live music in downtown pubs, especially on weekends. King Street and Piper's Lane, off the 300 block of King Street, have a number of spots. **Bugaboo Creek** (⊠ 422 Queen St. ☎ 506/453–0582) features R&B and blues. An eclectic collection of live jazz, blues, oldies, and folk can be found at the **Capital** (⊠ 362 Queen St. ☎ 506/459–3558). **Dolan's Pub** (⊠ 349 King St. ☎ 506/454–7474) has Maritime acts every weekend. The **Lunar Rogue** (⊠ 625 King St. ☎ 506/450–2065) has an old-world pub atmosphere and occasionally showcases acoustic folk, rock, and Celtic music. **Moe's Garage** (⊠ 375 King St. ☎ 506/458–1254) is a venue for rock, blues, folk, and pretty much anything other than country. **Rye's Deli & Pub** (✉ 73 Carleton St. ☎ 506/472–7937) goes for cozy and romantic with leather booths and soft lights.

Sports & the Outdoors

Canoeing & Kayaking

Shells, canoes, and kayaks can be rented by the hour or day at the **Small Craft Aquatic Center** (✉ Behind Victoria Health Centre where Brunswick St. becomes Woodstock Rd. ☎ 506/460–2260), which also arranges guided tours and instruction.

Golf

The **Lynx At Kingswood Park** (✉ 31 Kingswood Park ☎ 506/443–3333 or 877/666–0001) is an 18-hole, par-72 championship course designed by Cooke-Huxham International.

Skiing

Many of Fredericton's 70 km (44 mi) of walking trails, especially those along the river and in Odell and Wilmot parks, are groomed for cross-country skiing. Other trails are broken and useful for skate skiing, which doesn't require set tracks.

Ski Crabbe Mountain (✉ 50 Crabbe Mountain Rd., Central Hainesville, 55 km [34 mi] west of Fredericton ☎ 506/463–8311 ⊕ www. crabbemountain.com) has 17 trails, a vertical drop of 853 feet, snow-board and ski rentals, instruction, a skating pond, baby-sitting, and a lounge and restaurant.

Walking

Fredericton has a fine network of walking trails, one of which follows the river from the Green, past the Victorian mansions on Waterloo Row, behind the Beaverbrook Art Gallery, and along the riverbank to the Sheraton. The **visitor information center** (✉ City Hall, Queen St. at York St. ☎ 506/460–2129) has a trail map.

Shopping

Indoor mammoth crafts markets are held in fall. A Labor Day–weekend outdoor crafts fair is held in Officers' Square. Shop for pottery, blown glass, pressed flowers, turned wood, leather, and other items, all made by members of the New Brunswick Craft Council.

★ **Aitkens Pewter** (✉ 408 Queen St. ☎ 506/453–9474) makes its own pewter goblets, belt buckles, candlesticks, and jewelry. **Botanicals** (✉ 65 Shore St. ☎ 506/454–7361) sells crafts by juried Maritime artisans only. **Carrington & Co.** (✉ 225 Woodstock Rd. ☎ 506/450–8415), in the Sheraton, is a gem for crafts and Tilley Endurables clothing. **Eloise** (✉ 83 York St. ☎ 506/453–7715) carries women's fashions with flowing lines, made with natural fibers. **Gallery 78** (✉ 96 Queen St. ☎ 506/454–5192) has original works by local artists. The **New Brunswick Fine Craft Gallery** (✉ 87 Regent St. ☎ 506/450–8989) exhibits and sells juried crafts. The **Urban Almanac General Store** (✉ 59 York St. ☎ 506/450–4334) has an eclectic collection of unique housewares and other items of exemplary design.

Gagetown

40 *50 km (31 mi) southeast of Fredericton. Rte. 2 is fast and direct; Rte. 102 from Fredericton is scenic.*

Historic Gagetown bustles in summer. Artists welcome visitors, many of whom arrive by boat and tie up at the marina, to their studios and galleries. Several small restaurants have interesting menus. The **Queens County Museum** is growing by leaps and bounds. Its original building, **Tilley House** (a National Historic Site) was the birthplace of Sir Leonard Tilley, one of the Fathers of Confederation. It displays Loyalist and First Nations artifacts, early-20th-century medical equipment, Victorian glassware, and more. The nearby old **Queens County Court House** (⊠ Court House Rd. ☎ 506/488–2966) is part of the museum and has archival material and courthouse furniture. It hosts changing exhibits. ⊠ *Front St.* ☎ *506/488–2966* ⊠ *$2, $3 with courthouse* ⊘ *Mid-June–mid-Sept., daily 10–5.*

Where to Stay

¢–$ 🔲 **Steamers Stop Inn and Thistle Pub.** This grand old waterside inn is furnished in antiques and has a hot tub on the screened veranda. Other relaxing venues include an art gallery and a smoke-free Scottish-style pub. The pub is open in the evening only. Rent a canoe or kayak for exploration of the nearby creek. ⊠ *74 Front St., E5M 1A1* ☎ *506/488–2903 or 877/991–9922* 🖶 *506/488–1116* ✉ *stewartv@nbnet.nb.ca* ⇌ *6 rooms* ♨ *Outdoor hot tub, boating, pub, meeting rooms; no a/c, no room TVs, no smoking* 🖃 *MC, V* ⊘ *Closed Oct.–Apr.* ⭑❶ *BP.*

Shopping

Grimcross Crafts (⊠ 17 Mill Rd. ☎ 506/488–2832) represents 30 area craftspeople. **Flo Grieg's** (⊠ 36 Front St. ☎ 506/488–2074) carries superior pottery made on the premises. **Juggler's Cove** (⊠ 32 Tilley Rd. ☎ 506/488–2574) is a studio-gallery featuring pottery, paintings, and woodwork. **Loomcrofters** (⊠ Loomcroft La. off Main St. ☎ 506/488–2400) is a good choice for handwoven items.

NEW BRUNSWICK A TO Z

To research prices, get advice from other travelers, and book travel arrangements, visit www.fodors.com.

AIR TRAVEL

Airports in Saint John, Moncton, and Fredericton are served by Air Canada and Saint John is also served by Jetsgo and Pan Am (from Bangor, Maine). Moncton is also served by Delta, CanJet, and WestJet; Fredericton also is served by Canjet.

🔳 Airlines & Contacts **Air Canada** ☎ 800/776-3000 ⊕ www.aircanada.ca. **CanJet Airlines** ☎ 800/809-7777 ⊕ www.canjet.com. **Delta Airlines** ☎ 800/221-1212 ⊕ www.delta.com. **Jetsgo** ☎ 866/440-0441 ⊕ www.jetsgo.ca. **Pan Am** ☎ 800/359-7262 ⊕ www.flypanam.com. **WestJet Airlines** ☎ 800/538-5696 ⊕ www.westjet.ca.

AIRPORTS

New Brunswick has three major airports. Saint John Airport is about 15 minutes east, Moncton Airport about 10 minutes east, and Fredericton Airport about 10 minutes east of their respective downtowns.

🔳 Airport Information **Fredericton Airport** ⊠ Lincoln Rd. Lincoln ☎ 506/460-0920. **Moncton Airport** ⊠ Champlain Rd. Dieppe ☎ 506/856-5444. **Saint John Airport** ⊠ Loch Lomond Rd. ☎ 506/638-5555.

BOAT & FERRY TRAVEL

BAY Ferries runs from Saint John, New Brunswick, to Digby, Nova Scotia, 1–3 times per day, depending on the season. The passenger fare is $35 for the three-hour, one-way trip July–September and $20 at other times. Car fares (driver not included) are $75 in peak season, $70 off-season. Coastal Transport has up to seven crossings per day from Black's Harbour to Grand Manan July–August. Round-trip fares are $28 for a car and $9.35 per person. A one-way crossing takes about 1½ hours.

The half-hour ferry crossing from Letete to Deer Island is free. The July and August crossings from Deer Island to Campobello take about 40 minutes. The fare is $13 per car with driver; the passenger fare is $2.

🚢 Boat & Ferry Information **BAY Ferries** ☎ 902/245-2116 ⊕ www.nfl-bay.com. **Coastal Transport** ☎ 506/662-3724

BUS TRAVEL

Acadian Lines runs buses within the province and connects with most major bus lines.

🚌 Bus Information **Acadian Lines** ☎ 506/859-5100 or 800/567-5151.

CAR RENTAL

🚗 Major Agencies **Avis** ☎ 800/331-1084, 800/879-2847 in Canada ⊕ www.avis.com. **Budget** ☎ 800/527-0700 ⊕ www.budget.com. **Hertz** ☎ 800/654-3131, 800/263-0600 in Canada ⊕ www.hertz.com. **National Car Rental** ☎ 800/227-7368 ⊕ www.nationalcar.com.

🚗 Local Agency **Trius Car & Truck Rental** ☎ 506/457-9000.

CAR TRAVEL

From Québec, the Trans-Canada Highway (Route 2) enters New Brunswick at St-Jacques and follows the St. John River through Fredericton and on to Moncton and the Nova Scotia border. From Maine, I–95 crosses at Houlton to Woodstock, New Brunswick, where it connects with the Trans-Canada Highway. Those traveling up the coast of Maine on Route 1 cross at Calais to St. Stephen, New Brunswick. New Brunswick's Route 1 extends through Saint John and Sussex to join the Trans-Canada Highway near Moncton.

New Brunswick has an excellent highway system with numerous facilities. The Trans-Canada Highway, marked by a maple leaf, is the same as Route 2. Route 7 joins Saint John and Fredericton. Fredericton is connected to Miramichi City by Route 8. Route 15 links Moncton to the eastern coast and to Route 11, which follows the coast to Miramichi City, around the Acadian Peninsula, and up to Campbellton. Get a good map at a visitor information center. Tourism New Brunswick has mapped five scenic routes: the Fundy Coastal Drive, the River Valley Scenic Drive, the Acadian Coastal Drive, the Miramichi River Route, and the Appalachian Range.

EMERGENCIES

🚨 Emergency Services **Ambulance, fire, police** ☎ 911.

🏥 Hospitals **Campbellton Regional Hospital** ✉ 189 Lilly Lake Rd., Campbellton ☎ 506/789-5000. **Chaleur Regional Hospital** ✉ 1750 Sunset Dr., Bathurst ☎ 506/548-8961. **Dr. Everett Chalmers Hospital** ✉ Priestman St., Fredericton ☎ 506/452-5400. **Dr. Georges Dumont Hospital** ✉ 330 Archibald St., Moncton ☎ 506/862-4000. **Edmundston Regional Hospital** ✉ 275 Hébert Blvd., Edmundston ☎ 506/739-2200. **Miramichi Regional Hospital** ✉ 500 Water St., Miramichi City ☎ 506/623-3000. **Moncton City Hospital** ✉ 135 MacBeath Ave., Moncton ☎ 506/857-5111. **Saint John Regional Hospital** ✉ Tucker Park Rd., Saint John ☎ 506/648-6000.

SPORTS & OUTDOORS

Whale-watching, sea kayaking, trail riding, bird-watching, garden touring, river cruising, and fishing are just a few of the province's Day Adventure programs. Packages cover a variety of skill levels and include equipment. All adventures last at least a half day; some are multiday. Information is available at New Brunswick Day Adventure centers (in some information offices, hotels, and attractions), or contact Tourism New Brunswick.

ℹ️ **Tourism New Brunswick** ☎ 800/561-0123 ⊕ www.tourismnewbrunswick.ca.

BIKING B&Bs frequently have bicycles for rent. Tourism New Brunswick has listings and free cycling maps. Baymount Outdoor Adventures operates along the Fundy shore near Hopewell Cape.

🚩 **Baymount Outdoor Adventures** ⊠ 17 Elwin Jay Dr., Hillsborough ☎ 506/734-2660. **Tourism New Brunswick** ☎ 800/561-0123 ⊕ www.tourismnewbrunswick.ca.

FISHING New Brunswick Fish and Wildlife has information on sporting licenses and can tell you where the fish are.

🚩 **New Brunswick Fish and Wildlife** ☎ 506/453-2440.

GOLF The most up-to-date information about new courses and upgrades to existing courses is available at the New Brunswick Golf Association.

🚩 **New Brunswick Golf Association** ☎ 506/451-1349 or 877/833-4662 ⊕ www.golfnb.com.

HIKING The New Brunswick Trails Council has complete information on the province's burgeoning trail system.

🚩 **New Brunswick Trails Council** ☎ 506/459-1931 or 800/526-7070.

TOURS

Saint John visitor information centers have brochures for three good self-guided walking tours. Guided walking tours sponsored by the City of Saint John are also available. The 80-passenger *Carleton II* is used for sightseeing river cruises in Fredericton. It departs from Regent St. Wharf.

🚩 *Carleton II* ☎ 506/454-2628. **City of St. John** ☎ 506/658-2855

TRAIN TRAVEL

VIA Rail offers passenger service every day but Tuesday from Campbellton, Newcastle, and Moncton to Montréal and Halifax.

🚩 Train Information **VIA Rail** ☎ 800/561-8630 in Canada, 800/561-3949 in the U.S.

VISITOR INFORMATION

Tourism New Brunswick can provide information on day adventures, scenic driving routes, accommodations, and the seven provincial tourist bureaus. Also helpful are the city information services in Bathurst, Edmundston–St-Jacques, Fredericton, Grand Falls, Moncton, St. Andrews, Saint John, and St. Stephen.

🚩 Tourist Information **City of Bathurst** ☎ 506/548-0400 ⊕ www.bathurst.ca. **Edmundston–St-Jacques Tourism** ☎ 506/735-2747. **Fredericton Tourism** ☎ 506/460-2041. **Go Moncton** ☎ 506/853-3590 or 800/363-4558 ⊕ www.gomoncton.com. **St. Andrews Chamber of Commerce** ⊠ 46 Reed Ave., St. Andrews ☎ 506/529-3555 or 800/563-7397. **Tourism New Brunswick** ✍ Box 12345, Fredericton E3B 5C3 ☎ 800/561-0123 ⊕ www.tourismnewbrunswick.ca. **Tourism Saint John** ☎ 506/658-2990 or 866/463-8639 ⊕ www.tourismsaintjohn.com. **Town of Grand Falls** www.grandfalls.com. **Town of St. Stephen** ⊠ 34 Milltown Blvd., St. Stephen ☎ 506/466-7700 ⊕ www.town.ststephen.nb.ca.

PRINCE EDWARD ISLAND

3

FODOR'S CHOICE

Blue Heron Drive

cycling the Confederation Trail

Dunes Café, *Brackley Beach*

Fairholm National Historic Inn, *Charlottetown*

Islander Motor Lodge, *Charlottetown*

The Pilot House, *Charlottetown*

Port-La-Joye–Fort Amherst

Prince Edward Island National Park, *Cavendish*

Province House, *Charlottetown*

sea-kayaking

West Point Lighthouse, *West Point*

West Point Lighthouse inn, *West Point*

West Point Lighthouse restaurant, *West Point*

HIGHLY RECOMMENDED

SIGHTS   Green Gables, Prince Edward Island National Park, *Cavendish*

Province House National Historic Site, *Charlottetown*

St. Dunstan's Basilica, *Charlottetown*

*Many other great hotels and restaurants enliven Prince Edward Island.
For other favorites, look for the black stars as you read this chapter.*

AN ENCHANTING MEDLEY OF RICH COLOR, Prince Edward Island is a unique landmass with verdant patchwork fields that stretch out beneath an endless cobalt sky to meet the surrounding sea. At just 195 km (121 mi) long and 64 km (40 mi) wide, the accessible size is part of the Island's appeal. Warm hospitality welcomes you, and the laid-back, slow-paced Island lifestyle entices visitors back year after year. Almost every attraction and property is family-owned and -operated.

Genuine graciousness and charm are the true signatures of PEI. You might understand, then, why Lucy Maud Montgomery's novel of youth and innocence, *Anne of Green Gables,* was framed against this land. The story burst on the world in 1908 and is still selling untold thousands of copies every year. After potatoes and lobsters, Anne is the Island's most important product.

In 1864 Charlottetown, the Island's capital city, hosted one of the most important meetings in Canadian history, which eventually led to the creation of the Dominion of Canada in 1867. Initially, Prince Edward Island was reluctant to join, having spent years fighting for the right to an autonomous government. Originally settled by the French in 1603, the Island was handed over to the British under the Treaty of Paris in 1763. Tensions grew as absentee British governors and proprietors failed to take an active interest in the development of the land, and the resulting parliamentary government proved ineffective for similar reasons. Yet the development of fisheries and agriculture at the beginning of the 19th century strengthened the economy. Soon settlement increased, and those who were willing to take a chance on the Island prospered.

Around the middle of the 19th century, a modern cabinet government was created, and relations between tenants and proprietors worsened. At the same time, talk of creating a union with other North American colonies began. After much deliberation, and although political upheaval had begun to subside, delegates decided that it was in the Island's best economic interest to join the Canadian Confederation.

The Confederation Bridge, linking Prince Edward Island's Borden-Carleton with New Brunswick's Cape Jourimain, physically seals the Island's connection with the mainland. To create this engineering marvel, massive concrete pillars—65 feet across and 180 feet high—were sunk into waters more than 110 feet deep in order to cope with traffic that now brings more than 1 million visitors annually. When the bridge first opened, some residents feared the loss of the Island's tranquillity, and as you explore the crossroads villages and fishing ports, it's not hard to understand why. Outside the tourist mecca of Cavendish, otherwise known as Anne's Land, the Island seems like an oasis of peace in an increasingly busy world.

About the Restaurants

Dining in one of PEI's restaurants is always a casual, relaxed experience, even in fine-dining establishments. Most restaurants, cafés, and pubs are no-smoking. Water views are not hard to come by.

About the Hotels

Full-service resorts, luxury hotels, family-run farms, and moderately priced motels, cottages, and lodges are just some of your choices in PEI. Book 3–6 months in advance for July and August.

Numbers in the text correspond to numbers in the margin and on the Prince Edward Island and Charlottetown maps.

3

If you have
1 day

Leaving ⊡**Charlottetown** ①– ⑩▶ on Route 2 west, take Route 15 north to **Brackley Beach** ⑫. This puts you onto a 137-km-long (85-mi-long) scenic drive, marked with signs depicting a blue heron. Route 6 west takes you to **Cavendish** ⑬, an entryway to **Prince Edward Island National Park** ⑪. This area has enough attractions for a full day, but if you prefer to keep exploring, continue west on Route 6, with its fishing wharfs and scenic vistas. Blue Heron Drive (Route 20) takes you to the Anne of Green Gables Museum in Park Corner. Continue west, then south on Route 20 to Route 2 south (at Kensington) and turn onto Route 1A east (at Travellers Rest). Just north of the Confederation Bridge, follow the Trans-Canada Highway (Route 1) east back to Charlottetown. At seaside **Victoria** ⑮, stroll along the dock, with restaurant and craft shops.

If you have
3 days

From **Charlottetown** ①– ⑩▶, explore the peaceful suburbs of ⊡**Summerside** ㉒ before heading for its bustling waterfront. The relatively undiscovered area west of Summerside is perfect for those who like a slow pace. Follow Lady Slipper Drive through Acadian country to the Acadian Museum of Prince Edward Island in Miscouche. Leave midafternoon and take Route 12 to the scenic and peaceful ⊡**Tyne Valley** ㉔. From here, visit the Mi'Kmaq community at Lennox Island, where some fine traditional crafts are sold. The Mi'Kmaq Cultural Centre and Lennox Island Nature Trail are not to be missed. Stop by the historic Green Park in nearby **Port Hill** ㉓ to stroll through a former shipyard or visit the fine museum. On Day 3 make your way up to **North Cape** ㉖ and explore its reef and the Atlantic Wind Test Site and Interpretative Centre. Plan to arrive early in the afternoon at ⊡**West Point** ㉗, where you can enjoy the beach and walking trails and visit the lighthouse. Finish with a south-shore tour to **Mont-Carmel** ㉘, home to one of the province's best French dinner theaters.

If you have
7 days

Following a morning of shopping in ⊡**Charlottetown** ①– ⑩▶, travel along Route 10 to **Victoria** ⑯. Enjoy lunch at the restaurant at the end of the dock, then visit the crafts shops. Drive north to Breadalbane, on Route 246, to Stanley Pottery. Continue to the ⊡**Northwest Corner** to the restored stone train station at Kensington. The next day drive north to the Woodleigh Gardens in Burlington. Then head east for lunch and an afternoon at the Rainbow Valley Family Fun Park in ⊡**Cavendish** ⑬. Start Day 3 at Green Gables and end at ⊡**Prince Edward Island National Park** ⑪, where you can relax on the beach. On Day 4 visit the Anne of Green Gables Museum in Park Corner. Then follow Blue Heron Drive to ⊡**Summerside** ㉒ for shopping and a performance at the Jubilee Theatre. The next day follow Lady Slipper Drive (Route 11) to Cap-Egmont to view the bottle houses. Continue on to Route 178 and the pastoral hamlet of ⊡**Tyne heritable Valley** ㉔. In nearby **Port Hill** ㉓, wander through the Shipbuilding Museum. Don't miss the Mi'Kmaq handicrafts on Lennox Island, off Route 12 on Route 163. End the day at ⊡**North Cape** ㉖, overlooking one of the world's longest natural rock reefs. On Day 6 hike or bike along the Confederation Trail, which begins at Mile 0 in Tignish. Complete your tour at ⊡**West Point** ㉗, whose lighthouse-museum has guest rooms.

WHAT IT COSTS (in Canadian Dollars)				
	$$$$	$$$	$$	$	¢
RESTAURANTS	over $30	$20–$30	$12–$20	$8–$12	under $8
HOTELS	over $250	$175–$250	$125–$175	$75–$125	under $75

Restaurant prices are per-person for a main course at dinner. Hotel prices are for two people in a standard double room in high season.

Exploring Prince Edward Island

Prince Edward Island is irregular in shape, with deep inlets and tidal streams that nearly divide the province into three equal parts, known locally by their county names of Kings, Queens, and Prince (east to west). Roughly resembling a crescent, the Island is 195 km (121 mi) long from one end to the other, with a width ranging from 4 km (2½ mi) to 60 km (37 mi). Despite the gentle hills in the eastern and central regions of PEI, the land never rises to a height of more than 500 feet above sea level. To the west, from Summerside to North Cape, the terrain is flatter.

Timing

Although the Island is generally considered a summer destination, don't overlook the "shoulder" seasons: May, June, September, and October usually have spectacular weather and few visitors, although some sights and restaurants are closed. Fall is an excellent time to hike and explore the 350-km-long (217-mi-long) Confederation Trail, which crosses the Island. Migratory birds arrive in vast numbers toward the end of summer, many staying until the snow falls. Winters are unpredictable but offer some of the Island's most overlooked activities: cross-country skiing, snowmobiling, and ice-skating.

CHARLOTTETOWN

Prince Edward Island's oldest city, on an arm of the Northumberland Strait, is named for the stylish consort of King George III. This small city, peppered with gingerbread-clad Victorian houses and tree-shaded squares, is the largest community (population 33,000) on the Island. It's often called the Cradle of Confederation, a reference to the 1864 conference that led to the union of Nova Scotia, New Brunswick, Ontario, and Québec in 1867 and, eventually, Canada itself.

Charlottetown's main activities center on government, tourism, and private commerce. While suburbs were springing up around it, the core of Charlottetown remained unchanged, and the waterfront has been restored to recapture the flavor of earlier eras. Today the waterfront includes the Delta Prince Edward Hotel; an area known as Peake's Wharf and Confederation Landing Park, with informal restaurants and handicraft and retail shops; and a walking path painted as a blue line on the sidewalk leading visitors through some of the most interesting historical areas of the Old City. Irene Rogers's *Charlottetown: The Life in Its Buildings*, available locally, gives much detail about the architecture and history of downtown Charlottetown.

Exploring Charlottetown

You can see Charlottetown's historic homes, churches, parks, and waterfront on foot. The city center is compact, so walking is the best way to explore the area.

3

Beaches

You are never more than 15 minutes by car from a beach or waterway on Prince Edward Island. Ask a dozen islanders to recommend their favorites, and you'll hear many different answers. Basin Head Beach, near Souris, is one choice, with its miles of singing sands. West Point has lifeguards, restaurants nearby, and showers at the provincial park. At Greenwich, near St. Peters Bay, a half-hour walk along the floating boardwalk brings you to an endless empty beach. In summer, thanks to a branch of the Gulf Stream, the ocean beaches have the warmest water north of the Carolinas, making for fine swimming.

Bicycling

The Island is popular with bike-touring companies for its moderately hilly roads and stunning scenery; trips take place throughout the province, and the Island's tourism department can recommend tour operators. There are plenty of level areas, especially east of Charlottetown to Montague and along the north shore. However, shoulderless, narrow secondary roads in some areas and summer's car traffic can be challenging. A 9-km (5½-mi) path near Cavendish Campground loops around marsh, woods, and farmland. The Confederation Trail, which extends almost the complete length of the Island, has more than 350 km (217 mi) of flat surface covered with rolled stone dust, making it an excellent family cycling path. Plum-color entry gateways are near roadways at many points.

Deep-Sea Fishing

Deep-sea fishing boats are available along the eastern end of the Island as well as in the north-shore region. Although some boats can be chartered for fishing bluefin tuna, most operators offer excursions to fish for mackerel. These trips stay within 6 km (4 mi) of the shore and usually last for three or four hours. The vessels have washroom facilities, approved safety equipment, and all the required gear and bait. Some operators clean and bag the catch if passengers request it.

Golf Courses

More than two dozen 9- and 18-hole courses are open to the public on the Island. Several of the more beautiful ones have scenic ocean vistas, and almost all have hassle-free golfing, with easily booked tee times (now on-line), inexpensive rates, and uncrowded courses, particularly in fall. The 45-hole Brudenell River Resort incorporates Brudenell River Golf Course, Dundarave Golf Course, and the Canadian Golf Academy. Tee times are readily available outside the July–August peak tourist season.

Seafood

You are guaranteed fresh seafood on the Island. Talented chefs prepare mouthwatering Malpeque oysters and Island Blue mussels, but lobster gets top honors. Lobster suppers—with lobster, rolls, salad, and mountains of home-baked sweets—are offered commercially and by church and civic groups. Local papers, bulletin boards at grocery stores, and visitor information centers have information about these feasts.

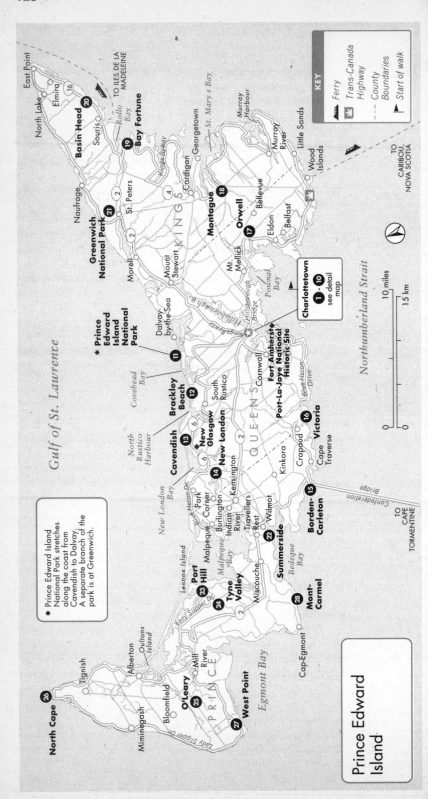

Prince Edward Island

KEY

✈ Ferry
Trans-Canada Highway
- - - County Boundaries
▲ Start of walk

* Prince Edward Island National Park stretches along the coast from Cavendish to Dalvay. A separate branch of the park is at Greenwich.

Gulf of St. Lawrence

TO ÎLES DE LA MADELEINE

East Point
Elmira 16
North Lake
Naufrage
Basin Head 20
Souris
Bay Fortune 19
Rollo Bay
Greenwich National Park 21
St. Peters 2
Kings Byway
Cardigan
Georgetown
St. Mary's Bay
Murray Harbour
Morell 2
Mount Stewart
Montague 18
Little Sands
Murray River
Orwell 17
Bellevue
Mt. Mellick
Eldon
Belfast
Wood Islands ✈
Charlottetown 1 - 10 see detail map
Pownal Bay
Hillsborough Bridge
Kingsway
Fort Amherst Port-La-Joye National Historic Site
Cornwall
Blue Heron Drive
TO CARIBOU, NOVA SCOTIA

Prince Edward Island National Park
Dalvay-by-the-Sea
Coverhead Bay
Brackley Beach 12 11
South Rustico
North Rustico Harbour
Cavendish 13
New Glasgow 6
New London 14
QUEENS
Victoria 16
Cape Traverse
Crapaud
Kinkora

North London Bay
Park Corner
Black Heron Dr.
Malpeque
Burlington
Indian River
Kensington
Travellers Rest
Wilmot
Summerside 22
Borden-Carleton 15
Bedeque Bay
Confederation Bridge
TO CAPE TORMENTINE

Malpeque Bay
Lennox Island
Port Hill 23
Tyne Valley 24
Miscouche 2
Mont-Carmel 28
Egmont Bay
Cap-Egmont

Oultons Island
Alberton
Lady Slipper Dr.
Tignish
North Cape 26
Miminegash
Bloomfield
O'Leary 25
Mill River
West Point 27
PRINCE

Northumberland Strait

0   10 miles
0   15 km

a good walk

Before setting out to explore Charlottetown, brush up on local history at the **Confederation Centre of the Arts ❶**, on Richmond Street in the heart of downtown. Next door, the **Province House National Historic Site ❷** is the site of the first meeting to discuss federal union. Turn left off Richmond Street onto Prince Street to see **St. Paul's Anglican Church ❸**. Backtrack on Richmond Street two blocks and turn left onto Great George Street, home to **St. Dunstan's Basilica ❹**, with its towering twin Gothic spires. Great George Street ends at the waterfront, where the boardwalks of **Confederation Landing Park ❺** lead past small eateries, shops, and **Founder's Hall ❻**. Break for lunch at the Merchantman Pub. On the city's west end, the work of Robert Harris, Canada's foremost portrait artist, adorns the walls of **St. Peter's Cathedral ❼** in Rochford Square, bordered by Rochford and Pownal streets. It's a bit of a walk (¾ km, or ½ mi) to get there, but **Victoria Park ❽** provides a grassy respite edging the harbor front. Next, visit one of the finest residential buildings in the city, **Beaconsfield Historic House ❾**, for panoramic views of its quiet garden and Charlottetown Harbour. Leave time to observe a favorite Prince Edward Island pastime—harness racing at **Charlottetown Driving Park ❿**, which is a 15-minute walk from downtown.

TIMING The downtown area can be explored on foot in a couple of hours, but the wealth of historic sites and harbor views warrants a full day.

Sights to See

❾ **Beaconsfield Historic House.** Designed by architect W. C. Harris and built in 1877 for wealthy shipbuilder James Peake, Jr., this gracious Victorian home near the entrance to Victoria Park is one of the Island's finest historic homes, with 11 furnished rooms. You can tour the first and second floors and enjoy views of the garden and Charlottetown Harbour. An on-site bookstore has museum publications as well as community histories. Special events such as musical performances and history-based lectures are held regularly. A carriage house on the grounds has activities for children June through early September, including a weekday-morning Children's Festival in July and August (call for exact times and price). ✉ *2 Kent St.* ☎ *902/368–6603* ⊕ *www.peimuseum.com* ☞ *$3.50* ⊙ *June–early Sept., daily 10–5; early Sept.–May, daily, call for hrs.*

❿ **Charlottetown Driving Park.** Since 1890 this track at the eastern end of the city has been the home of a sport dear to islanders—harness racing. Standardbred horses are raised around the Island, and harness racing on the ice and on country tracks has been popular for generations. In fact, there are more horses per capita on the Island than in any other Canadian province. August brings **Old Home Week**, when eastern Canada's best converge for 15 races in eight days. ✉ *Kensington Rd.* ☎ *902/892–6823* ☞ *Free* ⊙ *Races June, July, and most of Aug., 3 nights per wk; Old Home Week mid-Aug., Mon.–Sat. twice daily.*

❶ **Confederation Centre of the Arts.** In historic Charlottetown, the Confederation Centre of the Arts houses a 1,102-seat main-stage theater, a 1,000-seat outdoor amphitheater, and a 190-seat second-stage theater off-site. The center is most famous for the award-winning **Charlottetown Festival,** which runs from mid-May to mid-October, with concerts, comedy performances, art exhibitions, and musical theater productions, including *Anne of Green Gables—The Musical*™. Weather permitting, the festival offers free lunchtime theater performances and concerts in the amphitheater and on the plaza. During fall and winter the center presents a dynamic mix of touring and local productions, choral music concerts, and special events. The art gallery has a varied year-round exhibition program showcasing contemporary and historical Canadian art, with special reference to Confederation. The center also has a café and

Beaconsfield
Historic
House 9

Charlottetown
Driving
Park....... 10

Confederation
Centre
of the Arts 1

Confederation
Landing
Park........ 5

Founders'
Hall 6

Province
House
National
Historic Site... 2

St. Dunstan's
Basilica 4

St. Paul's
Anglican
Church....... 3

St. Peter's
Cathedral..... 7

Victoria
Park........ 8

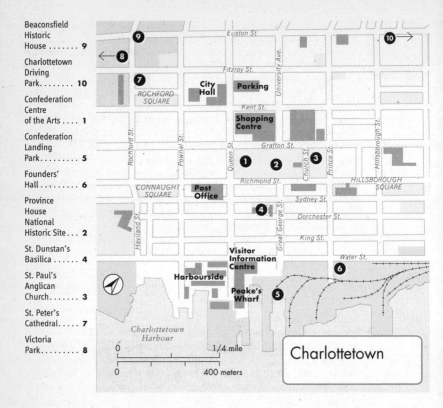

a public library. ✉ *145 Richmond St.* ☎ *902/566–1267 or 800/565–0278* ⊕ *www.confederationcentre.com* ☉ *Nov.–Apr., daily 9–5; hrs extended May–Oct.*

5 **Confederation Landing Park.** This waterfront recreation area at the bottom of Great George Street marks the site of the historic landing of the Fathers of Confederation in 1864. Walkways and park benches offer plenty of opportunities to survey the activity of the harbor. During summer performers in period costume stroll about the area re-creating historical events leading up to Canadian Confederation. **Peake's Wharf,** in the park next to Founders' Hall, has casual restaurants and bars, souvenir and crafts shops, and a marina where boat tours may be arranged. ✉ *Water St. between Queen and Hillsborough Sts.* ⊠ *Free* ☉ *Daily dawn–dusk.*

6 **Founders' Hall.** State-of-the-art displays at this museum in Confederation Landing Park transport visitors back in time to the Charlottetown Conference of 1864, eventually returning to the present day with a greater appreciation of this important event in Canadian history. ✉ *Confederation Landing Park, 6 Price St., at Water St.* ☎ *902/368–1864 or 800/955–1864* ⊕ *www.foundershall.ca* ⊠ *$7* ☉ *May 16–June 26 and Sept. 1–Oct. 18, Mon.–Sat. 9–5, Sun. 9–4; June 27–Aug. 31, Mon.–Sat. 9–8, Sun. 9–4.*

need a break? **Cows Ice Cream** (✉ *Queen St.* ☎ *902/892–6969* ⊕ *www.cows.ca/icecream* ✉ *Peake's Wharf* ☎ *902/566–4886*) is the most famous ice cream on the Island. Fresh milk from PEI cows and other natural ingredients are carefully combined to create 36 flavors of premium ice cream that should be slowly savored. Cows Ice Cream can be purchased at the two Charlottetown locations, as well as at

Cavendish Boardwalk (on Route 6), in Summerside (Water St., across from Spinaker's Landing), in PEI Factory Shops in North River, in Gateway Village at the approach to the Confederation Bridge, and on board the PEI–Nova Scotia passenger ferry *The Confederation*.

② **Province House National Historic Site.** This three-story sandstone building, completed in 1847 to house the colonial government and now the seat of the Provincial Legislature, has been restored to its mid-19th-century Victorian appearance. The many restored rooms include the historic Confederation Chamber, where representatives of the 19th-century British colonies met. Special guided tours are offered for a nominal charge, historical programs may be viewed daily during summer months, and a gift shop has mementos. The short history film shown here should not be missed. ⊠ *Richmond St.* ☎ *902/566–7626* ⊕ *www.pc.gc.ca* ✉ *By donation* ☉ *Mid-Oct.–May, weekdays 9–5; June and Sept.–mid-Oct., daily 9–5; July and Aug., daily 9–6.*

FodorsChoice ★

★ **④** **St. Dunstan's Basilica.** One of Canada's largest churches, St. Dunstan's is the seat of the Roman Catholic diocese on the Island. The church is known for its fine Italian carvings and twin Gothic spires. ⊠ *Great George St.* ☎ *902/894–3486* ⊕ *www.stdunstans.pe.ca.*

③ **St. Paul's Anglican Church.** Erected in 1896, this is actually the third church building on this site. The first was built in 1769, making this the Island's oldest parish. ⊠ *101 Prince St.* ☎ *902/892–1691* ⊕ *www.isn.net/~stpauls.*

⑦ **St. Peter's Cathedral.** The murals here by artist Robert Harris are found in **All Souls' Chapel,** designed in 1888 by his brother W. C. "Willy" Harris, the most celebrated of the Island's architects and the designer of many historic homes and buildings. This small chapel, which is attached to the side of the cathedral, may be open for viewing by chance; if not, you should inquire inside the cathedral. ⊠ *Rochford St.* ☎ *902/566–2102* ☉ *Weekdays 9–5.*

⑧ **Victoria Park.** At the southern tip of the city and overlooking Charlottetown Harbour are 40 beautiful acres that provide the perfect place to stroll, picnic, or watch a baseball game. Next to the park, on a hill between groves of white birches, is the white colonial **Government House,** built in 1835 as the official residence for the province's lieutenant governors (the house is not open to the public). The collection of antique cannons that still "guard" the city's waterfront provides a play area for children; runners can take advantage of the pathway that edges the harbor. ⊠ *Lower Kent St.* ☉ *Daily sunrise–sunset.*

Where to Eat

$$$–$$$$ ✕**The Selkirk.** With its wing chairs and live piano entertainment, the Selkirk is the Island's most sophisticated dining room. The imaginative menu concentrates on regional Canadian fare—locally grown potatoes, smoked Atlantic salmon, lobster, mussels, Malpeque oysters, and Canadian beef, to name a few—served with herbs straight from the garden. A four-course extravaganza aims to satisfy even the largest appetite. ⊠ *Delta Prince Edward Hotel, 18 Queen St.* ☎ *902/894–1208* ⌖ *Reservations essential* ▭ *AE, DC, MC, V.*

★ **$$–$$$** ✕**Claddagh Room Restaurant.** Some of the best seafood in Charlottetown is served here. The "Galway Bay Delight," one of the Irish owner's specialties, is a savory combination of fresh scallops and shrimp sautéed with onions and mushrooms, flambéed in Irish Mist, and doused with fresh cream. Nonseafarers can choose from a variety of chicken, beef, and fresh pasta dishes. The Olde Dublin Pub upstairs has live Irish entertainment every night from mid-June to mid-September and Thursday–Saturday the rest of the year. This friendly pub has the largest selection of beer on tap on the Island. ⊠ *131 Sydney St.* ☎ *902/892–9661* ▤ *AE, DC, MC, V.*

$$–$$$ ✕ **Culinary Institute of Canada.** Students at this internationally acclaimed school cook and present lunch and dinner under the supervision of their master chef–instructor as part of their training. Here's an opportunity to enjoy excellent food and top service at reasonable prices. At the very end of Sydney Street, next to Charlottetown Harbour, the institute has an elegant dining room with large windows that provide lovely water vistas. Many local residents come to this tastefully decorated dining room for a special culinary experience. Call for a schedule. ⊠ *4 Sydney St.* ☎ *902/894–6868* ⚖ *Reservations essential* ▤ *AE, MC, V.*

$$–$$$ ✕ **Griffon Dining Room.** This cozy restaurant in a Queen Anne–style inn is filled with antiques, copper, and brass. The French Continental cuisine includes fresh Atlantic salmon, beef tenderloin, and sea scallops. The Hearth and Cricket Pub serves light meals and a good selection of local and imported beers. ⊠ *Dundee Arms Inn, 200 Pownal St.* ☎ *902/ 892–2496 or 877/638–6333* ▤ *AE, DC, MC, V.*

$–$$$ ✕ **Merchantman Pub.** The best in pub food is served in this historic building with antique brick and original open-beam ceilings. The waterfront walking path near Confederation Landing Park is just steps away. House specialties include fresh seafood and steaks as well as Thai and Cajun creations. Both local and imported draft beers are available. ⊠ *Corner of Queen and Water Sts.* ☎ *902/892–9150* ▤ *AE, DC, MC, V.*

$–$$$ ✕ **Off Broadway.** Popular with Charlottetown's professional set, this restaurant offers an inventive menu of French-influenced food prepared with fresh local ingredients. The private booths won't reveal your indiscretions, including your indulgence in dessert. Upstairs, with large windows overlooking the street, is the 42nd Street Lounge, where a comfortable, casual atmosphere prevails. Light fare from the restaurant kitchen is available. ⊠ *125 Sydney St.* ☎ *902/566–4620* ▤ *AE, DC, MC, V.*

$–$$$ ✕ **Sirenella Ristorante.** Specializing in northern Italian cuisine, this eatery in downtown Charlottetown serves veal, grilled seafood, and homemade pasta. The intimate atmosphere is enhanced by soft music, candlelight, and excellent service. In addition to a private room that seats up to 30 guests, there is an outdoor patio for summer dining. The restaurant imports wines directly from Italy. ⊠ *83 Water St.* ☎ *902/628–2271* ▤ *AE, DC, MC, V* ☺ *Closed Jan.*

$$ ✕ **Peake's Quay Restaurant and Bar.** This great summer spot on Charlottetown's restored waterfront has daily lunch and evening specials during the summer season. The large heated patio overlooks Confederation Landing Park and the adjoining marina. Specialties include seafood chowder, fresh scallops, and Atlantic salmon. Lobster is a menu feature. There's a large selection of snack foods available, and live Celtic music is provided seven nights a week from May until the end of September. ⊠ *2 Great George St.* ☎ *902/368–1330* ▤ *AE, DC, MC, V* ☺ *Closed Nov.–late Apr.*

$$ ✕ **Piece a Cake Restaurant.** The young chef-owner, Wesley Gallant, cooks what he likes—and it appears that the public likes what he cooks. Canadian cuisine with ethnic influences is served at this upstairs restaurant overlooking Grafton Street near the Confederation Centre (and with a rear entrance to Confederation Mall). Working in an open kitchen, Gallant uses fresh ingredients and spices and sauces inspired from around the world. The changing menu always includes a good selection of pastas. A jazz or blues group usually entertains patrons Tuesday night. Be sure to ask for one of the six window tables. ⊠ *119 Grafton St.* ☎ *902/ 894–4585* ▤ *AE, DC, MC, V* ☺ *Closed Sun.*

$$ ✕ **The Pilot House.** In the historic Roger's Hardware Building, this restau-
Fodor'sChoice rant has fine dining and light pub fare. Original wood beams, brick
★ columns, and a unique bar top made of black granite inlaid with bird's-
eye maple enhance the cozy atmosphere. Certified Black Angus beef and
fresh seasonal seafood are popular items on the creative dinner menu.
⊠ *70 Grafton St.* ☎ *902/894–4800* ▤ *AE, DC, MC, V.*

¢ ✕ **Beanz Espresso Bar.** This hip café with an outside patio is an excel-
lent spot for hearty sandwiches, soups, salad, and coffee. The desserts
are right out of an *Anne of Green Gables* church social. Bakers who
know how to prepare these old-fashioned treats are a dying breed. The
pies, squares, and cakes are mouthwatering, huge, and cheap. Beanz serves
breakfast and lunch and closes at 6 Monday–Saturday and at 5 on Sun-
day. ⊠ *38 University Ave.* ☎ *902/892–8797* ▤ *MC, V* ✆ *No dinner.*

Where to Stay

★ **$$–$$$$** 🏨 **Delta Prince Edward Hotel.** Next to Peake's Wharf, the Delta Prince
Edward has an ideal location from which to explore both the water-
front and historic downtown areas on foot. The hotel has all the comforts and luxuries of its first-rate Delta counterparts, including a grand
ballroom, a golf simulator, and three dining choices: an elegant restaurant, a café that serves specialty sandwiches and gourmet coffees, and
a seasonal outdoor restaurant overlooking the marina and boardwalk.
Two-thirds of the guest rooms in the 10-story hotel have waterfront views.
⊠ *Box 2170, 18 Queen St., C1A 8B9* ☎ *902/566–2222* ⊟ *902/566–
1745* ⊕ *www.deltaprinceedward.pe.ca* ⇱ *211 rooms, 33 suites* ⚬ *2
restaurants, café, room service, in-room data ports, cable TV, indoor
pool, gym, health club, massage, spa, bar, shop, baby-sitting, dry cleaning, laundry facilities, laundry service, concierge, Internet, business services, convention center, meeting rooms, car rental, parking (fee), some
pets allowed (fee), no-smoking rooms* ▤ *AE, DC, MC, V.*

$$$ ✕🏨 **Rodd Charlottetown—A Rodd Signature Hotel.** This five-story redbrick
hotel with white pillars and a circular driveway is just one block from
the center of Charlottetown. The rooms have the latest amenities but re-
tain the hotel's old-fashioned flavor (it was built in 1931) with repro-
ductions of antique furnishings. The grandeur and charm of the Carvery
Dining Room ($$–$$$) capture the elegance of an earlier era. ⊠ *Box
159, Kent and Pownal Sts., C1A 7K4* ☎ *902/894–7371 or 800/565–7633*
⊟ *902/368–2178* ⊕ *www.rodd-hotels.ca* ⇱ *108 rooms, 7 suites* ⚬ *Restau-
rant, indoor pool, gym, hot tub, sauna, lounge* ▤ *AE, DC, MC, V.*

★ **$$–$$$** 🏨 **Elmwood Heritage Inn.** One of the Atlantic Provinces' leading architects,
W. C. Harris, designed this handsome Victorian home in 1889. Elmwood
was originally owned by Arthur Peters, grandson of Samuel Cunard,
founder of the famous shipping line. The antiques-laden home has been
restored, and the tastefully decorated rooms have either a claw-foot tub
(in three rooms) or a whirlpool bath. Some rooms have a working fire-
place. A common living room has its own fireplace and second-floor bal-
cony as well as a refrigerator, CD player, and video collection. Breakfast
is an elegant candlelight affair. ⊠ *121 N. River Rd., C1A 3K7* ☎ *902/
368–3310 or 877/933–3310* ⊟ *902/628–8457* ⊕ *www.elmwoodinn.pe.
ca* ⇱ *7 rooms* ⚬ *In-room VCRs* ▤ *AE, DC, MC, V* ⊠ *BP.*

$$–$$$ 🏨 **Fairholm National Historic Inn.** Originally built in 1838 for Thomas
Fodor'sChoice Heath Haviland, a noteworthy man in the early development of Prince
★ Edward Island, Fairholm is the finest Maritime example of the British
"picturesque" architectural movement. The seven spaciously elegant suites
include fireplaces and fax access; some rooms have whirlpool tubs. En-
hanced with inlaid hardwood floors, antiques, Island art, and wallpa-
per imported from England, this inn is a perfect alliance of British roots

and Island hospitality. A hearty breakfast is included. It's close to shopping, restaurants, and theater. ⊠ *230 Prince St., C1A 1S3* ☎ *902/892–5022 or 888/573–5022* 🖷 *902/892–5060* ⊕ *www.fairholm.pe.ca* ⇆ *7 rooms* ♨ *Cable TV, business services* ☐ *MC, V* ⦿ *BP.*

★ **$$–$$$** ⊡ **Inns on Great George.** Closely linked with the founding of Canada as a nation (the so-called Fathers of Confederation stayed in these buildings during the 1864 Charlottetown Conference), this complex includes several historic 1800s structures: the 24-room Pavilion, the five-room Wellington/Carriage House, and a couple of romantic hideaway town houses. Many restored buildings date to 1811. A Continental breakfast feast of homemade muffins, dessert breads, scones, and cookies—along with fruit and yogurt—is served in the Pavilion reception area each morning. ⊠ *58 Great George St., C1A 4K3* ☎ *902/892–0606 or 800/361–1118* 🖷 *902/628–2079* ⊕*www.innsongreatgeorge.com* ⇆ *29 rooms, 5 suites, 2 houses* ♨ *Cable TV, no-smoking rooms* ☐ *AE, DC, MC, V* ⦿ *CP.*

$–$$$ ⊡ **Hillhurst Inn.** In the heart of downtown, this grand 1897 mansion was once the home of George Longworth, a prominent Charlottetown merchant who made a fortune from building and operating ships. The reception area, dining room, and living room are paneled with burnished oak and beech, the work of the shipwrights Longworth employed. Each of the unique guest rooms has period furniture, and many have exquisite handmade beds. Two rooms have whirlpool baths. ⊠ *181 Fitzroy St., C1A 1S3* ☎ *902/894–8004 or 877/994–8004* 🖷 *902/892–7679* ⊕*www. hillhurst.com* ⇆ *9 rooms* ☐ *AE, MC, V* ⦿ *BP.*

$–$$$ ⊡ **Shipwright Inn B.** In a lovely 1860s home originally owned by the local shipbuilder James Douse are eight unique guest rooms and one apartment. The nautical theme is continued throughout the house in both construction and decoration. All rooms have original wood floors and Victorian memorabilia. Some units have fireplaces, whirlpool baths, and balconies. Enjoy the memorable breakfast and afternoon tea. ⊠ *51 Fitzroy St., C1A 1R4* ☎ *902/368–1905 or 888/306–9966* 🖷 *902/628–1905* ⊕ *www.shipwrightinn.com* ⇆ *8 rooms, 1 apartment* ♨ *In-room VCRs, Internet, no-smoking rooms* ☐ *AE, MC, V* ⦿ *BP.*

$$ ✕⊡ **Dundee Arms Inn.** Depending on your mood, you can choose to stay in either a 1960s motel or a 1903 Queen Anne–style inn. The motel is simple, modern, and neat; the inn is homey and furnished with brass and antiques. The Dundee Arms is only minutes from downtown. The Griffon Dining Room ($$–$$$) serves excellent Continental cuisine, and the Hearth and Cricket Pub serves hearty British fare. ⊠ *200 Pownal St., C1A 3W8* ☎ *902/892–2496 or 877/638–6333* 🖷 *902/368–8532* ⊕ *www.dundeearms.com* ⇆ *15 rooms, 3 suites* ♨ *Restaurant, pub; no smoking* ☐ *AE, DC, MC, V.*

$ ✕⊡ **Islander Motor Lodge.** In downtown Charlottetown, this motel has
Fodor'sChoice spacious, comfortable units: doubles, twin doubles, kings, queens, suites,
★ and apartments. The central location of the lodge is within walking distance of fine restaurants, theaters, and shops. The restaurant (¢–$) serves home-style food such as salt cod and liver and onions. ⊠ *146–148 Pownal St., C1A 7N4* ☎ *902/892–1217 or 800/268–6261* 🖷 *902/566–1623* ⇆ *50 rooms* ♨ *Coffee shop, dining room, some pets allowed* ☐ *AE, MC, V.*

¢–$ ⊡ **Sherwood Motel.** The friendly owners of this family-oriented motel help you reserve tickets for events and plan day trips. Don't be daunted by the Sherwood's proximity to the airport—very little traffic passes in front of this property. There are 28 motel rooms in the main building and 18 units in the newer motor inn behind the motel. ⊠ *281 Brackley Point Rd.–Rte. 15, C1E 2A3, 5 km (3 mi) north of downtown Charlottetown* ☎ *902/892–1622 or 800/567–1622* ⇆ *46 rooms* ♨ *Some kitchenettes, cable TV* ☐ *MC, V.*

Nightlife & the Arts

The **Benevolent Irish Society Hall** (✉ 582 N. River Rd. ☎ 902/892–2367) stages concerts on Friday, mid-May through October. *Ceilidhs*—live traditional entertainment combining dancing, fiddling, and stories—can be found in and around Charlottetown. For information on locations and times contact the **visitor information center** (☎ 902/368–4444). One of

★ ☺ Canada's most popular attractions is the **Charlottetown Festival** (✉ Grafton and Queen Sts. ☎ 902/628–1864 or 800/565–0278 ⊕ www. confederationcentre.com/festival.asp), home to the nation's longest-running musical, *Anne of Green Gables—The Musical*™. Professional comedies and musical theater are presented in three venues, and free outdoor performances take place on the property. Every evening during summer, you can catch live music under the stars—for free—on Victoria Row at the **Charlottetown Jazz Festival.** Dine at one of the restaurants with patios facing the stage. Bands start up at 7:30. The **Eddie May Murder Mystery Dinner Theatre** (✉ Piazza Joe's, 189 Kent St. ☎ 902/569–1999) combines madcap improvisation with sleuthing and dining. The **Feast Dinner Theatre** (✉ Rodd Charlottetown, corner of Kent and Pownal Sts. ☎ 902/629–2321) stages a lively show while you feast on chicken and ribs, mussels, and homemade bread. **Homefree Productions** (✉ Beaconsfield Historic House ☎ 902/368–6603) offers a summer-long program that may include musicals and dramas, as well as children's presentations, storytelling, and concerts. Just steps from the waterfront in a historic building with antique brick and original open-beam ceilings, the

★ **Merchantman Pub** (✉ Corner of Queen and Water Sts., ☎ 902/892–9150) is a great spot to enjoy seafood, Thai, and Cajun cuisines. Local and imported draft beers are available.

Sports & the Outdoors

Biking

Bicycling is a favorite sport in PEI. There are several companies in Charlottetown that offer bicycle repairs and rentals as well as guided city bicycle tours, among them **Smooth Cycle** (✉ 172 Prince St. ☎ 902/566–5530).

Golf

The 18-hole **Fox Meadow Golf and Country Club** (✉ 167 Kinlock Rd., Stratford ☎ 902/569–4653) is 5 km (3 mi) from town. The challenging par-72 championship course was designed by Rob Heaslip and overlooks the community of Stratford and Charlottetown Harbour.

Water Sports

For day sailing contact **Saga Sailing Adventures** (✉ Charlottetown Harbour ☎ 902/672–1222). You can arrange pickup service from your hotel for north-shore sea kayaking. A good way to discover the area's natural beauty is to contact **Outside Expeditions** (✉ 890 Grand Pere Rd., off Rte. 242, 8 km [5 mi] east of Cavendish, South Rustico ☎ 902/963–
☺ 3366 or 800/207–3899 ⊕ www.getoutside.com). **Peake's Wharf Boat Tours/ Seal Watching** (✉ 1 Great George St., Peake's Wharf ☎ 902/566–4458) arranges seal-watching tours.

Shopping

The most interesting stores are at Peake's Wharf, in Confederation Court Mall (off Queen Street), and in Victoria Row, on Richmond Street between Queen and Great George streets. There are also a dozen factory outlet stores along the Trans-Canada Highway at North River Causeway, near the western entrance to the city.

The zany **Cows** (⊠ Queen St. across from Confederation Centre ☎ 902/892–6969) sells all things bovine—from T-shirts embellished with cartoon cows to delicious ice cream. **Great Northern Knitters** (⊠ 133 Queen St. ☎ 902/566–5302) has a terrific selection of handmade woolen sweaters. **Island Craft Shop** (⊠ 156 Richmond St. ☎ 902/892–5152) sells handmade pottery, weaving, rug hooking, and woodworking crafted by members of the PEI Craft Council. **Moonsnail Soapworks and Aromatherapy** (⊠ 87 Water St. ☎ 902/892–7627) produces handmade soaps using olive, coconut, and palm oils with herbs, spices, and pure essential oils for scent. **Roots** (⊠ Confederation Court Mall off Queen St. ☎ 902/566–1877) is an upscale leather-goods and clothing company with stores across Canada.

BLUE HERON DRIVE

FodorśChoice ★ From Charlottetown, Blue Heron Drive follows Route 15 north to the north shore, then winds along Route 6 through north-shore fishing villages, past the spectacular white-sand beaches of Prince Edward Island National Park, through Anne of Green Gables country, and finally along the south shore, with its red-sandstone seascapes and historic sites. The drive takes its name from the great blue heron, a stately waterbird that migrates to Prince Edward Island every spring to nest in the shallow bays and marshes. The whole circuit roughly outlines Queens County and covers 190 km (118 mi). It circles some of the Island's most beautiful landscapes and best beaches. The northern section around Cavendish and the Green Gables farmhouse is cluttered with commercial tourist operations, but if you look beyond the fast-food outlets and tacky gift shops, you can envision the Island's simpler days. Unspoiled beauty still exists in the magnificent sunsets, refreshing open spaces, distinctive red headlands, white sandy beaches, and changeable sculpted coastline.

Prince Edward Island National Park

⓫ *24 km (15 mi) north of Charlottetown.*

FodorśChoice ★ Prince Edward Island National Park, a narrow strip of mostly beach and dunes, stretches for more than 40 km (25 mi) along the north shore of the Island, from Cavendish to Tracadie Bay plus a separate extension, about 24 km (15 mi) farther east at Greenwich. The park is blessed with nature's broadest brush strokes—sky and sea meet red-sandstone cliffs, rolling dunes, and long stretches of sand. There are six entrances to the park system off Routes 6, 13, and 15. National park information centers are at Cavendish and Brackley. The Gulfshore Highway runs through the park, giving tantalizing views of the beach and dunes. Beaches invite swimming, picnicking, and walking. Trails lead through woodlands and along streams and ponds. Among the more than 200 species of birds that pass through the area are the northern phalarope, the Swainson's thrush, and the endangered piping plover. Spanning the park are many campgrounds with varying fees and seasons. In autumn and winter it's difficult to reach park staff; call in spring or summer for exact rates and schedules if you're planning a camping trip. From mid-September through May, there are no park services, though the beach and trails are open. A seasonal pass is $25. ☎ 902/672–6350, 800/213–7875 *campground reservations* ⊕ *www.pc.gc.ca* ☒ *$5, free early Sept.–early June* ☉ *Daily dawn–dusk.*

Where to Stay & Eat

$$–$$$ ✕ **Cafe St. Jean.** Next to Rustico Harbour, this restaurant has a warm, rustic post-and-beam interior, rich upholstery, and views of oceanfront

dunes or the Wheatley River from the high-back booths. Pepper steak, seafood dishes, and Cajun sauces are menu specialties. Brackley, Dalvay, and Cavendish are just minutes away. ⊠ *Rte. 6* ☎ *902/675–4175* ⌂ *Reservations essential* ▤ *AE, DC, MC, V* ⊙ *Closed Oct.–mid-June.*

$$$–$$$$ ▦ **Dalvay-by-the-Sea.** Just within the eastern border of Prince Edward Island National Park is this Victorian house, built in 1895 as a private summer home. This historic property is the only seaside country inn on Prince Edward Island. Rooms are furnished with antiques and reproductions. You can sip cocktails or tea on the porch while viewing the inn's gardens, Dalvay Lake, or the nearby beach. Canoes and rowboats are available. In addition to the rooms in the inn, Dalvay also has eight upscale overnight cottages. Park entrance fees apply. ⊠ *Rte. 6. York, near Dalvay Beach* ⌂ *Box 8, PEI National Park, Grand Tracadie C0A 1P0* ☎ *902/672–2048* ⊕ *www.dalvaybythesea.com* ➥ *26 rooms, 8 cottages* ⌂ *Restaurant, driving range, 2 tennis courts, boating, croquet, bar, shop; no smoking* ▤ *AE, DC, MC, V* ⊙ *Closed mid-Oct.–early June* ⧖ *MAP.*

$$–$$$$ ▦ **Blue Heron Hideaways Beach Houses.** Blue Heron comprises two large (five- and six-bedroom) beach houses at Blooming Point (on Tracadie Bay) and two beach houses plus a studio cottage on Point Deroche, 5 km (3 mi) to the east. The private 10-km-long (6-mi-long) beach is perfect for beachcombing and has sand dunes and wildlife along with rowboats and kayaks for guest use. Units have gas barbecues and CD players. Most have whirlpool baths. From mid-June to mid-September there are weekly rentals only. ⊠ *Meadowbank, R.R. 2, Cornwall C0A 1H0* ☎ *902/566–2427* ⌂ *902/368–3798* ⊕ *www.blueheronhideaways. com* ➥ *4 houses, 1 cottage* ⌂ *Kitchens, microwaves, refrigerators, in-room VCRs, pool, beach, boating* ▤ *No credit cards* ⊙ *Closed mid-Oct.–early June.*

Sports & the Outdoors

The **Links at Crowbush Cove** (⊠ Off Rte. 2 on Rte. 350, Lakeside ☎ 902/961–7300 or 800/377–8337), an 18-hole, par-72 Scottish-style course with ocean views, is about 40 km (25 mi) east of the national park. The 18 holes of the links-style par-72 course at **Stanhope Golf and Country Club** (⊠ Off Rte. 6, Stanhope ☎ 902/672–2842) are among the most challenging and scenic on the Island. The course is a couple of miles west of Dalvay, along Covehead Bay.

Brackley Beach

⑫ *15 km (9 mi) north of Charlottetown.*

Just outside Prince Edward Island National Park, Brackley Beach offers a variety of country-style accommodations and eating establishments. The town has a national park information service building about a mile from the tollbooth at the actual park entrance. Its bays and waterways attract migratory birds and are excellent for canoeing or kayaking and windsurfing.

Where to Stay & Eat

$$–$$$ ✕ **Dunes Café.** A pottery studio, art gallery, artisans' outlet, and outdoor **Fodor's**Choice gardens share a property with this stunning café. Wood ceilings soar above ★ the indoor dining room, and a deck overlooks the dunes and marshlands of Covehead Bay. The chef's specialty is local seafood and lamb prepared with locally grown, fresh produce, much of which comes from the café's own gardens. ⊠ *Rte. 15, 1 km (½ mi) south of national park* ☎ *902/672–2586* ▤ *AE, MC, V* ⊙ *Closed early Oct.–late May.*

★ $$$ ✕▦ **Shaw's Hotel and Cottages.** Each room is unique in this 1860s hotel with antique furnishings, hardwood floors, and country elegance. Shaw's is one of only two remaining hotels on the Island that have been operating for more than a century. The hotel and cottages have lovely bay vistas. Half the cottages have fireplaces. Canoes and kayaks are available. The fine-dining restaurant ($$–$$$) has four-course menus of salmon, chicken, or steak. Lobster is served twice weekly. Seafood is served at the Sunday-evening buffet ($$$$), a popular local tradition. ✉ *Rte. 15, Brackley Beach, C1E 1Z3* ☎ *902/672–2022* 📠 *902/672–3000* 🌐 *www.shawshotel.ca* *17 rooms, 3 suites, 25 cottages* *Restaurant, beach, boating, bicycles, bar, playground* 💳 *AE, MC, V* *Closed early Oct.–May; 6 cottages open year-round* *MAP.*

$$–$$$ **Barachois Inn.** South Rustico is one of the oldest communities on the Island, and the Barachois Inn blends into the historic region with its 1880 Victorian elegance. Built as the stately home for a local merchant, the original heritage house has four spacious suites with period antiques and fine art. The adjacent MacDonald House has four suites, each with a fireplace, a kitchenette, and a whirlpool tub. The inn overlooks a Victorian garden and the lovely countryside as it leads to nearby Rustico Bay. ✉ *Rte. 243, Rustico, off Rte. 6, 8 km (5 mi) west of Brackley Beach* *RR3, Hunter River C0A 1N0* ☎ *902/963–2194* *902/963–2906* 🌐 *www.barachoisinn.com* *8 suites* *Some kitchenettes, in-room VCRs, gym, sauna, Internet, meeting room; no smoking* 💳 *AE, MC, V* *BP.*

Sports & the Outdoors

Northshore Rentals (✉ Rte. 15 at Shaw's Hotel ☎ 902/672–2022) rents canoes, river kayaks, and rowboats.

Shopping

The **Cheeselady's Gouda** (✉ Rte. 223, Winsloe North, 8 km [5 mi] off Rte. 2 ☎ 902/368–1506) not only demonstrates how genuine Gouda is produced but also offers samples of uniquely flavored cheeses. **The Dunes Studio Gallery** (✉ Rte. 15 south of the national park ☎ 902/672–2586) sells the work of dozens of leading local artists and of craftspeople from around the world. The pottery studio is open for viewing, and a rooftop garden has vistas of saltwater bays, dunes, and hills.

Cavendish

⓭ *21 km (13 mi) west of Brackley Beach.*

Cavendish is the most visited Island community outside Charlottetown because of the heavy influx of visitors to Green Gables, Prince Edward Island National Park, and amusement park–style attractions. Recreational options range from bumper-car rides and water slides to pristine sandy beaches. In 1908 Lucy Maud Montgomery (1874–1942) entered immortality as a beloved Canadian writer of fiction. It was in that year that she created a most charming and enduring character, Anne Shirley, whom Mark Twain described as "the dearest and most lovable child in fiction since the immortal Alice [in Wonderland]." Montgomery's novel *Anne of Green Gables* is still enjoyed today, and thousands of adoring fans flock to the Cavendish area to visit some of the homes associated with Montgomery and to explore the places described in the book.

The **Site of Lucy Maud Montgomery's Cavendish Home** is where the writer lived with her maternal grandparents following the untimely death of her mother. Though the foundation and surrounding white picket fence of the home where Montgomery wrote *Anne of Green Gables* are all that remain, the homestead's fields and old apple-tree gardens provide lovely walking grounds. A bookstore and museum are also on the property, which is operated by descendants of the family. ✉ *Rte. 6, just east* *of Green Gables* ☎ 902/963–2231 ✆ *$5.75* ◷ *June and Sept.–mid-Oct., daily 10–5; July–Aug., daily 9–7.*

★ **Green Gables, Prince Edward Island National Park,** ½ km (¼ mi) west of Lucy Maud Montgomery's Cavendish homesite, is the green-and-white farmhouse that served as the setting for *Anne of Green Gables*. Held dearly by Montgomery, it belonged to her grandfather's cousins. The house, farm buildings, and grounds re-create some of the settings found in the book, as do the posted walking trails Haunted Wood (2 km [1 mi]), and Balsam Hollow (1 km [½ mi]). The site has been part of Prince Edward Island National Park since 1937. ☒ *Rte. 6 west of Rte. 13* ☎ 902/963–7874 ⊕ *www.pc.gc.ca* ✆ *$5.50* ◷ *May–late June and Sept.–Oct., daily 9–5; late June–Aug., daily 9–8; limited schedule Nov., Dec., Mar., and Apr.; by appointment only in Jan. and Feb.*

There are many amusement parks throughout the Cavendish area, but
☾ **Rainbow Valley Family Fun Park** is unique. Not only is it one of the oldest attractions in the region, but as a family-operated business, it provides a full day of activities for visitors of all ages. Spread over 40 acres, this clean, friendly operation includes three boating lakes, many rides for each age group, six water slides, and an exciting flume ride using rubber rafts, as well as live performances. Food service is available or you can bring a picnic lunch. ☒ *Rte. 6* ☎ 902/963–2221 ⊕ *www.rainbowvalley.pe.ca* ✆ *$12* ◷ *Early June–early Sept., Mon.–Sat. 9–8, Sun. 11–8.*

Where to Stay & Eat

Accommodations in the Cavendish area are often booked a year in advance for July and most of August. Don't despair—hotels in Charlottetown and elsewhere in the central region are still within minutes of "Anne's Land."

$$–$$$$ ✕ **New Glasgow Lobster Supper.** Established in 1958, New Glasgow Lobster Supper brings fresh lobster direct from a pond on the premises to your plate. Breaded scallops, hot roast beef, haddock, and ham are other choices. All guests receive unlimited fresh-baked rolls, cultivated steamed mussels, seafood chowder, garden salad, homemade desserts, and beverages. Bar service is also available, and there's a children's menu. The dining area can seat up to 500 guests at one time, and it often fills up, but because turnover is fast, there isn't usually a long wait. ☒ *Rte. 258 at New Glasgow* ☎ 902/964–2870 ☐ 902/964–3116 ⊕ *www.peilobstersuppers. com* ☐ *AE, DC, MC, V* ◷ *Closed mid-Oct.–late May.*

★ **$$$** ☷ **Sundance Cottages.** On a quiet little lane near the center of Cavendish is this friendly family operation, a collection of 20 one- to four-bedroom cottages in a gently sloping field. The modern, spacious cottages are nicely decorated and have queen-size beds, decks with views of the countryside, picnic tables, and barbecues. Many cottages have whirlpool baths, dishwashers, and propane fireplaces. From the vegetable garden, you can pick fresh vegetables for meals free of charge. A national park pass is provided for each day of your stay. ☒ *R.R. 2 off Rte. 6, C0A 1N0* ☎ 902/963–2149 or 800/565–2149 ☐ 902/963–2100 ⊕ *www.sundancecottages.ca* ☖ 20 cottages ☖ *In-room VCRs, pool, gym, hot tub, mountain bikes, playground, laundry facilities, Internet* ☐ *AE, DC, MC, V.*

$–$$$ ☷ **Kindred Spirits Country Inn and Cottages.** Green hills surround this lovely country estate, a short walk from Green Gables House and Golf Course. You can relax by the parlor fireplace and then retreat to a large room or suite, decorated in country Victorian style with local antiques. Surrounding extensive lawns and gardens are 14 large cottages that range from economy to luxury (the upper-end cottages have fireplaces and hot tubs). All cottages are fully equipped for cooking; some have dishwashers, and all have barbecues. ☒ *Memory La. off Rte. 6, C0A 1N0*

☎ 902/963–2434 🖷 902/963–2619 ⊕ www.kindredspirits.ca 🔊 25 rooms, 14 cottages ⚹ Dining room, some kitchens, some kitchenettes, cable TV, some in-room VCRs, pool, hot tub, gym, playground, Internet ☰ MC, V ۞ Closed mid-Oct.–mid-May ⑩ BP.

$ 🏨 **Bay Vista Motor Inn and Cottage.** This spotlessly clean and friendly motel caters to families. Parents can sit on the outdoor deck and take in the New London Bay panorama while keeping an eye on their children in the large playground. There's a good hiking trail opposite the motel, and a restaurant is next door. Beaches and all area attractions are nearby. A separate three-bedroom cedar cottage is available for weekly rental. ✉ Rte. 6 🏠 R.R. 2, Hunter River C0A 1N0 ☎ 902/963–2225 or 800/846–0601 ⊕ www.bayvistamotorinn.com 🔊 28 rooms, 2 apartments, 1 cottage ⚹ Cable TV, pool, playground, laundry facilities, some pets allowed, no-smoking rooms ☰ AE, DC, MC, V ۞ Closed late Sept.–mid-June.

CAMPING 🏕 **Marco Polo Land Campground.** Of the many camping options in the Cavendish region—some inside national and provincial parks—this is one of the best private campgrounds. The site has a tennis court, miniature golf course, and supervised activities, including hayrides. The serviced lots are often reserved well in advance for July and August. A beach is a 2-km (1-mi) walk or a 4-km (2½-mi) drive away. Some tent sites have electricity and water. ✉ Rte. 13 ☎ 902/963–2352 or 800/665–2352 🖷 902/963–3727 ⊕ www.marcopololand.com 🔊 243 tent sites, 263 RV sites ⚹ Flush toilets, full RV hookups, partial RV hookups (electric and water), dump station, running water, laundry facilities, showers, food service, fire pits, picnic tables, general store, play area, 2 pools 🏕 Tent sites $25–$28, RV sites $30–$32 🔖 Reservations essential ☰ MC, V ۞ Closed late May–mid-Oct.

Sports & the Outdoors

GOLF The scenic, 18-hole, par-72 **Green Gables Golf Course** (✉ Prince Edward Island National Park, Rte. 6 ☎ 902/963–2488 May–Oct., 902/368–8045 Nov.–Apr. ⊕ www.greengablesgolf.com) is one of a half-dozen golf courses in the north-shore region. It was based on an original design by the golf-course architect Stanley Thompson. The clubhouse lounge serves refreshments and light meals. Tee times may be booked by phone; the course is closed November–April.

SEA KAYAKING Trips with **Outside Expeditions** (✉ 890 Grand Pere Rd., off Rte. 242, 8 km [5 mi] east of Cavendish, South Rustico ☎ 902/963–3366 or 800/ 207–3899 ⊕ www.getoutside.com), in North Rustico Harbour, can be geared to suit beginning or experienced paddlers. Tours include food from light snacks to full-fledged lobster boils, depending on the expedition.

New London

⑭ 11 km (7 mi) southwest of Cavendish.

This tiny village is best known as the birthplace of Lucy Maud Montgomery. It's also home to several seasonal gift and crafts shops and a tea shop. The wharf area is a great place to stop, rest, and watch fishing boats come and go. The **Lucy Maud Montgomery Birthplace** is a modest white-and-green house overlooking New London Harbour; the author of Anne of Green Gables was born here in 1874. The interior of the house has been furnished with Victorian antiques to re-create the era. Among memorabilia on display are her wedding dress and personal scrapbooks filled with many of her poems and stories. ✉ Rtes. 6 and 20 ☎ 902/886–2099 or 902/436–7329 🔖 $2 ۞ Mid-May–June and Sept.–mid-Oct., daily 9–5; July and Aug., daily 9–6.

Northwest Corner

Blue Heron Dr. begins 12 km (7 mi) west of New London, and extends 66 km (41 mi) to Borden-Carleton.

Some of the most beautiful scenery on the Island is on Blue Heron Drive along the north shore. As the drive follows the coastline south to the other side of the Island, it passes rolling farmland and the shores of Malpeque Bay. There are a couple of lovely beaches in this area. Just north of Darnley, off Route 20, is a long sand beach with a number of sandstone caves at the end. This beach—Darnley Beach—does not have developed facilities, and it is often almost entirely deserted except for the seabirds.

Not far from the village of Malpeque is **Cabot Beach Provincial Park,** which has camping facilities, a beach, and a playground. You can tour the sets used for filming the television series *Emily of New Moon,* based on another of L. M. Montgomery's fictional characters. In summer the beach area is supervised during the day, and the playground is open from dawn to dusk. ⊠ *Rte. 20, 16 km (10 mi) north of Kensington* ☎ *902/836–8945, 888/734–7529 camping reservations* ⊠*Free* ☉*July–Sept., daily dawn–dusk.*

☝ **Woodleigh Replicas and Gardens,** in Burlington, southwest of New London, is a 45-acre park with 30 scale replicas of Great Britain's best-known architectural structures, including the Tower of London and Dunvegan Castle. The models, some large enough to enter, are furnished with period antiques. Children especially enjoy climbing to the top of the lookout tower that crowns a small hill surrounded by flower gardens. A medieval maze and 10 acres of English country gardens are also on the grounds, as is a picnic area, a children's playground, and a snack bar with items such as hot dogs, fries, and ice cream. ⊠ *Rte. 234, Burlington* ☎ *902/836–3401* ⊕ *www.woodleighreplicas.com* ⊠ *$10* ☉ *June, Sept., and Oct., daily 9–5; July and Aug., daily 9–7.*

☝ The **Anne of Green Gables Museum at Silver Bush** was once the home of Lucy Maud Montgomery's aunt and uncle. Montgomery herself lived here for a time and was married in the parlor in 1911. Inside the house are mementos such as photographs and a quilt worked on by the writer. One of the highlights of a visit to Silver Bush is a ride in Matthew's carriage (Matthew is one of the characters in *Anne of Green Gables*). Short trips around the farm property are available as well as longer excursions. The property also includes a lovely crafts shop and an antiques store. ⊠ *Rte. 20, Park Corner* ☎*902/886–2884* ⊕*www.annesociety.org/anne* ⊠*$2.75* ☉ *May, June, Sept., and Oct., daily 10–4; July and Aug., daily 9–6.*

Where to Stay

$–$$ ▥ **Malpeque Cove Cottages.** Within walking distance of Cabot Beach Provincial Park and only 21 km (13 mi) from Cavendish, these two- and three-bedroom cottages sit in an open field and have magnificent views of the rising sun over Darnley Basin. The interiors are pine, and each unit has a barbecue and picnic table; some have a whirlpool bath, and all have a roofed patio overlooking the harbor. In July and August there are weekly reservations only. ⊠ *Rte. 105, Malpeque* ✉ *Box 714, Kensington C0B 1M0* ☎*902/836–5667 or 888/283–1927* ⊕*www.malpeque. ca* ➦ *13 cottages* ⚴ *Kitchens, laundry facilities* ⊟ *MC, V* ☉ *Closed mid-Oct.–early June.*

$–$$ ▥ **Stanley Bridge Country Resort.** This collection of quality cottages, lodge rooms, and inn rooms overlooks picturesque New London Bay. The cottages, in a large open area, are available in several price ranges, with or without kitchens, and with 1–3 bedrooms. The lodge rooms have kitchenettes. The property's central location makes it an ideal base for exploring the whole north-shore region. ⊠ *Rte. 6, Stanley Bridge*

🏠 *Box 8203, Kensington C0B 1M0* ☎ *902/886–2882 or 800/361–2882* 🖨 *902/886–2940* 🌐 *www.peisland.com/stanleybridge* 🛏 *16 cottages, 10 lodge rooms, 28 inn rooms* ⚭ *Restaurant, some kitchens, some kitchenettes, pool, gym, hot tub, lounge, playground, laundry facilities* ☰ *MC, V* ☾ *Closed late Oct.–early May* ◉⬤ *CP.*

Nightlife & the Arts

St. Mary's Church (⊠ Hwy. 104, Indian River, 5 km [3 mi] south of Park Corner ☎ 902/836–4933 or 800/565–3688 🌐 www.indianriverfestival. com 🎫 $10–$18) has performances by visiting artists in July and August as part of the Indian River Festival of Music.

Borden-Carleton

🟤 *35 km (22 mi) south of New London*

Once home port to the Marine-Atlantic car ferries, Borden-Carleton is now linked to the mainland via the Confederation Bridge. The 13-km (8-mi) behemoth spans the Northumberland Strait and ends in Cape Jouri-

⟳ main, New Brunswick. **Gateway Village** (⊠ Foot of Confederation Bridge, near tollbooths ☎ 902/437–8539) has an interesting exhibit of the unique construction techniques used to create the Confederation Bridge. A fascinating interactive display, **Island Home Museum,** traces the history of the Northumberland Strait crossings. A government-run visitor information center (open year-round) is within the village complex, along with crafts and gift shops and food-service outlets (including a Cows Ice Cream shop). The PEI section of the Trans-Canada Highway begins here and continues through Charlottetown to the Wood Islands Ferry terminal. Many visitors to PEI enter the province across the Confederation Bridge, explore the Island, then continue on to Nova Scotia via ferry from Wood Islands.

en route   Prior to the late 1800s, when ferry service began, passengers and mail were taken across the Northumberland Strait in iceboats that were rowed and alternately pushed and pulled by men across floating ice. A **monument** (⊠ Rte. 10, Cape Traverse) commemorates their journeys.

Victoria

★ 🟤 *22 km (14 mi) east of Borden-Carleton.*

Victoria-by-the-Sea, as this charming community is known locally, is a fishing village filled with antiques, art galleries, and handicrafts shops. But the real beauty of Victoria is that it has retained its peace and integrity. The little shops and eateries are all owned by local people. Many of the artists and craftspeople who live here do so to escape the hectic life of larger centers. To truly appreciate Victoria, park on one of its several streets and walk. Stroll about the community, browse its shops, watch the fishing boats beside the wharf, admire the harbor lighthouses, and take time to chat with the locals. Be sure to take in a performance at the Victoria Playhouse. The usually uncrowded **Victoria Provincial Park** is just outside the village. Here beach lovers enjoy the warm, calm waters of the Northumberland Strait. You can walk on the sand flats at low tide.

Where to Stay & Eat

$$–$$$ ✕ **Landmark Café.** This funky little spot serves homemade soups, pasta, seafood dishes, and delicious desserts. Favorite dishes include steamed salmon and scallops sautéed in garlic butter and dill. ⊠ Main St. ☎ 902/ 658–2286 ☰ MC, V ☾ Closed mid-Sept.–late June.

$ ✕🏠 **Victoria Village Inn and Restaurant.** Rooms are in a three-story Victorian house at this inn next to the Victoria Playhouse. The Actor's Retreat Café ($$–$$$) has dinner and theater packages for the Victoria Playhouse. The owner of the inn, a culinary chef, offers casual meals of fresh seafood from the wharf a block away. ⊠ *Box 1, 22 Main St., C0A 2G0* ☎ *902/658–2483* ⊕ *www3.pei.sympatico.ca/victoriavillageinn* ⇨ *3 rooms* ⚭ *Café; no room TVs* ⊟ *AE, MC, V* ⑩| *BP.*

$ ⌂ **Orient Hotel.** One of two hotels on PEI that have been in continuous operation for more than a century, this small B&B has cozy guest rooms and suites. Most of the individually decorated and spacious rooms have expansive water views. Breakfast is served in the downstairs breakfast room. ⊠ *Box 55, 34 Main St., C0A 2G0* ☎ *902/658–2503 or 800/565–6743* ⧠ *902/658–2366* ⊕ *www.theorienthotel.com* ⇨ *6 rooms* ⚭ *Dining room, cable TV* ⊟ *MC, V* ⊘ *Closed mid-Oct.–mid-May* ⑩| *BP.*

Nightlife & the Arts
In summer the historic **Victoria Playhouse** (⊠ Howard and Main St. ☎ 902/658–2025, 800/925–2025 in the Maritimes) has a renowned professional theater program that celebrates Maritime comedy. From late June through September, the company mounts three plays plus the Monday-night Musical Showcase Series. In the Community Hall (circa 1914), the theater has just 150 seats and excellent acoustics. Dinner packages with the Actor's Retreat Café next door and the Paddler's Pub, across the street on the wharf, are available.

Shopping
Island Chocolates (⊠ Main St. ☎ 902/658–2320 or 800/565–2320), a chocolate factory in a 19th-century general store, sells treats made from Belgian chocolate and flavored with fruit and liqueur fillings.

Port-La-Joye–Fort Amherst National Historic Site

Fodor'sChoice ★ *36 km (22 mi) east of Victoria.*

In 1720 the French founded the first European settlement on the Island, Port-La-Joye, which was usurped by the British 38 years later and renamed Fort Amherst. Take time to stroll around the original earthworks of the fort and to appreciate its magnificent panoramic views. The site has wooded trails and a collection of antique cannons guarding the harbor, next to the picnic area. The visitor center has informative exhibits, an audiovisual presentation, and a 1720s-era café. The drive from Victoria to Rocky Point passes through the Argyle Shore to this site, which is at the mouth of Charlottetown Harbour. ⊠ *Palmers La. off Rte. 19* ☎ *902/566–7626 or 902/675–2220* ⊕ *www.pc.gc.ca* ⧠ *$3.50* ⊘ *Visitor center mid-June–late Aug., daily 9–5; grounds May–Nov., daily 9–5.*

THE KINGS BYWAY

For 375 km (233 mi), the Kings Byway follows the coastline of green and tranquil Kings County on the eastern end of the Island. The route passes wooded areas, patchwork-quilt farms, fishing villages, historic sites, and long, uncrowded beaches. In early summer, fields of blue, white, pink, and purple wild lupines slope down to red cliffs and blue sea. To get here from Charlottetown, take Route 1 east and follow the Kings Byway counterclockwise.

Orwell

★ ⑰ *27 km (17 mi) east of Charlottetown.*

For those who like the outdoors, Orwell, lined with farms that welcome guests and offer activities, is ideal. The **Orwell Corner Historic Village** is a living-history farm museum that re-creates a 19th-century rural settlement by employing methods used by Scottish and Irish settlers in the 1800s. The village contains a beautifully restored 1864 farmhouse, a school, a general store, a church, a community hall, a blacksmith shop, a refurbished shingle mill, and barns with handsome draft horses. From spring to fall the site runs fairs and crafts shows, and in summer the community hall hosts traditional music performances four evenings a week. ⊠ *Rte. 1 off Trans-Canada Hwy.* ☎ *902/651–8510* 🖷 *902/368–6608* ⊕ *www.orwellcorner.isn.net* 🖎 *$5* ☉ *Mid-May–mid-June, weekdays 10–3; mid-June–early Sept., daily 9–5; early Sept.–mid-Oct., Tues.–Sun. 9–5.*

The **Sir Andrew Macphail Homestead,** a National Historic Site, is a 140-acre farm property that contains an ecological forestry project, gardens, and three walking trails. The restored 1829 house and 19th-century outbuildings commemorate the life of Sir Andrew Macphail (1864–1938), a writer, professor, physician, and soldier. A licensed tearoom-restaurant serves traditional Scottish and contemporary fare and is open for lunch daily and for dinner Sunday through Friday until 8. Local entertainers accompany Thursday dinner (at 6) July through August; make a reservation. ⊠ *Off Rte. 1* ☎ *902/651–2789* ⊕ *www.isn.net/~dhunter/ macphailfoundation.html* 🖎 *Free* ☉ *Late June–early Sept., daily 10–5; July–Aug., daily 10–9.*

---

off the beaten path

BEN'S LAKE TROUT FARM – This pleasant attraction is especially appreciated by aspiring young anglers. You're almost guaranteed a fish, and the staff cleans it and supplies the barbecue (for a small fee) and picnic table for a great meal. Fly-fishing can also be arranged.
ⓒ ⊠ *Rte. 24, Bellevue* ☎ *902/838–2706* 🖎 *Free, catch $4 per pound* ☉ *Apr.–Sept., daily 8–8; Oct., weekends 8–8 or by reservation.*

Where to Stay

¢ 🏠 **Forest and Stream Cottages.** This collection of one- and two-bedroom cottages in a forest grove provides a secluded stay overlooking a large pond. You can use one of the rowboats to explore the winding stream or to take advantage of the property's nature trails. These traditional-style cottages have screened verandas, and each has a barbecue and picnic table. ⊠ *Murray Harbour, C0A 1V0* ☎ *800/227–9943* 🖷 *902/ 962–3537* 🛏 *5 cottages* ⚭ *Cable TV, boating, playground, some pets allowed* ▤ *MC, V* ☉ *Closed Nov.–Apr.*

---

en route

One of the Island's most historic churches, St. John's Presbyterian, is in **Belfast,** off Route 1 on Route 207. This pretty white church on a hill was built by settlers from the Isle of Skye who were brought to the Island from Scotland in 1803 by Lord Selkirk. At **Little Sands,** on Route 4, is Canada's only saltwater winery, Rossignol Estate Winery, which has tastings for which it charges a small fee. The lighthouse at **Cape Bear** is the site of the first wireless station in Canada to receive the distress call from the *Titanic.*

Montague

🔞 *20 km (12 mi) northeast of Orwell.*

The business hub of eastern Prince Edward Island, Montague is a lovely small town that straddles the Montague River and serves as a depar-
ⓒ ture point for seal-watching boat tours. **Cruise Manada Seal-Watching Boat Tours** (☎ 902/838–3444 or 800/986–3444 ⊕ www.tourpei.ca/seals) sails past a harbor-seal colony and mussel farms. Boats leave from Montague Marina on Route 4 and Brudenell Resort Marina on Route 3 from

mid-May through September. The tour price is $20; call to reserve. The restored **railway station** overlooking the marina has a tourist information center and a number of small crafts shops inside. The Confederation Trail continues past the station and is ideal for a leisurely stroll.

Where to Stay & Eat

$$–$$$ ✕ **Windows on the Water Café.** Overlooking the former railway station is this old house furnished with antiques. In warm weather you can eat on the large deck with views of the Montague Marina. Winner of the Island Shellfish Chowder Competition, this lovely little eatery has tasty seafood, vegetarian fare, and chicken dishes. ⊠ *106 Sackville St.* ☎ *902/ 838–2080* ⊟ *AE, DC, MC, V* ⊘ *Closed Nov.–early May.*

$–$$$ ▦ **Roseneath Bed & Breakfast.** This fine heritage home, built in 1868, faces the Brudenell River. You can golf at the adjacent Brudenell and Dundarave courses, walk or bike the Confederation Trail (which crosses the property), go trout fishing, or explore the 90 acres of woodlands. All rooms have views of the river or the property's extensive gardens. Morning brings coffee delivered to your room and a home-cooked breakfast downstairs. A lobster dinner may be arranged in advance during May and June. ⊠ *R.R. 6, Cardigan C0A 1G0* ☎ *902/838–4590 or 800/823–8933* ▦ *902/838–4590* ⊕ *www.rosebb.ca* ⇆ *3 rooms, 1 suite* ⚘ *Fishing, bicycles* ⊟ *MC, V* ⊘ *Closed Oct.–late May; open off-season by reservation* ⦿ *BP.*

Bay Fortune

⑲ *23 km (14 mi) north of Montague*

For two generations, Bay Fortune, a little-known scenic village, has been a secret refuge of American vacationers, who return year after year to relax in the peace and quiet of this charming little community.

> off the beaten path

SOURIS – The Souris area, 14 km (9 mi) north of Bay Fortune, is noted for its fine traditional musicians. An outdoor Scottish concert at Rollo Bay in July, with fiddling and step dancing, attracts thousands every year. At Souris a car ferry links Prince Edward Island with Québec's scenic **Magdalen Islands** (☎ 887/624–4437).

Where to Stay & Eat

$$$–$$$$ ✕▦ **Inn at Spry Point.** The sister property of the Inn at Bay Fortune, this luxury retreat hugs the end of a 110-acre peninsula. In addition to 4 km (2½ mi) of shoreline walking trails, the property has a 1-km (½-mi) sandy beach. Each of the rooms has a king bed and either a private balcony or a garden terrace. Seafood and locally grown fresh produce are served in the restaurant ($$$–$$$$); pan-seared scallops, halibut, and salmon take top billing. Desserts are glorious. ⊠ *Spry Point Rd.* ☎ *902/ 583–2400, 860/563–6090 off-season* ▦ *902/583–2176* ⊕ *www. innatsprypoint.com* ⇆ *15 rooms* ⚘ *Restaurant, cable TV, meeting room; no smoking* ⊟ *MC, V* ⊘ *Closed early Oct.–late May* ⦿ *BP.*

★ $$–$$$$ ✕▦ **Inn at Bay Fortune.** Superb dining and genteel living await at this enticing, unforgettable getaway, the former summer home of Broadway playwright Elmer Harris. The inn overlooks Fortune Harbour and the Northumberland Strait. Local fresh-caught and fresh-harvested ingredients are served in an old-time ambience at the restaurant ($$$–$$$$). Tread Softly Cottage, a restored farmhouse, has five bedrooms. Howe Point Cottage is a modern wood-paneled lodge with two bedrooms, a loft, and a view of the Northumberland Strait. ⊠ *Rte. 310 off Rte. 2, C0A 2B0* ☎ *902/687–3745, 860/563–6090 off-season* ⊕ *www. .innatbayfortune.com* ⇱ *18 rooms, 2 houses* ☆ *Restaurant, some kitchens, cable TV in some rooms, no-smoking rooms* ▤ *MC, V* ◷ *Closed late Oct.–mid-May* |◯| *BP.*

Basin Head

⑳ *13 km (8 mi) north of Souris.*

This town is noted for an exquisite silvery beach that stretches northeast for miles, backed by high grassy dunes. The lovely sand beach has been "discovered," but it's still worth spending some time here. Scuff your feet in the sand and hear it squeak, squawk, and purr. Known locally as "singing sand," it is a phenomenon found in only a few locations worldwide. The high silica content in the sand helps to produce the sound. A boardwalk leads from the museum area at the top of the hill down to the beach area. There's a small takeout next to the museum where fish-and-chips and other fast food may be purchased and eaten at picnic tables overlooking the ocean. **Red Point Provincial Park** (⊠ Rte. 16, 13 km [8 mi] east of Souris, 2 km [1 mi] west of Basin Head ☎ 902/357–3075) makes an excellent base for campers. The park has a supervised ocean beach and an interpretive program.

The **Basin Head Fisheries Museum** is on a headland overlooking the Northumberland Strait and has views of one of the most beautiful white-sand beaches on the Island. The museum depicts the ever-changing nature of PEI's historic inshore fishing tradition through interesting displays of artifacts. The museum has an aquarium, a smokehouse, a cannery, and coastal ecology exhibits. ⊠ *Off Rte. 16, east of Souris, turn onto dirt road marked with sign indicating Basin Head Beach and Basin Head Fisheries Museum* ☎ *902/357–7233 or 902/368–6600* ⊕ *www. peimuseum.com* ⊡ *$3.50* ◷ *Late May–Aug., daily 9–6; Sept., daily 9–5.*

Greenwich National Park

㉑ *19 km (12 mi) southwest of Basin Head*

The national park in Greenwich is known for its superior beach and massive sand dunes. These dunes are moving, gradually burying the nearby woods. Here and there the bleached skeletons of trees thrust up through the sand like wooden ghosts. To get to the national park, follow Route 16 to St. Peters Bay and Route 313 to Greenwich. The road ends at an interpretive center that offers programs that explain to visitors the ecology of this rare land formation. Visitors are permitted to walk along designated pathways among sand hills and through beige dunes to reach the beach. Due to the rather delicate nature of the dune system, visitors must stay on the trails and refrain from touching the flora. ⊠ *Rte. 313, 6 km (4 mi) north of St. Peters Bay* ☎ *902/672–6350* ⊡ *$4* ◷ *May 24–June 20 and Aug. 26–Oct. 31, daily 9–5; June 21–Aug. 25, daily 9–8.*

Where to Eat

★ **$$$–$$$$** ✕ **The McCulloch Room.** Away from the hustle and bustle, this restaurant overlooks the serene waters of St. Peters Bay. Enjoy superb cuisine while watching the sun set slowly over the horizon. In addition to Island mussels and oysters, the imaginative menu includes cardamom-scented roast rack of lamb, Arctic char, and duck. The surrounding property has acres of gardens filled with over 25,000 flowers, as well as herbs and vegetables. ⊠ *Inn at St. Peters, 1668 Greenwich Rd., St. Peters Bay, C0A 2A0.* ☎ *902/961–2135* ▭ *AE, MC, V.*

<table>
<tr><td>en route</td><td>Ships from many nations have been wrecked on the reef running northeast from East Point Lighthouse (⊠ Rte. 16, East Point ☎ 902/357–2106). Guided tours are offered in July and August, and many books about life at sea are available at the gift shop in the 1908 fog-alarm building. Due to the high erosion in this area, caution should be used when approaching the high cliffs overlooking the ocean.</td></tr>
</table>

LADY SLIPPER DRIVE

Many visitors to the western end of PEI tend to follow straight, flat Route 2 most of the distance, which gives a rather boring view of the Island. To truly appreciate what the western region has to offer, divert along the coastline. Follow Route 14 to West Point and continue northward along the Northumberland Strait. Try returning along the Gulf of St. Lawrence area by using Route 12, which passes the lovely beach area of Jacques Cartier Provincial Park. Both these highways are part of Lady Slipper Drive. This drive—named for the delicate lady's slipper orchid, the province's official flower—winds along the coast of the narrow, indented western end of the Island, known as Prince County, through very old, very small villages that still adhere to a traditional way of life. Many of these hamlets are inhabited by Acadians, descendants of the original French settlers. The area is known for its oysters and Irish moss (the dried plants of red sea algae) but most famously for its potato farms: the province is a major exporter of seed potatoes worldwide, and half the crop is grown here.

Summerside

② *71 km (44 mi) west of Charlottetown.*

Summerside, the second-largest city on the Island, has a beautiful waterfront area. A self-guided walking tour arranged by the Eptek Exhibition Centre is a pleasant excursion along leafy streets lined with large houses. A number of buildings in Summerside have murals painted on the sides, most depicting historical events. The Confederation Trail passes through the city, and the former railway station makes an excellent starting point for walking or biking excursions. It takes about a half hour to drive by car from Summerside to major attractions like Cavendish in the central region of PEI. During the third week of July, all of Summerside celebrates the eight-day **Summerside Lobster Carnival,** with livestock exhibitions, harness racing, fiddling contests, and of course, lobster suppers.

The **International Fox Museum and Hall of Fame** describes some unique local history. Silver foxes were first bred in captivity in western Prince Edward Island, and for several decades Summerside was the headquarters of a virtual gold rush based on fox ranching. Some of the homes in Summerside built with money from this enterprise are known as fox houses. ⊠ *286 Fitzroy St.* ☎ *902/436–2400* ☒ *Small admission price* ☉ *June–early Sept., daily 9–5.*

Eptek Exhibition Centre on the waterfront has a spacious main gallery with changing Canadian-history and fine-arts exhibits, often with a strong emphasis on Prince Edward Island. In the same buildings are the 527-seat **Harbourfront Jubilee Theatre** and the **PEI Sports Hall of Fame.** ⊠ *130*

Harbour Dr., Waterfront Properties ☎ *902/888–8373* 🖨 *902/888–8375* 💺 *$3.50 June–early Oct., by donation early Oct.–May* ☉ *Hrs vary; call ahead.*

Spinnaker's Landing, a boardwalk along the water's edge, is lined with shops and eateries. The area has a good blend of shopping, history, and entertainment. The visitor information center is a re-created lighthouse that may be climbed for panoramic views of Bedeque Bay and the city. In summer there's often free evening entertainment (usually at 7) on the outdoor stage over the water, weather permitting. ⊠ *130 Harbour Dr.* ☎ *902/436–6692* ⊕ *www.summersidewaterfront.com.*

Many descendants of the Island's early French settlers live in the Miscouche area, 10 km (6 mi) northwest of Summerside, and the **Acadian Museum** (Musée Acadien), a National Historic Site, commemorates their history. There's a permanent exhibition on Acadian life as well as an audiovisual presentation depicting the history and culture of Island Acadians. It also has a genealogical center and an Acadian gift shop. ⊠ *23 Main Dr. E (Rte. 2), Miscouche* ☎ *902/432–2880* 💺 *$3.50* ☉ *July–Aug., daily 9:30–7; reduced hrs off-season.*

Where to Stay & Eat

$–$$ ✕ **The Homeplace Inn and Restaurant.** This licensed restaurant is in a historic home built in 1915 by local merchant Parmenus Orr. The dining room, which seats up to 45 people, has a varied menu of home cooking at its best. An item not to be missed is the panfried Malpeque oysters. ⊠ *21 Victoria St., Kensington, 13 km (8 mi) northeast of Summerside* ☎ *902/836–5686* ▤ *MC, V* ☉ *Closed mid-Oct.–mid-June.*

¢–$$ ✕ **Brothers Two Restaurant.** Next to the Quality Inn Garden of the Gulf, this restaurant is popular with local residents. Service is friendly, and seating is in booths, at tables, and in a roofed-patio area in summer. As with most restaurants in PEI, fish is a staple on the menu, and dishes such as fish-and-chips can be found along with more elaborate creations. The pride of the restaurant is the homemade bread served with each meal. ⊠ *618 Water St.* ☎ *902/436–9654* ▤ *AE, DC, MC, V.*

$$–$$$$ 🏨 **Quality Inn Garden of the Gulf.** Close to the city's rich cultural attractions, this hotel has a high-ceiling courtyard with rooms on both sides. New Orleans–style decor creates a pleasant atmosphere. There is a separate lodge-style building next to the main structure; both are adjacent to the Brothers Two Restaurant. ⊠ *618 Water St., C1N 2V5* ☎ *902/436–2295 or 800/265–5551* 🖨 *902/432–2911* ⊕ *www.qualityinnpei.com* 🛏 *94 rooms* ⚖ *Coffee shop, 9-hole golf course, outdoor pool, indoor pool, bicycles, shuffleboard, shop, no-smoking rooms* ▤ *AE, DC, MC, V.*

★ $$ 🏨 **Loyalist Country Inn.** Throughout this waterfront inn are detailed touches that create a traditional elegance. The Loyalist combines the atmosphere of a country inn with the professionalism of a large hotel. In the heart of Summerside, the property overlooks the city waterfront, a yacht club, and a marina. The rear of the hotel faces the main downtown area, the former railway station, and the Confederation Trail— good for biking. The Prince William Dining Room has an innovative menu of seafood, steaks, and island delicacies. Some rooms have whirlpool baths. ⊠ *195 Harbour Dr., C1N 5R1* ☎ *902/436–3333 or 800/ 361–2668* 🖨 *902/436–4304* 🛏 *100 rooms, 3 suites* ⚖ *Restaurant, indoor pool, gym, sauna, lounge* ▤ *AE, DC, MC, V.*

$ 🏨 **Silver Fox Inn.** A fine old Victorian house and a designated historic property, this bed-and-breakfast houses a tearoom, where homemade scones and Devonshire cream are served each afternoon, and a small antiques shop. Breakfasts include homemade quiche, muffins, and croissants. If you make prior arrangements, the chef will prepare dinner. Outside, a two-tier deck provides a lovely view of the garden with three koi-stocked pools. ⊠ *61 Granville St., C1N 2Z3* ☎ *902/436–1664 or 800/565–4033* ⊕ *www.silverfoxinn.net* ⊷ *6 rooms* ⚭ *Cable TV, shop* ⊟ *AE, DC, MC, V* ⎮⊙⎮ *CP.*

Nightlife & the Arts

The **College of Piping and Celtic Performing Arts of Canada** (⊠ 619 Water St. E ☎ 902/436–5377 or 877/224–7473 ⊕ www.collegeofpiping.com) puts on a summer-long Celtic Festival incorporating bagpiping, Highland dancing, step dancing, and fiddling. The **Harbourfront Jubilee Theatre** (⊠ 124 Harbour Dr. ☎ 902/888–2500 or 800/708–6505 ⊕ www.jubileetheatre.com) celebrates the tradition and culture of the region with dramatic and musical productions year-round in the 527-seat main-stage theater. Call for information on current productions and schedule. At **Feast Dinner Theatre** (⊠ Brothers Two Restaurant, 618 Water St. ☎ 902/436–7674 or 888/748–1010), established in 1978, musical comedy is served up with heaping platefuls of Atlantic salmon, chicken, barbecue ribs, and fresh desserts mid-June through early September and from the second week in November to December 23.

Port Hill

㉓ *35 km (22 mi) north of Miscouche on Rte. 12.*

Port Hill was one of the many communities in the Tyne Valley that benefited from the shipbuilding boom of the 1800s, the era of tall-masted wooden schooners. Some beautifully restored 19th-century homes testify to the prosperity of those times. By the mid-1840s shipbuilder James Yeo, Jr., was the most powerful businessman on the Island. His former home is here at the **Green Park Shipbuilding Museum and Yeo House.** The 19th-century mansion is topped by a cupola from which Yeo observed his nearby shipyard with a spyglass. The museum details the history of the shipbuilder's craft. Those skills are brought to life at a re-created shipyard with carpentry and blacksmithing shops. The museum has lectures, concerts, and activities throughout summer. ⊠ *Green Park Provincial Park, Rte. 12* ☎ *902/831–7947* ⊠ *$4* ⊙ *June–Sept., daily 9–5.*

Tyne Valley

㉔ *8 km (5 mi) south of Port Hill.*

The charming community of Tyne Valley has some of the finest scenery on the Island. Watch for fisherfolk standing in flat boats wielding rakes to harvest the famous Malpeque oysters. A gentle river flows through the middle of the village, with lush green lawns and sweeping trees edging the water. The **Tyne Valley Oyster Festival** takes place here the first week of August. This three-day event includes fiddling, step dancing, oyster shucking, a talent contest, and a community dance. The festival is a good time to sample a fried-oyster and scallop dinner. Call **Tourism PEI** (☎ 902/368–7795 or 888/734–7529) for dates and times.

Where to Stay & Eat

$ ✕ **The Landing Oyster House and Pub.** In the heart of charming Tyne Valley, this restaurant serves Malpeque oysters and Island Blue mussels, locally grown vegetables, and fresh-brewed Island beers. Live music is offered nightly from Thursday to Saturday in a warm, smoke-free atmosphere. The restaurant shares facilities with the River Bend Language School. ⊠ *1329 Port Hill Station Rd.* ☎ *902/831–3138* ⊟ *AE, MC, V.*

¢ ✕⊡ **Doctor's Inn Bed & Breakfast.** Beautifully landscaped, this 1860s village home is a joy in summer with its garden of herbs and flowers. In winter cross-country skiers gather around the woodstove or living-room fireplace and share conversation over a warm drink. At the dining-room table, the local catch of the day is complemented by produce from the inn's own organic gardens. Dinner ($$$$) is prix fixe and available by reservation only. There are free tours of the inn's gardens. ⊠ *Box 92, Rte. 167, C0B 2C0* ☎ *902/831–3057* ⊕ *www.peisland.com/ doctorsinn* ➴ *2 rooms without bath* ♻ *Restaurant* ⊟ *MC, V* ¶◎¶ *CP.*

Shopping

Lennox Island, one of the largest Mi'Kmaq communities in the province, has a few shops that sell First Nations crafts. To get here, take Route 12 west to Route 163 and follow the road over the causeway leading to a large island projecting into Malpeque Bay. **Indian Art & Craft of North America** (⊠ Rte. 163 ☎ 902/831–2653) specializes in Mi'Kmaq ash-split baskets as well as pottery, jewelry, carvings, and beadwork. The shop, which sits on the edge of the water, has a screened-in porch where visitors may enjoy a complimentary cup of coffee along with the scenery. Earthenware figurines depicting local legends can be found at **Micmac Productions** (⊠ Rte. 163 ☎ 902/831–2277). The company is Canada's only producer of such Mi'Kmaq figurines depicting the legends and exploits of the Mi'Kmaq hero Glooscap. At **Shoreline Sweaters and Tyne Valley Studio Art Gallery** (⊠ Rte. 12 ☎ 902/831–2950) Lesley Dubey produces Shoreline handcrafted woolen sweaters, which have a unique lobster pattern, and sells local crafts and honey June through October. The store is open 9–5:30 daily, noon–5 Sunday. A gallery displays works by Island artists.

O'Leary

㉕ *37 km (23 mi) northeast of Tyne Valley.*

The center of Prince County is composed of a loose network of small towns; many are merely a stretch of road. In the tradition of their forebears, a majority of the local residents are engaged in farming and fishing. Farmers driving their tractors through fields of rich, red soil, and colorful lobster boats braving the seas are common scenes in this area. This region is well known for its magnificent red cliffs, majestic lighthouses, and glistening sunsets. Woodstock, north of O'Leary, has a resort where opportunities for outdoor activities abound. The town is also a good base from which to visit one of the Island's best golf courses and a rare woolen crafts shop.

Many things in the friendly Acadian town of **Tignish** are cooperative, including the supermarket, insurance company, seafood plant, service station, and credit union. The imposing parish church of **St. Simon and St. Jude** (⊠ 315 School St. ☎ 902/882–2049), across from Dalton Square, has a superb 1882 Tracker pipe organ, one of the finest such instruments in eastern Canada. The church is often used for recitals by world-renowned musicians. ⊠ *Rte. 2, 12 km (7½ mi) north of O'Leary.*

Where to Stay & Eat

$ ✕▥ **Rodd Mill River—A Rodd Signature Resort.** With activities ranging from night skiing to golfing, canoeing, and kayaking, this is truly an all-season resort. One of the highlights of the resort, which is inside Mill River Provincial Park, is the Mill River Golf Course. Every table at the restaurant ($$–$$$) has a view of the course. Menu items include seafood specialties like planked salmon and a lobster platter, plus pastas, steak, and chicken. The heated pool has a 90-foot slide. ⊠ *Box 399, Rte. 136, Woodstock, 5 km (3 mi) east of O'Leary, C0B 1V0* ☎ *902/ 859–3555 or 800/565–7633* 🖷 *902/859–2486* ⊕ *www.rodd-hotels.ca* ➴ *80 rooms, 10 suites* ♻ *Restaurant, 18-hole golf course, tennis court, pro shop, indoor pool, fitness classes, gym, hot tub, sauna, windsurf-*

*ing, boating, bicycles, squash, cross-country skiing, ice-skating, tobog-
ganing, bar ▤ AE, DC, MC, V ⊙ Closed Nov.–Jan. and Apr.*

Sports & the Outdoors

Among the most scenic and challenging courses in eastern Canada is
the 18-hole, par-72 **Mill River Provincial Golf Course** (✉ Mill River Provincial Park, Rte. 136, Woodstock ☎ 902/859–8873 or 800/377–8339).
It is ranked among the country's top 50 courses and has been the site
of several championship tournaments. Book in advance.

Shopping

The **Old Mill Craft Company** (✉ Rte. 2, Bloomfield, 8 km [5 mi] north
of O'Leary ☎ 902/859–3508) sells hand-quilted and woolen crafts
July–August, daily 9:30–6:30 (reduced hours June and September). Adjacent to the Old Mill Craft Company, **MacAusland's Woollen Mill** (✉ Rte.
2, Bloomfield ☎ 902/859–3005) has been producing famous MacAusland blankets since 1932. It's the only producer of 100% pure virgin
wool blankets in Atlantic Canada.

North Cape

★ ㉖ *27 km (17 mi) north of O'Leary*

In the northwest the Island narrows to a north-pointing arrow of land,
at the tip of which is North Cape with its imposing lighthouse. At low
tide one of the longest reefs in the world gives way to tidal pools teeming with marine life. Seals often gather offshore here. The curious structures near the reef are wind turbines at the Atlantic Wind Test Site, set
up on this breezy promontory to evaluate the feasibility of using wind
power to generate electricity.

The **Interpretive Centre and Aquarium** has information about marine life,
local history, and turbines and windmills. ✉ *End of Rte. 12* ☎ *902/882–
2991* 🖾 *$2* ⊙ *July–Aug., daily 9–8; late May–June and Sept.–mid-Oct.,
daily 10–6.*

Near North Cape, just off Lady Slipper Drive on the western side of the
Island, is the rock formation called **Elephant Rock,** which lost its trunk
in a winter storm. You may also see horse mossers—man, horse, and
rake—working the surf to harvest Irish moss, a valuable sea plant containing carrageenan, which is used as a thickener in products such as
ice cream and toothpaste.

The **Irish Moss Interpretive Centre,** in the tiny ocean-side town of Miminegash, tells you everything you wanted to know about Irish moss, the
fan-shape red algae found in abundance on this coast and used as a thick-
ening agent in foods and other products. "Seaweed pie," made with Irish
moss, is served at the adjacent Seaweed Pie Café. ✉ *Rte. 14, 20 km (12
mi) south of North Cape* ☎ *902/882–4313* 🖾 *$1* ⊙ *Early June–Sept.,
daily 10–7.*

Where to Stay & Eat

$$–$$$ ✕ **The Pier Restaurant.** An authentic renovated boatbuilding shop houses
this restaurant with a panoramic view of the marina from its multilevel
dining room and outdoor patio. The varied menu includes scallops
Newburg, chicken breast stuffed with asparagus, and Brie and fresh Atlantic cod fried in beer batter. ✉ *296 Harbourview Dr. (Rte. 152),
Northport, 33 km (21 mi) south of North Cape* ☎ *902/853–4510*
⊕ *www.northportpier.ca* ▤ MC, V ⊙ *Closed Oct.–June.*

$–$$$ ✕ **Wind & Reef Restaurant.** This restaurant serves good seafood, such as
Island clams, mussels, and lobster, as well as steaks, prime rib, and chicken.
There's a fine view of the Gulf of St. Lawrence and the Northumber-

land Strait. ⊠ *End of Rte. 12* ☎ *902/882–3535* ▤ *MC, V* ⊘ *Closed Oct.–May.*

¢–$ 🏨 **Tignish Heritage Inn.** Originally built as a convent in 1868, this large inn is close to North Cape, Mile 0 of the Confederation Trail, and the facilities offered in the town of Tignish. Rooms range in size from cozy to spacious, and all have wooden headboards. Each room has a view of the grounds, which includes a quiet pathway weaving through tall maple trees. Some of the bathrooms have cast-iron claw-foot tubs. ⊠ *Box 398, Maple St. behind St. Simon and St. Jude Church, C0B 2B0* ☎ *902/882–2491 or 877/882–2491* 🖷 *902/882–2500* ⊕ *www.tignish.com/heritageinn* ↪ *17 rooms, 1 suite* ⟁ *Dining room, cable TV, laundry facilities, meeting room, no-smoking rooms* ▤ *AE, DC, MC, V* ⊘ *Closed mid-Oct.–mid-May, except for groups by reservation only* |⊙| *CP.*

West Point

❷❼ *35 km (22 mi) south of Miminegash.*

At the southern tip of the western shore, West Point has a tiny fishing
Fodor'sChoice harbor, campsites, and a supervised beach. **West Point Lighthouse,** built
★ in 1875, is the tallest lighthouse on the Island. When it was automated, the community took over the building and converted it into an inn and museum, with a moderately priced restaurant. The lighthouse is open daily, late May through late September. Don't miss the sunsets here.

Lady Slipper Drive meanders from West Point back to Summerside through the **Région Évangéline,** the Island's main Acadian district. At **Cap-Egmont** (⊠ 72 km [45 mi] east of West Point) stop for a look at the Bottle Houses, two tiny houses and a chapel built by a retired carpenter entirely out of glass bottles—over 25,000 of them—mortared together like bricks. The chapel even has pews made from glass.

Where to Stay & Eat

$–$$ ✕🏨 **West Point Lighthouse.** Few people can say they've actually spent the
Fodor'sChoice night in a lighthouse, but here's your chance to do just that. Rooms, most
★ with ocean views, are pleasantly furnished with local antiques and handmade quilts. You can enjoy clam-digging, a favorite local pastime, or perhaps try finding the buried treasure reputed to be hidden nearby. The restaurant ($–$$$) serves fresh lobster, scallops, mussels, chowder, and other seafood. A seaside deck, open summer months, provides a spectacular view of the Northumberland Strait. Make your reservations early. ⊠ *Rte. 14* 🖃 *Box 429, O'Leary C0B 1V0* ☎ *902/859–3605 or 800/764–6854* 🖷 *902/859–1510* ⊕ *www.westpointlighthouse.com* ↪ *9 rooms* ⟁ *Restaurant, beach, fishing* ▤ *AE, DC, MC, V* ⊘ *Closed Oct.–May.*

Mont-Carmel

❷❽ *63 km (39 mi) southeast of West Point.*

This community has a magnificent brick church overlooking the Northumberland Strait. **Le Village de l'Acadie** (Acadian Pioneer Village), a reproduction of an 1820s French settlement, has a church, school, and blacksmith shop. A crafts shop sells locally produced goods. There are also modern accommodations and a restaurant where you can sample authentic Acadian dishes. ⊠ *Rte. 11* ☎ *902/854–2227 or 800/567–3228* 🎟 *$3.25* ⊘ *Early June–late Sept., daily 9–7.*

Nightlife & the Arts

Typical Acadian step dancing and fiddle music, comedy, and song are all part of **La Cuisine à Mémé** (⊠ Rte. 11 ☎ 902/854–2227 or 800/567–3228), a dinner theater running June 29–September 1. The evening, which lasts from 6:30 to about 10:15, is $30 for adults.

PRINCE EDWARD ISLAND A TO Z

To research prices, get advice from other travelers, and book travel arrangements, visit www.fodors.com.

AIR TRAVEL

Air Canada and its regional carriers offer daily nonstop service from Charlottetown to Halifax and Toronto, both of which have connections to the rest of Canada, the United States, and beyond. JetsGo is a discount airline that flies within Canada and to Newark and Ft. Lauderdale. Prince Edward Air is available for private charters.

🛪 Airlines & Contacts **Air Canada** ☎ 888/247-2262 ⊕ www.aircanada.ca. **Jetsgo** ☎ 866/440-0441 ⊕ www.jetsgo.ca. **Prince Edward Air** ☎ 902/566-4488 ⊕ www.peair.com.

AIRPORTS

Charlottetown Airport is 5 km (3 mi) north of town.

🛈 Airport Information **Charlottetown Airport** ⊠ 250 Maple Hills Ave. ☎ 902/566-7997.

BOAT & FERRY TRAVEL

Northumberland Ferries sails between Wood Islands and Caribou, Nova Scotia, from May to mid-December. The crossing takes about 75 minutes, and the round-trip costs approximately $50 per vehicle, $65 for a recreational vehicle; foot passengers pay $12 (you pay only when leaving the Island). There are 18 crossings per day in summer. Reservations are not accepted.

🛥 Boat & Ferry Information **Northumberland Ferries** ☎ 888/249-7245 ⊕ www.nflbay.com.

CAR TRAVEL

The 13-km-long (8-mi-long) Confederation Bridge connects Cape Jourimain, in New Brunswick, with Borden-Carleton, Prince Edward Island. The crossing takes about 12 minutes. The toll is about $39 per car, $44 for a recreational vehicle; it's collected when you leave the Island. The lack of public transportation on the Island makes having your own vehicle almost a necessity. There are more than 3,700 km (2,300 mi) of paved road in the province, including the three scenic coastal drives: Lady Slipper Drive, Blue Heron Drive, and Kings Byway. A helpful highway map of the province is available from Tourism PEI and at visitor centers on the Island.

Designated Heritage Roads are surfaced with red clay, the local soil base. The unpaved roads meander through rural and undeveloped areas, where you're likely to see lots of wildflowers and birds. A four-wheel-drive vehicle is not necessary, but in spring and inclement weather the mud can get quite deep, and the narrow roads become impassable. Keep an eye open for bicycles, motorcycles, and pedestrians.

EMERGENCIES

🚑 Emergency Services **Ambulance, fire, police** ☎ 911 or 0.

🏥 Hospitals **Queen Elizabeth Hospital** ⊠ 60 Riverside Dr., Charlottetown ☎ 902/894-2200 or 902/894-2095.

SPORT & THE OUTDOORS

BIKING Several tour companies rent bicycles and provide custom-made tours. The Confederation Trail allows people to cycle from one end of the Island to the other. Island Explorations Custom Bicycle Tours provides custom-designed, self-guided tour packages. A two-sided map and information sheet is available from Tourism PEI.

🏴 Outfitter**Island Explorations Custom Bicycle Tours** ✉ Wood Islands, Belle River R.R. 1 ☎ 902/962-3500 or 800/868-7734 ⊕ www.peisland.com/homeport/tours.html. **Tourism PEI** ☎ 902/368-7795 or 888/734-7529 ⊕ www.peiplay.com.

FISHING A nonresident one-day fishing license may be purchased for $7 at more than 100 businesses (hardware, tackle, convenience stores) throughout PEI. A few operations rent fishing tackle and offer "no license required" fishing on private ponds. The PEI government Web site lists businesses that sell fishing licenses.

🏴 Fishing Information **Government of Prince Edward Island** ⊕ www.gov.pe.ca/egovernment

GOLF For a publication listing golf courses in Prince Edward Island and to book online, contact Tourism PEI. Most courses may be booked directly or by contacting Golf PEI.

🏴 Golf Information **Golf PEI** ☎ 902/566-4652 ⊕ www.golfpei.com. **Tourism PEI** ☎ 902/368-4444 or 888/734-7529 information, 800/235-8909 booking ⊕ www.golflinkspei.com.

SEA KAYAKING With its quiet coves and cozy bays, PEI has become a haven for those who enjoy sea kayaking. Outside Expeditions provides rentals and tours designed for all levels of expertise.

🏴 Outfitter**Outside Expeditions** ✉ 890 Grand Pere Rd., off Rte. 242, 8 km [5 mi] east of Cavendish, South Rustico ☎ 902/963-3366 or 800/207-3899 ⊕ www.getoutside.com.

SHOPPING

For information on crafts outlets around Prince Edward Island, contact the Prince Edward Island Crafts Council.

🏴 Shopping Information**Prince Edward Island Crafts Council** ✉ 156 Richmond St., Charlottetown C1A 1H9 ☎ 902/892-5152.

TOURS

The Island has about 20 sightseeing tours, including double-decker bus tours, taxi tours, cycling tours, harbor cruises, and walking tours. Most tour companies are based in Charlottetown and offer excursions around the city and to the beaches.

DRIVING TOURS Yellow Cab can be booked for tours by the hour or the day.

🏴 Fees & Schedules**Yellow Cab** ☎ 902/892-6561.

WALKING TOURS Island Nature Trust sells a nature-trail map of the Island. Tourism PEI has maps of the 350-km (217-mi) multiuse Confederation Trail.

🏴 Fees & Schedules**Island Nature Trust** ✉ Box 265, Charlottetown C1A 7K4 ☎ 902/566-9150. **Tourism PEI** ✉ Box 940, Charlottetown C1A 7M5 ☎ 902/368-7795 or 888/734-7529 🖨 902/566-4336 ⊕ www.peiplay.com.

VISITOR INFORMATION

Tourism PEI publishes an informative annual guide for visitors and maintains 10 visitor information centers (VICs) on the Island. It also produces a map of the 350-km (217-mi) Confederation Trail. The main visitor information center is in Charlottetown and is open daily from mid-May to October and weekdays from November to mid-May.

🏴 Tourist Information **Tourism PEI** ✉ Box 940, Charlottetown C1A 7M5 ☎ 902/368-4444 or 888/734-7529 🖨 902/368-6613 ⊕ www.peiplay.com. **Visitor Information Center** ✉ 178 Water St. ☎ 902/888-8364 in summer.

NEWFOUNDLAND & LABRADOR

4

FODOR'S CHOICE

boat tours off the east coast of Newfoundland

Brittoner Bed & Breakfast, *Brigus*

The Cellar, *St. John's*

Ches's, *St. John's*

Compton House, *St. John's*

Discovery Trail, *near Clarenville*

Gros Morne National Park

hiking the East Coast Trail, *Avalon Peninsula*

L'Anse aux Meadows National Historic Site

The Norseman Restaurant, *L'Anse aux Meadows*

Signal Hill National Historic Site, *St. John's*

Valhalla Lodge Bed & Breakfast, *near L'Anse aux Meadows*

HIGHLY RECOMMENDED

SIGHTS   Cape Spear National Historic Site, *St. John's*

Battle Harbour National Historic Site, *Labrador*

Memorial University Botanical Garden, *St. John's*

Red Bay National Historic Site, *Labrador*

*Many other great hotels and restaurants enliven Newfoundland and
Labrador. For other favorites, look for the black stars as you read
this chapter.*

Updated by
Tracy Barron

CANADA STARTS HERE, from the east, on the island of Newfoundland in the North Atlantic. Known as Mile One, the province's capital of St. John's is North America's most easterly point and its oldest city. The province also includes Labrador to the northwest, on the mainland bordering Québec. Along Newfoundland and Labrador's nearly 17,699 km (11,000 mi) of coastline, humpback whales feed near shore, millions of seabirds nest, and 10,000-year-old icebergs drift by fishing villages.

The first European settlement in North America was established in Newfoundland with the arrival of Vikings from Iceland and Greenland over 1,000 years ago. Vikings assembled a sod hut village at what is now a National Historic Site at L'Anse aux Meadows, calling their new home Vinland. They stayed less than 10 years and then disappeared into the mists of history for centuries. The site was discovered in the 1960s.

Early as they were, the Vikings were preceded by people who lived in the region 9,000 years ago, as the glaciers melted. A 7,500-year-old burial ground in southern Labrador is the oldest-known cemetery in North America. When explorer John Cabot arrived at Bonvista from England in 1497, he reported an ocean so full of fish they could be caught in a basket lowered over the side. Within a decade St. John's had become a crowded harbor. Soon, fishing boats from France, England, Spain, and Portugal vied for a chance to catch Newfoundland's lucrative cod, which would shape the province's history.

At one time, 700 outports dotted Newfoundland's coast, devoted to the world's most plentiful fish. Today only about 400 of these settlements survive. By 1992 cod had become so scarce from overfishing that the federal government called a moratorium, throwing thousands out of work. The cod have not yet returned, forcing generations of people to retrain for other industries or leave. The fishing industry has since diversified into other species, mainly crab. The development of one of the world's richest and largest nickel deposits at Voisey's Bay in northern Labrador, near Nain, holds hope for new prosperity, as does the growing offshore oil and gas industry.

In 1949 Newfoundland and Labrador joined the Canadian Confederation. Despite over 50 years as a Canadian province, the people are still independent and maintain a unique language and lifestyle. Whether Confederation was a good move is still a matter of great debate. E. Annie Proulx's Pulitzer prize–winning novel *The Shipping News* and subsequent film adaptation in 2001 brought the province to the attention of the world. Now Newfoundland writers such as Wayne Johnston (*The Colony of Unrequited Dreams, The Navigator of New York*), Michael Crummey (*River of Thieves*), and Lisa Moore (*Open*) are bringing the province to an international audience.

Visitors find themselves straddling the centuries. Old Irish, French, and English accents and customs still exist in small towns and outports despite television and the Internet. The cities of St. John's in the east and Corner Brook to the west are very much part of the 21st century.

Wherever you travel in the province, you're sure to meet some of the warmest, wittiest people in North America. Strangers have always been welcome in Newfoundland. To help develop an ear for the provincial dialects, the *Dictionary of Newfoundland English* has more than 5,000 words, most related to fishery, weather, and scenery. Your first task is to master the name of the island portion of the province—it's New-fund-*land,* with the accent on "land." The effects of globalization and the changing economy are eroding the old dialects as young people leave for larger cities. Still, it's these same young people who are devoted fans

Numbers in the text correspond to numbers in the margin and on the St. John's, Avalon Peninsula, and Newfoundland and Labrador maps.

4

If you have 3 days

Pick either the west or east coast of Newfoundland. On the west coast, after arriving by ferry at **Port aux Basques 44**, drive through the Codroy Valley, heading north to **Gros Morne National Park 38** and its fjords, and overnight in nearby Rocky Harbour or Woody Point. The next day visit **L'Anse aux Meadows National Historic Site 40**, where the Vikings built a village 1,000 years ago; there are reconstructions of the dwellings. Spend the night in **St. Anthony 41** or nearby.

On the east coast, the ferry docks at Argentia. Explore the Avalon Peninsula, beginning in **St. John's 1 – 15**, where you should spend your first night. The next day visit **Cape Spear,** the most easterly point in North America, and the **Witless Bay Ecological Reserve 16**, where you can see whales, seabirds, and icebergs. Drive though **Placentia 22** and spend your third day at **Cape St. Mary's Ecological Reserve 24**, known for its gannets and dramatic coastal scenery.

If you have 6 days

On Newfoundland's west coast, add southern Labrador to your trip. A ferry takes you from St. Barbe to Blanc Sablon on the Québec–Labrador border. Drive 96 km (60 mi) to **Red Bay 47** to explore the remains of a 17th-century Basque whaling station; then head to **L'Anse Amour 46** to see Canada's second-tallest lighthouse. Overnight at **L'Anse au Clair 45**. Return through **Gros Morne National Park 38** and explore **Corner Brook 42**, where you should stay overnight. The next day travel west of **Stephenville 43** to explore the Port au Port Peninsula, home of Newfoundland's French-speaking population.

On the east coast add **Trinity 27** to your must-see list, and spend the night there or in **Clarenville 25**. The north shore of Conception Bay is home to many picturesque villages, including **Cupids 20** and **Harbour Grace 21**. Several half-day, full-day, and two-day excursions are possible from St. John's, and in each direction a different personality of the region unfolds.

If you have 9 days

In addition to the places already mentioned on the west coast, take a drive into central Newfoundland and visit the lovely villages of Notre Dame Bay. Overnight in **Twillingate 35**. Catch a ferry to **Fogo** or the **Change Islands.** Accommodations are available on both islands, but book ahead.

On the east coast add the Burin Peninsula and a trip to France—yes, France—to your itinerary. You can reach the French territory of **St-Pierre and Miquelon 32** by passenger ferry from Fortune. Explore romantic **Grand Bank 31**, named for the famous fishing area just offshore, and climb Cook's Lookout in **Burin 30**, where Captain James Cook kept watch for smugglers from St-Pierre.

of the Newfoundland band Great Big Sea and other modern exponents of traditional music breaking into the international market.

Exploring Newfoundland & Labrador

The provincial capital of St. John's, on the Avalon Peninsula, is a starting point for most visits to Newfoundland. Moving clockwise around the perimeter of the peninsula, you traverse the Cape Shore. Farther west, on the main island of Newfoundland, is the Burin Peninsula, and to the north, the Bonavista Peninsula and Notre Dame Bay. The Great Northern Peninsula, on the west side of Newfoundland, stretches up toward Labrador. Corner Brook, at the base of the Great Northern Peninsula, is a good starting point for exploring the mountains. To the north and west, Labrador, on the mainland, begins at the Straits. Moving west, make your way through some of the wildest parts of the country and finally to the twin towns of Labrador City and Wabush, which combine natural phenomena, wilderness adventure, history, and culture.

About the Restaurants

Generally, only the large urban centers, especially St. John's and Corner Brook, have sophisticated restaurants. Fish is a safe dish just about everywhere. Excellent meals are offered in the province's network of bed-and-breakfasts, where home cooking goes hand in hand with warm hospitality.

About the Hotels

Lodgings in Newfoundland and Labrador range from modestly priced B&Bs, which you can find through local tourist offices, to luxury accommodations. In remote areas, be prepared to find very basic lodgings, though some of the best lodging in the province can be found in rural areas. Home-cooked meals and great hospitality often makes up for a lack of amenities.

WHAT IT COSTS In Canadian Dollars				
$$$$	**$$$**	**$$**	**$**	**¢**
RESTAURANTS over $30	$20–$30	$12–$20	$8–$12	under $8
HOTELS over $250	$175–$250	$125–$175	$75–$125	under $75

Restaurant prices are per person for a main course at dinner. Hotel prices are for two people in a standard double room in high season, excluding 15% harmonized sales tax (HST).

Timing

Seasons vary dramatically in Newfoundland and Labrador. In spring icebergs float down from the north, and in late spring fin, pilot, minke, and humpback whales arrive to hunt for food along the coast and stay until August. In summer Newfoundland's bogs and meadows turn into a colorful riot of wildflowers and greenery, and the sea is dotted with boats and buoys marking traps and nets. Fall is a favored season: the weather is usually fine; hills and meadows are loaded with berries; and the woods are alive with moose, caribou, partridge, and rabbits. In winter ski hills attract downhillers and snowboarders, and the forest trails hum with the sounds of snowmobiles and all-terrain vehicles taking anglers to lodges and lakes. Cross-country ski trails in provincial and national parks are oases of quiet.

The tourist season runs from June through September, when the province celebrates with festivals, fairs, concerts, plays, and crafts shows. The temperature hovers between 24°C (75°F) and 29°C (85°F) and gently cools off in the evening, providing a good night's sleep.

4

Festivals

The province is filled with music of all kinds. Newfoundlanders love a party, and from the cities to the smallest towns they celebrate their history and unique culture with festivals and events throughout the summer. "Soirees" and "times"—big parties and small parties—offer a combination of traditional music, recitation, comedy, and local food, sometimes in a dinner-theater setting.

Fishing

Newfoundland has more than 200 salmon rivers and thousands of trout streams. Fishing these unpolluted waters is an angler's dream. The Atlantic salmon is king of the game fish. Top salmon rivers in Newfoundland include the Gander, Humber, and Exploits, while Labrador's top-producing waters are the Sandhill, Michaels, Flowers, and Eagle rivers. Lake trout, brook trout, and landlocked salmon are other favorite species. In Labrador northern pike and Arctic char can be added to that list. Nonresidents must hire a guide or outfitter for anything other than roadside angling.

Tastes of Newfoundland & Labrador

Today, despite the fishing moratorium, seafood is an excellent value in Newfoundland and Labrador. Many restaurants offer seasonal specialties with a wide variety of traditional wild and cultured species. Cod is still readily available and can be found panfried, baked, and poached. Aquaculture species such as steelhead trout, salmon, mussels, and sea scallops are available in better restaurants. Cold-water shrimp, snow crab, and lobster are also good seafood choices.

Two other foods to try are partridgeberries and bakeapples. Partridgeberries, also called mountain cranberries, cowberries, and lingonberries (among other names), are used in pies, jams, cakes, pancakes, and as a meat sauce. Bakeapples, also known as cloudberries, look like yellow raspberries and grow on low plants in bogs. They ripen in August, and pickers sell them by the side of the road in jars. If the ones you buy are hard, wait a few days, and they'll ripen into rich-tasting fruit. The berries are popular on ice cream, cheesecake, and as a spread on bread.

Wilderness Hikes

The island portion of the province is a hiker's paradise, with much emphasis in recent years on building and improving a vast network of trails, some of which cut through resettled communities. Many provincial parks and both national parks have hiking and nature trails, and coastal and forest trails radiate out from most small communities. The East Coast Trail on the Avalon Peninsula covers 520 km (322 mi) of coastline; the trail begins in Conception Bay South and moves north to Cape St. Francis and then south all the way down to Trepassey. It passes through two dozen communities and along cliff tops that provide ideal lookouts for icebergs and seabirds. You can call individual parks or the tourist information line for specifics.

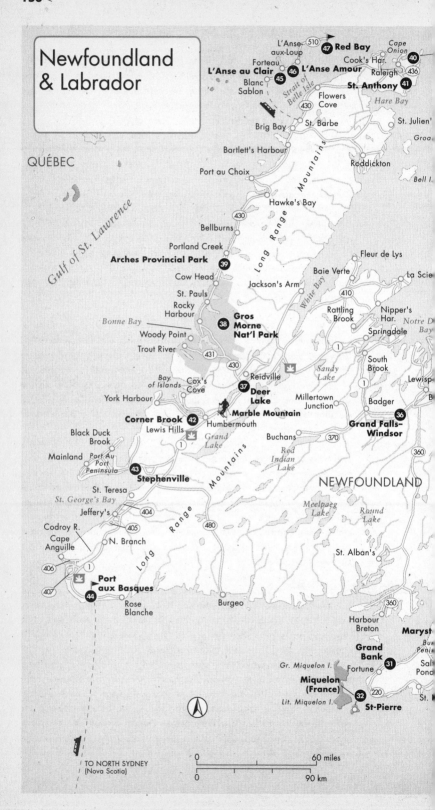

Newfoundland & Labrador

QUÉBEC

NEWFOUNDLAND

Gulf of St. Lawrence

Strait of Belle Isle

L'Anse-aux-Loup · 510 · 47 **Red Bay** · Cape Onion

Forteau · 46 **L'Anse Amour** · Cook's Har. · 40

L'Anse au Clair · 45 · Raleigh · 436

Blanc Sablon · **St. Anthony** · 41

Flowers Cove · *Hare Bay*

Brig Bay · St. Barbe · 430 · St. Julien'

Bartlett's Harbour · *Groa*

Roddickton

Port au Choix · *Bell I.*

Hawke's Bay

Bellburns · 430

Portland Creek · Fleur de Lys

Arches Provincial Park · 39 · la Scie

Cow Head · Baie Verte

Jackson's Arm · 410

St. Pauls · Rattling · Nipper's

Rocky Harbour · Brook · Har. · *Notre D Bay*

Bonne Bay · 38 · **Gros Morne Nat'l Park** · Springdale

Woody Point · *White Bay*

Trout River · 431 · *Sandy Lake* · South Brook

430 · Reidville · Lewisp

Bay of Islands · Cox's Cove · 37 · **Deer Lake**

York Harbour · Millertown Junction · Badger

Corner Brook · 42 · Humbermouth · **Marble Mountain** · **Grand Falls-Windsor** · 36

Lewis Hills · *Grand Lake* · Buchans · 370 · 360

Black Duck Brook · 1

Mainland · Port Au Port Peninsula · *Red Indian Lake*

Stephenville · 43

St. Teresa · *Meelpaeg Lake* · *Round Lake*

St. George's Bay · Jeffery's · 404

Codroy R. · 405 · St. Alban's

Cape Anguille · N. Branch · 480

406 · 1

407 · **Port aux Basques** · 44 · Burgeo

Rose Blanche · Harbour Breton · 360

Maryst

Grand Bank · *Bu Peni*

Gr. Miquelon I. · 31 · Sal Pond

Fortune

Miquelon (France) · 32 · 220 · St.

Lit. Miquelon I. · **St-Pierre**

Long Range Mountains

Long Range Mountains

TO NORTH SYDNEY (Nova Scotia)

0 — 60 miles

0 — 90 km

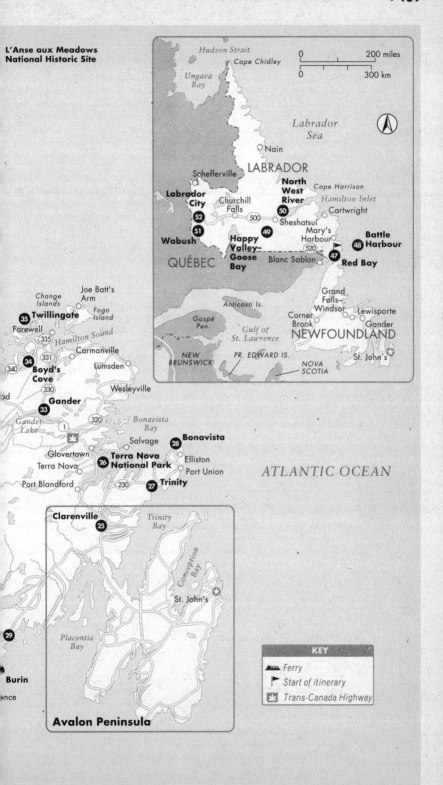

L'Anse aux Meadows
National Historic Site

Hudson Strait
Cape Chidley

Ungava
Bay

200 miles

300 km

Labrador
Sea

Nain

LABRADOR

Schefferville

**North
West
River**
50

Cape Harrison

Hamilton Inlet

Cartwright

**Labrador
City**
52

Churchill
Falls

500

51

Sheshatsui

Mary's
Harbour

**Battle
Harbour**
48

Wabush

49

520

**Happy
Valley–
Goose
Bay**

47

Red Bay

QUÉBEC

Blanc Sablon

Grand
Falls–
Windsor

Anticosti Is.

Lewisporte

Change
Islands

Joe Batt's
Arm

Corner
Brook

Gander

35 **Twillingate**

Fogo
Island

Gaspé
Pen.

Gulf of
St. Lawrence

NEWFOUNDLAND

Farewell

335

Hamilton Sound

St. John's

331

Carmanville

NEW
BRUNSWICK

PR. EDWARD IS.

NOVA
SCOTIA

340

331

34

Lumsden

**Boyd's
Cove**

330

Wesleyville

od

33 **Gander**

Gander
Lake

1

320

Bonavista
Bay

Salvage

28 **Bonavista**

Glovertown

**Terra Nova
National Park**
26

Elliston

Terra Nova

Port Union

Port Blandford

230

27 **Trinity**

ATLANTIC OCEAN

Clarenville

Trinity
Bay

25

29

Conception
Bay

St. John's

Burin

Placentia
Bay

nce

Avalon Peninsula

KEY

Ferry

Start of itinerary

Trans-Canada Highway

ST. JOHN'S

When Sir Humphrey Gilbert sailed into St. John's to establish British colonial rule for Queen Elizabeth in 1583, he found Spanish, French, and Portuguese fishermen working the harbor, all fighting for a spot in Newfoundland's lucrative cod fishery. For centuries Newfoundland was the largest supplier of salt cod in the world, and St. John's Harbour was the center of the trade. As early as 1627, the merchants of Water Street—then known as the Lower Path—were doing a thriving business buying fish, selling goods, and supplying alcohol to soldiers and sailors.

Today old meets new in the province's capital (population 99,181). Modern office buildings are surrounded by heritage shops and colorful row houses. St. John's mixes English and Irish influences, Victorian architecture and modern convenience, and traditional music and rock and roll into a heady brew. The arts scene is lively, but overall the city has a relaxed pace.

Exploring St. John's

The city encircles St. John's Harbour, expanding past the hilly, narrow streets of old St. John's. Downtown has the most history and character. The city was destroyed by fire many times. Much of the row housing dates back to the last major blaze, known as the Great Fire, in 1892. Heritage houses on Waterford Bridge Road, winding west from the harbor along the Waterford River, and Rennies Mill Road and Circular Road to the east (backing onto Bannerman Park), were originally the homes of sea captains and merchants. Duckworth Street and Water Street, running parallel to the harbor, are where you find the shops and restaurants, but duck down the narrow lanes and paths as you get farther from the harbor to get the best sense of the history of the city. A walk downtown takes in many historic buildings, but a car is needed to explore some farther-flung sights.

a good
walk

Begin at **Harbourside Park** ❶ ▶ on Water Street, where Gilbert planted the staff of England and claimed Newfoundland. When you leave, turn left on Water Street, right on Holloway Street, and then right onto **Duckworth Street** ❷. The east end of this street is full of crafts shops and other stores. After walking east for five blocks, turn left onto Ordinance Street, just one of several streets that recall St. John's military past. Cross Military Road to **St. Thomas Anglican (Old Garrison) Church** ❸, built in the 1830s as a place of worship for British soldiers.

Turn left as you leave St. Thomas and walk up King's Bridge Road. The first building on the left is **Commissariat House** ❹, an officer's house restored to the style of the 1830s and one of the oldest buildings in the province. North of Commissariat House, a shady lane on the left leads to the gardens of **Government House** ❺. **Circular Road** ❻, where the business elite moved after a fire destroyed much of the town in 1846, is across from the gardens in front of the house. Back on Military Road, cross Bannerman Road to the **Colonial Building** ❼, the former seat of government. Walk west on Military Road until it becomes Harvey Road. The Roman Catholic **Basilica Cathedral of St. John the Baptist** ❽, finished in 1855, is on the right; you pass the Basilica Museum in the Bishop's Palace just before you get there. Cross Bonaventure Avenue as you leave the Basilica to visit **the Rooms** ❾, the province's one-stop shopping for arts, culture, and heritage. The Rooms is the home of the provincial archives, museum, and art gallery.

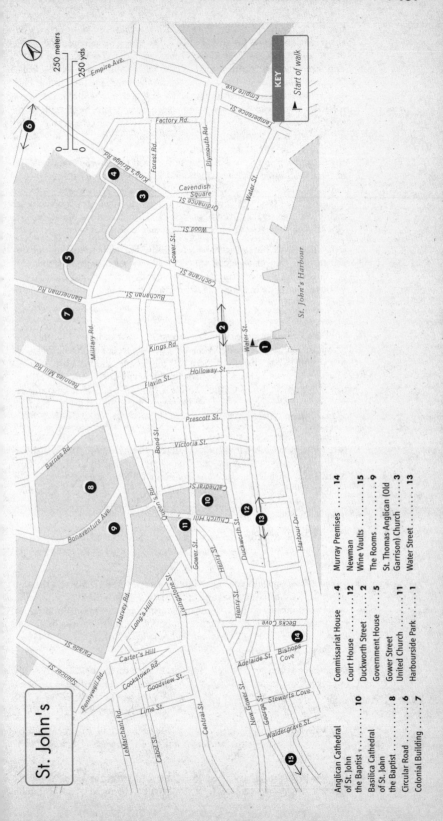

St. John's

KEY

▲ Start of walk

250 meters
250 yds

St. John's Harbour

Empire Ave.
Temperance St.
Empire Ave.
Factory Rd.
Plymouth Rd.
Water St.
King's Bridge Rd.
Forest Rd.
Cavendish Square
Ordnance St.
Wood St.
Gower St.
Cochrane St.
Bannerman Rd.
Buchanan St.
Military Rd.
Kings Rd.
Water St.
Holloway St.
Rennie's Mill Rd.
Flavin St.
Prescott St.
Bond St.
Victoria St.
Barnes Rd.
Cathedral St.
Queen's Rd.
Church Hill
Duckworth St.
Harbour Dr.
Bonaventure Ave.
Gower St.
Henry St.
Henry St.
Becks Cove
Harvey Rd.
Livingstone St.
Long's Hill
Parade St.
Carter's Hill
Cookstown Rd.
Adelaide St.
Bishops Cove
Spencer St.
Goodview St.
New Gower St.
George St.
Stewarts Cove
LeMarchant Rd.
Rennie's Mill Rd.
Lime St.
Cabot St.
Central St.
Waldegrave St.

Anglican Cathedral
of St. John
the Baptist **10**
Basilica Cathedral
of St. John
the Baptist **8**
Circular Road **6**
Colonial Building **7**

Commissariat House ... **4**
Court House **12**
Duckworth Street **5**
Government House **5**
Gower Street
United Church **11**
Harbourside Park **1**

Murray Premises **14**
Newman
Wine Vaults **15**
The Rooms **9**
St. Thomas Anglican (Old
Garrison) Church **3**
Water Street **13**

Cross Harvey Road as you leave the Rooms and turn right down Garrison Hill, so named because it once led to Fort Townshend, now home to fire and police stations. Cross Queen's Road and walk down Cathedral Street to Gower Street and the Gothic Revival **Anglican Cathedral of St. John the Baptist ⑩**. The entrance is on the west side on Church Hill. **Gower Street United Church ⑪** is directly across from the cathedral on the west side of Church Hill. Continue to the bottom of Church Hill to see the Duckworth Street **Court House ⑫**, with its four turrets, each one different. Exit the courthouse and turn right; then go down the long set of steps to **Water Street ⑬**, one of the oldest commercial streets in North America. Turn right on Water Street to reach the **Murray Premises ⑭**, a restored mercantile complex with boutiques, a science center, offices, restaurants, a coffee bar, and a wine cellar. Exit Murray Premises and continue left on Water Street to the last stop, the historic **Newman Wine Vaults ⑮**, at 440 Water Street, just west of the corner of Water and Springdale Streets, where for 200 years the legendary Newman's Port has been aged.

TIMING   Downtown St. John's is compact but hilly. The walk avoids major uphill climbs. Expect to spend up to a full day visiting these sights, depending on how much time you stay at each location and the number of stores you take in along the way. This walk is best undertaken from spring to fall.

Sights to See

⑩ **Anglican Cathedral of St. John the Baptist.** A fine example of Gothic Revival architecture designed by Sir George Gilbert Scott, this church was first completed in the mid-1800s; it was rebuilt after the 1892 fire. Women of the parish operate a tearoom in the crypt 2:30–4:40 daily June through August. ✉ *22 Church Hill* ☎ *709/726–5677* ⊕ *www.infonet. st-johns.nf.ca/cathedral* ✆ *Free* ☉ *Tours June–Sept., daily 10–5 or by appointment.*

❽ **Basilica Cathedral of St. John the Baptist.** This 1855 Roman Catholic cathedral in the Romanesque style has a commanding position above Military Road, overlooking the older section of the city and the harbor. A museum with vestments and religious objects is next door in the Bishop's Palace. ✉ *200 Military Rd.* ☎ *709/754–2170* ⊕ *www. stjohnsarchdiocese.nf.ca* ✆ *Museum $2* ☉ *Museum June–Sept., weekdays 9–5 or by appointment.*

❻ **Circular Road.** After the devastating fire of 1846, the business elite of St. John's moved to Circular Road. The street contains some very fine Victorian houses and shade trees.

❼ **Colonial Building.** This columned building (erected 1847–50) was the seat of the Newfoundland government from the 1850s until 1960, when the legislature moved to its current home, the Confederation Building, in the north end of the city. The limestone for the building was imported from Cork, Ireland. ✉ *Military and Bannerman Rds.* ☎ *709/729–3065* ✆ *Free* ☉ *Weekdays 9–4:15.*

❹ **Commissariat House.** The residence and office of the British garrison's supply officer in the 1830s has been restored to reflect that era. Interpreters dress in period costume. ✉ *King's Bridge Rd.* ☎ *709/729–6730 or 709/729–0592* ✆ *$2.50* ☉ *Mid-June–early Oct., daily 10–5:30.*

⑫ **Court House.** The late-19th-century courthouse has an eccentric appearance: each of its four turrets is a different style. ✉ *Duckworth St. at bottom of Church Hill.*

❷ **Duckworth Street.** Once called the Upper Path, this has been St. John's "second street" for centuries. (Water Street is the main street.) Stretching from the bottom of Signal Hill in the east to near City Hall in the west, Duckworth Street has restaurants, bars, antiques and crafts shops, and lawyers' offices. Lanes and stairways lead off the street down to Water Street and up to higher elevations.

5 **Government House.** This is the residence of the lieutenant governor, the Queen's representative in Newfoundland. Myth has it the moat around Government House was designed to keep out snakes, though Newfoundland is one of a handful of regions in the world (along with Ireland and New Zealand) that does not have snakes. The house, so the story goes, was originally intended for the governor of a warmer colony, where serpents might be a problem. In fact, the moat was actually designed to allow more light into the basement rooms. Built in the 1830s, the house is not open for tours but has a marvelous garden you can explore. ✉ *Military Rd.* ☎ *709/729-4494* ⊕ *www.mun.ca/govhouse* ✆ *Free* ☉ *Garden daily 8–6.*

11 **Gower Street United Church.** This 1896 church has a redbrick facade, green turrets, 50 stained-glass windows, and a massive pipe organ. ✉ *99 Gower St., at Queen's Rd.* ☎ *709/753-7286* ⊕ *www.sji.ca/providers/ goweunited* ✆ *Free* ☉ *Daily 9–5; tours July–Aug., daily 2–4:30.*

▶ **1** **Harbourside Park.** Here Sir Humphrey Gilbert claimed Newfoundland for Britain in 1583, much to the amusement of the French, Spanish, and Portuguese fishermen in port at the time. They thought him a fool, a judgment borne out a few days later when he ran his ship aground and drowned. The small park is a good vantage point from which to watch the boats come and go and to rest from your walk, but the larger parks have more green space and are better for picnics. This area, known as the Queen's Wharf, is where the harbor-pilot boat is docked. ✉ *Water St. E.*

14 **Murray Premises.** One of the oldest buildings in St. John's, the Murray Premises dates from only 1846, since the city was destroyed many times by fire. The last and worst fire was in 1892. This restored warehouse now houses shops, offices, an elite business hotel, and restaurants. The ☉ **Newfoundland Science Centre** (☎ 709/754–0823), open daily, with hands-on exhibits and special demonstrations, is within the Murray Premises. Admission is $6. ✉ *Water St. and Harbour Dr., at Beck's Cove* ☎ *709/754–0823* ⊕ *www.sciencecentre.nf.ca* ✆ *Free* ☉ *Weekdays 10–5, Sat. 10–6, Sun. noon–6.*

15 **Newman Wine Vaults.** This 200-year-old building with stone barrel vaults is where the renowned Newman's Port was aged. According to legend, a Newman and Company vessel loaded with port wine was driven off course by pirates in 1679 and forced to winter in St. John's. Upon return to London, her cargo was found to have improved in flavor, and the historic wine vaults on an island in the North Atlantic were built. The vaults are now a Provincial Historic Site, with guides who interpret the province's long and unique association with port. You can purchase more than 20 brands of port on-site. ✉ *440 Water St.* ☎ *709/ 739-7870* ⊕ *www.historictrust.com/newman* ✆ *By donation* ☉ *Mid-June–early Sept., daily 10–4:30.*

9 **The Rooms.** Provincial archives, a museum, and an art gallery are encompassed in the Rooms, set at this writing to open in summer 2004. The Rooms has replaced the Basilica as the dominant structure on the St. John's skyline. The design was taken from the traditional "fishing rooms," which were tracts of land by the waterside where fishing activities took place. Rooms were composed of a variety of structures that included fishing stages, stores, flakes, and wharves. The art gallery contains 5,500 contemporary works of art, while permanent exhibitions tell the story of the province and the hardships of its people. You can dine at the restaurant and browse the gift shop. Admission price and hours of operation are not set at this writing; call for information. ✉ *9 Bonaventure Ave.* ☎ *709/729–0862.*

③ St. Thomas Anglican (Old Garrison) Church. English soldiers used to worship at this black wooden church, the oldest in the city, during the early- and mid-1800s. ✉ *8 Military Rd.* ☎ *709/576–6632* ✉ *Free* ☉ *Tours June 24–Aug. 30, daily 9:30–5:30; call ahead for off-season hrs.*

⑬ Water Street. Originally called the Lower Path, Water Street has been the site of businesses since at least the 1620s. The older architecture resembles that of seaports in southwestern England and Ireland.

Greater St. John's

A number of must-see attractions can be found a short drive from the downtown core. When you stand with your back to the ocean at Cape Spear National Historic Site—the easternmost point of North America—the entire population is to the west of you. Cape Spear and the historic Signal Hill National Historic Site are excellent places to see icebergs and whales in spring and early summer. Plan to spend a full day exploring Greater St. John's to give yourself some time at each spot.

Sights to See

The Battery. This tiny fishing village perches precariously at the base of steep cliffs between Signal Hill and St. John's Harbour. Narrow lanes snake around the houses, which empty directly onto the street, making this a good place to get out and walk.

Bowring Park. An expansive Victorian park west of downtown, Bowring resembles the famous city parks of London, after which it was modeled. Dotting the grounds are ponds and rustic bridges; the statue of Peter Pan just inside the east gate was cast from the same mold as the one in Kensington Park in London. The wealthy Bowring family donated the park to the city in 1911. ✉ *Waterford Bridge Rd.* ☎ *709/576–6134* ✉ *Free* ☉ *Daily dawn–dusk.*

Cabot Tower. This tower at the summit of Signal Hill was constructed in 1897 to commemorate the 400th anniversary of Cabot landing in Newfoundland. The ride here along Signal Hill Road affords fine harbor, ocean, and city views, as does the tower. Guides lead tours in summer. ✉ *Signal Hill Rd.* ☎ *709/772–5367* ⊕ *www.pc.gc.ca* ✉ *Free* ☉ *June–Aug., daily 8:30–9; Sept.–Dec. and Mar.–May, daily 9–5.*

★ Cape Spear National Historic Site. At the easternmost point of land on the continent, songbirds begin their chirping in the dim light of dawn, and whales (in early summer) feed directly below the cliffs, providing an unforgettable start to the day. From April through July you may well see icebergs floating by. **Cape Spear Lighthouse,** Newfoundland's oldest such beacon, has been lovingly restored to its original form and furnishings. ✉ *Rte. 11* ☎ *709/772–5367* ⊕ *www.pc.gc.ca* ✉ *Site free, lighthouse $3.50* ☉ *Site daily dawn–dusk; lighthouse mid-May–mid-Oct., daily 10–6.*

☼ The Fluvarium. Underwater windows look onto a brook at the only public facility of its kind in North America. In season you can observe spawning brown and brook trout in their natural habitat. Feeding time for the fish, frogs, and eels is 4 PM daily. ✉ *Nagle's Pl., C. A. Pippy Park* ☎ *709/754–3474* ⊕ *www.fluvarium.ca* ✉ *$5* ☉ *June–Aug., daily 9–5; call for off-season hrs.*

Maddox Cove and Petty Harbour. These neighboring fishing villages lie along the coast between Cape Spear and Route 10. The wharves and sturdy seaside sheds, especially those in Petty Harbour, harken back to a time not long ago when the fishery was paramount in the economy and lives of the residents.

★ **Memorial University Botanical Garden.** The many gardens at this 110-acre natural area include rock gardens and scree, a Newfoundland historic-plants bed, peat and woodland beds, an alpine house, a medicinal garden, and native plant collections. There are also four pleasant walking trails. You can see scores of varieties of rhododendron here, as well as many kinds of butterflies and the rare hummingbird hawkmoth. Guided walks are available with advance notice for groups of 10 or more. ⊠ *C. A. Pippy Park, Oxen Pond, 306 Mt. Scio Rd.* ☎ *709/737–8590* ⊕ *www. mun.ca/botgarden* ⊠ *$3.50* ☉ *May–Nov., daily 10–5.*

Quidi Vidi. No one knows the origin of this fishing village's name. It's one of the oldest parts of St. John's. The town is best explored on foot, as the roads are narrow and make driving difficult. In spring the inlet, known as the Gut, is a good place to catch sea-run brown trout. The Gut is a traditional outport in the middle of a modern city, making it a contrast worth seeing. ⊠ *Take first right off King's Bridge Rd. (left of Fairmont Hotel) onto Forest Rd., which heads into the village.*

Quidi Vidi Battery. This small redoubt has been restored to the way it appeared in 1812 when soldiers stood guard to fight off a possible American attack during the War of 1812–14. Costumed interpreters tell you about the hard, unromantic life of a soldier of the empire. The site has no washroom facilities, so make a stop before you go. ⊠ *Off Cuckold's Cove Rd.* ☎ *709/729–2977 or 709/729–0592* ⊕ *www.education. gov.nl.ca/dis_hist_quidi.htm* ⊠ *$2.50* ☉ *Mid-June–early Sept., daily 10–5:30; early Sept.–mid-Oct., by appointment only.*

★ ☺ **Signal Hill National Historic Site.** In spite of its height, Signal Hill was difficult to defend: throughout the 1600s and 1700s it changed hands with every attacking French, English, and Dutch force. In 1762 this was the site of the final battle between the French and British in the Seven Years' War (called the French and Indian War in the United States). A wooden palisade encircles the summit of the hill, indicating the boundaries of the old fortifications. In July and August cadets in 19th-century British uniform perform a tattoo of military drills and music. En route to the hill is the **Park Interpretation Centre,** with exhibits describing St. John's history, and the **Johnson GEO Centre,** which describes the 550-million-year-old rocks that make up Signal Hill and the province's oldest rocks that date back 3.87 billion years. In 1901 Guglielmo Marconi received the first transatlantic wire transmission near **Cabot Tower,** at the top of Signal Hill. From the top of the hill it's a 500-foot drop to the narrow harbor entrance below; views are excellent. walking trails take you to the base of the hill and closer to the ocean. Dress warmly; it's always windy. ⊠ *Signal Hill Rd.* ☎ *709/772–5367* ⊕ *www.pc.gc.ca* ⊠ *Site free; visitor center $3.50 mid-May–mid-Oct., free mid-Oct.–mid-May* ☉ *Site daily dawn–dusk. Visitor center mid-June–early Sept., daily 8:30–8; early Sept.–Oct. and mid-Apr.–mid-June, daily 8:30–4:30; Nov.–mid-Apr., weekdays 8:30–4:30.*

Where to Stay & Eat

$$–$$$$
Fodor'sChoice
★ ✕ **The Cellar.** Despite its name, this restaurant is on the fourth floor, overlooking one of the oldest streets in the city, Water Street. The restaurant moved from the basement of a historic building in 2002 but kept

its recognizable name and reputation for fine dining. Menu selections include chicken, pork, beef, and fish dishes. ⊠ *152 Water St.,* ☎ *709/ 579–8900* ⌕ *Reservations essential* ▭ *AE, MC, V.*

$$–$$$$ ✕ **Nageira's Restaurant.** In a 1920s-era building with dark-wood decor, Nageira's has fine dining on the main floor and an upscale bar with pub fare upstairs. The menu on the main floor includes salads, pastas, and soups, with entrée choices of chicken, beef, lamb, and one of a variety of fish. ⊠ *283 Duckworth St.* ☎ *709/753–1924* ▭ *AE, DC, MC, V* ◔ *No lunch weekends.*

$$–$$$ ✕ **Bianca's.** Modern paintings lend this bright eatery the air of an art gallery. The menu changes seasonally but emphasizes fish dishes such as salmon marinated in Scotch whiskey. There's a private cigar room, a wine cellar, and an adjoining jazz club. ⊠ *171 Water St.,* ☎ *709/726– 9016* ▭ *AE, DC, MC, V* ◔ *Closed Sun.*

$$–$$$ ✕ **Django's.** This elegant and modern restaurant serves dishes that are well made and satisfying. The lunch menu includes pastas, salads, and sandwiches; dinner fare consists of chicken and steak dishes, but seafood is the specialty. ⊠ *190–192 Duckworth St.* ☎ *709/738–4115* ▭ *AE, DC, MC, V* ◔ *No lunch Sat.*

$$–$$$ ✕ **Hungry Fishermen.** Salmon, scallops, halibut, mussels, cod, and shrimp top the menu here. If you're not a fish eater, try the chicken, lamb, or steak. This restaurant in a historic 19th-century building overlooking a courtyard has great sauces; homemade desserts change daily. ⊠ *Murray Premises, 5 Beck's Cove, off Water St.* ☎ *709/726–5790* ▭ *AE, DC, MC, V.*

★ $–$$$ ✕ **Chez Briann.** Pâtés, crepes, and other French standards are served on the second floor of a downtown Victorian town house. The dark-stained wood trim is well masked by subdued decor. Heavier dishes include scallops and garlic sautéed in olive oil and served over pasta; medallions of lamb stuffed with spinach and feta; and several steak dishes. ⊠ *290 Duckworth St.* ☎ *709/579–0096* ▭ *AE, DC, MC, V* ◔ *No lunch.*

¢–$$ ✕ **Velma's Place.** For traditional Newfoundland fare such as fish and *brewis* (bread and fish soaked in water and boiled) and Jigg's dinner (boiled beef served with potatoes, carrots, cabbage, and turnips), Velma's is the place to go. The service here is friendly, and the maritime look tastefully transcends the usual lobster-pot kitsch. ⊠ *264 Water St.* ☎ *709/ 576–2264* ▭ *AE, DC, MC, V.*

¢–$ ✕ **The Big R.** Popular among locals, this fish-and-chips place with two locations in the city draws diners from all walks of life. Be warned: schoolkids eat at the Harvey Road location at lunchtime, and it can be noisy. ⊠ *69 Harvey Rd.* ☎ *709/722–2256* ⊠ *201 Blackmarsh Rd.* ☎ *709/722–6549* ▭ *V.*

¢–$ ✕ **Ches's.** Since the 1950s this restaurant has been serving fish-and-chips to a steady stream of customers from noon until well after midnight. They come from all walks of life to sample the flaky fish fried in a batter whose recipe the owner keeps under lock and key (literally). There are four locations in the city. Ches's is strictly laminated tabletops, booths, and plastic chairs, but the fish is hot and fresh. ⊠ *9 Freshwater Rd.* ☎ *709/722–4083* ⊠ *655 Topsail Rd.* ☎ *709/368–9473* ⊠ *29– 33 Commonweath Ave., Mount Pearl* ☎ *709/364–6837* ⊠ *8 Highland Dr.* ☎ *709/738–5022* ▭ *MC, V.*

FodorśChoice ★

¢–$ ✕ **Pasta Plus Café.** Pasta is the specialty here, but the local chain also serves curries, salads, and pizza. Try pasta, a curry dish served with banana-date chutney, or a crepe stuffed with seasonally available seafood. ⊠ *233 Duckworth St.* ☎ *709/739–6676* ⊠ *Avalon Mall, Thorburn Rd.,* ☎ *709/722–6006* ⊠ *Churchill Sq., Elizabeth Ave.* ☎ *709/739–5818* ▭ *AE, DC, MC, V.*

¢ ✕ **International Flavours.** Don't be fooled by the unvarnished walls and six small tables: the place may not look like much, but the curry dishes are delicious. You can also buy Indian spices to use in making your own curries. ✉ *124 Duckworth St.* ☎ *709/738–4636* ▭ *V* ☉ *Closed Sun.*

$$–$$$ ✕▥ **Delta St. John's.** Rooms in this popular convention hotel in downtown St. John's are standard, but they overlook the harbor and the city. The staff is friendly and the lobby bright, with foliage, mahogany trim, and polished brass. Rooms facing New Gower Street have the best view. The restaurant, Capital Grill and Steakhouse ($$–$$$$), serves steak and seafood, but restaurants of all types are in abundance nearby. ✉ *120 New Gower St., A1C 6K4* ☎ *709/739–6404 or 800/563–3838* 🖷 *709/570–1622* ⊕ *www.deltahotels.com* ✎ *276 rooms, 9 suites* ⚫ *Restaurant, room service, in-room data ports, minibars, cable TV, indoor pool, gym, bar, dry cleaning, laundry service, business services, convention center, meeting rooms, car rental, parking (fee), some pets allowed, no-smoking floors* ▭ *AE, DC, MC, V.*

★ $$–$$$$ ✕▥ **Fairmont Newfoundland.** Charming rooms overlook the harbor at this nine-story hotel where uniformed bellhops meet you at the door. The hotel is noted for its Sunday and evening buffets in the Bonavista restaurant ($$–$$$) and for the fine evening cuisine of the Cabot Club ($$$–$$$$), which serves Newfoundland specialties and seafood. An indoor garden atrium overlooks the Narrows, and is an ideal spot for breakfast or afternoon tea. The Cabot Club is worth taking in, whether you're staying at the hotel or not. ✉ *Box 5637, 115 Cavendish Sq., A1C 5W8* ☎ *709/726–4980* 🖷 *709/725–2025* ⊕ *www.fairmont.com* ✎ *301 rooms, 14 suites* ⚫ *2 restaurants, room service, in-room data ports, minibars, cable TV, indoor pool, gym, hair salon, bar, dry cleaning, laundry service, business services, meeting rooms, free parking, some pets allowed* ▭ *AE, DC, MC, V.*

$$–$$$$ ▥ **Holiday Inn.** The surprise at this chain hotel is the location: walking trails meander around small lakes and link into the Grand Concourse. Pippy Park, which has two golf courses, is directly across the street, and a miniature golf course is nearby. The in-house restaurant, East Side Marios, serves Italian food and burgers. The hotel is in the center of the city, near the airport and shopping mall. ✉ *180 Portugal Cove Rd., A1B 2N2* ☎ *709/722–0506* 🖷 *709/722–9756* ⊕ *www.holidayinnstjohns.com* ✎ *250 rooms* ⚫ *Restaurant, in-room data ports, cable TV, pool, gym, bar, dry cleaning, laundry service, business services, meeting rooms, free parking, some pets allowed, no-smoking rooms* ▭ *AE, D, DC, MC, V.*

$$–$$$ ▥ **Winterholme Heritage Inn.** This National Historic Site in the center of old St. John's is a movie star: the gorgeous dark-wood-paneled interiors were prominently featured in the 1999 film *The Divine Ryans.* Some rooms in this Queen Anne–style inn have working fireplaces. All rooms have double whirlpool tubs. ✉ *79 Rennies Mill Rd., A1C 3R1* ☎ *709/739–7979 or 800/599–7829* 🖷 *709/753–9411* ⊕ *www.winterholmeheritageinn.com* ✎ *11 suites* ⚫ *Fans, in-room data ports, cable TV, laundry facilities, free parking; no smoking* ▭ *AE, DC, MC, V* ❒ *BP.*

$–$$$ ▥ **The Battery Hotel and Suites.** Halfway up Signal Hill, this hotel has an unequaled view of the harbor and downtown St. John's. Not all rooms have views, so make sure you request one that's up front. The rooms are standard, but the quality of staff and service is top-notch. The restaurant has a menu of pasta, fish, chicken, beef, and munchies. ✉ *100 Signal Hill Rd., A1A 1B3* ☎ *709/576–0040 or 800/563–8181* 🖷 *709/576–6943* ⊕ *www.batteryhotel.com* ✎ *106 rooms, 19 suites* ⚫ *Restaurant, room service, in-room data ports, some kitchenettes, cable TV, indoor pool, hot tub, sauna, bar, dry cleaning, laundry services, meeting rooms, free parking, no-smoking rooms; no a/c* ▭ *MC, V.*

$–$$$ ☗ **Compton House.** A charming historic residence in the west end of the
Fodor'sChoice city, the Victorian inn is professionally run and beautifully decorated.
★ Twelve-foot ceilings and wide halls give the place a majestic feeling. Suites
have fireplaces and whirlpool tubs. ✉ *26 Waterford Bridge Rd., A1E
1C6* ☏ *709/739–5789* ⊟ *709/738–1770* ⊕ *www3.nf.sympatico.
ca/comptonhouse* ⇝ *5 rooms, 5 suites* ⚭ *Fans, in-room data ports, cable
TV, laundry service, free parking; no-smoking* ⊟ *AE, DC, MC, V.*

$–$$$ ☗ **Waterford Manor.** This Queen Anne–style inn on the river in leafy Wa-
terford Valley has won a heritage restoration award. The Pink House,
as it was originally known because of the color of the exterior, has deep
moldings and an intricately carved wooden staircase and retains the
house's original colors. The King Arthur Suite has a king-size bed, a fireplace, and a double whirlpool bath. The inn is within a few minutes'
drive of Bowring Park and the downtown area. ✉ *185 Waterford
Bridge Rd., A1E 1C7* ☏ *709/754–4139* ⊟ *709/754–4155* ⊕ *www.
waterfordmanor.nf.ca* ⇝ *4 rooms, 3 suites* ⚭ *Dining room, room service, fans, cable TV, lounge, Internet, free parking; no smoking* ⊟ *AE,
MC, V* ⦿ *BP.*

$$ ☗ **Quality Hotel Harbour Front.** This harbor-front hotel is in the down-
town core, directly overlooking the harbor. Friendly staff members im-
mediately flash a welcoming smile when you enter the sand-color tile
lobby. The five floors of rooms are clean and comfortable. The restau-
rant, Rumpelstiltskins, has a splendid view and an unpretentious menu.
✉ *Hill O'Chips, A1C 6B1* ☏ *709/754–7788* ⊟ *709/754–5209* ⊕ *www.
choicehotels.ca/cn246* ⇝ *160 rooms* ⚭ *Restaurant, room service, some
in-room data ports, cable TV, dry cleaning, laundry service, meeting rooms,
free parking, no-smoking rooms* ⊟ *AE, DC, MC, V.*

$–$$ ☗ **McCoubrey Manor.** This Queen Anne–style heritage home was built
in 1904 for Henry T. McCoubrey, manager of a prominent St. John's
merchant firm. The front veranda and back garden are perfect places
to spend a quiet evening. The house is near the base of Signal Hill and
in walking distance of shops, restaurants, and historical landmarks. Three
suites have whirlpool tubs and fireplaces. Evening wine and cheese is
included in the rate. Apartments are available for groups and longer stays.
✉ *6–8 Ordnance St., A1C 3K7* ☏ *709/722–7577 or 888/753–7577*
⊟ *709/579–7577* ⊕ *www.mccoubrey.com* ⇝ *4 suites* ⚭ *In-room data
ports, cable TV, in-room VCRs, laundry facilities, free parking; no-
smoking* ⊟ *AE, MC, V* ⦿ *BP.*

$–$$ ☗ **Airport Plaza Hotel.** Although this four-story hotel is a half mile from
the airport, noise is not a problem. Rooms are clean and modern, and
those on the upper floors have balconies. The hotel lacks an elevator
and is not within walking distance of downtown. ✉ *106 Airport Rd.,
A1A 5B2* ☏ *709/753–3500 or 800/563–2489* ⊟ *709/753–3711* ⊕ *www.
cityhotels.ca* ⇝ *98 rooms, 3 suites* ⚭ *Restaurant, room service, cable
TV, bar, laundry facilities, Internet, meeting rooms, airport shuttle, free
parking; no a/c in some rooms* ⊟ *AE, DC, MC, V* ⦿ *CP.*

¢–$ ☗ **Gower House.** This B&B, the gracious former home of the late pho-
tographer Elsie Holloway, has been designated by the Newfoundland
Historic Trust as a point of interest. The area is a favorite setting for
paintings by prominent local artists. The restored Victorian town house
is within walking distance of the city's main attractions. A full breakfast is included in the rate May through October. ✉ *180 Gower St., A1C
1P9* ☏ *800/563–3959* ⊟ *709/754–0058* ⇝ *4 rooms* ⚭ *Room service, fans, cable TV, laundry facilities, Internet, business services; no smoking* ⊟ *AE, MC, V.*

★ **¢–$** ☗ **Prescott Inn.** Local artwork decorates the walls of this house, one of
the city's most established and popular B&Bs. The owners have created
a name for themselves in the business through word-of-mouth referrals.

The helpful staff will help to coordinate car rentals and tourist excursions. The inn tastefully blends the new and the old. It's central to shops and downtown attractions, but the return climb up the hill might leave you winded. ✉ *21 Military Rd., A1C 2C3* ☎ *709/753–7733 or 888/263–3786* 🖷 *709/753–6036* ⊕ *www.prescottinn.nf.ca* ⌨ *8 rooms* ⚭ *Kitchenettes, cable TV; no-smoking* ⊟ *AE, DC, MC, V* 🍽 *BP.*

Nightlife & the Arts

St. John's has tremendous variety and vitality for such a small population. Theater settings include traditional spaces, courtyards, and parks. Celtic-inspired traditional music and traditional rock are the city's best-known music genres, although there are also vibrant blues and alternative rock scenes.

The Arts

The Arts and Culture Centre (✉ Allandale Rd. ☎ 709/729–3650) has a 1,000-seat main theater and a well-stocked library. The center hosts musical and theatrical events from September through June. The library is open year-round, Tuesday–Thursday 10–9, Friday 10–5:30; and, September–May, Saturday 10–5:30. The **Resource Centre for the Arts** (✉ LSPU Hall, 3 Victoria St. ☎ 709/753–4531) is an innovative theater with professional main-stage and experimental second-space productions year-round. It has been the launching pad for the province's best-known and successful theatrical exports. The **Ship Inn** (✉ Solomon's La. between Duckworth and Water Sts. ☎ 709/753–3870) serves as the local arts watering hole. Nighttime performances showcase local musical talent of all genres. The **Newfoundland and Labrador Folk Festival** (☎ 709/576–8508 ⊕ www.sjfac.nf.net), held in St. John's the first weekend in August, is the province's best-known traditional music festival.

Nightlife

St. John's well-deserved reputation as a party town has been several hundred years in the making. **Erin's Pub** (✉ 186 Water St. ☎ 709/722–1916) is famous for Irish music. Downtown **George Street** is the city's most famous street, with more bars per capita than any other street in North America. The short cobblestone street has dozens of pubs and restaurants. Seasonal open-air concerts, which close off the street, are held here as well.

Sports & the Outdoors

Golf

Neither high winds nor unforgiving temperatures can keep golfers off the links in St. John's. If you want to play, call several days in advance to book a tee time. The par-71, 18-hole Admiral's Green and the par-35, 9-hole Captain's Hill are two adjacent public courses in **C. A. Pippy Park** (✉ 460 Allandale Rd. ☎ 709/753–7110) that overlook St. John's. **Clovelley** (✉ Off Stavanger Dr. ☎ 709/722–7170) has two 18-hole courses: the 72-par Osprey and the 62-par Black Duck, in the east end of St. John's. The **Woods** (✉ Off Rte. 2 in the city's west end ☎ 709/368–4747) has wide, forgiving fairways on its 18-hole, par-70 layout. It caters to players of moderate skill.

Scuba Diving

The ocean around Newfoundland and Labrador rivals the Caribbean in clarity but certainly not in temperature. There are thousands of known shipwreck sites. One, a sunken whaling ship, is only yards from the shore of the Conception Bay community of Conception Harbour. The wrecked ship and a wealth of sea life can be explored with a snorkel and wet suit. Classes are available for beginners. **Dive Adventures Network** (✉ 524 Water St. ☎ 709/754–8687 or 866/819–8687 ⊕ www. newfoundlandtours.com) organizes excursions of the shipwrecks of the southern shore and Conception Bay. **Ocean Quest** (✉ Foxtrap Marina, Foxtrap ☎ 709/685–4565 or 709/834–1098 ⊕ www.oceanquestcharters. com) leads ocean tours aboard Zodiacs and a 38-foot custom boat to popular scuba diving sites, including the world-class WWII shipwrecks off Bell Island.

Sea Kayaking

One of the best ways to explore the coastline is by sea kayaking, which lets you visit sea caves and otherwise inaccessible beaches. There's also a very good chance you'll see whales, icebergs, and seabirds. **O'Brien's Whitecap Adventures** (✉ Bay Bulls ☎ 709/753–4850 ⊕ www. obriensboattours.com), about 30 minutes outside St. John's, conducts half-day sea-kayaking trips. **Wilderness Newfoundland Adventures** (✉ 67 Circular Rd., ☎ 709/579–6353 or 888/747–6353 ⊕ www.wildnfld. ca) offers excursions leaving from Cape Broyle through world-famous sanctuaries, under waterfalls, and inside caves. In season, paddle with whales and icebergs.

Walking

A well-developed, marked trail system, the **Grand Concourse** (☎ 709/737–1077), crisscrosses the city of St. John's, covering more than 100 km (62 mi). Some trails traverse river valleys, parks, and other open areas, while others are sidewalk routes. Well-maintained trails encircle several lakes, including Long Pond and Quidi Vidi Lake, both of which are great for bird-watching. Detailed maps are available at tourist information centers and many hotels.

Whale-Watching

The east coast of Newfoundland, including the area around St. John's, provides spectacular whale-watching opportunities, with up to 22 species of dolphins and whales visible along the coast. Huge humpback whales weighing up to 30 tons come close to shore to feed in late spring and early summer. You may be able to spot icebergs and large flocks of nesting seabirds in addition to whales on many boat tours. For tour times and rates, visit the tour company booths at harbor side in summer, near Pier 7, or inquire at your hotel. **Adventure Tours** (☎ 709/726–5000 or 800/779–4253 ⊕ www.nfld.com/scademia) operates the tour boat *Scademia* from Pier 7 at St. John's Harbour. The two-hour tour includes live entertainment and the company of a Newfoundland dog. **Dee Jay Charters** takes passengers to Cape Spear and Quidi Vidi aboard the *Shanadithi II*. **Morissey's Boat Tours** conducts whale-watching excursions on a 76-foot vessel to the backdrop of live traditional music.

Shopping

The **Art Gallery of Newfoundland and Labrador** (✉ The Rooms, 9 Bonaventure Ave. ☎ 709/729–0862) is the province's largest public gallery and exhibits historical and contemporary Canadian arts and crafts with an emphasis on local artists and artisans. **Christina Parker Fine Art** (✉ 7 Plank Rd. ☎ 709/753–0580) carries mainly the work of local artists in all mediums, including painting, sculpture, drawing, and prints. The **Cod Jigger** (✉ 245 Duckworth St. ☎ 709/726–7422) carries crafts and handmade wool sweaters and mittens. The **Craft Council Shop** (✉ 59 Duckworth St. ☎ 709/753–2749) displays the work of local craftspeople and showcases innovative designs. The **Eastern Edge Gallery** (✉ Clift's–Baird's Cove at Harbour Dr. ☎ 709/739–1882) is a contemporary gallery that shows the works of emerging artists. **Emma Butler Gallery** (✉ 111 George St.

☎ 709/739–7111 ⊕ www.emmabutler.com) represents some of the more prominent and established artists in the province. **Fred's Records** (✉ 198 Duckworth St. ☎ 709/753–9191) has the best selection of local recordings, as well as other music.

The **Glasshopper Studio** (✉ 206 Duckworth St. ☎ 709/738–5585) carries locally made glass items, including sun catchers and jewelry. The **Holloway Heights Galleria** (✉ 14 Holloway St., off Duckworth St. ☎ 709/754–5560) is a small gallery that carries oil paintings, watercolors, and clay sculptures by two local artists that depict the St. John's area. The **Lane Gallery** (✉ Fairmont Hotel, 1st floor, Cavendish Sq. ☎ 709/753–8946) has seascapes, landscapes, and other works by photographer Don Lane. **Livyers** (✉ 202 Duckworth St. ☎ 709/726–5650) has a little of everything, from furniture and books to maps and prints. **Murray's Antiques** (✉ 414 Blackmarsh Rd. ☎ 709/579–7344) is renowned for silver, china, and fine mahogany and antique walnut furniture.

The **Newfoundland Weavery** (✉ 177 Water St. ☎ 709/753–0496) sells rugs, prints, lamps, books, crafts, and other gift items. **NONIA** (Newfoundland Outport Nurses Industrial Association; ✉ 286 Water St. ☎ 709/753–8062) was founded in 1920 to give women in the outports a way to earn money so they could provide nursing services in these remote communities. Homespun wool was used to create exquisite clothing. Today the shop continues to sell these fine homespun articles as well as lighter, more modern handmade items. **Polyanna Art and Antique Gallery** (✉ 214 Duckworth St. ☎ 709/726–0936) carries antiques as well as paintings and photographs.

Red Ochre Gallery (✉ 96 Duckworth St. ☎ 709/726–6422) exhibits the works of 10 professional local artists, as well as those of Inuit carvers from Labrador. The bookstore **Saltwater Chronicles** (✉ 188 Duckworth St. ☎ 709/726–7323) specializes in the works of local writers and the offerings of local publishers. Most bookstores have a section dedicated to local writers. **Wild Things** (✉ 124 Water St. ☎ 709/722–3123) sells nature-theme crafts and jewelry.

AVALON PENINSULA

On the southern half of the peninsula, small Irish hamlets are separated by large tracts of wilderness. You can travel part of the peninsula's southern coast in one or two days, depending on how much time you have. Quaint towns line Route 10, and the natural sights are beautiful. La Manche and Chance Cove, both abandoned communities–turned–provincial parks, attest to the region's bounty of natural resources. At the intersection of Routes 90 and 91 in Salmonier you can either head north toward Salmonier Nature Park and on to the towns on Conception Bay, or head west and then south to Route 100 to Cape St. Mary's Ecological Reserve. Both take about three hours. On the former route, stop in Harbour Grace; if you plan to travel on to Bay de Verde, at the northern tip of the peninsula, and down the other side of the peninsula on Route 80 along Trinity Bay, consider overnighting in the Harbour Grace–Carbonear area. Otherwise turn around and follow the same route back to Route 1.

Witless Bay Ecological Reserve

⓰ *29 km (18 mi) south of St. John's.*

Four small islands and the water surrounding them make up the reserve, which is the summer home of millions of seabirds—puffins, murres, kit-

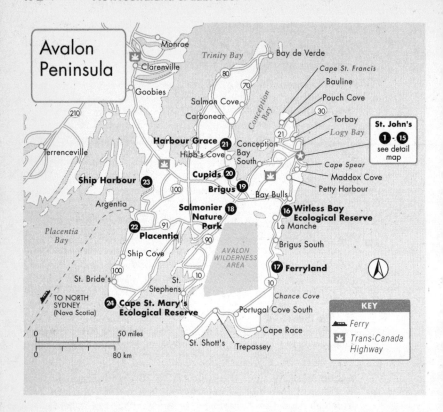

Avalon Peninsula

Monroe
Trinity Bay
Bay de Verde
Clareville
Cape St. Francis
Bauline
Goobies
Pouch Cove
Salmon Cove
Carbonear
Torbay
Logy Bay
Harbour Grace 21   Conception Bay South
Hibb's Cove
St. John's
1 - **15**
see detail map
Terrenceville
Cupids 20
Cape Spear
Maddox Cove
Ship Harbour 23
Brigus 19
Petty Harbour
Argentia
Bay Bulls
Salmonier Nature Park 18
Witless Bay Ecological Reserve 16
Placentia Bay
22   **Placentia**
La Manche
Ship Cove
Brigus South
AVALON WILDERNESS AREA
St. Bride's
St. Stephens
Ferryland 17
TO NORTH SYDNEY (Nova Scotia)
24   **Cape St. Mary's Ecological Reserve**
Chance Cove
Portugal Cove South
KEY
Cape Race
Ferry
St. Shott's
Trepassey
Trans-Canada Highway

0   50 miles
0   80 km

tiwakes, razorbills, and guillemots. The birds, and the humpback and minke whales that linger here before moving north to the summer grounds in the Arctic, feed on capelin that swarm inshore to spawn. It's an excellent place to see icebergs in late spring and early summer. The best views of birds and icebergs are from tour boats that operate here. ⊠ *Rte. 10; take Pitts Memorial Dr. (Rte. 2) from downtown St. John's and turn right onto Goulds off-ramp, then left onto Rte. 10* ☎ *709/729–2424* ⊕ *www.gov.nl.ca/parks&reserves* ⊠ *Free* ⊙ *Daily 24 hrs.*

Sports & the Outdoors

From mid-May to mid-October, **Gatherall's Puffin and Whale Watch** (☎ 709/334–2887 or 800/419–4253 ⊕ www.gatheralls.com) leads between six and eight 90-minute trips per day into the reserve on a high-speed catamaran. Shuttle service is available from St. John's hotels. **O'Brien's Whale and Bird Tours** (☎ 709/753–4850 or 877/639–4253 ⊕ www.obriensboattours.com) offers two-hour excursions to view whales, icebergs, and seabirds. Dress warmly. Icebergs can linger in Newfoundland waters into June and sometimes July, cooling the temperature before falling victim to the milder climate. The loud crack as an iceberg breaks apart can be heard from shore, but a boat can get you a closer look at these natural ice sculptures. Icebergs have spawned a lucrative business in Newfoundland beyond tourism. Iceberg water and iceberg vodka are now on the market, made from ice chipped from the 10,000-year-old bergs as they float by.

en route   Although there are many pretty hamlets along the way from Witless Bay to Ferryland on Route 10, **La Manche,** accessible only on foot, and **Brigus South** have especially attractive settings and strong traditional flavors. La Manche is an abandoned fishing community between Tors Cove and Cape Broyle. The former residents moved to other towns after a storm destroyed part of the community in 1966. Brigus South, between Witless Bay and Cape Broyle, is a fishing village whose name is derived from an old French word for intrigue.

Ferryland

17 *43½ km (27 mi) south of Witless Bay Ecological Reserve.*

The major ongoing **Colony of Avalon archaeological dig** at Ferryland has uncovered the early 17th-century colony of Lord Baltimore, who abandoned the area after a decade for the warmer climes of Maryland. The site includes an archaeology laboratory, exhibit center and museum, gift shop, period gardens, and reconstructed 17th-century kitchen. Guided tours are available. ⊠ *Rte. 10, Ferryland* ☎ *709/432–3200 or 877/326–5669* ⊕ *www.heritage.nf.ca/avalon* ⊠ *$5* ☉ *Mid-May–mid-Oct., daily 9–7.*

> **en route** Between Chance Cove and Portugal Cove South, on a stretch of land about 58 km (36 mi) long, hundreds of **caribou** and their calves gather in the springtime on the barrens near Route 10. They migrate to this southern area from farther north in the Avalon Wilderness Area.

Sports & the Outdoors

Kayaking excursions with **Wilderness Newfoundland Adventures** (⊠ 67 Circular Rd., St. John's ☎ 709/579–6353 or 888/747–6353 ⊕ www.wildnfld.ca) leave from Cape Broyle. The family company also runs guided hiking tours of the East Coast Trail.

Salmonier Nature Park

18 *88 km (55 mi) northwest of Ferryland, 14½ km (9 mi) north of the intersection of Rtes. 90 and 91.*

Many indigenous animal species, including moose, caribou, lynx, and otters, can be seen at this 3,000-acre wilderness reserve area. An enclosed 100-acre exhibit allows up-close viewing. ⊠ *Salmonier Line, Rte. 90* ☎ *709/229–7189* ⊕ *www.gov.nl.ca/snp* ⊠ *Free* ☉ *Early June–early Sept., daily 10–6; early Sept.–mid-Oct., daily 10–4.*

> **en route** From Salmonier Nature Park to Brigus, take Route 90, which passes through the scenic **Hawke Hills** before meeting up with the Trans-Canada Highway (Route 1). This reserve is the best representative of alpine barrens in Canada east of the Rockies. Turn off at Holyrood Junction (Route 62) and follow Route 70, which skirts Conception Bay.

Brigus

19 *19 km (12 mi) north of intersection of Rtes. 1 and 70.*

This historic village on Conception Bay has a wonderful public garden, winding lanes, and a tea house. Brigus is best known as the birthplace of Captain Bob Bartlett, the famed Arctic explorer who accompanied Admiral Peary on polar expeditions during the first decade of the 20th century.

Hawthorne Cottage, Captain Bartlett's home, is one of the few surviving examples of picturesque cottage style, with a veranda decorated with ornamental wooden fretwork. It dates from 1830 and is a National Historic Site. ⊠ *Irishtown Rd.* ☎ *709/753–9262, 709/528–4004 June–Aug.*

✉ *$3.50* ⊙ *Mid-May–late June and early Sept.–mid-Oct., daily 10–6; late June–early Sept., daily 10–8.*

The **Olde Stone Barn Museum** (John L. Leamon Museum) displays historic town photos and artifacts, especially objects relating to the museum's connection with the fishery. ⊠ *4 Magistrate's Hill* ☎ *709/528–3391* ✉ *$1* ⊙ *Mid-June–early Sept., daily 11–6.*

Where to Stay

¢ ▥ **Brittoner Bed & Breakfast.** This 160-year-old restored historic home

Fodor's Choice is in the heart of Brigus, near Hawthorne Cottage, the Olde Stone Barn

★ Museum, and hiking trails. It has a large area for picnics or for just sitting outside and enjoying the splendid view. ⊠ *Box 163, 12 Water St., A0A 1K0* ☎ *709/528–3412, 709/579–5995 Nov.–Apr.* 🖷 *709/528–3412* ⮑ *3 rooms, 2 with bath* ⚲ *Playground, laundry facilities, some pets allowed; no smoking* ▭ *No credit cards* ⦿ *BP.*

¢ ▥ **Brookdale Manor.** This old farmhouse is in a quiet country setting just outside town. A common area has a fireplace, television, and phone that guests can use. Rooms are spacious. ⊠ *Box 121, Farm Rd., A0A 1K0* 🖷 *709/528–4544* ⮑ *4 rooms* ⚲ *Fans, room service; no a/c, no room phones, no room TVs* ▭ *MC, V* ⦿ *CP.*

Cupids

⑳ *5 km (3 mi) north of Brigus.*

Cupids is the oldest English colony in Canada, founded in 1610 by John Guy, to whom the town erected a monument in 1910. Nearby flies a replica of the enormous Union Jack that flew during that 300th-anniversary celebration. When the wind snaps the flag, you can hear it half a mile away. In 1995 archaeologists at the **Cupids Archaeological Site,** began unearthing the long-lost remains of the original colony here. Some of the recovered artifacts—including pots, pipes, and trade beads—are on display in the on-site community museum. ⊠ *Main Rd.* ☎ *709/528–3500* ✉ *$2, includes museum and site* ⊙ *July–Sept., weekdays 8:30–4:30.*

Where to Stay

¢ ▥ **Skipper Ben's** This 100-year-old heritage home has been restored to maintain its original character, with wood ceilings and antique furnishings. The four spacious rooms of this B&B share two bathrooms. The dining room is open for lunch, afternoon tea, and dinner. ⊠ *Box 137, 408 Seaforest Dr., A0A 2B0* ☎ *877/528–4436* 🖷 *709/528–4436* ⮑ *4 rooms without bath* ⚲ *Dining room, picnic area, cable TV, Internet, business services; no smoking* ▭ *No credit cards* ⦿ *BP.*

¢ ▥ **Guy View Manor.** On a hillside overlooking the ocean, this ranch-style home is near the Cupids Archaeological Site and good hiking and walking trails. The brightly painted rooms each have their own entrance, giving guests added privacy. A TV and telephone are available in the common room. ⊠ *Box 122, First Colony Dr., A0A 2B0* ☎ *877/528–4248* 🖷 *709/528–4248* ⮑ *4 rooms* ⚲ *Fans, no-smoking rooms; no a/c, no room phones, no room TVs* ▭ *V* ⦿ *CP.*

Harbour Grace

㉑ *21 km (13 mi) north of Cupids.*

Harbour Grace, once the headquarters of 17th-century pirate Peter Easton, was a major commercial town in the 18th and 19th centuries. Beginning in 1919, the town was the departure point for many attempts to fly the Atlantic. Amelia Earhart left Harbour Grace in 1932 to become the first woman to fly solo across the Atlantic. The town has two fine churches and several registered historic houses.

Where to Stay

$ 🏨 **Rothesay House Inn Bed & Breakfast.** This Queen Anne–style B&B was built in the early 20th century. The front of the house has a lovely porch, and the greens, yellows, and reds of the exterior are echoed in the room colors. ✉ *34 Water St., A0A 2M0* ☎ *709/596–2268* 🖷 *709/596–0317* ⊕ *www.rothesay.com* 🛏 *4 rooms* ♿ *Dining room; no smoking* ▭ *MC, V* ⋔ *BP.*

ROUTE 100: THE CAPE SHORE

This area is the site of an outstanding seabird colony at Cape St. Mary's. It's also culturally and historically rich. The French settlers had their capital here in Placentia. The Irish influence is also strong here, in music and manner. You can reach the Cape Shore on the western side of the Avalon Peninsula from Route 1, at its intersection with Route 100. The ferry from Nova Scotia docks in Argentia, near Placentia.

Placentia

㉒ *48 km (30 mi) south of Rte. 1.*

Placentia was Newfoundland's French capital in the 1600s. It was first settled by 16th-century Basque fishermen. The remains of an old fort built on a hill look out over Placentia and beyond to the placid waters and wooded, steep hillsides of the inlet. The **Castle Hill National Historic Site,** just north of town, is what remains of the French fortifications. The visitor center has an exhibit on life at Plaisance that shows the hardships endured by early English and French settlers. Performances of *Faces of Fort Royal,* a historical play about the French era, take place twice daily during July and August. ✉ *Off Rte. 100* ☎ *709/227–2401* ⊕ *www.pc.gc.ca* 🎟 *Site $3.50, play $2* ⊙ *Mid-June–early Sept., daily 8:30–8; early Sept.–mid-June, daily 8:30–4:30.*

Where to Stay

¢ 🏨 **Northeast Arm Motel.** Ten minutes by ferry to Nova Scotia via Argentia, this motel overlooks the 8-km (5-mi) arm of water on which the community of Northeast Arm is built. Rooms are standard, without much in the way of frills, but they're painted in cheery, bright colors. Rooms in the back have the better view. ✉ *Main St., Dunville A0B 1S0* ☎ *709/227–3560 or 877/227–3560* 🖷 *709/227–5430* 🛏 *13 rooms* ♿ *Restaurant, room service, cable TV, bar, laundry facilities, Internet, some pets allowed, no-smoking rooms* ▭ *AE, DC, MC, V.*

¢ 🏨 **Seaside Bed and Breakfast.** A great place to stay with kids, this B&B overlooking Southeast Arm has an outdoor covered swimming pool and, inside, a pinball machine and other games. Rooms are small and sparse, but clean. The house is a typical 30-year-old split level. The owners are friendly. ✉ *Rte. 91, A0B 2Y0* ☎ *709/227–2825* 🖷 *709/227–2583* ⊕ *www.angelfire.com/nf/seasidebandb* 🛏 *5 rooms* ♿ *Dining room, cable TV, pool, exercise equipment, billiards, recreation room, no-smoking rooms* ▭ *V* ⋔ *BP.*

Ship Harbour

㉓ *34 km (21 mi) north of Placentia.*

An isolated, edge-of-the-world place, Ship Harbour has historic significance. In 1941, on a ship in these waters, Franklin Roosevelt and Winston Churchill signed the Atlantic Charter and formally announced the "Four Freedoms," which still shape the politics of the world's most successful democracies: freedom of speech, freedom of worship, freedom from want, and freedom from fear. Off Route 102, amid the splendor of Placentia Bay, an unpaved road leads to an Atlantic Charter monument.

Cape St. Mary's Ecological Reserve

★ ㉔ *65 km (40 mi) south of Placentia.*

Cape St. Mary's Ecological Reserve is the third-largest nesting colony of gannets in North America and the most accessible seabird colony on the continent. A paved road takes you within a mile of the colony. You can visit the interpretation center—guides are on-site in summer—and then walk to within 100 feet of the colony of nesting gannets, murres, black-billed kittiwakes, and razorbills. Most birds are March-through-August visitors. The reserve has some of the most dramatic coastal scenery in Newfoundland and is a good place to spot whales. From May through September the interpretation center hosts performances of traditional music by local artists; call for information and times. ⊠ *Off Rte. 100* ☎ *709/337-2473* ⊕ *www.gov.nl.ca/parks&reserves* ⊠ *Site free, center $3* ☉ *Site daily dawn–dusk; center May and early–mid-Oct., daily 9–5; June–Sept., daily 8–7.*

Where to Stay

¢–$ 🏨**Bird Island Resort.** This pleasant lodging is a half-hour drive from Cape St. Mary's. The motel units are standard, but cottages are carpeted, have decks and kitchens, and overlook the water. ⊠ *Off Rte. 100, St. Bride's A0B 2Z0* ☎ *709/337-2450 or 888/337-2450* 🖷 *709/337-2903* 💤 *5 rooms, 15 cottages* ⏶ *Some kitchens, cable TV, gym, laundry facilities* 🖃 *AE, MC, V.*

¢ 🏨**Capeway Motel.** The main attraction of this basic motel is its proximity to the seabird sanctuary at Cape St. Mary's. Built in 1968, the two-story building was originally a convent. It was refurbished and opened as a motel in the 1990s. Rooms are very bright, but blinds effectively filter out the morning sun. In-room phones are available by request. ⊠ *Rte. 100, General Delivery, St. Bride's A0B 2Z0* ☎ *709/337-2163 or 866/ 337-2163* 🖷 *709/337-2028* 💤 *7 rooms* ⏶ *Fans, kitchenettes, cable TV, laundry facilities; no room phones* 🖃 *MC, V.*

CLARENVILLE & THE BONAVISTA PENINSULA

Clarenville, about two hours northwest of St. John's via the Trans-Canada Highway (Route 1), is the departure point for two different excursions: the Discovery Trail, on the Bonavista Peninsula, and Terra Nova National Park.

Clarenville

㉕ *189 km (117 mi) northwest of St. John's.*

If history and quaint towns appeal to you, follow the **Fodor's**Choice ★**Discovery Trail,** which begins in Clarenville on Route 230A. The trail includes two gems: the old town of Trinity, famed for its quaint architecture and theater festival, and Bonavista, one of John Cabot's reputed landing spots.

Where to Stay

¢–$$ 🏨**Restland Motor Inn.** The bland name doesn't do justice to the lovely garden at this inn. The rooms are small but clean and cozy. The restaurant, Brownings, is open all day and serves a selection of Canadian dishes, including seafood. ⊠ *Memorial Dr., A0E 1J0* ☎ *709/466-7636 or 800/205-3993* 🖷 *709/466-2743* 💤 *25 rooms* ⏶ *Restaurant, room* *service, cable TV, laundry service, Internet, some pets allowed, no-smoking rooms* ☐ *AE, DC, MC, V.*

$ ☐ **St. Jude Hotel.** Rooms are spacious and comfortable, if somewhat spartan, at this modern hotel with the sports bar Don Cherry's under its roof. Rooms fronting the highway have a good view of the bay, but those in the back are quieter. ☒ *Box 2500, Rte. 1, A0E 1J0* ☎ *709/466–1717 or 800/563–7800* ☐ *709/466–1714* ⊕ *www.stjudehotel.nf.ca* ⌁ *63 rooms* ☐ *Restaurant, room service, bar, laundry service, Internet, some pets allowed, no-smoking rooms* ☐ *AE, MC, V.*

¢ ☐ **Clarenville Inn.** This hotel on the Trans-Canada Highway has a million-dollar view of Random Sound. Rooms are standard, with wall-to-wall carpeting. It's a convenient home base for tourists looking to take day trips along the Discovery Trail, down the Burin Peninsula, or even to the Avalon region. Rooms on the top floor are brighter, and the ones in the back have the better view. It's popular with families because children under 10 eat free, and there's a heated swimming pool. ☒ *Box 967, Rte. 1, A0E 1J0* ☎ *709/466–7911 or 877/466–7911* ☐ *709/466–3854* ⌁ *62 rooms, 1 suite* ☐ *Restaurant, room service, pool, bar, laundry facilities, Internet, no-smoking rooms* ☐ *AE, DC, MC, V.*

Terra Nova National Park

㉖ *24 km (15 mi) northwest of Clarenville.*

Newfoundland's first national park was Terra Nova Park, established in 1957. On Bonavista Bay, it has natural beauty, a dramatic coastline, and rugged woods. Moose, black bear, and other wildlife move about freely in the forests and marshy bogs. Pods of whales play within sight of the shores of the park, and many species of birds inhabit the cliffs and shores encompassed by the 396-square-km (246-square-mi) park. Rugged terrain, golf, sea kayaking, fishing, and camping are draws at this park on the exposed coastline of Bonavista Bay. The park also has the Marine Interpretation Center, nature walks, whale-watching and sea-kayaking tours, and a small but decent snack bar–cafeteria. Eight backcountry camping areas are accessible by trail or canoe. ☒ *Trans-Canada Hwy., Glovertown A0G 2L0* ☎ *709/533–2801* ⊕ *www.pc.gc.ca* ☒ *$5 mid-May–mid-Oct., free mid-Oct.–mid-May* ☉ *Site daily dawn–dusk; center July and Aug., daily 9–8, May, June, Sept., and Oct., daily 10–5.*

Where to Stay

$$ ☐ **Terra Nova Golf Resort.** Two of the most beautiful golf courses in Canada are at this resort at Port Blandford. The 18-hole course is traversed by two salmon rivers. Nestled in the beautiful Clode Sound near Terra Nova National Park, the high-end lodgings have all the big-city hotel luxuries rolled into the charm of a country inn. Rooms are large and bright with spectacular views. The property is sprawling, with lots to do, from hiking and swimming to an array of recreational activities. The golf courses are in high demand, so it's best to book two or three months in advance to be assured a tee time. ☒ *Port Blandford* ☎ *709/543–2525, 709/543–2626 golf reservations* ☐ *709/543–2201* ⊕ *www.terranovagolf.com* ⌁ *83 rooms* ☐ *Dining room, room service, some microwaves, some refrigerators, cable TV, 18-hole golf course, 9-hole golf course, tennis court, pool, basketball, volleyball, pub, children's programs (ages 7–18); no a/c in some rooms* ☐ *AE, D, MC, V.*

△ **Malady Head Campground.** The smaller of Terra Nova's two campgrounds, Malady Head is nestled in a wooded area. Malady Head is essentially an overflow for nearby Newman Sound Campground, and the entry permit gets you access to both campgrounds. Laundry facilities, a grocery store, and most activities are at nearby Newman Sound.

✉ Rte. 310 ☎ 866/533–3186 ⇄ 99 RV and tent sites ⚱ Flush toilets, dump station, running water, showers, fire pits ▦ $13 ▤ AE, MC, V ◷ Open July–Sept.

⚠ **Newman Sound Campground.** Organized in clusters around playgrounds, this campground is nestled in the woods, with hiking trails that hug the perimeter of the camping area and take you to longer trails along the shore. It has an activity center for children, an outdoor theater, and guided hikes, all of which are free. The on-site store is small, so it's best to stock up on groceries before arriving. Bicycle rentals and winter camping are available. ✉ Rte. 1 ☎ 866/533–3186 July–Sept., 709/ 533–2801 Oct.–June ⇄ 387 tent and RV sites ⚱ Flush toilets, partial RV hookups (electric), running water, laundry facilities, showers, fire pits, general store ▦ Tent sites $21, RV sites $26, plus entry permit of $5 ▤ AE, MC, V ◷ Open July–Sept.; call ahead Oct.–June.

Trinity

★ ㉗ 71 km (44 mi) northeast of Clarenville.

Trinity is one of the jewels of Newfoundland. The village's ocean views, winding lanes, and snug houses are the main attractions. Several homes have been turned into museums and inns. In the 1700s Trinity competed with St. John's as a center of culture and wealth. Its more contemporary claim to fame, however, is that its intricate harbor was a favorite anchorage for the British navy. Here, too, the smallpox vaccine was introduced to North America by a local rector. On West Street an information center with costumed interpreters is open daily mid-June through October. To get here, take Route 230 to Route 239.

The **Garland Mansion** is a re-creation of a fish merchant's house that was one of the most prominent 18th-century homes in Newfoundland. Next door is a 19th-century store. An interpretation center traces the history of the town, once a mercantile center. ✉ West St. ☎ 709/464–2042 or 800/563–6353 ▦ $2.50 ◷ Mid-June–early Oct., daily 10–5:30.

From mid-June through Labor Day, the **Rising Tide Theatre** (☎ 709/464–3232 or 888/464–3377) conducts New-Founde-Land Trinity Pageant walking tours of the lanes, roads, and sites of the town (Wednesday and weekends at 2) that are more theater than tour, with actors in period costume.

Where to Stay & Eat

★ ¢–$$ ✗ **Dock Restaurant.** Right on the wharf, this restaurant is in a restored 300-year-old fish merchant's headquarters. The menu includes traditional Newfoundland meals and seafood as well as standard Canadian fare: burgers, chicken, and steak. Upstairs is an art gallery and crafts shop. ✉ Trinity Waterfront ☎ 709/464–2133 ▤ AE, DC, MC, V ◷ Closed Nov.–Apr.

$–$$$ ⊞ **Campbell House Bed & Breakfast.** This mid-19th-century house is decorated with antiques and has low-ceilinged, light-filled rooms, two-bedroom suites, and a large studio with full kitchen. A working artist's studio is on-site. Guests can use the studio or watch a visiting artist at work. Art exhibitions are common. ✉ High St., A0C 2S0 ☎ 877/464–7700 ☎☎ 709/464–3377 ⊕ www.trinityvacations.com ⇄ 2 rooms, 2 suites, 1 studio ⚱ Dining room, cable TV, laundry service, Internet; no-smoking ▤ AE, DC, MC, V ◷ Closed Nov.–Apr. ◉| BP.

$–$$ ⊞ **Eriksen Premises.** This two-story mansard-style building was built in the late 1800s as a general store and tearoom. It has since been restored to its original elegance and character. The rooms here are larger than at its sister property, Bishop White Manor. They're also furnished with antiques and have views of the bay. ⌧ *Box 58, West St., A0C 2S0* ☎ *709/464–3698, 709/464–3299, or 877/464–3698* ☷ *709/464–2104* ⊕ *www.trinityexperience.com* ⇨ *7 rooms* ⌂ *Dining room, fans, shop; no room phones, no room TVs* ▭ *AE, MC, V* ⊙ *Closed Nov.–Apr.* ◉ *BP.*

$–$$ ▦ **Fishers' Loft Inn.** Whales sometimes swim among small fishing boats in the harbor in sight of this inn, and icebergs drift by farther out in the bay. Rooms are bright and airy, with down duvets, handcrafted furniture, and original artwork. Four rooms have cathedral ceilings. The owners pack you a lunch and give you a map and guidance for hiking in the area. ⌧ *Mill Rd., Port Rexton A0C 2H0, 15 km (9 mi) northeast of Trinity* ☎ *877/464–3240* ☎☎ *709/464–3240* ⊕ *www.fishersloft.com* ⇨ *8 rooms, 4 suites* ⌂ *Dining room, in-room data ports; no-smoking* ▭ *MC, V* ⊙ *Closed Nov.–Apr.*

$ ▦ **Bishop White Manor.** Built at the turn of the 19th century, this history-filled Victorian-style lodging is one of the oldest standing homes in Trinity and was the childhood home of Newfoundland's first native-born Anglican bishop, William Charles White. The four-poster canopy bed White used is in one of the rooms; all rooms are furnished with local antiques and have nice views. ⌧ *Gallavan's La., A0C 2S0* ☎ *709/464–3698, 709/464–3299, or 877/464–3698* ☷ *709/464–2104* ⊕ *www.trinityexperience.com* ⇨ *9 rooms* ⌂ *Fans; no a/c, no room phones, no room TVs* ▭ *AE, MC, V* ⊙ *Closed Nov.–Apr.* ◉ *BP.*

¢–$ ▦ **Peace Cove Inn.** Once a schooner captain's residence, this restored inn is one of the few remaining modified Second Empire houses in Newfoundland that have front and back mansard roofs and bonneted windows. Antiques-filled rooms are large. ⌧ *Trinity Rd. E* ✑ *Box 123, Port Rexton A0C 2H0* ☎ *709/464–3738* ☷ *709/464–2167* ⊕ *www.atlanticadventures.com* ⇨ *6 rooms* ⌂ *Dining room, no-smoking rooms* ▭ *MC, V* ⊙ *Closed Nov.–Apr.*

¢–$ ▦ **Sherwood Suites.** The cottages here are spacious and have living rooms and private patios. Opt for a cottage if you plan to do your own cooking. The motel rooms are large and bright with private entrances. ⌧ *Rocky Hill Rd., Port Rexton A0C 2H0* ☎☎ *709/464–2130 or 877/464–2133* ⊕ *www.sherwoodsuites.nfld.net* ⇨ *4 rooms, 10 cottages* ⌂ *Some kitchens, cable TV, playground, laundry facilities, no-smoking rooms* ▭ *MC, V* ⊙ *Closed Oct.–May.*

Nightlife & the Arts

Shakespeare productions, dinner theater, and local dramas and comedies run throughout July and August at the Summer in the Bight festival at the **Rising Tide Theatre** (⌧ Rte. 230 to Rte. 239, then left onto road into Trinity ☎ 709/464–3232 or 888/464–3377 ⊕ www.risingtidetheatre.com) The theater, on the waterfront, is styled like an old mercantile warehouse.

Sports & the Outdoors

Atlantic Adventures Charters and Tours (☎ 709/464–2133 or 709/781–2255) operates a 46-foot motorized sailboat for whale-watching or just cruising Trinity Bay. The boat departs daily at 10 and 2, depending on the weather and on charter bookings. Tours are 2½–3 hours and cost about $40 per person. A group of six or more people can charter the boat for an 8- to 10-hour tour, which includes a meal, for about $85 per person. The vessel departs from the Dockside Marina.

Shopping

Trinity Crafts (⌧ Church Rd. ☎ 709/464–3823) specializes in locally made quilts, woolens, and knitted goods. **Trinity Folk Art** (⌧ Water St. ☎ 709/464–3760) sells a wide array of crafts from all over the province, including Innu tea dolls from Labrador.

Bonavista

28 *28 km (17 mi) north of Trinity.*

No one knows exactly where explorer John Cabot landed when he came to Atlantic Canada in 1497, but many believe it to have been at Bonavista, based on his descriptions of the newfound land. The **Ryan Premises National Historic Site** on the waterfront depicts the almost-500-year history of the commercial cod fishery in a restored fish merchant's property. ⊠ *Off Rte. 230* ☎ *709/468–1600 or 800/213–7275* ⊕ *www. pc.gc.ca* ☞ *$3.50* ⊙ *Mid-June–early Oct., daily 10–6.*

The **Cape Bonavista Lighthouse** on the point, about 1 km (½ mi) outside town, was built in 1843. It's been restored to the way it looked in 1870. ☎ *709/468–7444 or 800/563–6353* ☞ *$2.50, includes Mockbeggar Plantation* ⊙ *Mid-June–early Oct., daily 10–5:30.*

The **Mockbeggar Plantation** teaches about the life of an outport merchant in the years immediately before Confederation. Guides in period costume lead you through an early-18th-century fish store, carpentry shop, and cod-liver-oil factory. ⊠ *Off Rte. 230* ☎ *709/468–7300 or 800/563–6353* ☞ *$2.50, includes Cape Bonavista Lighthouse* ⊙ *Mid-June–early Oct., daily 10–5:30.*

BURIN PENINSULA, GANDER & NOTRE DAME BAY

The Burin Peninsula's history is tied to the rich fishing grounds of the Grand Bank, which established this area as a center for European fishery as early as the 1500s. By the early 1900s one of the world's largest fishing fleets was based on the Burin Peninsula. Today its inhabitants hope for a recovery of the fish stocks that have sustained their economy for centuries. Marystown is the peninsula's commercial center.

Gander, in east-central Newfoundland, is known for its airport and its aviation history. North of it is Notre Dame Bay, an area of rugged coastline and equally rugged islands that were once the domain of the now extinct Beothuk tribe. Only the larger islands are currently inhabited. Before English settlers moved into the area in the late 18th and early 19th centuries, it was seasonally occupied by French fisherfolk. Local dialects preserve centuries-old words that have vanished elsewhere. The bay is swept by the cool Labrador Current, which carries icebergs south through Iceberg Alley; the coast is also a good whale-watching area.

The journey down to the Burin Peninsula is a three- to four-hour drive from the intersection of Routes 230 and 1 through the craggy coastal landscapes along Route 210.

Marystown

29 *283 km (175 mi) south of Bonavista.*

Marystown is built around beautiful Mortier Bay, so big it was considered large enough for the entire British fleet during the early days of World War II. Shipbuilding is the main industry. Of note is the 20-foot statue of the Virgin Mary that looks out over the bay.

Where to Stay

¢–$ 🏨 **Hotel Marystown.** This is the largest hotel on the Burin Peninsula; rooms are standard but comfortable. Rooms on the upper floors are a bit brighter. In the restaurant, P. J. Billington's, the peninsula's history of rum smuggling and connection to gangster Al Capone is told in photographs on the wall. ⊠ *76 Ville Marie Dr., A0E 2M0* ☎ *709/279–1600 or 800/563–2489* ☐ *709/279–4088* ⊕ *www.cityhotels.ca* ⏎ *131 rooms* ⚑ *Restaurant, room service, some kitchenettes, cable TV, bar, business services, meeting rooms, some pets allowed* ▭ *AE, DC, MC, V.*

Burin

③ *17 km (11 mi) south of Marystown.*

A community built amid intricate cliffs and coves, Burin was an ideal setting for pirates and privateers, who used to lure ships into the rocky dead-end areas in order to plunder them. When Captain James Cook was stationed here to chart the coast in the 1760s, one of his duties was to watch for smugglers bringing in rum from the island of St-Pierre. Smuggling continues to this day. Cook's Lookout, a hill overlooking Burin, is where Cook kept watch. Trail directions for Cook's Lookout are available at **Island Treasure Woodcrafts** (⊠ 34 Penney's Pond Rd., off Main St. ☎ 709/891–2516).

Heritage Museum, considered one of the best community museums in Newfoundland, gives you a sense of what life used to be like in this fishing community. It has a display of the 1929 tidal wave that struck Burin and the surrounding coastal communities and information on the famous gangster Al Capone, who helped raise money for the local cottage hospital and arts center when he ran rum through the Burin Peninsula during prohibition. ⊠ *Seaview Dr. off Rte. 221* ☎ *709/891–2217* ⊕ *www.schooner.nf.ca* ⊙ *Mid-May–June and early Sept.–Oct., daily 10–6; July–early Sept., daily 10–8.*

Where to Stay

¢ 🏠 **Sound of the Sea Bed and Breakfast.** The sound of waves crashing on the shore drifts into this three-story B&B to create an utterly relaxing experience. The owners restored this 70-year-old merchant's house and have decorated it with antiques from the area. One room is furnished all in antiques. The owners can help to plan the day's itinerary or arrange boat tours. ⊠ *11A Seaview Dr., A0E 1E0* ☎ *709/891–2115* ☐ *709/891–2377* ⏎ *3 rooms* ⚑ *Cable TV, laundry facilities, Internet; no-smoking* ▭ *MC, V* ⊙❙ *BP.*

Grand Bank

③ *62 km (38 mi) west of Burin.*

One of the loveliest communities in Newfoundland, Grand Bank has a fascinating history as an important fishing center. Because of trading patterns, the architecture here was influenced more by Halifax, Boston, and Bar Harbor, Maine, than by the rest of Newfoundland. A sail-shape building holds the **Provincial Seamen's Museum,** a memorial to the many Newfoundlanders who lost their lives at sea. ⊠ *54 Marine Dr.* ☎ *709/832–1484* ☑ *$2.50* ⊙ *Apr. 22–Oct. 25, daily 9:30–4:45.*

Where to Stay

¢ 🏠 **Granny's Motor Inn.** The rooms here may be small, but they're cozy and the owners friendly. The rooms are clean, with teak furnishings, carpeting, and private entrances. The location is convenient, with easy access to the ferry to St-Pierre. The town's soccer field is also nearby—take a five-minute walk after dinner to catch the most popular sport on the Burin Peninsula. ⊠ *33 Grandview Blvd., A0E 1W0* ☎ *709/832–2355 or 888/275–1098* ☐ *709/832–0009* ⏎ *10 rooms* ⚑ *Restaurant, room service, bar, laundry service, Internet* ▭ *AE, DC, MC, V.*

¢   ☒ **Thorndyke Bed and Breakfast.** This 1917 Queen Anne–style mansion, a former sea captain's house, is a designated historic structure. The blown-glass objects, colored panels, and sunporch have been part of the house since it was first built. The ferry to St-Pierre is a five-minute drive. ⊠ *33 Water St., A0E 1W0* ☎ *709/832–0820* ↩ *5 rooms* ♿ *No smoking* ▱ *V* ⊙ *Closed Oct.–Apr.* ⦿ *BP.*

St-Pierre & Miquelon

❸❷ *70-min ferry ride from Fortune, which is 10 km (6 mi) south of Grand Bank*

The islands of St-Pierre and Miquelon, France's only territory in North America, are a ferry ride away if you crave French cuisine or a bottle of perfume. Shopping and eating are both popular pastimes here. The bakeries open early, so there's always piping-hot fresh bread for breakfast. Bargain hunters can find reasonably priced wines from all over France. An interesting side trip via boat takes you to see seals, seabirds, and other wildlife, plus the huge sandbar (formed on the bones of shipwrecks) that now connects formerly separate Great and Little Miquelon. Visitors to the islands must carry proof of citizenship—even U.S. citizens must have a passport, and Canadians should have a passport or a government-issued photo ID. Because of the ferry schedule, a trip to St-Pierre means an overnight stay in a hotel or a pension, the French equivalent of a B&B. Call the **St-Pierre Tourist Board** (☎ 011/508/41–22–22 or 800/565–5118) for information about accommodations.

A passenger ferry operated by **St-Pierre Tours** (☎ 709/832–2006, 709/722–4103, or 800/563–2006) leaves Fortune (south of Grand Bank) daily from mid-June to late September; the crossing takes 90 minutes. Call for schedule and rates.

Where to Stay

$ ☒ **Hotel Robert.** Reservations for this hotel must be made through St-Pierre Tours, listed above. Packages include transportation and hotel, resulting in a much cheaper room rate. The hotel is a short walk from where the boat docks and is the most popular accommodation for tourists from Newfoundland and Labrador because of the tour packages. Gangster Al Capone stayed in a wing of the hotel when he ran rum through St-Pierre during prohibition. The rooms are spacious, but be warned that smoke lingers in the air. The owner is fluently bilingual and eager to educate tourists about St-Pierre. He gives a history of the islands, which takes place in a room off the lobby upon arrival. ⊠ *Rue du 11 Novembre, St-Pierre, 97500* ☎ *011/508/41–24–19, 709/832–2006, 709/722–4103, or 800/563–2006 reservations* 🖶 *011/508/41–28–79* ↩ *46 rooms* ♿ *Restaurant, cable TV, laundry facilities, no a/c, no room phones* ▱ *MC, V* ⦿ *CP.*

Gander

❸❸ *367 km (228 mi) north of Grand Bank.*

Gander, a busy town of 9,651 people, is notable for its aviation history. It also has many lodgings and makes a good base for travel in this part of the province. After September 11, 2001, Gander gained the attention of the world for having sheltered thousands of airline passengers whose planes were rerouted to this small town.

During World War II, **Gander International Airport** (⊠ James Blvd.) was chosen by the Canadian and U.S. air forces as a major strategic air base because of its favorable weather and secure location. After the war the airport became an international hub for civilian travel; today it's a major air-traffic control center. The **Aviation Exhibition** (☎ 709/256–6677), in the domestic passenger lounge, traces Newfoundland's role in the history of air travel and in accommodating thousands of stranded airline passengers after the September 11, 2001, terrorist attacks on the United States.

The **North Atlantic Aviation Museum** gives an expansive view of Gander's and Newfoundland's roles in aviation. In addition to viewing the expected models and photographs, you can climb into the cockpit of a real DC-3 parked outside next to a World War II Hudson bomber and a Canadian jet fighter. ⊠ *Rte. 1 between hospital and visitor information center* ☎ *709/256–2923* ⊠ *$3* ☉ *June–Sept., daily 9–9; Oct.–May, weekdays 9–5.*

From April to November, **Gander River Tours** (☎ 709/679–2271) organizes salmon-fishing and hunting trips and guided tours of the river and wilderness areas around Gander.

Where to Stay

$–$$ 🏨 **Hotel Gander.** The largest hotel in Gander has a decent dining room that serves standard Canadian fare. Children under 12 stay and eat for free. The view at this hotel on the Trans-Canada Highway is unremarkable, but rooms are spacious, modern, and clean. ⊠ *100 Trans-Canada Hwy., A1V 1P5* ☎ *709/256–3931 or 800/563–2988* 🖶 *709/ 651–2641* ⊕ *www.hotelgander.com* ⬧ *154 rooms* ⚇ *Dining room, room service, indoor pool, bar, laundry facilities, no-smoking rooms* ▭ *AE, DC, MC, V.*

¢–$$ 🏨 **Sinbad's Hotel and Suites.** Near nightclubs and restaurants, Sinbad's is popular with young couples. The hotel also has a lively bar of its own. Rooms are spacious but standard. ⊠ *Bennett Dr., A1V 1W6* ☎ *709/ 651–2678 or 800/563–8330* 🖶 *709/651–3123* ⊕ *www.sinbadshotel.nf. ca* ⬧ *103 rooms, 9 suites* ⚇ *Dining room, some kitchenettes, cable TV, gym, bar, laundry facilities, business services, no-smoking rooms* ▭ *AE, DC, MC, V.*

Boyd's Cove

④ *66 km (41 mi) north of Gander.*

Between 1650 and 1720, the Beothuks' main summer camp on the northeast coast was at the site of what is now Boyd's Cove. The coastline in and near Boyd's Cove is somewhat sheltered by Twillingate Island and New World Island. Short causeways link the shore to the islands.

The **Boyd's Cove Beothuk Interpretation Centre** offers a fresh look at the lives of the Beothuks, an extinct First Nations people who succumbed in the early 19th century to a combination of disease and battle with European settlers. The center uses traditional Beothuk building forms and adjoins an archaeological site that was inhabited from about 1650 to 1720, when pressure from settlers drove the Beothuks from this part of the coast. ⊠ *Rte. 340* ☎ *709/656–3114 or 800/563–6353* ⊕ *www. heritage.nf.ca/aboriginal/beo_boydscove.html* ⊠ *$2.50* ☉ *Mid-June–early Oct., daily 10–5:30.*

Twillingate

⑤ *31 km (19 mi) north of Boyd's Cove.*

The inhabitants of this scenic old fishing village make their living from the sea and have been doing so for nearly two centuries. Colorful houses, rocky waterfront cliffs, a local museum, and a nearby lighthouse add to the town's appeal. One of the best places on the island to see icebergs, Twillingate is known to the locals as Iceberg Alley. These majestic and dangerous mountains of ice are awe inspiring to see while they're grounded, in early summer.

Every year on the last full weekend in July, the town hosts the **Fish, Fun & Folk Festival** (☎ 709/884–2678 ⊕ www.fishfunfolkfestival.com), where fish are cooked every possible way.

Where to Stay

¢ ⊞ **Hillside Bed & Breakfast.** You can relax on the veranda and watch the sun set over the bay from this heritage home that's been in the owner's family since it was built in 1874. The rooms are bright and cozy. Handmade quilts complement a decor that is distinctly country. ⊠ *5A Young's La., A0G 4M0* ☎ *709/884–5761, 902/463–1970 off-season* ⇔ *3 rooms* ⚐ *Cable TV, laundry service; no room phones, no room TVs, no smoking* ⊟ *V* ⏐◯⏐ *BP.*

¢ ⊞ **Toulinquet Inn Bed & Breakfast.** In this 1920s-era home on the harbor front, rooms are old-fashioned, bright, and airy. Each room has two windows, and two of the rooms have views of the harbor. A second-story balcony looks out over the Atlantic Ocean. You can wind down in the living room or den and admire the antiques and original character of the heritage house. ⊠ *56 Main St., A0G 4M0* ☎ *709/884–2080* ⎙ *709/ 256–8410* ⇔ *3 rooms* ⚐ *Cable TV, laundry facilities, Internet, some pets allowed; no smoking* ⊟ *V* ⊙ *Closed Oct.–Apr.* ⏐◯⏐ *BP.*

Sports & the Outdoors

Twillingate Adventure Tours (☎ 709/884–5999 or 888/447–8687) conducts two-hour guided cruises on the M. V. *Daybreak* to see icebergs, whales, and seabirds. **Whales & Birds Inc.** (☎ 709/682–7688) offers half- and full-day excursions around the islands of Notre Dame Bay by kayak, sailboat, and powerboat, departing from Lewisporte, an hour east of Twillingate heading toward Grand Falls–Windsor. **Twillingate Island Boat Tours** (☎ 709/884–2242 or 800/611–2374) offers two-hour cruises to see whales, icebergs, and birds. Iceberg photography is the company's specialty, and there are tours that take amateur photographers out to get that perfect shot. Tours are $30–$40 per person.

Grand Falls–Windsor

36 *95 km (59 mi) west of Gander.*

This central Newfoundland town is an amalgamation of two towns that were joined in 1991. The papermaking town of Grand Falls is the quintessential company town, founded by British newspaper barons early in the 20th century. Windsor was once an important stop on the railway. The paper mill still ships newsprint all over the world, but the railway is no more.

A Logger's Life Provincial Museum. The hard lives of those who supplied wood for the paper mill are explored in this re-created 1920s-era logging camp. ⊠ *Off Rte. 1, Exit 17, 2 km (1 mi) west of Grand Falls–Windsor* ☎ *709/292–4522* ⎙ *$2.50, includes Mary March Provincial Museum* ⊙ *May 20–Sept. 27, daily 9:30–4:45.*

Mary March Provincial Museum. Mary March was the European name given to Demasduit, one of the last Beothuks. Displays trace the existence of aboriginal cultures in Newfoundland and Labrador and their lives and customs. ⊠ *16 St. Catherine's St.* ☎ *709/292–4522* ⎙ *$2.50, includes A Logger's Life Museum* ⊙ *Apr. 22–Oct. 25, daily 9:30–4:45.*

off the beaten path

CHANGE ISLANDS AND FOGO ISLAND – These islands give the impression of places frozen in time. Modernity came late to these outposts of the past, where old expressions and accents still survive. You can take a ferry (☎ 709/486–0733) from Farewell to either the Change Islands or Fogo Island. To get to Farewell from Grand Falls–Windsor, go east on the Trans-Canada Highway to get to Route 340. Take Route 340 from Grand Falls–Windsor to Route 335, which takes you through scenic coastal communities.

Hart's Bed & Breakfast (☎ 709/621–3133) is the best place to stay on the Change Islands.

Where to Stay

$$$ 🏨 **Mount Peyton Hotel.** This lodging establishment has hotel and motel rooms, apartments with kitchenettes, and a good steak house. The hotel rooms have more services than the motel rooms and have easy access to the restaurant and bar. The motel rooms are across a divided highway from the hotel, making access to the bar and restaurant tricky. ✉ *214 Lincoln Rd., A2A 1P8* ☎ *709/489–2251 or 800/563–4894* 🖷 *709/489–6365* ⊕ *www.mountpeyton.com* 🛏 *98 hotel rooms, 32 motel rooms, 16 housekeeping units, 4 suites ⓑ 2 restaurants, some kitchenettes, cable TV, bar, Internet, some pets allowed, no-smoking rooms* ⊟ *AE, DC, MC, V* ⊘ *Motel rooms closed Sept.–Mar.*

THE GREAT NORTHERN PENINSULA

The Great Northern Peninsula is the northernmost visible extension of the Appalachian Mountains. Its eastern side is rugged and sparsely populated. The Viking Trail—Route 430 and its side roads—snakes along its western coast through a national park, fjords, sand dunes, and communities that have relied on lobster fishing for generations. At the tip of the peninsula, the Vikings established the first European settlement in North America 1,000 years ago. For thousands of years before their arrival, Native peoples made this area their home, where they hunted, fished, and gathered berries and herbs.

Deer Lake

❸❼ *208 km (129 mi) west of Grand Falls–Windsor.*

Deer Lake was once just another small town on the Trans-Canada Highway, but the opening of Gros Morne National Park in the early '70s and the construction of a first-class paved highway passing right through to St. Anthony changed all that. Today, with an airport and car rentals available, Deer Lake is a good starting point for a fly-drive vacation.

ⓒ The **Newfoundland Insectarium** holds an intriguing collection of live and preserved insects, spiders, scorpions, and the like. A big attraction is the greenhouse, with live tropical butterflies. It's in a suburb of Deer Lake. ✉ *Rte. 430, Reidville* ☎ *709/635–4545* ⊕ *www.nfinsectarium.com* 🎟 *$6.50* ⊘ *Mid-Apr.–June and Sept.–mid-Oct., Tues.–Fri. 9–5 and weekends 10–5; July and Aug., daily 9–9.*

Where to Stay

$–$$ 🏨 **Deer Lake Motel.** The motel is clean and comfortable, but it's best to request a room in the back as the front rooms face the highway and can be noisy. ✉ *15 Trans-Canada Hwy., A8A 2E5* ☎ *709/635–2108, 800/563–2144 in Newfoundland* 🖷 *709/635–3842* ⊕ *www.deerlakemotel.com* 🛏 *54 rooms, 2 suites ⓑ Coffee shop, dining room, room service, cable TV, bar, no-smoking rooms* ⊟ *AE, MC, V.*

Gros Morne National Park

③⑧   *46 km (29 mi) north of Deer Lake on Rte. 430.*

FodorsChoice
★

Because of its geological uniqueness and immense splendor, this park has been named a UNESCO World Heritage Site. Among the more breathtaking visions are the expanses of wild orchids in springtime. Camping and hiking are popular recreations, and boat tours are available. To see Gros Morne properly, you should allow yourself at least two days. An excellent **interpretation center** (✉ Rocky Harbour ☎ 709/458–2417) has displays and videos about the park. Scenic **Bonne Bay**, a deep, mountainous fjord, divides the park in two. You can drive around the perimeter of the fjord on Route 430 going north.

Woody Point, a charming community of old houses and imported Lombardy poplars, is in the south of the park, on Route 431. The **Tablelands,** rising behind Norris Point, is a unique rock massif that was raised from the earth's mantle through tectonic upheaval. Its rocks are toxic to most plant life, and Ice Age conditions linger in the form of persistent snow and moving rock glaciers. The **Discovery Centre** (✉ Rte. 431 on the outskirts of Woody Point heading west toward Trout River ☎ 709/458–2417) is the main interpretation center for the park and has educational programs on the park's geology and natural history. The small community of **Trout River** is at the western end of Route 431 on the Gulf of St. Lawrence. You pass the scenic **Trout River pond** along the way. The **Green Gardens Trail,** a spectacular hike, is also nearby, but be prepared to do a bit of climbing on your return journey. The trail passes through the Tablelands barrens and descends sharply to a coastline of eroded cliffs and green meadows. Head to the northern side of the park, along coastal Route 430, to visit **Rocky Harbour** with its range of restaurants, lodgings, and a luxurious indoor public pool and large hot tub—the perfect place to soothe tired limbs after a strenuous day.

The most popular attraction in the northern portion of Gros Morne is the boat tour of **Western Brook pond.** You park at a lot on Route 430 and take a 45-minute walk to the boat dock through an interesting mix of bog and woods. Cliffs rise 2,000 feet on both sides of the gorge, and high waterfalls tumble over ancient rocks. Hikers in good shape can tackle the 16-km (10-mi) hike up **Gros Morne Mountain,** at 2,644 feet the second-highest peak in Newfoundland. Weather permitting, the reward for your effort is a unique arctic landscape and spectacular views. The park's **northern coast** has an unusual mix of sand beaches, rock pools, and trails through tangled dwarf forests (which locally are called tuckamore forests). Sunsets seen from **Lobster Cove Head Lighthouse** are spectacular. Keep an eye out for whales, and visit the lighthouse museum, devoted to the history of the area. ✉ *Viking Trail (Rte. 430) from Deer Lake* ☎ *709/458–2417* 🖷 *709/458–2059* ⊕ *www.pc.gc.ca* 🖙 *$7.50* ◷ *Mid-May–mid-June and Sept.–mid-Oct., daily 9–5; mid-June–Aug., Mon., Tues., and Thurs.–Sat. 9–6, Wed. and Sun. 9–9.*

Where to Stay & Eat

$$ ✕ **Fisherman's Landing.** The food is good here and ranges from seafood dishes (in season) to standard Canadian fare like club and hot turkey sandwiches or pork chops and steak. ✉ *Main St., Rocky Harbour* ☎ *709/458–2060* ▭ *AE, MC, V.*

$–$$ ✕ **Seaside Restaurant.** This restaurant overlooking the ocean prepares fresh seafood in traditional Newfoundland style. Try scallops and shrimp sautéed or in a stir-fry, or choose from a wide selection of seafood dinners including salmon, catfish, and cod tongue. ✉ *Main St., Trout River* ☎ *709/451–3461* ▭ *MC, V* ◷ *Closed Nov.–late May.*

$$–$$$ 🏨 **Fisherman's Landing Inn** This resort has two arms of rooms reaching from either side of the main complex. The rooms are spacious and bright and have private outside entrances. They're set up like modern hotel rooms, with a country charm. The coffee shop–bar is the nerve center, where you can get three meals a day and linger for a few drinks. ⊠ *Box 124, West Link Rd. off Rte. 430, Rocky Harbour A0K 4N0* 🕾 *709/458–2711, 866/458–2711 toll-free* 🖷 *709/458–2168* ⊕ *www. fishermans-landing.com* ⇌ *20 rooms* ☼ *Coffee shop, room service, in-room data ports, cable TV, outdoor hot tub, bar, shop, laundry facilities; no smoking* ☰ *AE, DC, MC, V.*

$$–$$$ 🏨 **Gros Morne Resort.** Rooms in the front of this hotel overlook the ocean; those in the rear face the Long Range mountains and St. Pauls Inlet. The rooms are spacious and have private balconies or patios. Some suites have whirlpool tubs. Guests can choose from a restaurant serving traditional meals or fine dining. The resort is in St. Pauls, a small community encircled by Gros Morne Park. ⊠ *Box 100, Rte. 430, St. Pauls A0K 4Y0* 🕾 *709/243–2606 or 888/243–2644* 🖷 *709/243–2615* ⇌ *8 rooms, 12 suites* ☼ *2 restaurants, some minibars, hair salon, bar* ☰ *AE, DC, MC, V.*

$–$$$ 🏨 **Sugar Hill Inn.** Host Vince McCarthy's culinary talents and educated palate have earned this inn a reputation for fine wining and dining. There's only one sitting, at 7:30, for the three-course meal in the dining room. Afterward sit back under the vaulted cedar ceiling of the common, or relax in the cedar-lined hot-rub room with attached sauna. A stay here is hospitable and a delight. ⊠ *Box 100, 115–129 Sexton Rd., Norris Point A0K 3V0* 🕾 *709/458–2147 or 888/299–2147* 🖷 *709/458–2166* ⊕ *www.sugarhillinn.nf.ca* ⇌ *3 rooms, 3 suites* ☼ *Dining room, room service, cable TV, hot tub, sauna, laundry facilities; no smoking* ☰ *AE, MC, V* ☉ *Closed Nov.–mid-Jan.*

$–$$ 🏨 **Gros Morne Cabins.** These modern log chalets, which overlook the Gulf of St. Lawrence, are near restaurants and stores in Rocky Harbour. Cabins have hardwood floors, log walls, and a tremendous ocean view. They can accommodate up to four people. ⊠ *Main St., Rocky Harbour A0K 4N0* 🕾 *709/458–2020 or 888/603–2020* 🖷 *709/458–2882* ⇌ *22 cabins* ☼ *Grocery, fans, kitchens, cable TV, playground, laundry facilities* ☰ *AE, DC, MC, V.*

$–$$ 🏨 **Ocean View Motel.** This large two-story motel is right on the water and has an on-site kiosk for Bon Tours, which conducts sightseeing boat trips on Western Brook pond and Bonne Bay. A pub on the premises features a house band. The brightly decorated standard rooms are clean; the rooms at the front of the building have water views. ⊠ *Box 129, Main St., Rocky Harbour A0K 4N0* 🕾 *709/458–2730 or 800/563–9887* 🖷 *709/458–2841* ⊕ *www.oceanviewmotel.com* ⇌ *48 rooms, 4 suites* ☼ *Dining room, cable TV, pub, no-smoking rooms* ☰ *AE, DC, MC, V.*

$ 🏨 **Frontier Cottages.** These rustic log cabins can hold up to six people and are ideal if you wish to do your own cooking while visiting Gros Morne. The cabins are close together, but the view of the hills from the deck is spectacular, and the cabins are clean, spacious, and private. The grocery store, which has a pay phone for guests' use, stocks most items, but for greater variety pick up your staples at a larger store beforehand. ⊠ *Box 172, Rte. 430, Wiltondale A0K 4N0* 🕾 *709/453–7266 or 800/ 668–2520* 🖷 *709/453–7272* ⇌ *6 cabins* ☼ *Restaurant, grocery, fans, kitchens, cable TV, miniature golf, snowmobiling, playground, laundry facilities; no a/c, no room phones* ☰ *AE, DC, MC, V.*

$ 🏨 **Shallow Bay Motel and Cabins.** Near the northern boundary of the park, Shallow Bay has standard motel rooms and spacious rustic cottages. The theater on-site hosts the Gros Morne Theatre Festival's comedic dinner theater productions from June to September. ⊠ *Main St., Cow Head*

A0K 2A0 ☎ *709/243–2471 or 800/563–1946* 🖷 *709/243–2816* ⊕ *www. shallowbaymotel.com* 💬 *38 rooms, 17 cottages* ⚐ *Restaurant, cable TV in some rooms, miniature golf, pool, sauna, lounge, shop, laundry facilities* ▭ *AE, DC, MC, V.*

¢–$ 🖭 **Crocker Cabins.** These spacious two-bedroom cabins with two double beds are in Trout River in the quieter, less-developed southern part of Gros Morne National Park. They're in a wooded area between the boundary of the community and the park. Each building contains two cabins, which share a common deck. Rooms are standard, clean, and can accommodate up to four people. ✉ *57 Duke St., Trout River A0K 5P0* 🖳 *709/451–3236* 💬 *4 cabins* ⚐ *Cable TV, fishing, playground, laundry facilities, some pets allowed; no a/c, no room phones, no room TVs* ▭ *AE, MC, V.*

¢–$ 🖭 **Victorian Manor Heritage Properties.** At this property you have a choice of three lodgings. Jane's Place has three B&B rooms in a beautiful historic house overlooking Bonne Bay. At Uncle Steve's you can rent the entire neighboring three-bedroom guest house—or just one room. Steve's has beamed ceilings and the traditional small staircase and is painted in historic colors. Victorian Manor has three suites, one with a whirlpool tub. Your choice depends on whether you're looking for privacy and to cook your own meals, or for the social contact of a B&B. All three properties have been lovingly restored to preserve the architectural integrity of the old homes. ✉ *Box 165, Woody Point A0K 1P0* 🖳 *709/ 453–2485* ⊕ *www.grosmorne.com/victorianmanor* 💬 *3 rooms, 3 suites, 1 3-bedroom house* ⚐ *Cable TV in some rooms, laundry facilities, no-smoking rooms* ▭ *AE, MC, V.*

¢–$ 🖭 **Blanchard House.** Built in 1904, this heritage home has since been renovated but has retained its original character, accented by antique furniture. ✉ *12 Blanchard La., Woody Point A0K 1P0* ☎ *709/451–3236 or 877/451–3236* 💬 *4 rooms* ⚐ *Laundry facilities; no room TVs, no smoking* ▭ *AE, MC, V* ⦿ *CP.*

⚠ **Parks Canada at Gros Morne.** To make reservations at Gros Morne campgrounds, contact Parks Canada. ☎ *800/414–6765.* **Berry Hill Campground** (✉ Rte. 430 ☎ 800/563–6353) in the forest 4 km (2½ mi) north of Gros Morne National Park, has 152 sites and fire pits, kitchen shelters, flush toilets, a dump station, hot showers, and playgrounds. Close to the ocean, the **Green Point Campground** (✉ Rte. 430, 10 km [6 mi] north of Rocky Harbour ☎ 800/563–6353) has 31 sites, fire pits, and kitchen shelters, but no showers. It's the only campground that operates on a first-come, first-served basis.

Surrounded by trees and in view of Bonne Bay and the Long Range Mountains, **Lomond Campground** (✉ Rte. 431 ☎ 800/563–6353) has 29 sites, fire pits, kitchen shelters, flush toilets, a dump station, hot showers, and a playground. **Shallow Bay Campground** (✉ Off Rte. 430, 52 km [32 mi] north of Rocky Harbour, near Cow Head ☎ 800/563–6353), in the northern part of the park, is sheltered from the ocean by sand dunes and trees. It has 62 sites, kitchen shelters, fire pits, flush toilets, a dump station, hot showers, a playground, and a huge sandy beach.

Trout River Campground (✉ Trout River ☎ 800/563–6353) has 44 sites, fire pits, kitchen shelters, flush toilets, hot showers, a playground, and a beach nearby.

Nightlife & the Arts

The **Gros Morne Theatre Festival** (☎ 709/243–2899) provides summer entertainment in Cow Head and other venues throughout the park. Most productions are comedies, though there are some dramas based on local stories, plus an outdoor children's show.

Sports & the Outdoors

Bon Tours (☎ 709/458–2730 or 800/563–9887 ⊕ www.oceanviewmotel. com) runs sightseeing boat tours of Western Brook pond in Gros Morne National Park and on Bonne Bay and Seal Island. **Gros Morne Adventures** (☎ 709/458–2722 or 800/685–4624 ⊕ www.grosmorneadventures. com) has sea kayaking up the fjords and landlocked ponds of Gros Morne National Park, as well as a variety of hikes and adventures in the area. **Tableland Boat Tours** (☎ 709/451–2101) leads tours on Trout River pond near the southern boundary of Gros Morne National Park.

Arches Provincial Park

39 *20 km (12 mi) north of Gros Morne National Park.*

Arches Provincial Park is a geological curiosity: its rock formations were made millions of years ago by wave action and undersea currents. The succession of caves through a bed of dolomite was later raised above sea level by tectonic upheaval. ⊠ *Rte. 430* ☎ *800/563–6353* ⊕ *www. gov.nl.ca/parks&reserves* ☒ *Free* ⊙ *Mid-June–mid-Sept.*

en route Continuing north on Route 430, parallel to the Gulf of St. Lawrence, you find yourself refreshingly close to the ocean and the wave-tossed beaches. The **Long Range Mountains,** to your right, reminded Jacques Cartier, who saw them in 1534 as he was exploring the area on behalf of France, of the long, rectangular-shape farm buildings of his home village in France. Small villages are interspersed with rivers where salmon and trout grow to be "liar size." Remains of Maritime Archaic and Dorset peoples have been found in abundance along this coast, and **Port au Choix National Historic Site** has an interesting interpretation center on them. An archaeological dig also has discovered an ancient village. Ask at the interpretation center for directions to the site of the dig. ⊠ *Off Rte. 430* ☎ *709/458–2417, 709/861–3522 mid-June–Aug.* ⊕ *www.pc.gc.ca* ☒ *$3.50* ⊙ *Early June and Sept.–mid. Oct., daily 9–5; mid-June–Aug., daily 9–8.*

L'Anse aux Meadows National Historic Site

40 *210 km (130 mi) northeast of Arches Provincial Park.*

Fodor'sChoice ★ Around the year AD 1000, Vikings from Greenland and Iceland founded the first European settlement in North America near the northern tip of Newfoundland. They arrived in the New World 500 years before Columbus but stayed only a few years and were forgotten for centuries. It was only in 1960 that the Norwegian team of Helge and Anne Stine Ingstad discovered the remains of the Viking settlement's long sod huts. Today L'Anse aux Meadows is a UNESCO World Heritage Site. Parks Canada has a fine visitor center and has reconstructed some of the huts to give you a sense of centuries past. An interpretation program introduces you to the food, games, and way of life of that long-ago time. ⊠ *Rte. 436* ☎ *709/623–2608 or 709/458–2417* ☒ *709/623–2028 summer only* ⊕ *www.pc.gc.ca* ☒ *$7* ⊙ *Mid-May–mid-June, daily 9–5; mid-June–early Sept., daily 9–8; early Sept.–mid-Oct., daily 9–5.*

Two kilometers (1 mile) east of L'Anse aux Meadows is a Viking attraction, **Norstead.** This reconstruction of an 11th-century Viking port has a chieftain's hall, church, and ax-throwing arena. Much of the site is aimed at kids, but the Viking boatbuilding course is designed for all ages. Interpreters in period dress can answer questions as they go about their Viking business. ⊠ *Rte. 436* ☎ *709/454–8888* ☒ *$7* ⊙ *Early June–late Sept., daily 10–6.*

Where to Stay & Eat

$–$$ ✕ **Norseman Restaurant.** This restaurant on the harbor front allows you
Fodor'sChoice   to pick your own lobster from a crate. An extensive wine list accom-
★   panies a menu ranging from seafood and pasta to caribou tenderloins
and butternut squash soup. There's a dinner theater performance every
Tuesday and Friday in July and August. ⊠ *Turn right at end of Rte. 436,
L'Anse aux Meadows* ☎ 877/623–2018 ⊟ *DC, MC, V.*

¢–$ ✕ **Smith's Restaurant.** Don't let the modest facade and roadside location
of Smith's Restaurant fool you—inside, huge windows frame a magnificent
view of a shallow harbor protected by an island dotted with grazing sheep,
with seabirds circling overhead. The food's not bad, either. Try the
Mediterranean chowder, halibut, or cod and walk it off with a stroll on
the deck. The attached store sells crafts and books. ⊠ *Rte. 436, St. Lunaire–Griquet* ☎ 709/623–2431 ⊟ *AE, DC, MC, V.*

¢–$ 🛏 **Valhalla Lodge Bed & Breakfast.** On a hill overlooking the ocean, the
Fodor'sChoice   Valhalla is 8 km (5 mi) from L'Anse aux Meadows. Some fossils are part
★   of the rock fireplace in the common room. The owner quickly becomes
known by her guests for her pancakes with local berry sauce. Rooms
are quiet and brightly painted, with large windows and handmade
quilts. The rooms all have Viking names. E. Annie Proulx, author of *The
Shipping News*, stayed here while writing the novel. ⊠ *Gunner's Cove,
St. Lunaire–Griquet A0K 2X0* ☎ 709/623–2018 *or* 877/623–2018
mid-May–Sept., 709/896–5476 *Oct–mid-May* 🖷709/623–2144 ⊕*www.
valhalla-lodge.com* 🛏 *5 rooms* ⟂ *Dining room, sauna; no TV in some
rooms, no smoking* ⊟ *MC, V* ⊙❘ *BP.*

¢   🛏 **Southwest Pond Cabins.** These basic cabins are a 10-minute drive
from L'Anse aux Meadows. There are two cabins under one roof, but
the units are totally self-contained and private. The cabins have log ex-
teriors, with spacious, bright, and clean interiors. ⊠ *Box 58, Rte. 436,
St. Lunaire–Griquet A0K 2X0* ☎ 709/623–2140 *or* 800/515–2261
🖷 709/623–2145 🛏 *8 cabins* ⟂ *Grocery, fans, cable TV, playground,
laundry facilities* ⊟ *AE, DC, MC, V* ⊙ *Closed Nov.–mid-May.*

¢   ✕🛏 **Tickle Inn at Cape Onion.** This refurbished, century-old fisherman's
house on the beach is probably the northernmost residence on the island of Newfoundland. Relax by the Franklin stove in the parlor after
exploring the coast or L'Anse aux Meadows (about 45 km [28 mi] away).
The kitchen serves seafood, baked goods, and homemade jams. ⊠ *Box
62, R.R. 1, Cape Onion A0K 4J0* ☎ 709/452–4321, 866/814–8567
June–Sept., 709/739–5503 *Oct.–May* ⊕ *www.tickleinn.net* 🛏 *4 rooms
without bath* ⟂ *Dining room, no-smoking room* ⊟ *MC, V* ⊙❘ *CP.*

¢   🛏 **Viking Nest/Viking Village Bed & Breakfast.** Each of the four rooms at
the Viking Nest is named after a famous person or boat from Viking
legends or history. Only one of the rooms has a private bathroom. The
Viking Village is a five-room inn on the same property, with patio doors
opening onto a fenced patio. Rooms at the Viking Village have spruce
walls and Scandinavian furniture. Room phones are available only by
request. The Viking settlement at L'Anse aux Meadows is 1 km (½ mi)
away. ⊡ *Box 127, Hay Cove A0K 2X0* ☎ 877/858–2238 🖷🖷 709/
623–2238 🛏 *9 rooms, 6 with bath* ⟂ *2 dining rooms; no room TVs,
no room phones* ⊟ *MC, V* ⊙❘ *BP.*

St. Anthony

④   *16 km (10 mi) south of L'Anse aux Meadows.*

The northern part of the Great Northern Peninsula served as the setting for *The Shipping News*, E. Annie Proulx's Pulitzer prize–winning
novel. St. Anthony is built around a natural harbor on the eastern side

of the Great Northern Peninsula, near its tip. If you take a trip out to the lighthouse, you may see an iceberg or two floating by.

The **Grenfell Mission** was founded by Sir Wilfred Grenfell, a British medical missionary who established nursing stations and cooperatives and provided medical services to the scattered villages of northern Newfoundland and the south coast of Labrador in the early 1900s. It remains the town's chief employer. The main foyer of the **Charles S. Curtis Memorial Hospital** (⊠ 178–200 West St. ☎ 709/454–4010) has a decorative tile mural depicting scenes from the life of Grenfell.

The **Grenfell Historic Properties** comprise a museum, house, and interpretation center, all focusing on Dr. Grenfell's life and work. ⊠ *West St.* ☎ *709/454–4010* ⊕ *www.grenfell-properties.com* ✉ *$5* ☉ *May 1–Sept. 30, daily 9–8.*

Where to Stay & Eat

$ ✕ **Light Keeper's Cafe.** Good seafood and solid Canadian fare are served in this former lighthouse keeper's home overlooking the ocean. Halibut, shrimp, and cod are usually good bets. ⊠ *Fishing Point Rd.* ☎ *709/454–4900* ▭ *MC, V* ☉ *Closed Oct.–Apr.*

$–$$ 🏨 **Tuckamore Country Inn.** The Scandinavian-style lodges of the Tuckamore Country Inn provide a comfortable base from which to explore the wilderness of the area. Adventure packages include sea kayaking, wilderness viewing, and snowmobiling. The inn is about an hour from St. Anthony. ⊠ *Box 100, 1 Southwest Pond Rd., Main Brook A0K 3N0* ☎ *709/865–6361 or 888/865–6361* ☎ *709/865–2112* ⊕ *www.tuckamore-lodge.nf.net* ✏ *5 rooms, 3 suites* ♿ *Sauna, laundry service, airport shuttle; no smoking* ▭ *AE, DC, MC, V.*

$ 🏨 **Vinland Motel.** These are standard rooms, but the motel is in the center of town, so what it lacks in a view, it makes up for in convenience. Two rooms and the suite have whirlpool baths. Rooms are clean, and the staff is friendly and helpful. ⊠ *19 West St., A0K 4S0* ☎ *709/454–8843 or 800/563–7578* ☎ *709/454–8468* ✏ *43 rooms, 1 suite* ♿ *Restaurant, cable TV, gym, sauna, bar, laundry facilities, meeting rooms* ▭ *AE, DC, MC, V.*

Sports & the Outdoors

Northland Discovery Boat Tours (⊠ Behind Grenfell Interpretation Centre off West St. ☎ 709/454–3092 or 877/632–3747 ⊕ www.discovernorthland.com) leads specialized trips to see whales, icebergs, and seabirds, as well as salmon-fishing excursions.

Shopping

Be sure to visit **Grenfell Handicrafts** (⊠ 227A West St. ☎ 709/454–4010) in the Grenfell Historic Properties complex. Training villagers to become self-sufficient in a harsh environment was one of Grenfell's aims. A windproof cloth that villagers turned into well-made parkas came to be known as Grenfell cloth. Mittens, caps, and coats are embroidered with motifs such as polar bears; the selection of items for sale is extensive.

THE WEST COAST

Western Newfoundland is known for the unlikely combination of world-class Atlantic salmon fishing and papermaking at two newsprint mills. This area includes Corner Brook, a major center. To the south, the Port au Port Peninsula west of Stephenville shows the French influence in Newfoundland; the farming valleys of the southwest were settled by Scots. A ferry from Nova Scotia docks at Port aux Basques in the far southwest corner.

Corner Brook

㊷ *50 km (31 mi) southwest of Deer Lake.*

Newfoundland's second-largest city, Corner Brook is the hub of the island's west coast. Mountains fringe three sides of the city, which has beautiful views of the harbor and the Bay of Islands. The town is also home to one of the largest paper mills in the world (you'll probably smell it while you're here). Captain James Cook, the British explorer, charted the coast in the 1760s, and a memorial to him overlooks the bay.

Corner Brook is a convenient hub and point of departure for exploring the west coast. It's only a three-hour drive (allowing for traffic) from the Port aux Basques ferry from Nova Scotia. The town enjoys more clearly defined seasons than most of the rest of the island, and in summer it has many pretty gardens. The nearby Humber River is the best-known salmon river in the province.

The north and south shores of the Bay of Islands have fine paved roads—Route 440 on the north shore and Route 450 on the south—and both are a scenic half-day drive from Corner Brook. On both roads, farming and fishing communities exist side by side.

Where to Stay & Eat

★ $$–$$$ ✕ **13 West.** Start your meal off with oysters and chase them down with one of the wonderful salmon specials: strawberry salmon, mango salmon, blackened salmon, or salmon with rosemary and peppercorns. For those not interested in seafood, the rack of lamb and pork tenderloin are good choices. ✉ *13 West St.* ☎ *709/634–1300* ▭ *AE, MC, V.*

★ $–$$ ✕▥ **Glynmill Inn.** This Tudor-style inn was once the staff house for the visiting top brass of the paper mill. Rooms are cozy, and the dining room serves basic and well-prepared Newfoundland seafood, soups, and specialty desserts. There's also a popular steak house ($$–$$$) in the basement. ✉ *Box 550, 1B Cobb La., A2H 6E6* ☎ *709/634–5181, 800/563–4400 in Canada* 🖶 *709/634–5106* ⊕ *www.glynmillinn.ca* ⤢ *58 rooms, 23 suites* ⚬ *2 restaurants, cable TV, bar, meeting rooms, no-smoking rooms* ▭ *AE, DC, MC, V.*

$ ✕▥ **Mamateek Inn.** The restaurant (¢–$$$) here is well known for its exquisite view of the city and serves a wide selection of cuisines from Tex-Mex and seafood to chicken and steak. The sunsets are remarkable, so get a table close to the window. Rooms are standard, bright, and clean, but it's the panoramic view of the city and the Bay of Islands that is the selling point for this hotel. ✉ *Box 787, Maple Valley Rd., A2H 6G7* ☎ *709/639–8901 or 800/563–8600* 🖶 *709/639–7567* ⊕ *www.mamateekinn.com/default.asp* ⤢ *55 rooms* ⚬ *Restaurant, in-room data ports, bar, business services, meeting rooms, no-smoking rooms* ▭ *AE, DC, MC, V.*

$$–$$$$ ▥ **Strawberry Hill Resort.** Once an exclusive retreat for the owner of the Corner Brook Mill, this resort has Newfoundland's finest salmon fishing, hiking, skiing, and snowmobiling. At the end of the day you can relax in the hot tub or sauna and retire to your room or chalet. Some rooms have fireplaces and sitting areas. Chalets, which sleep up to seven, have all the conveniences of home, with washers and dryers, kitchens, several bedrooms, and full-size living rooms. The resort has boat, helicopter, and snowmobile tours of the area, plus guided fishing, sea kayaking, hiking, and spelunking trips. ✉ *Box 2200, Rte. 1 Little Rapids A2H 2N2, 12 km (7 mi) east of Corner Brook* ☎ *709/634–0066 or 877/434–0066* 🖶 *709/639–7604* ⊕ *www.strawberryhill.net* ⤢ *6 rooms, 8 chalets* ⚬ *Restaurant, some kitchens, cable TV, hot tub, sauna, dock, boating, fishing, hiking, horseshoes, cross-country skiing, snow-*

mobiling, library, business services, meeting room; no smoking ☰ *AE, D, DC, MC, V* ⊚ *CP.*

Sports & the Outdoors

The growing **Marble Mountain Resort** (⊠ Rte. 1, Steady Brook, 5 km [3 mi] east of Corner Brook ☎ 709/637–7600 or 888/462–7253 ⊕ www.skimarble.com) has 34 downhill runs and four lifts capable of moving 6,500 skiers an hour, as well as a large day lodge, ski shop, day-care center, and restaurant. The vertical drop is 1,700 feet. A full-day lift ticket is $42.

Stephenville

43 *77 km (48 mi) south of Corner Brook.*

The former Harmon Air Force Base is in Stephenville, a town best known for its summer festival. Stephenville is the only airstrip in Canada able to land the space shuttle. It also has a large, modern paper mill. To the west of town is the Port au Port Peninsula, which was largely settled by the French, who brought their way of life and language to this small corner of Newfoundland.

The **Stephenville Theatre Festival** (☎ 709/643–4982 ⊕ www.stf.ca), held from mid-July to mid-August, is the province's major annual summer theatrical event, with a mix of light musicals and serious drama.

> **en route** As you travel down the Trans-Canada Highway toward Port aux Basques, Routes 404, 405, 406, and 407 bring you into the small Scottish communities of the **Codroy Valley.** Some of the most productive farms in the province are nestled in the valley against the backdrop of the Long Range Mountains and the Lewis Hills, from which gales strong enough to stop traffic hurtle down to the coast. Winds in the area known as Wreckhouse have overturned tractor trailers. The Codroy Valley is great for bird-watching, while the Grand Codroy River is ideal for kayaking. Walking trails, a golf course, and mountain hikes make the area an appealing stop for nature lovers.

Port aux Basques

▶ **44** *166 km (103 mi) south of Stephenville.*

Port aux Basques was one of seven Basque ports along Newfoundland's west coast and in southern Labrador during the 1500s and early 1600s and was given its name by the town's French successors. It's now the main ferry port connecting the island to Nova Scotia. In J. T. Cheeseman Provincial Park, 15 km (9 mi) north of town on the Trans-Canada Highway, and at Grand Bay West you may see the endangered piping plover, which nests in the sand dunes along this coast.

Where to Stay

$–$$ ⊞ **Hotel Port aux Basques.** There's nothing special about the rooms here, but this is a good choice for families since children stay free. The food in the restaurant is good, with a choice of local dishes and seafood. This modern hotel is closer to the ferry than any other in town. Suites have whirlpool baths. ⊠ *1 Grand Bay Rd., A0M 1C0* ☎ *709/695–2171 or 877/695–2171* 🖷 *709/695–2250* ⊕ *www.hotelpab.com* ⊅ *50 rooms, 3 suites* ⊖ *Restaurant, room service, some kitchenettes, cable TV, bar, Internet, meeting rooms, some pets allowed (fee), no-smoking rooms* ☰ *AE, DC, MC, V.*

$ ⊞ **St. Christopher's Hotel.** This clean, comfortable two-story hotel has quiet rooms and good food. Minutes from the ferry, the rooms are bright and modern, with heavy curtains to keep out the light if desired. The suites are spacious, with hardwood flooring and fireplaces. ⊠ *Box 2049, Caribou Rd., A0M 1C0* ☎ *709/695–7034 or 800/563–4779* 🖷 *709/695–9841* ⊕ *www.stchrishotel.nf.net* ⇨ *52 rooms, 3 suites* ⚐ *Restaurant, cable TV, bar, playground, laundry facilities, meeting rooms, no-smoking rooms* ⊟ *AE, DC, MC, V.*

¢ 🛏 **Caribou Bed and Breakfast.** The Caribou tends to be a quiet B&B because most people have an early breakfast before catching the nearby ferry. The rooms are small and plain. Three rooms have a double and a single bed. ⊠ *42 Grand Bay Rd., A0N 1K0* ☎ *709/695–3408* ⊕ *home. thezone.net/~gibbons* ⇨ *5 rooms, 3 with bath* ⚐ *No room phones, no room TVs, no smoking* ⊟ *MC, V* ⊗ *Closed Nov.–Apr.* †◎† *CP.*

THE STRAITS

The Straits in southeastern Labrador were a rich hunting-and-gathering ground for the area's earliest peoples, the Maritime Archaic tribes. The oldest industrial site in the New World is here—the 16th-century Basque whaling station at Red Bay.

L'Anse au Clair

45 *5 km (3 mi) from Blanc Sablon, Québec (ferry from St. Barbe, Newfoundland docks in Blanc Sablon).*

In L'Anse au Clair—French for "clear water cove"—anglers can try their luck for trout and salmon on the scenic Forteau and Pinware rivers. The French place-name dates from the early 1700s, when this area was settled by French speakers from Québec. Ask at the local museum for directions to the Doctor's Path, sno named because it was here in the 19th century that the local doctor searched out herbs and medicinal plants.

Where to Stay

$ 🛏 **Northern Light Inn.** Loads of bus-tour passengers make this a stop in summer because the Northern Light is the only accommodation of any size along Route 510. The hotel is pretty ordinary, but breakfasts, lunches, and dinners are decent, the rooms spacious, and the furnishings of good quality. ⊠ *58 Main St. (Rte. 510), A0K 3K0* ☎ *709/931–2332 or 800/563–3188* 🖷 *709/931–2708* ⇨ *49 rooms, 10 suites* ⚐ *Restaurant, some kitchenettes, cable TV, bar, shop, laundry facilities, meeting rooms* ⊟ *AE, DC, MC, V.*

L'Anse Amour

46 *19 km (12 mi) east of L'Anse au Clair.*

The elaborate **Maritime Archaic Indian burial site** (⊠ *Rte. 510*) discovered near L'Anse Amour is 7,500 years old. A plaque marks a site that is the oldest-known aboriginal funeral monument in North America. Constructed in 1857, the **L'Anse Amour Lighthouse,** at 109 feet tall, is the second-tallest lighthouse in Canada. Interpreters in period costume tell the story of the lighthouse and the history of southern Labrador. You can climb to the top. ☎ *709/931–2013* ⊒ *$2.50* ⊗ *Mid-June–early Oct., daily 10–5:30.*

⌜en route⌝ The **Labrador Straits Museum and Craft Store** has exhibits themed *150 years on the Labrador* and explores women's roles in Labrador Straits history. ⊠ *Rte. 510, between Forteau and L'Anse au Loup* ☎ *709/931–2067 mid-June–mid-May, 709/927–5237 mid-Sept.–mid-June* ⊒ *$2* ⊗ *June 15–Sept. 15, Mon.–Sat. 9–5:30.*

Red Bay

⚑ **47** *35 km (22 mi) northeast of L'Anse Amour.*

The area's main attraction lies at the very end of Route 510: Red Bay, the site of a 16th-century Basque whaling station and a National Historic Site. Basque whalers began harpooning migrating whales from flimsy boats in frigid waters a few years after Cabot's discovery of the coast in 1497. Between 1550 and 1600 Red Bay was the world's whaling capital. The **Red Bay National Historic Site** has a visitor center that interprets the Basque heritage with film and artifacts. A boat takes you on a five-minute journey to the excavation site on Saddle Island. ⊠ *Rte. 510* ☎ *709/920–2051* ⊕ *www.pc.gc.ca* 💷 *$3.50* 🕓 *Mid–late June and Sept.–mid-Oct., daily 9–5; July and Aug., daily 9–8.*

★

COASTAL LABRADOR

Along the southern coast, most villages are inhabited by descendants of Europeans, whereas farther north they are mostly Inuit and Innu. Over the years the European settlers have adopted Native skills and survival strategies, and the Native peoples have adopted many European technologies. In summer the ice retreats and a coastal steamer delivers goods, but in winter small airplanes and snowmobiles are the only ways in and out. To get to the south coast of Labrador, you can catch the ferry at St. Barbe on Route 430 in Newfoundland to Blanc Sablon, Québec. From here you can drive to Mary's Harbour, and on to Cartwright, along Route 510. **Newfoundland and Labrador Tourism** (☎ 800/563–6353) has information about ferry schedules. A coastal boat takes passengers into a number of small communities. For information and schedules, call **Coastal Labrador Marine Services** (☎ 866/535–2567) or visit the government Web site at www.gov.nl.ca/ferryservices. **Coastal Cruising Adventures** (☎ 709/454–8888 or 877/778–4546 ⊕ www.vikingtrail.org), operated by the Viking Trail Tourism Association, offers a way to see the Northern Peninsula and Labrador on board the expedition-style cruise vessel, the *Atlantis*, a 190-foot, three-mast vessel with three passenger decks and 18 self-contained cabins with air-conditioning and private washroom and shower facilities. On board are a bar, dining room, and professional guides. Packaged itineraries can be tailored, depending on whether you want to explore the bays and visit the major attractions and isolated fishing communities or to hike, cycle, or kayak to remote locations.

Battle Harbour National Historic Site

★ **48** *12 km (7 mi) by boat from Mary's Harbour.*

This island site has the only remaining intact outport fishing merchant's premises in the province. Settled in the 18th century, Battle Harbour was the main fishing port in Labrador and the economic and social center of the southern Labrador coast until the first half of the 20th century. After fires destroyed some of the community, the people moved to nearby Mary's Harbour. The Battle Harbour Historic Trust has restored the community to its former glory with historic structures and artifacts. The oldest Anglican church in Labrador is also at this site. You can stay overnight on the island at accommodations that range from individual cottages to a hostel-type bunkhouse. Information is available from the **Battle Harbour Historic Trust** (☎ 709/921–6677 ⊕ www.southeastern-labrador. nf.ca/battleharbour/historictrust.htm). To get to the site, contact **Jones Charters and Tours** (☎ 709/921–6249, 709/921–6948 Riverlodge Hotel), which makes the one-hour trip from Mary's Harbour at 10 daily. The boat leaves Battle Harbour again at 3. Tickets are $40 round-trip, and can be bought right at the boat or from the Riverlodge Hotel, on the main road in Mary's Harbour. There's no need to buy tickets in advance; space is not an issue. ⊠ *Southern Labrador coast, accessible by boat from Mary's Harbour* 🕾🕾 *709/921–6216 or 709/921–6325* ⊕ *www.battleharbour. com* ⊠ *$5* ☉ *June–Sept., daily 10–6.*

Where to Stay

$–$$ 🖫 **Battle Harbour Inn.** Perched on a hilltop with a commanding view of the Labrador Sea from every window, this fully restored two-story house overlooks the merchant premises and Great Caribou Island. The rooms share two baths. The house is furnished with antiques and has a sunporch on which to relax and soak up the view. The inn doesn't have a phone or television, in keeping with the idea of taking visitors back to the 18th century. There is a phone at the general store. ⊠ *Battle Harbour Historic Site* ⌖ *Box 140, Mary's Harbour A0K 3P0* ☎ *709/ 921–6216* 🕾🕾 *709/921–6325* ⟿ *5 rooms without bath* ⚲ *Dining room; no a/c, no room phones, no room TVs, no smoking* ⊟ *MC, V* ☉ *Closed Oct.–May* ⍾◖ *FAP.*

Happy Valley–Goose Bay

49 *525 km (326 mi) east of Labrador City.*

Happy Valley–Goose Bay is the chief service center for coastal Labrador. Anyone coming to Labrador to fish will probably pass through here. The town was founded in the 1940s as a top-secret air base used to ferry fleets of aircraft to Europe. It's still used as a low-level flying training base by the British, Dutch, and German air forces.

Where to Stay

$ 🖫 **Aurora Hotel.** Rooms at this hotel, though basic, are the best of the limited selection in this town. None has a view or any special characteristics, but all are clean and quiet. The Aurora is a five-minute drive from the airport. ⊠ *382 Hamilton River Rd., A0P 1C0* ☎ *709/896– 3398 or 800/563–3066* 🖷 *709/896–9608* ⊕ *www.aurorahotel.com* ⟿ *37 rooms, 3 suites* ⚲ *Dining room, room service, bar, meeting rooms* ⊟ *AE, DC, MC, V.*

Sports & the Outdoors

Ski Mont Shana (⊠ Rte. 520 ☎ 709/896–8162), with 10 downhill runs, is between Happy Valley–Goose Bay and North West River. The vertical drop is 525 feet. A full-day lift ticket is $25.

North West River

50 *32 km (20 mi) northeast of Happy Valley–Goose Bay.*

North West River was founded as a Hudson's Bay trading post in the 1830s. The town was also the starting point for the Wallace–Hubbard expedition of 1903. Leonidas Hubbard and Dillon Wallace were American adventurers who attempted a journey from Lake Melville to Ungava Bay along a previously untraveled route. They took a wrong turn and got lost, and Hubbard died in the wilderness from starvation. His wife, Mina, never forgave Wallace and completed her husband's journey in 1905. Her book, *A Woman's Way Through Unknown Labrador*, is still considered a classic. The Wallace–Hubbard expedition and other historic events are examined at the **Labrador Heritage Museum**, in the 1923 Hudson Bay Company Building. Artifacts and displays relate the history of the Hudson Bay Company and International Grenfell Association, trapping, and the trappers' families. ⊠ *Main St.* ☎ *709/497–8858* ⊠ *$2* ☉ *Wed.–Sun. 8:30–4:30.*

LABRADOR WEST

Labrador West's subarctic landscape is challenging and unforgettable. The two towns here, Wabush and Labrador West, were built in the 1960s to accommodate employees of the Iron Ore Company of Canada. The area is home to the largest iron ore deposits in the world. The best way to see this area is to ride the **Québec North Shore and Labrador Railway** (☎418/ 968–7808 or 709/944–8205), which leaves Sept-Isles, Québec, for Labrador City three times a week in summer and twice a week in winter. The seven- to eight-hour trip takes you through nearly 600 km (372 mi) of virgin forest, past spectacular waterfalls and majestic mountains.

Wabush

🖲 *525 km (326 mi) west of Happy Valley–Goose Bay.*

The modern town of Wabush has all the amenities of larger centers, including accommodations, sports and recreational facilities, good shopping, and some of the warmest hospitality found anywhere. Labrador City and Wabush—or the "twin towns," as they are called—exist because of the rich iron ore deposits, and the Iron Ore Company of Canada offers free tours of Wabush Mines Wednesday and Sunday at 1:30 in July and August. Arrangements should be made through the Labrador West Tourism Association (✉ Labrador Mall, Wabush ☎ 709/ 944–7631)

Sports & the Outdoors
The **Smokey Mountain Alpine Skiing Center** (✉ Rte. 500 ☎ 709/944–2129), west of Wabush, is open from mid-November to late April and has 18 groomed runs that can accommodate both beginners and advanced skiers. The vertical drop is 1,000 feet. A full-day lift ticket is less than $30.

Labrador City

🖲 *525 km (326 mi) west of Happy Valley–Goose Bay.*

Labrador City has all the facilities of nearby Wabush, but more of them. At just under 10,000 people, the city has more than three times the population of Wabush.

Sports & the Outdoors
The **Carol Curling Club** (✉ Booth St. ☎ 709/944–5889) is the home club of the onetime world junior champions. The club has four sheets of ice, has produced some of the province's finest curlers, and has hosted the provincial finals. Each March Labrador City and Wabush play host to the 192-km (120-mi) **Labrador 120 International Sled Dog Race.** The event is well attended locally, with teams coming mostly from Labrador and Québec. The **White Wolf Snowmobile Club** (☎ 709/944–7401) organizes the Winter Odyssey, a March snowmobile rally that includes tours to see the world's largest caribou herd (about 600,000 animals). White Wolf also maintains an extensive groomed trail system all winter; snowmobile rentals are available.

NEWFOUNDLAND & LABRADOR A TO Z

To research prices, get advice from other travelers, and book travel arrangements, visit www.fodors.com.

AIR TRAVEL
Air Canada flies into St. John's. Regional connectors include Air Labrador, Provincial Airlines, and Jazz. CanJet Airlines has flights into the province

from most Canadian cities. JetsGo has discount flights to Goosey Bay, Stephenville, St. John's, and Gander from other Canadian cities and from Newark and Ft. Lauderdale. At this writing, the reliability of air travel to cities around Newfoundland—other than to St. John's—is in a state of flux. Call the airlines to get up-to-date information on routes.

🛈 Airlines & Contacts **Air Canada** ☎ 888/247-2262 ⊕ www.aircanada.ca. **Air Labrador** ☎ 800/563-3042. **CanJet Airlines** ☎ 800/809-7777 ⊕ www.canjet.ca. **Jazz** ☎ 888/247-2262 ⊕ www.flyjazz.ca. **Jetsgo** ☎ 866/440-0441 ⊕ www.jetsgo.ca. **Provincial Airlines** ☎ 709/576-1666, 800/563-2800 in Atlantic Canada.

AIRPORTS

The province's main airport is St. John's International Airport, although another international airport is at Gander, farther north. The domestic airports in Newfoundland are in Stephenville, Deer Lake, and St. Anthony. The airports in Labrador are in Happy Valley–Goose Bay, Wabush, and Churchill Falls.

🛈 Airport Information **Gander International Airport** ✉ James Boulevard Dr., Gander ☎ 709/256-6677. **St. John's International Airport** ✉ Off Portugal Cove Rd., St. John's ☎ 709/758-8515.

BOAT & FERRY TRAVEL

Marine Atlantic operates a car ferry from North Sydney, Nova Scotia, to Port aux Basques, Newfoundland (crossing time is six hours), and, from June through September, from North Sydney to Argentia three times a week (crossing time 12–14 hours). In all cases reservations are required. To explore the south coast of Labrador, catch the ferry at St. Barbe on Route 430 in Newfoundland to Blanc Sablon, Québec. From here you can drive to Cartwright along Route 510. Newfoundland and Labrador Tourism has information about ferry schedules. Coastal Cruising Adventures, operated by the Viking Trail Tourism Association, offers a way to see the Northern Peninsula and Labrador on board the *Atlantis*. Coastal Labrador Marine Services takes passengers to smaller communities in Labrador.

🛈 Boat & Ferry Information **Coastal Labrador Marine Services** ☎ 866/535-2567 ⊕ www.gov.nl.ca/ferryservices. **Marine Atlantic** ☎ 800/341-7981, 902/794-8109 TTY. **Newfoundland and Labrador Tourism** ☎ 800/563-6353. **Viking Trail Tourism Association** ☎ 877/778-4546 or 709/454-8888 ⊕ www.vikingtrail.org.

BUS TRAVEL

DRL Coachlines runs a transisland bus service in Newfoundland. Buses leave daily at 8 from St. John's and Port aux Basques. Outport taxis connect the major centers with surrounding communities.

🛈 Bus Information **DRL Coachlines** ☎ 709/738-8088.

CAR TRAVEL

In winter some highways may close during and after severe snowstorms. The government of Newfoundland and Labrador's Department of Works, Services & Transportation Web site has up-to-date information on road conditions and closures. The Department of Tourism, Culture, and Recreation can help with any travel-related problems.

Newfoundland has an excellent highway system, and all but a handful of secondary roads are paved. The province's roads are generally uncrowded, adding to the pleasure of driving. Travel time along the Trans-Canada Highway (Route 1) from Port aux Basques to St. John's is about 13 hours, with time out for a meal. The trip from Corner Brook to St. Anthony, at the northernmost tip of the island, is about five hours. The drive from St. John's to Grand Bank on the Burin Peninsula takes about four hours. If you're heading for the southern coast of the Avalon

Peninsula, pick up Route 10 just south of St. John's and follow it toward Trepassey.

The southeastern coast of Labrador is becoming more accessible by car. Route 510 now goes all the way to Cartwright. Route 500 links Labrador City with Happy Valley–Goose Bay via Churchill Falls. Conditions on this 526-km (326-mi) wilderness road are best from June through October. Labrador's road system is being extended and upgraded. If you plan on doing any extensive driving in any part of Labrador, contact the Department of Tourism, Culture, and Recreation for advice on the best routes and road conditions.

🄵 Department of Tourism, Culture, and Recreation ☎ 709/729-2830 or 800/563-6353 ⊕ www.gov.nl.ca/tcr. Department of Works, Services & Transportation ☎ 709/635-4144 in Deer Lake, 709/292-4444 in Grand Falls-Windsor and Central Newfoundland, 709/466-4160 in Clarenville, 709/729-7669 in St. John's, 709/896-7888 in Happy Valley-Goose Bay ⊕ www.gov.nl.ca/roads.

EMERGENCIES

🄵 Emergency Services Ambulance, fire, police ☎ 911 or 0.

🄵 Hospitals Captain William Jackman Hospital ⊠ 410 Booth Ave., Labrador City ☎ 709/944-2632. Charles S. Curtis Memorial Hospital ⊠ West St., St. Anthony ☎ 709/454-3333. General Hospital ⊠ 300 Prince Philip Dr., St. John's ☎ 709/777-6300. George B. Cross Hospital ⊠ Manitoba Dr., Clarenville ☎ 709/466-3411. James Paton ⊠ 125 Trans-Canada Hwy., Gander ☎ 709/651-2500. St. Clare's Mercy Hospital ⊠ 154 Le Marchant Rd., St. John's ☎ 709/777-5000. Western Memorial ⊠ Brookfield Ave., Corner Brook ☎ 709/637-5000.

SPORTS & THE OUTDOORS

Seasonal and regulatory fishing information can be obtained from the Department of Tourism, Culture, and Recreation.

🄵 Department of Tourism, Culture, and Recreation ☎ 709/729-2830 or 800/563-6353 ⊕ www.gov.nl.ca/tcr.

TOURS

ADVENTURE TOURS Local operators offer sea kayaking, ocean diving, canoeing, wildlife viewing, mountain biking, white-water rafting, heli-hiking, and interpretive walks in summer. In winter snowmobiling and caribou- and seal-watching expeditions are popular. In spring and early summer a favored activity is iceberg watching. Before choosing an operator, contact the Department of Tourism, Culture, and Recreation to make sure you're calling an established outfit.

Eastern Edge Kayak Adventures leads east-coast sea-kayaking tours and gives white-water kayaking instruction. Maxxim Vacations in St. John's organizes packaged adventure and cultural tours. Tuckamore Wilderness Lodge, in Main Brook, uses its luxurious lodge on the Great Northern Peninsula as a base for viewing caribou, seabird colonies, whales, and icebergs, and for winter snowmobile excursions. Wildland Tours in St. John's has three weeklong guided tours that view wildlife and visit historically and culturally significant sites across Newfoundland.

🄵 Fees & Schedules Department of Tourism, Culture, and Recreation ☎ 709/729-2830 or 800/563-6353 ⊕ www.gov.nl.ca/tcr. Eastern Edge Kayak Adventures ☎ 709/782-5925 ⊕ www.kayakjim.com. Maxxim Vacations ☎ 709/754-6666 or 800/567-6666 ⊕ www.maxximvacations.com. Tuckamore Wilderness Lodge ☎ 709/865-6361 or 888/865-6361 ⊕ www.tuckamore-lodge.nf.net. Wildland Tours ☎ 709/722-3123 ⊕ www.wildlands.com.

BUS TOURS Local tours are available for Port aux Basques, the Codroy Valley, Corner Brook, the Bay of Islands, Gros Morne National Park, the Great Northern Peninsula, and St. John's. Local information chalets—provincially run tourist centers located strategically along the Trans-Canada Highway—have contact names and numbers. The Department of Tourism, Culture, and Recreation can help out here as well. McCarthy's Party in St. John's has guided bus tours across Newfoundland, learning vacations, and charter services.

🚩 Fees & Schedules **Department of Tourism, Culture, and Recreation** ☎ 709/729-2830 or 800/563-6353 ⊕ www.gov.nl.ca/tcr. **McCarthy's Party** ☎ 709/781-2244 or 888/660-6060 ⊕ www.newfoundland-tours.com.

WALKING TOURS On the St. John's Haunted Hike, Reverend Thomas Wickam Jarvis (actor Dale Jarvis) leads popular walking tours of the city's haunted sites and urban legends on summer evenings; tours begin at the west entrance of the Anglican Cathedral on Church Hill.

🚩 Fees & Schedules **St. John's Haunted Hike** ☎ 709/576-2087 or 709/685-3444.

TRAIN TRAVEL

Iron Ore Company of Canada's Québec North Shore and Labrador Railway has service between Sept-Isles, Québec, and Labrador City.

🚩 Train Information **Iron Ore Company of Canada's Québec North Shore and Labrador Railway** ☎ 418/968-7808 or 709/944-8205.

VISITOR INFORMATION

Newfoundland and Labrador Tourism distributes brochures from its offices in St. John's. The province maintains a 24-hour tourist-information line year-round that can help with accommodations and reservations.

From June until Labor Day a network of visitor information centers, open daily 9–9, dots the province. These centers have information on events, accommodations, shopping, and crafts stores in their areas. The airports in Gander and St. John's operate in-season visitor-information booths. The city of St. John's operates an information center in a restored railway carriage next to the harbor.

🚩 Tourist Information **Newfoundland and Labrador Tourism** ✉ Department of Tourism, Culture, and Recreation, Confederation Bldg., West Block, 2nd floor ⊘ Box 8730, St. John's A1B 4K2 ☎ 709/729-2831, 800/563-6353 in North America ⊕ www.gov.nl.ca/tourism.

UNDERSTANDING ATLANTIC CANADA

OF SEA AND LAND

BOOKS & MOVIES

OF SEA & LAND

Helga Loverseed

CANADA'S ATLANTIC PROVINCES ARE BOUND TO THE SEA by tradition and geography. Each province has a distinct personality, but the Atlantic Ocean and the other great bodies of water that flow into it from further inland—the Bay of Fundy with its mighty tides, the warm Baie des Chaleurs, and the Gulf of St. Lawrence, which in pioneer days was part of Canada's nautical highway to the world—have influenced the lifestyle and culture of the more than 2 million people who live in the Maritime provinces—Nova Scotia, New Brunswick, and Prince Edward Island—along within the province of Newfoundland and Labrador.

The culture manifests itself in the region's language, art, and music. It has been shaped by strong ties to Europe, decades of economic hardship, and a struggle to tame the land. Celtic music, for example, a strong tradition in Cape Breton and other parts of Nova Scotia, has thrived for centuries. The haunting melodies of a lost homeland traveled over the Atlantic in the 18th century when the first Highlanders arrived from Scotland, and mingled with musical influences from the Acadians and Irish. Today Celtic music is being "exported" in a modern form, via young avant-garde performers, to the Scottish homeland from whence it came. In New Brunswick the toe-tapping fiddle music of the French-speaking Acadians echoes the rhythms of the jigs and reels of Ireland, Scotland, and France. In Newfoundland, too, a lively musical tradition is tempered with folkloric, humorous tales of yesteryear and a vocabulary full of twists and turns that delight the ear.

The Atlantic provinces are strongly rooted in the past, but they are not isolated from the rest of North America—far from it. Those who live in the region have always looked beyond their own borders to wheel and deal with the outside world. The bounty of the ocean (now sadly in decline in certain areas, in part because of mismanagement of resources), marine commerce, and shipbuilding once provided the economic lifeblood of the region, and people sold (and continue to sell) their catches and their expertise around the globe.

Tourism and other service industries have taken over where some of the more traditional occupations have left off. Many national and international technology companies have set up shop here (especially in New Brunswick, which has a large bilingual workforce), attracted by the quality of life and by labor and housing costs that are lower than those in the rest of Canada.

Even Prince Edward Island, Canada's smallest province and a rural enclave of manicured farmland and picturesque villages, is no longer the sleepy backwater of yesteryear. Connected, since 1997, to the mainland by the Confederation Bridge, it is visited by more than 1 million people annually, almost half the entire population of Atlantic Canada.

The Island offers a multitude of outdoor attractions in scenic surroundings, as do all the Atlantic provinces. Gently rolling roads (no hill is higher than 500 feet) make it ideal for cycling. Beaches, many in spectacular settings, abound throughout the region. The Bay of Fundy, which divides Nova Scotia from New Brunswick, is renowned for its whale-watching. On Newfoundland, the birdlife is abundant, and moose are so plentiful (125,000 at last count) that locals may warn you not to drive at night.

Atlantic Canada isn't all moose and maritime landscapes, though. Its cities, while small, are attractive, safe, clean, and historic. Charlottetown, on Prince Edward Island, is an intimate, walkable community with old wooden houses and quiet tree-lined streets. Fredericton, New Brunswick's capital, is a university town on the St. John River. It too, has gracious old buildings, as well as an exceptional regional art museum—the Beaverbrook Art Gallery—named after its benefactor and one of New Brunswick's most famous citizens, Lord Beaverbrook, a renowned Canadian and British press magnate.

St. John's, Newfoundland, has terrific crafts stores (many locals still while away the long winters by knitting sweaters, socks, and woolen hats) and lively pubs, many of them housed in colorfully painted, renovated wooden buildings that march up from the waterfront.

Halifax, Nova Scotia, is the self-proclaimed "capital" of Atlantic Canada. The business center of the region, it is also the area's most populous and sophisticated city. Old and new blend comfortably here. Gracing its harbor skyline are a 19th-century fortress (the Citadel), high-rise hotels, a renovated waterfront collectively known as Historic Properties, and several glass-wall office towers. The present is here but, as in the rest of the region, the past is not forgotten.

BOOKS & MOVIES

Books

General *A Traveller's History of Canada,* by Robert Bothwell, provides a good overview of Canadian history. For information on seabirds and ocean life in the Maritimes, pick up the *Guide to the Offshore Wildlife of the Northern Atlantic,* by Michael H. Tove. *Sea of Slaughter, A Chronicle of the Destruction of Animal Life in the North Atlantic,* by Farley Mowat, explores marine life that is now threatened or extinct.

Acadian culture is unique to this region. Clive Doucet's *Notes from Exile: On Being Acadian* is a thoughtful memoir that explores what it means to be Acadian and incorporates the history of Acadie and the Acadians. *Acadia of the Maritimes,* by Jean Daigle, is an exhaustive collection of historic documents that give an overview of Acadian society, politics, and economics. The historical novel *Acadie—Prelude to Derangement,* by Peter N. Coleman and Andre Dupuis, follows the trials of Acadian families as they exiled from their homes in the Bay of Fundy. Janette Oke and T. Davis Bunn have written five books in the series *Song of Acadia,* in which the conflicts between French and British settlers in Acadie unfold amid turbulent romance and heart-wrenching drama. The first three books—*The Meeting Place, The Sacred Shore,* and *The Birthright*—take place in Canada, after which the setting moves to England.

Newfoundland & Labrador The difficult lives of Atlantic fishermen were exposed to the world with Sebastian Junger's novel *The Perfect Storm* in 1997, which became a feature film in 2000. Newfoundland native Linda Greenlaw, who some consider the best swordfish captain in the world and whose ship was the sister ship of the one that inspired Junger's book, has written a captivating account of her experiences in *The Hungry Ocean. The North Bay Narrative,* by Walter Staples (Peter E. Randall), is the true story of the evolution of a remote outpost into a bustling fishing town. In the 1960s the excavation of a Norse site at L'Anse aux Meadows revealed it to be the oldest settlement in North America. *The Viking Discovery of America,* by

Helge and Anne Stine Ingstad, is a non-fiction account of that finding.

English is spoken almost everywhere in Atlantic Canada, but the *Dictionary of Newfoundland English,* by G. M. Story, can shed light on some of the words that may be new to you. To get in the mood for Newfoundland and Labrador's breathtaking scenery, flip through *This Marvelous Terrible Place: Images of Newfoundland and Labrador,* by Yva Momatiuk and John Eastcott (Firefly Books).

The Shipping News, by E. Annie Proulx, has gained much attention since the book was adapted into a major motion picture in 2001. Wayne Johnston's *Baltimore's Mansion* is a memoir depicting his childhood on the Avalon Peninsula. Bernice Morgan has written three novels about a family living on Cape Random in the 1800s: *Random Passage, Waiting For Time,* and *Cape Random.*

New Brunswick David Adams Richards is one of New Brunswick's best-known writers. His novels *Mercy Among the Children* and *Bay of Love and Sorrows,* both set in northern New Brunswick, explore bleak themes. Richards has also authored *Lines on the Water,* a tale of the fishing community on the Miramichi River. In the memoir *Home: Chronicle of a North Country Life,* by Beth Powning, journey with the author as she and her husband relocate from Connecticut to a farm near the Bay of Fundy.

It's hard to escape the Maritimes without hearing a ghost story or two; to discover New Brunswick's best haunts before you go, read *Ghosts, Pirates and Treasure Trove: the Phantoms that Haunt New Brunswick,* by Stuart Trueman. New Brunswick has 64 historic covered bridges. If you can't catch them all while you're in the province, at least you can scan the lovely photographs in *No Faster Than a Walk: The Covered Bridges of New Brunswick,* by Stephen and John Gillis.

Nova Scotia Henry Wadsworth Longfellow's poem *Evangeline* tells the story of lovers separated when the British deported the Acadians in 1755. The poem has been the inspiration for a number of tourist attractions in the province. The sweeping novel *Fall on your Knees,* by Ann-Marie MacDonald, takes place partly on Cape Breton Island. *Island, The Complete Stories,* by Alistair MacLeod, is a collection of tales about everyday life in Nova Scotia. MacLeod's first novel, *No Great Mischief,* is the story of a Scottish family that builds a new life on Cape Breton Island. Suspense story *Burden of Desire,* by Robert MacNeil, is set in Halifax during WWI.

Prince Edward Island It almost goes without saying that *Anne of Green Gables* is a must-read. Serious Anne fans (or L. M. Montgomery fans) might try *The Annotated Anne of Green Gables,* which provides insight into the characters, places, flora, fauna, and geography of the Island. Despite the numerous footnotes, the book remains thoroughly engaging. Montgomery's most recently popular PEI-based series is *Emily of New Moon.*

Movies

The documentary *Ghosts of the Abyss* (2003) has excellent footage of the *Titanic,* which sank off the coast of Newfoundland. *Rain, Drizzle, and Fog* (1998) is a documentary about Newfoundland through the eyes of a "townie," or resident of St. John's. *Sunrise at Campobello* (1960), a

film about FDR's bout with polio, was shot on Campobello Island, NB. *The Shipping News* (2001), set in Newfoundland, was filmed primarily in Corner Brook, New Bonaventure, and Trinity, NL. Other high-profile movies filmed either entirely or in part in Atlantic Canada include *K-19 Widowmaker* (2002; Halifax); *Simon Birch* (1998; Lunenburg, NS); *Contact* (1997; Gros Morne National Park, NL); *Titanic* (1997; Halifax); *Leaving Las Vegas* (1995; Halifax); *The Scarlet Letter* (1995; Shelburne and Yarmouth, NS); and *Children of a Lesser God* (1986; Beaver Harbour, Rothesay, and Saint John, NB).

Many lesser-known movies filmed and set in the Atlantic provinces show more of the landscape and culture. Some of these are *The Bay of Love and Sorrows* (2002; Miramichi, NB); *The Bay Boy* (1984; Cape Breton, NS); *Echoes of a Summer* (1976; Chester Bay, NS); *Margaret's Museum* (1995; Cape Breton, NS); *New Waterford Girl* (1999; Cape Breton, NS); *A Rumor of Angels* (2000; Crescent Beach, Halifax, Lunenburg, and Sambro, NS); *Virginia's Run* (2002; Shelburne, NS); *The Divine Ryans* (2000; St. John's, NL); *John and the Missus* (1987; Petty Harbour, NL); *Rare Birds* (2001; Cape Spear, Petty Harbour, and St. John's, NL).

INDEX

A

Aberdeen Cultural Centre, 99
Acadia (ship), 11
Acadian Coast and Peninsula
(New Brunswick),
103–109
Acadian culture, 108
Acadian Festival, 107
Acadian Historical Village,
107
Acadian Museum (Moncton),
99
Acadian Museum
(Summerside), 146
Acadian Pioneer Village, 150
Acadian Wax Museum, 107
Acton's Grill & Café, F21, 38
Admiral Digby Museum, 33
Adventure tours, 199
Advocate Harbour, 50
Age of Sail Museum Heritage
Centre, 50
Air travel, F26–F28
luggage, F40–F41
New Brunswick, 118
*Newfoundland and Labrador,
197–198*
Nova Scotia, 69–70
Prince Edward Island, 151
Airports, F28, 182–183
Alexander Graham Bell
National Historic Site of
Canada, 64
Alma, 96
Amherst, 49–50
Amherst Shore Country Inn
✕⊡ , 49
Andrew and Laura McCain
Gallery, 111
Anglican Cathedral of St. John
the Baptist, 162
Anna Leonowens Gallery, 9
Annapolis Royal, 34–36
Annapolis Royal Historic
Gardens, 34
Annapolis Royal Tidal Power
Project, 35
Anne Murray Centre, 49
Anne of Green Gables Museum
at Silver Bush, 139
Antigonish, 43–45
Antigonish Heritage Museum,
44
Apartment and villas rentals,
F37
Aquarium and Marine Centre
(Shippagan), 106
Aquariums, 89, 105, 106,
149
Archalaus Smith Museum, 30
Arches Provincial Park, 189
Arichat, 68–69
Arisaig, 44
Army Museum, 10
Art Gallery of Nova Scotia, 9

Aspotogan Peninsula, F22
Atlantic Salmon Museum and
Aquarium, 105
Atlantic Theatre Festival, 39
ATMs, F39
Automobile racing, 16
Avalon Peninsula, 171–175
Aviation Exhibition, 183

B

Baddeck, 63–65
Balmoral Grist Mill Museum,
47
Barbour's General Store, 78
Barrington, 29–30
Barrington Woolen Mill
Museum, 29
Basilica Cathedral of St. John
the Baptist, 162
Basin Head Fisheries Museum,
144
Battery (St. John's), 164
Battle Harbour National
Historic Site, 195–196
Bay Fortune, 143–144
Bay St. Lawrence, 61–62
Beaches, F17
*New Brunswick, 79, 87, 102,
103, 107*
Nova Scotia, 41, 42, 45, 50, 51
*Prince Edward Island, 125,
135, 139*
Beaconsfield Historic House,
127
Bear River, 34
Beauty and the Beastro ✕ , 85
Beaverbrook Art Gallery, 113
Bed-and-breakfasts, F37
Belfast, 142
Bell Inn Restaurant ✕ , 101
Ben's Lake Trout Farm, 142
Bicycling, F17, F23, F28, F42
*New Brunswick, 88, 93, 95,
120*
Nova Scotia, 28, 71
*Prince Edward Island, 125,
133, 151–152*
Big and Little Tancook Islands,
20
Big Pond, 68
Bird Islands, 62
Bird-watching
*New Brunswick, 84, 92, 93, 96,
102–103, 119*
*Newfoundland and Labrador,
172, 184, 191*
*Nova Scotia, 5, 37–38, 49, 62,
71–72*
Black Cultural Center for Nova
Scotia, 18
Blomidon Inn ✕⊡ , 38
Blue Heron Drive (Prince
Edward Island), F22,
134–141
Bluenose II (schooner), 23

Boat and ferry travel, F29
New Brunswick, 92, 118–119
*Newfoundland and Labrador,
187, 198*
Nova Scotia, 36–37, 70
Prince Edward Island, 151
Boat tours, F23
New Brunswick, 110
*Newfoundland and Labrador,
184, 189, 191, 195*
Nova Scotia, 62, 72–73
Boating, F18, 55, 87, 92,
133, 136
Bonavista, 180
Bonavista Peninsula,
176–180
Borden-Carleton, 140
Bouctouche, 104–105
Bowring Park, 164
Boyce Farmers' Market
(Fredericton), 113
Boyd's Cove Beothuk
Interpretation Center, 183
Brackley Beach, 135–136
Bread and Roses Country Inn
⊡ , 36
Brewery Market (Halifax), 9
Bridgewater, 25–26
Brier Island, 36–37
Brigus, 172–173
Brittoner Bed & Breakfast ⊡ ,
174
Burin, 181
Burin Peninsula, 180–185
Bus tours, 73, 199–200
Bus travel, F29
New Brunswick, 119
*Newfoundland and Labrador,
198*
Nova Scotia, 70–71
Business hours, F29

C

Cabot Beach Provincial Park,
139
Cabot Tower, 164, 165
Cabot Trail, F22, 55–56
Cabot's Landing Provincial
Park, 61
Calendar of events, F14–F16
Cameras and photography,
F29–F30
Camp Gagetown, 111
Camping, F37
Campobello Island, 94–95
Canoeing, F42, 28, 72, 105,
117, 136
Canso Island National Historic
Site, 43
Cape Bear, 142
Cape Blomidon, 38
Cape Bonavista Lighthouse,
180
Cape Breton Highlands
National Park, F24, 60–61

Cape Breton Island (Nova Scotia), 55–69
Cape Chignecto, 50–51
Cape Chignecto Provincial Park, F24, 50
Cape d'Or, F24, 50–51
Cape Enrage, 97–98
Cape Mabou Highlands, F23–F24
Cape Sable Island, 30
Cape St. Mary's Ecological Reserve, 176
Cape Spear Lighthouse, 164
Cape Spear National Historic Site, 164
Cap-Egmont, 150
Capitol Theatre, 99
Car rental, F30
Car travel, F30–F31
New Brunswick, 119
Newfoundland and Labrador, 198–199
Nova Scotia, 71
Prince Edward Island, 151, 152
Caraquet, 107, 109
Caribou, 173
Carleton Martello Tower, 84
Castle Hill National Historic Site, 175
Cavendish, 136–138
Caves, 96, 97
Cellar ✕, F21, 165–166
Celtic Colours International Festival, 64
Central New Brunswick Woodmen's Museum, 106
Change Islands, 185
Charles C. Richards House B&B 🖭, 32
Charles S. Curtis Memorial Hospital, 191
Charlotte Lane Café ✕, 29
Charlottetown (Prince Edward Island), 124, 127–134
Charlottetown Driving Park, 127
Charlottetown Festival, 127–128
Cherry Brook Zoo, 84
Che's ✕, F21, 166
Chester, 20–21
Chéticamp, 58–60
Chez Briann ✕, 166
Children, travel with, F31–F32
Chimney Corner, 58
Chocolate Museum, 88
Christ Church Cathedral, 113
Churches
New Brunswick, 83, 89, 99, 101, 107, 113
Newfoundland and Labrador, 162, 163, 164
Nova Scotia, 12, 32–33, 61, 69
Prince Edward Island, 129, 148
Circular Road (St. John's), 162

Claddagh Room Restaurant ✕, 129–130
Clarenville, 176–177
Climate, F13
Climbing, F42, 97–98
Coastal Labrador, 195–196
Cobequid Interpretation Centre, 53
Codroy Valley, 193
Colonial Building (St. John's), 162
Colony of Avalon archaeological dig, 173
Commissariat House, 162
Compton House 🖭, F20, 168
Confederation Centre of the Arts, 127–128
Confederation Landing Park, 128
Confederation Trail, F23
Consulates, F36
Consumer protection, F32
Corner Brook, 192–193
Court House (St. Andrews by-the-Sea), 89
Cows Ice Cream, 128
Credit cards, F6, F39
Cruise travel, F32
Cuisine, 5, 79, 125, 157
Cupids Archaeological Site, 174
Curling, 197
Currency, F39–F40
Customs and duties, F32–F34

D

Da Maurizio Dining Room ✕, F21, 12
Dare the Dark for the Headless Nun! (guided tour), 106
Dartmouth, 4, 17–18
Deer Island, 93–94
Delta Beauséjour ✕🖭, 100
Delta Prince Edward Hotel 🖭, 131
DesBrisay Museum, 25–26
Digby, 33–34
Digby Scallop Days, 33
Dining, F17, F21–F22, F35. ⇨ Also under cities and provinces
price categories, F35, 4, 75, 124, 156
Disabilities and accessibility, F34–F35
Discounts and deals, F35
Discovery Centre, 186
Discovery Trail, F22, 176
Dock Restaurant ✕, 178
Dr. Elizabeth LeFort Gallery and Museum: Les Trois Pignons, 59
Dogsledding, 79, 197
Domaine de Grand Pré (winery), 38
Dorchester, 101–102

Drives, F22, 152
Duckworth Street (St. John's), 162–163
Dunes Cafe ✕, F21, 135

E

East Coast Trail, F24
East Point Lighthouse, 145
Economy Shoe Shop ✕, 13
Ecotourism, F36, 49
Edmundston, 109–110
Elephant Rock, 149
Embassies, F36
Emergencies
and car travel, F31
New Brunswick, 119
Newfoundland and Labrador, 199
Nova Scotia, 71
Prince Edward Island, 151
Englishtown, 63
Eptek Exhibition Centre, 145–146
Eskasoni, 66
Evangeline Express, 39–40

F

Faire Brayonne, 109
Fairholm National Historic Inn 🖭, F20, 131–132
Fairmont Algonquin 🖭, 91
Fairmont Newfoundland ✕🖭, 167
Fairview Cemetery, 9–10
Farmhouse Inn B & B 🖭, F20, 39
Ferry service. ⇨ See Boat and ferry travel
Ferryland, 173
Festival Antigonish, 43
Festival of the Tartans, 46
Festivals and seasonal events, F14–F16
Firefighters Museum of Nova Scotia, 31
Fish, Fun & Folk Festival, 184
Fisheries Museum of the Atlantic, 23
Fishing, F18, F42
New Brunswick, 79, 119, 120
Newfoundland and Labrador, 157, 183
Nova Scotia, 5, 27, 72
Prince Edward Island, 125, 152
Five Islands, 53–54
Five Islands Provincial Park, 53
Flight 111 Memorial, 19
Fluvarium, 164
Fodor's choice, F20–F25
Fogo Island, 185
Fort Anne National Historic Site, 34
Fort Beauséjour National Historic Site, 102
Fort Edward, 39
Fort Point Lighthouse Park, 26

208 < Index

Fortress of Louisbourg National Historic Site of Canada, F23, 67
Fossil hunting, 5, 50, 51–52
Founders' Hall, 128
Four Mile Beach Inn ☒, F31, 62
Fraser Cultural Centre, 47
Fredericton (New Brunswick), 112–118
Free Meeting House, 99
Fundy Coast (New Brunswick), 88–101
Fundy Geological Museum, 52
Fundy National Park, F22, F24, 96–97
Fundy Shore Ecotour, 49
Fundy Trail Parkway, 88, 95

G

Gabrieau's Bistro Restaurant ✕, F21, 44
Gagetown, 117–118
Gampo Abbey, 61
Gander, 180, 182–183
Gander International Airport, 182–183
Ganong Chocolatier, 88
Gardens
New Brunswick, 89, 109
Newfoundland, 165
Nova Scotia, 10, 34
Prince Edward Island, 139
Garland Mansion, 178
Gateway Village, 140
Gay and lesbian travel, F36
Giant MacAskill Museum, 63
Glace Bay Miners' Museum, 67
Glynmill Inn ✕☒, 192
Golf, F18, F42
New Brunswick, 87, 91, 96, 117, 120
Newfoundland and Labrador, 169
Nova Scotia, 16, 63, 65, 72
Prince Edward Island, 125, 133, 135, 138, 149, 152
Government House (Halifax), 10
Government House (St. John's), 163
Gower Street United Church, 163
Gowrie House ☒, F20, 66
Grand Bank, 181–182
Grand Falls (New Brunswick), 110–111
Grand Falls Historical Museum, 110
Grand Falls-Windsor (Newfoundland), 184–185
Grand Manan Island, 92–93
Grand Pré National Historic Site, 37–38
Great Hall of the Clans, 63
Great Northern Peninsula (Newfoundland), 185–191

Green Gables, Prince Edward Island National Park, 137
Green Gardens Trail, 186
Green Park Shipbuilding Museum and Yeo House, 147
Greenock Church, 89
Greenwich National Park, 144–145
Grenfell Historic Properties, 191
Grenfell Mission, 191
Gros Morne Mountain, 186
Gros Morne National Park, F24, 186–189

H

Haddon Hall Inn ✕☒, 21
Haliburton House Museum, 40
Halifax (Nova Scotia), 4–17
Halifax Citadel National Historic Site, 10
Halifax Public Gardens, 10
Halls Harbour, 38
Hank Snow Country Music Centre Museum, 26
Happy Valley-Goose Bay, 196
Harbour Grace, 174–175
Harbourfront Jubilee Theatre, 145–146
Harbourside Park, 163
Harris' Quick 'n Tasty ✕, F21, 31
Hawke Hills, 173
Hawthorne Cottage, 173–174
Hector Heritage Quay, 45
Heritage Discovery Tours, 89
Heritage Museum, 181
Herring Cove Provincial Park, 94
Highland Games, 44
Highland Village Museum, F24–F25, 65
Hiking, F23–F24
New Brunswick, 88, 93, 95, 109, 120
Newfoundland and Labrador, 157, 173, 189
Nova Scotia, 39, 44, 53, 58, 72
Historic Garrison District (Fredericton), 114
Historic Properties (Halifax), 10
History, F23
HMCS Sackville (ship), 11
Hockey, 16–17
Holidays, F36
Home exchanges, F37–F38
Hopewell Cape, 98
Hopewell Rocks, F23, 98
Horse racing, 55, 127
Horseback riding, 93, 96–97
Hostels, F38
Hotels, F38
Houses and buildings, historic, F23
New Brunswick, 82, 94, 99, 101
Newfoundland and Labrador, 162, 163, 173–174, 178, 191

Nova Scotia, 10, 11–12, 26, 29, 40, 52
Prince Edward Island, 127, 129, 136–137, 138, 142, 147
Huntsman Aquarium and Museum, 89

I

Icebergs, 184, 191
Île Miscou, 107
Ingonish, 62
Inn at Bay Fortune ✕☒, 143–144
Insurance, F36–F37
International Festival of Baroque Music, 107
International Fox Museum and Hall of Fame, 145
Interpretive Centre and Aquarium, 149
Iona, 65–66
Irish Moss Interpretive Centre, 149
Irving Eco-Centre: La Dune de Bouctouche (coastal ecosystem), 104
Irving Nature Park, 84
Island Home Museum, 140
Island Treasure Woodcrafts, 181
Islander Motor Lodge ✕☒, F20, 132

J

Joggins Fossil Center, 50
John Stanfield Inn ✕☒, 54–55
Johnson GEO Centre, 165
Jost Vineyards, 48
Julien's Pastry Shop & Bakery ✕, F22, 21

K

Kayaking, F24, F42
New Brunswick, 87, 92, 93, 94, 97, 98, 117, 119
Newfoundland and Labrador, 170, 173, 184, 189
Nova Scotia, 17, 28
Prince Edward Island, 133, 136, 138, 152
Keillor House & Coach House Museum and St. James Church, 101
Kejimkujik National Park, F24, 27–28
Kejimkujik Seaside Adjunct, 26–27
Keltic Lodge ✕☒, F20, 62–63
Kenomee Hiking and Walking Trails, 53
Khyber Center for the Arts, 10
King Street (Saint John), 78
Kings Byway (Prince Edward Island), 141–145
Kings Landing Historical Settlement, F23, 111

King's Square (Saint John), 78, 82
Kingsbrae Arms ⬜, F20, 90–91
Kingsbrae Horticultural Gardens, 89
Kouchibouquac National Park, 105

L

La Fine Grobe-Sur-Mer ✕, F21, 107
La Manche, 172–173
La Pirogue Museum, 59
Labrador. ⇨ See Newfoundland and Labrador
Labrador City, 197
Labrador Heritage Museum, 196
Labrador Straits Museum and Craft Store, 194
Lady Slipper Drive (Prince Edward Island), 145–150
Language, F37, 204–210
L'Anse Amour Lighthouse, 194
L'Anse au Clair, 194
L'Anse aux Meadows National Historic Site, F23, 189–190
Le Château à Pape ✕, 99–100
Le Pays de la Sagouine (theme park), 104
Le Village de l'Acadie, 150
LeNoir Forge, 69
Lion Inn B&B ✕⬜, 24
Lismore, 44–45
Little Anse, 69
Little Sands, 142
Little Shemogue Country Inn ✕⬜, F20, 104
Liverpool, 26–27
Lobster Cove Head Lighthouse, 186
Lodging, F20–F21, F37–F38. ⇨ Also under cities and provinces
price categories, F37, 4, 75, 124, 156
Logger's Life Provincial Museum, 184
Long Island, 36–37
Long Range Mountains, 189
Louisbourg, 67–68
Louisburg Playhouse, 67
Loyalist Country Inn ⬜, 146
Loyalist House, 82
Lucy Maud Montgomery Birthplace, 138
Luggage, F40–F41
Lunenburg, 23–25

M

Mabou, 56–57
Mabou Coal Mines, 58
Mactaquac Provincial Park, 111

Maddox Cove, 165
Magdalen Islands, 143
Magic Mountain (theme park), 99
Magnetic Hill, 99
Magnetic Hill Zoo, 99
Magnolia's Grill ✕, 24
Mahone Bay, 21–23
Mail and shipping, F38
Malabeam Tourist Information Center, 110
Malagash, 48
Marconi National Historic Site of Canada, 67
Margaree Salmon Museum, 58
Maritime Archaic Indian burial site, 194
Maritime Museum of the Atlantic, 11
Market Slip (Saint John), 82
Marshlands Inn ✕⬜, 102
Martinique Beach, 41
Mary E. Black Gallery, 11
Mary March Provincial Museum, 184
Marystown, 180–181
Marysville, 114
McCulloch Room ✕, 144–145
Meal plans, F7, F37
Meat Cove, 61
Media, F39
Melmerby Beach, 45
Memorial University Botanical Garden, 165
Memramcock, 101–102
Merchantman Pub, 133
Mermaid Theatre, 40
Mimi's Ocean Grill ✕, 22
Minas Basin, 51–52
Ministers Island, 89–90
Miquelon, 182
Miramichi City, 105–106
Mockbeggar Plantation, 180
Moncton, 98–101
Moncton Museum, 99
Money matters, F39–F40
Mont-Carmel, 150
Montague, 142–143
Montgomery, Lucy Maud, 136–137, 138, 139
Monument Lefebvre National Historic Site, 101–102
Moose River Gold Mines and Museum, 41
Morrisey Rock, F25
Mountaineering, F42
Murray Premises, 163
Museums and galleries, F23, F24–F25
New Brunswick, 78, 82, 88, 89, 92, 95, 97, 99, 101–102, 105, 106, 107, 110, 111, 113, 114–115, 118
Newfoundland and Labrador, 165, 174, 181, 183, 184, 186, 191, 194, 195, 196

Nova Scotia, 9, 10, 11, 18, 20, 23, 25–26, 29, 30, 31, 33, 34, 40, 41, 43, 44, 45, 47, 49, 50, 52, 58, 59, 60, 63, 64, 65, 67
Prince Edward Island, 127–128, 129, 139, 140, 141–142, 144, 145–146, 147, 149
Music
New Brunswick, 86–87, 100–101, 104, 107, 116–117
Newfoundland, 169
Nova Scotia, 5, 15, 46, 53, 57
Prince Edward Island, 133, 140, 141, 147, 150
Musquodoboit Harbour, 41–42
Musquodoboit Railway Museum, 41

N

Nature, F24
New Brunswick, F10, 75–120
Acadian Coast and Peninsula, 103–109
children, attractions for, 82, 84, 88, 89, 91, 98, 99, 101, 105–106, 107, 111, 114
dining and lodging, 75, 79
emergencies, 119
festivals and seasonal events, 107, 109
Fredericton, 112–118
Fundy Coast, 88–101
itinerary recommendations, 77
nightlife and the arts, 86–87, 100–101, 116–117
outdoor activities and sports, 79, 87, 94, 96–98, 101, 102–103, 105, 109, 110, 117, 119–120
Saint John, 76, 78, 82–87
St. John River Valley, F24, 109–111
shopping, 87, 103, 117, 118
Tantramar Region, 101–103
timing the visit, 76
tours, 89, 106, 120
transportation, 118–119, 120
visitor information, 120
New Brunswick Botanical Garden, 109
New Brunswick Museum, 82
New Glasgow, 46
New London, 138
New River Beach, 87
Newfoundland and Labrador, F10–F11, 154–200
Avalon Peninsula, 171–175
Burin Peninsula, Gander, and Notre Dame Bay, 180–185
children, attractions for, 164, 165, 173, 180, 185, 189
Clarenville and the Bonavista Peninsula, 176–180
Coastal Labrador, 195–196

dining and lodging, *156, 157*
emergencies, *199*
festivals and seasonal events, *157, 169, 179, 184, 188, 193, 197*
Great Northern Peninsula, *185–191*
itinerary recommendations, *155*
Labrador West, *197*
nightlife and the arts, *169, 188*
outdoor activities and sports, *157, 169–170, 189, 193, 196, 199*
Route 100: The Cape Shore, *175–176*
St. John's, *160–171*
shopping, *170–171, 179*
Straits, *194–195*
timing the visit, *156*
tours, *183, 199–200*
transportation, *197–199, 200*
visitor information, *200*
West Coast, *191–194*
Newfoundland Insectarium, *185*
Newman Wine Vaults, *163*
Newman's Restaurant ✕, *35*
Nightlife and the arts. ⇨ *See under cities and provinces*
Norseman Restaurant ✕, *F21, 190*
Norstead, *189*
North Cape, *149–150*
North West River, *196*
Northwest Corner, *139–140*
Notre Dame Bay, *180–185*
Notre Dame de l'Assumption, *69*
Nova Scotia, *F11, 2–73*
Cape Breton Island, *55–69*
children, attractions for, *11, 20, 23, 31, 35, 40, 50, 52, 60, 64, 67*
dining and lodging, *3, 4, 5*
Eastern Shore and Northern Nova Scotia, *41–55*
emergencies, *71*
festivals and seasonal events, *5, 15, 22, 33, 34, 39, 43, 44, 45, 46, 51, 64, 66*
Halifax and Dartmouth, *4–18*
itinerary recommendations, *3*
nightlife and the arts, *15–16, 18, 39, 46, 53, 57, 66, 67*
outdoor activities and sports, *5, 16–17, 27, 28, 37, 44, 55, 60, 61, 62, 64, 71–72*
shopping, *17, 20, 21, 23, 25, 32, 39, 44, 46, 48*
South Shore and Annapolis Valley, *18–40*
timing the visit, *4*
tours, *29, 49, 62, 72–73*
transportation, *69–71, 72*
visitor information, *73*
Nova Scotia Gem and Mineral Show, *51*

Nova Scotia Museum of Industry, *45*
Nova Scotia Museum of Natural History, *11*

O

Oakdene Centre, *34*
Old Burial Ground (Saint John), *82–83*
Old City Market (Saint John), *83*
Old Courthouse (Saint John), *83*
Old Gaol (St. Andrews by-the-Sea), *89*
Old Government House (Fredericton), *114*
Old Home Week, *127*
Old Meeting House Museum, *29*
Old Stone Barn Museum, *174*
O'Leary, *148–149*
Orwell Corner Historic Village, *141–142*
Ottawa House Museum-by-the-Sea, *52*
Outdoor activities and sports, *F17–F19, F23–F24, F42.* ⇨ *Also under cities and provinces*
Owens Art Gallery, *102*

P

Packing, *F40–F41*
Pansy Patch ✕🖬, *90*
Parc de l'Aboiteau, *103*
Park Interpretation Centre, *165*
Parks, national and provincial, *F17, F24, F25, F40*
New Brunswick, *94, 96–97, 105, 111*
Newfoundland and Labrador, *177–178, 186–189*
Nova Scotia, *27–28, 50, 53, 60–61*
Prince Edward Island, *134–135, 139, 140, 144–145*
Parlee Beach, *103*
Parrsboro, *51–53*
Parrsboro Rock and Mineral Shop and Museum, *52*
Partridge Island, *52*
Passports and visas, *F41*
PEI Sports Hall of Fame, *145–146*
Peggy's Cove, *19–20*
Petty Harbour, *165*
Pictou, *45–46*
Pier 21, *11*
Pilot House ✕, *F21, 131*
Pine Resort Hotel ✕🖬, *33*
Piper's Palate ✕, *115*
Placentia, *175*
Plane travel. ⇨ See Air travel
Pleasant Bay, *F24*
Point de l'Eglise, *32–33*

Point Pleasant Park (Halifax), *11*
Pope's Museum, *107*
Port au Choix National Historic Site, *189*
Port aux Basques, *193–194*
Port Bickerton Lighthouse Beach Park, *42*
Port Hill, *147*
Port Hood Island, *56*
Port-La-Joye-Fort Amherst National Historic Site, *F23, 141*
Port Royal National Historic Site, *36*
Powning Design (gallery), *95*
Prescott Inn 🖬, *168–169*
President Roosevelt's boyhood home, *94*
Price categories, *F35, F37*
New Brunswick, *75*
Newfoundland and Labrador, *156*
Nova Scotia, *4*
Prince Edward Island, *124*
Prince Edward Island, *F11–F12, 122–152*
Blue Heron Drive, *F22, 134–141*
Charlottetown, *124, 127–134*
children, attractions for, *127, 133, 137, 139, 140, 141–143*
dining and lodging, *122, 124, 125*
emergencies, *151*
festivals and seasonal events, *127–128, 133, 140, 145, 147*
itinerary recommendations, *123*
Kings Byway, *141–145*
Lady Slipper Drive, *145–150*
nightlife and the arts, *133, 141, 147, 150*
outdoor activities and sports, *125, 133, 135, 136, 138, 151–152*
shopping, *133–134, 136, 141, 148, 149, 152*
timing the visit, *124*
tours, *142–143, 152*
transportation, *151*
visitor information, *152*
Prince Edward Island National Park, *F24, F25, 134–135, 137*
Prince William Street (Saint John), *83*
Province House (Nova Scotia), *11–12*
Province House National Historic Site (Prince Edward Island), *F23, 129*
Provincial Legislature (New Brunswick), *114*
Provincial Seamen's Museum, *181*
Pubnico, *30*
Pump House Brewery ✕, *F21, 100*
Purdy's Wharf, *12*

Q

Québec North Shore and
  Labrador Railway, *197*
Queens County Museum, *118*
Quidi Vidi, *165*
Quidi Vidi Battery, *165*

R

Rainbow Valley Family Fun
  Park, *137*
Rappelling, *97–98*
Red Bay National Historc Site,
  195
Red Point Provincial Park, *144*
Regatta, *64*
Région Évangéline, *150*
Reversing Falls, *84*
Rickshaw tours, *73*
Rising Tide Theatre, *178*
Rita's Tea Room, *68*
Ritchie Wharf Park, *105–106*
Riverfront Music Jubilee, *46*
Riverview Ethnographic
  Museum, *34*
Robie Tufts Nature Center,
  37–38
Rockwood Park, *84*
Rocky Harbour, *186*
Rooms, The, *163–164*
Roosevelt Campobello
  International Park, *94*
Rose Arbour Café ✕, *F22, 40*
Ross Farm Living Museum of
  Agriculture, *20*
Ross Memorial Museum, *89*
Rossignol Cultural Centre, *26*
Ross-Thomson House, *29*
Ryan Premises National
  Historic Site, *180*

S

Sackville, *102–103*
Sackville Waterfowl Park, *102*
St. Andrews by-the-Sea, *88–92*
St. Anthony, *190–191*
St. Bernard Church, *33*
St. Croix Island, *88*
St. Dunstan's Basilica, *129*
St. Francis Xavier University,
  43
St-Jacques, *109*
Saint John (New Brunswick),
  76, 78, 82–87
St. John River Valley (New
  Brunswick), *F22, 109–111*
St. John's (Newfoundland),
  160–171
St. John's (Stone) Church, *83*
St. Martins, *95–96*
St. Mary's Church, *32–33*
St. Paul's Anglican Church, *129*
St. Paul's Church, *12*
St. Peter's, *68*
St. Peter's Cathedral, *129*
St-Pierre, *182*
St. Simon and St. Jude Church,
  148

St. Stephen, *88*
St. Thomas Anglican (Old
  Garrison) Church, *164*
Sainte Famille Winery, *40*
Sainte-Cécile church, *107*
Salem & Hillsborough Railroad
  Inc., *96*
Salmonier Nature Park, *173*
Salty's on the Waterfront ✕,
  12–13
Scarecrow Festival, *22*
Science East (Fredericton),
  114
Scuba diving, *F18, F42,
  169–170*
Seal Island Lighthouse, *30*
Seal-watching, *92, 133,
  142–143*
Secret Garden Restaurant ✕,
  35
Senior-citizen travel, *F41*
Serendipin' Art (gallery), *92*
Shadow Lawn Inn ✕🖼, *86*
Shaw's Hotel and Cottages
  ✕🖼, *135–136*
Shediac, *103–104*
Shelburne, *29*
Sherbrooke Village, *F23,
  42–43*
Sherman Hines Museum of
  Photography, *26*
Ship Harbour
  (Newfoundland), *175–176*
Ship Harbour (Nova Scotia),
  42
Shippagan, *106–107*
Shopping, *F18, F41–F42.*
  ⇨ *Also under cities and
  provinces*
Signal Hill National Historic
  Site, *F23, F25, 165*
Simeon Perkins House, *26*
Sir Andrew Macphail
  Homestead, *142*
Site of Lucy Maud
  Montgomery's Cavendish
  Home, *136–137*
Skiing, downhill and cross-
  country, *F18–F19*
*New Brunswick, 79, 96, 109,
  110, 117*
*Newfoundland and Labrador,
  193, 196, 197*
Nova Scotia, 72
Snowmobiling, *F19, 197*
Souris, *143*
South Gut St. Ann's, *63*
South Shore Tourism
  Association, *29*
Spelunking, *96, 97*
Spencer's Island Beach, *51*
Spinnaker's Landing, *146*
Sports and outdoor activities,
  F17, F19, F23–F24, F42.
  ⇨ *Also under cities and
  provinces*
Springhill Miners Museum,
  48–49

Stan Rogers Folk Festival, *43*
Stellarton, *45*
Stephenville Theatre Festival,
  193
Stonehame Lodge and Chalets
  🖼, *F20, 46*
Student travel, *F42*
Sugar Moon Farm Maple
  Products and Pancake House
  ✕, *F22, 54*
Summerside, *145–147*
Summerside Lobster Carnival,
  145
Sundance Cottages 🖼, *137*
Sunrise Trail, *44–45*
Sunrise Trail Museum, *47*
Swallowtail, *F25*
Sydney, *66*
Sydney and Louisbourg
  Railway Museum, *67*
Symbols, *F7*

T

Tablelands, *186*
Tantramar Marsh, *49*
Tantramar Region (New
  Brunswick), *101–103*
Tatamagouche, *47–48*
Taxes, *F42–F43*
Taxis, *72*
Tennis, *F42*
Terra Nova National Park,
  177–178
Theater
*New Brunswick, 86–87, 99,
  104, 116*
*Newfoundland and Labrador,
  169, 178, 179, 188, 193*
*Nova Scotia, 15–16, 18, 33, 39,
  40, 46, 53, 66, 67*
*Prince Edward Island,
  127–128, 133, 141, 145–146,
  147, 150*
13 West ✕, *192*
Tidal Bore (Moncton), *98–99*
Tignish, *148*
Time, *F43*
Timing the visit, *F13–F16*
Tipping, *F43*
Tours and packages,
  F43–F44
Train Station Inn 🖼, *48*
Train tours, *39–40, 73, 96,
  197*
Train travel, *F44*
New Brunswick, 120
*Newfoundland and Labrador,
  200*
Travel agencies, *F44*
Trinity, *178–179*
Trinity Church, *83*
Trout Point Lodge 🖼, *31–32*
Trout River Pond, *186*
Truro, *54–55*
Twillingate, *183–184*
Tyne Valley, *147–148*
Tyne Valley Oyster Festival,
  147

U

Uniacke Museum Park, *40*
Université Ste-Anne, *32*
Upper Clements Park
 (amusement park), *35*

V

Valhalla Lodge Bed &
 Breakfast ⌑ , *F20–F21,*
 190
Victoria, *140–141*
Victoria Park
 (Charlottetown), *129*
Victoria Park (Truro), *54*
Victoria Provincial Park, *140*
Victoria's Historic Inn and
 Carriage House B&B ⌑ , *38*
Views, *F24–F25*
Visas, *F41*
Visitor information, *F44*
New Brunswick, 120
Newfoundland and Labrador,
 200
Nova Scotia, 73
Prince Edward Island, 152

W

Wabush, *197*
Wagmatcook Culture &
 Heritage Centre, *64*
Walking tours, *73, 117, 152,*
 170, 200
Water Edge Gallery, *64*
Water sports, *92, 133*
Water Street (St. John's),
 164
Web sites, *F44*
West Point Lighthouse, *F25,*
 150
West Point Lighthouse ✕⌑ ,
 F20, F21, 150
Western Brook Pond, *186*
Whale Interpretive Centre, *60*
Whale watching, *F18, F24*
New Brunswick, 79, 92, 93, 94,
 119
Newfoundland and Labrador,
 170, 172, 184, 191
Nova Scotia, 25, 37, 60, 61, 62
White Point Beach Resort ⌑ ,
 28

Wild Blueberry & Maple
 Centre, *49*
Wile Carding Mill, *26*
Windsor (Nova Scotia),
 39–40
Windsor Hockey Heritage
 Centre, *40*
Wineries, *38, 40, 48*
Witless Bay Ecological
 Reserve, *171–173*
Wolfville, *37–39*
Wooden Boat Festival, *22*
Woodleigh Replicas and
 Gardens, *139*
Woody Point, *186*

Y

Yarmouth, *30–32*
Yarmouth County Museum, *31*
York Street (Fredericton), *114*
York-Sunbury Historical
 Museum, *114–115*

Z

Zoos, *84, 99*